1967

CLASSICS OF GREEK LITERATURE

CLASSICS

OF

GREEK LITERATURE

From the literary beginnings to the second century A. D.

Edited by

HARRY E. WEDECK

Lecturer in Classics, Brooklyn College of the City University of N. Y.

Member, Mediaeval Academy of America

PHILOSOPHICAL LIBRARY
New York

Printed in the United States of America

CONTENTS

v

HISTORY

PHILOSOPHY

ORATORY

SATIRE

PREFACE

The purpose of this anthology is to offer, in English translation, a conspectus of Greek achievement and its impact upon Western civilization, by means of the most characteristic, the most significant, and occasionally the uniquely interesting contributions, as its literary legacy: and in such a variety of genres as will confirm its impressive and dominant multiple activities.

The passages so selected are complete units in themselves or are so self-contained as to be readily explicable. For convenience of reference, the arrangement is according to categories, and within each classification the sequence is chronological.

In each case the selections are preceded by biographical or literary notes, and, whenever relevant, a brief summary of the circumstances and the context.

Some of the English translations have long been standard versions: while in other instances the renderings have been made by the editor himself.

Acknowledgment is gratefully expressed to Random House, Publishers, for permission to use the English translation of Aristophanes' *The Birds*.

* * *

The ancient Greeks have exercised the greatest influence on all Western culture. The West is indebted to them for their artistic, dramatic and philosophical achievement. The Greek ideal of perfection, *areté*, or *excellence*, pervades much of this transmitted written literature: in poetry and drama, in metaphysical speculation, and also in their attitude to the more material aspects of life—the emphasis on physical perfection in athletic contests as well as in statuary and sculpture and analogous spheres. In medicine and in the mathematical fields, in their creation of a polytheistic pantheon and in their imaginative mythological creations they displayed amazing pliancy and versatility. Endowed with intellectual inquisitiveness far beyond other nations, they were supreme pioneers. They probed into the meaning of life and the compo-

vii

sition of the cosmos. They investigated animate life and the relationships of men in a corporate society. They established the principles of logical reasoning and the bases of many sciences and fields of knowledge. They examined the nature of political man and the nature of imponderable concepts. They were both realistic and idealistic, and they contemplated man as a harmonious synthesis of these two attitudes.

In the fifth century B. C. the Greeks attained the apogee of human culture. The funeral oration of the statesman Pericles, which becomes a kind of essential core in Thucydides' *History of the Peloponnesian War*, is virtually the manifesto of that culture at its best and highest. And when the Athenian Empire, representative of Hellenic supremacy, began to disintegrate, Hellenism was still able to bequeath to the West its essential accomplishments, the epitome of its culture.

H. E. W.

POETRY

Homer

Hesiod

Tyrtaeus

Theognis

Sappho

Anacreon

Pindar

Theocritus

Bion

Moschus

1

HOMER

HOMER, the earliest Greek poet whose work has survived, is traditionally assigned to the ninth or the eighth century B. C. His birthplace is a matter of dispute. Even his two epic poems, the *Iliad* and the *Odyssey,* have been attributed to different authors.

The *Iliad,* in twenty-four books, describes the last days of Troy, which is usually dated 1184 B. C. The *Odyssey,* also in twenty-four books, traces the adventures of Odysseus, one of the heroes of the Greek expedition against Troy.

THE ILIAD

Book I — *The Contention of Achilles and Agamemnon*

The quarrel between two leaders of the Greek expedition, Achilles and Agamemnon, with regard to two captives, Chryseis and Briseis, provokes discord throughout the Greek camp and requires the intervention of the gods.

> Achilles' wrath, to Greece the direful spring
> Of woes unnumber'd, heavenly Goddess sing!
> That wrath which hurl'd to Pluto's gloomy reign
> The souls of mighty chiefs untimely slain:
> Whose limbs, unburied on the naked shore,
> Devouring dogs and hungry vultures tore:
> Since great Achilles and Atrides strove,
> Such was the sovereign doom, and such the will of Jove!
> Declare, O Muse! in what ill-fated hour
> Sprung the fierce strife, from what offended power
> Latona's son a dire contagion spread,
> And heap'd the camp with mountains of the dead;
> The king of men his reverend priest defied,
> And, for the king's offence, the people died.
> For Chryses sought with costly gifts to gain
> His captive daughter from the victor's chain.
> Suppliant the venerable father stands;
> Apollo's awful ensigns grace his hands:

2

By these he begs: and, lowly bending down,
Extends the sceptre and the laurel crown.
He sued to all; but chief implor'd for grace
The brother-kings of Atreus' royal race:
'Ye kings and warriors! may your vows be crown'd;
'And Troy's proud walls lie level with the ground;
'May Jove restore you, when your toils are o'er,
'Safe to the pleasures of your native shore.
'But oh! relieve a wretched parent's pain,
'And give Chryseis to these arms again;
'If mercy fail, yet let my presents move,
'And dread avenging Phoebus, son of Jove.'
　　　The Greeks in shouts their joint assent declare,
The priest to reverence, and release the fair.
Not so Atrides: he, with kingly pride,
Repuls'd the sacred sire, and thus replied:
'Hence on thy life, and fly these hostile plains,
'Nor ask, presumptuous, what the king detains:
'Hence, with thy laurel crown, and golden rod,
'Nor trust too far those ensigns of thy god.
'Mine is thy daughter, priest, and shall remain;
'And prayers, and tears, and bribes, shall plead in vain;
'Till time shall rifle every youthful grace,
'And age dismiss her from my cold embrace,
'In daily labours of the loom employ'd,
'Or doom'd to deck the bed she once enjoy'd.
'Hence then! to Argos shall the maid retire,
'Far from her native soil, and weeping sire.'
　　　The trembling priest along the shore return'd,
And in the anguish of a father mourn'd.
Disconsolate, not daring to complain,
Silent he wander'd by the sounding main:
Till, safe at distance, to his god he prays,
The god who darts around the world his rays.
　　　'O Smintheus! sprung from fair Latona's line,
'Thou guardian power of Cilla the divine,
'Thou source of light! whom Tenedos adores,
'And whose bright presence gilds thy Chrysa's shores;
'If ever with wreaths I hung thy sacred fane,
'Or fed the flames with fat of oxen slain;
'God of the silver bow! thy shafts employ,
'Avenge thy servant, and the Greeks destroy.'
　　　Thus Chryses pray'd: the fav'ring power attends,

3

And from Olympus' lofty tops descends.
Bent was his bow, the Grecian hearts to wound;
Fierce as he mov'd, his silver shafts resound.
Breathing revenge, a sudden night he spread,
And gloomy darkness roll'd around his head.
The fleet in view, he twang'd his deadly bow,
And hissing fly the feather'd fates below.
On mules and dogs th' infection first began;
And last, the vengeful arrows fix'd in man.
For nine long nights, through all the dusky air
The pyres thick-flaming shot a dismal glare.
But ere the tenth revolving day was run,
Inspir'd by Juno, Thetis' god-like son
Conven'd to council all the Grecian train;
For much the goddess mourn'd her heroes slain.

    Th'assembly seated, rising o'er the rest,
Achilles thus the king of men address'd:
'Why leave we not the fatal Trojan shore,
'And measure back the seas we cross'd before?
'The plague destroying whom the sword would spare,
''Tis time to save the few remains of war.
'But let some prophet or some sacred sage,
'Explore the cause of great Apollo's rage;
'Or learn the wasteful vengeance to remove
'By mystic dreams, for dreams descend from Jove.
'If broken vows this heavy curse have laid,
'Let altars smoke, and hecatombs be paid.
'So heaven aton'd shall dying Greece restore,
'And Phoebus dart his burning shafts no more.'

    He said, and sat; when Calchas thus replied
Calchas the wise, the Grecian priest and guide,
That sacred seer, whose comprehensive view
The past, the present, and the future knew:
Uprising slow the venerable sage
Thus spoke the prudence and the fears of age:
'Belov'd of Jove, Achilles! would'st thou know
'Why angry Phoebus bends his fatal bow?
'First give thy faith, and plight a prince's word
'Of sure protection, by thy pow'r and sword,
'For I must speak what wisdom would conceal,
'And truths, invidious to the great, reveal.
'Bold is the task, when subjects, grown too wise,
'Instruct a monarch where his error lies;

'For though we deem the short-liv'd fury past,
''Tis sure, the mighty will revenge at last.'
  To whom Pelides. 'From thy inmost soul
'Speak what thou know'st, and speak without control.
'Ev'n by that god I swear, who rules the day,
'To whom thy hands the vows of Greece convey,
'And whose blest oracles thy lips declare;
'Long as Achilles breathes this vital air,
'No daring Greek, of all the numerous band,
'Against his priest shall lift an impious hand:
'Not ev'n the chief by whom our hosts are led,
'The king of kings, shall touch that sacred head.'
  Encouraged thus, the blameless man replies:
'Nor vows unpaid, nor slighted sacrifice,
'But he, our chief, provok'd the raging pest,
'Apollo's vengeance for his injured priest.
'Nor will the god's awaken'd fury cease,
'But plagues shall spread, and funeral fires increase,
'Till the great king, without a ransom paid,
'To her own Chrysa send the black-ey'd maid.
'Perhaps, with added sacrifice and prayer,
'The priest may pardon, and the god may spare.'
  The prophet spoke; when, with a gloomy frown,
The monarch started from his shining throne;
Black choler fill'd his breast that boil'd with ire,
And from his eyeballs flash'd the living fire.
'Augur accurs'd! denouncing mischief still,
'Prophet of plagues, for ever boding ill!
'Still must that tongue some wounding message bring,
'And still thy priestly pride provoke thy king?
'For this are Phoebus' oracles explor'd,
'To teach the Greeks to murmur at their lord?
'For this with falsehoods is my honour stain'd;
'Is heaven offended, and a priest profan'd,
'Because my prize, my beauteous maid, I hold,
'And heav'nly charms prefer to proffer'd gold?
'A maid, unmatch'd in manners as in face,
'Skill'd in each art, and crown'd with every grace
'Not half so dear were Clytaemnestra's charms,
'When first her blooming beauties bless'd my arms.
'Yet, if the gods demand her, let her sail;
'Our cares are only for the public weal:
'Let me be deem'd the hateful cause of all,

5

'And suffer, rather than my people fall.
'The prize, the beauteous prize, I will resign,
'So dearly valued, and so justly mine.
'But since for common good I yield the fair,
'My private loss let grateful Greece repair;
'Nor unrewarded let your prince complain,
'That he alone has fought and bled in vain.'
'Insatiate king! (Achilles thus replies)
'Fond of the pow'er, but fonder of the prize.'
'Wouldst thou the Greeks their lawful prey should yield,
'The due reward of many a well-fought field?
'The spoils of cities raz'd, and warriors slain,
'We share with justice, as with toil we gain:
'But to resume whate'er thy avarice craves,
' (That trick of tyrants) may be borne by slaves.
'Yet if our chief for plunder only fight,
'The spoils of Ilion shall thy loss requite,
'Whene'er, by Jove's decree, our conqu'ring pow'rs
'Shall humble to the dust her lofty tow'rs.'
        Then thus the king: 'Shall I my prize resign
'With tame content, and thou possess'd of thine?
'Great as thou art, and like a god in fight,
'Think not to rob me of a soldier's right.
'At thy demand shall I restore the maid?
'First let the just equivalent be paid;
'Such as a king might ask; and let it be
'A treasure worthy her, and worthy me.
'Or grant me this, or with a monarch's claim
'This hand shall seize some other captive dame.
'The mighty Ajax shall his prize resign,
'Ulysses' spoils, or e'en thy own be mine.
'The man who suffers, loudly may complain;
'And rage he may, but he shall rage in vain.
'But this when time requires. It now remains
'We launch a bark to plough the watery plains,
'And waft the sacrifice to Chrysa's shores,
'With chosen pilots, and with lab'ring oars.
'Soon shall the fair the sable ship ascend,
'And some disputed prince the charge attend.
'This Creta's king, or Ajax shall fulfil,
'Or wise Ulysses see perform'd our will;
'Or, if our royal pleasure shall ordain,
'Achilles' self conduct her o'er the main;

6

'Let fierce Achilles, dreadful in his rage,
'The god propitiate and the pest assuage.'
    At this, Pelides, frowning stern, replied:
'O tyrant, arm'd with insolence and pride!
'Inglorious slave to interest, ever join'd
'With fraud, unworthy of a royal mind!
'What gen'rous Greek, obedient to thy word,
'Shall form an ambush, or shall lift the sword?
'What cause have I to war at thy decree?
'The distant Trojans never injured me:
'To Phthia's realms no hostile troops they led;
'Safe in her vales my warlike coursers fed;
'Far hence remov'd, the hoarse resounding main,
'And walls of rocks, secure my native reign,
'Whose fruitful soil luxuriant harvests grace,
'Rich in her fruits, and in her martial race.
'Hither we sail'd, a voluntary throng,
'T'avenge a private, not a public wrong:
'What else to Troy th'assembled nations draws,
'But thine, ungrateful, and thy brother's cause?
'Is this the pay our blood and toils deserve,
'Disgraced and injur'd by the man we serve?
'And dar'st thou threat to snatch my prize away,
'Due to the deeds of many a dreadful day?
'A prize as small, O tyrant! matched with thine,
'As thy own actions if compared to mine.
'Thine in each conquest is the wealthy prey,
'Though mine the sweat and danger of the day.
'Some trivial present to my ships I bear,
'Or barren praises pay the wounds of war.
'But know, proud monarch, I'm thy slave no more:
'My fleet shall waft me to Thessalia's shore.
'Left by Achilles on the Trojan plain,
'What spoils, what conquests, shall Atrides gain?'
    To this the king: 'Fly, mighty warrior! fly,
'Thy aid we need not, and thy threats defy:
'There want not chiefs in such a cause to fight,
'And Jove himself shall guard a monarch's right.
'Of all the kings (the gods' distinguish'd care)
'The pow'r superior none such hatred bear;
'Strife and debate thy restless soul employ,
'And wars and horrors are thy savage joy.
'If thou hast strength, 'twas Heav'n that strength bestow'd,

'For know, vain man! thy valour is from God.
'Haste, launch thy vessels, fly with speed away,
'Rule thy own realms with arbitrary sway:
'I heed thee not, but prize at equal rate
'Thy short-liv'd friendship, and thy groundless hate.
'Go, threat thy earth-born Myrmidons; but here
''Tis, mine to threaten, prince, and thine to fear.
'Know, if the god the beauteous dame demand,
'My bark shall waft her to her native land;
'But then prepare, imperious prince! prepare,
'Fierce as thou art, to yield thy captive fair:
'E'en in thy tent I'll seize the blooming prize,
'Thy lov'd Briseis, with the radiant eyes.
'Hence shalt thou prove my might, and curse the hour,
'Thou stood'st a rival of imperial pow'r;
'And hence to all our host it shall be known
'That kings are subject to the gods alone.'
    Achilles heard, with grief and rage oppress'd;
His heart swell'd high and labour'd in his breast.
Distracting thoughts by turns his bosom rul'd,
Now fir'd by wrath, and now by reason cool'd:
That prompts his hand to draw the deadly sword,
Force thro' the Greeks, and pierce their haughty lord;
This whispers soft, his vengeance to control,
And calm the rising tempest of his soul.
Just as in anguish of suspense he stay'd,
While half unsheath'd appear'd the glitt'ring blade,
Minerva swift descended from above,
Sent by the sister and the wife of Jove;
(For both the princes claim'd her equal care;)
Behind she stood, and by the golden hair
Achilles seiz'd; to him alone confess'd;
A sable cloud conceal'd her from the rest.
He sees, and sudden to the goddess cries,
(Known by the flames that sparkle from her eyes):
'Descends Minerva, in her guardian care,
'A heav'nly witness of the wrongs I bear
'From Atreus' son? Then let those eyes that view
'The daring crime, behold the vengeance too.'
'Forbear!' (the progeny of Jove replies)
'To calm thy fury I forsake the skies:
'Let great Achilles, to the gods resign'd,
'To reason yield the empire o'er his mind.

8

'By awful Juno this command is giv'n;
'The king and you are both the care of heav'n.
'The force of keen reproaches let him feel,
'But sheath, obedient, thy revenging steel.
'For I pronounce (and trust a heav'nly pow'r)
'Thy injur'd honour has its fated hour,
'When the proud monarch shall thy arms implore,
'And bribe thy friendship with a boundless store.
'Then let revenge no longer bear the sway,
'Command thy passions, and the gods obey.'
　　To her Pelides: 'With regardful ear,
''Tis just, O goddess! I thy dictates hear.
'Hard as it is, my vengeance I suppress:
'Those who revere the gods, the gods will bless.'
　　He said, observant of the blue-ey'd maid;
Then in the sheath return'd the shining blade.
The goddess swift to high Olympus flies,
And joins the sacred senate of the skies.
　　Nor yet the rage his boiling breast forsook,
Which thus redoubling on Atrides broke:
'O monster! mix'd of insolence and fear,
'Thou dog in forehead, but in heart a deer!
'When wert thou known in ambush'd fights to dare,
'Or nobly face the horrid front of war?
''Tis ours, the chance of fighting fields to try,
'Thine to look on, and bid the valiant die.
'So much 'tis safer through the camp to go,
'And rob a subject, than despoil a foe.
'Scourge of thy people, violent and base!
'Sent in Jove's anger on a slavish race,
'Who, lost to sense of generous freedom past,
'Are tam'd to wrongs, or this had been thy last.
'Now by this sacred sceptre hear me swear,
'Which never more shall leaves or blossoms bear,
'Which, sever'd from the trunk (as I from thee)
'On the bare mountains left its parent tree;
'This sceptre, form'd by temper'd steel to prove
'An ensign of the delegates of Jove,
'From whom the pow'r of laws and justice springs:
'(Tremendous oath! inviolate to kings:)
'By this I swear, when bleeding Greece again
'Shall call Achilles, she shall call in vain.
'When, flush'd with slaughter, Hector comes to spread

'The purpled shore with mountains of the dead,
'Then shalt thou mourn th'affront thy madness gave,
'Forced to deplore, when impotent to save:
'Then rage in bitterness of soul, to know
'This act has made the bravest Greek thy foe.'

He spoke; and furious hurl'd against the ground
His sceptre starr'd with golden studs around;
Then sternly silent sat. With like disdain,
The raging king return'd his frowns again.

To calm their passion with the words of age,
Slow from his seat arose the Pylian sage,
Experienc'd Nestor, in persuasion skill'd;
Words sweet as honey from his lips distill'd:
Two generations now had pass'd away,
Wise by his rules, and happy by his sway;
Two ages o'er his native realm he reign'd,
And now th'example of the third remain'd.
All view'd with awe the venerable man;
Who thus, with mild benevolence, began:
'What shame, what woe is this to Greece! what joy
'To Troy's proud monarch, and the friends of Troy!
'That adverse gods commit to stern debate
'The best, the bravest of the Grecian state.
'Young as you are, this youthful heat restrain,
'Nor think your Nestor's years and wisdom vain.
'A godlike race of heroes once I knew,
'Such as no more these aged eyes shall view.
'Lives there a chief to match Pirithous' fame,
'Dryas the bold, or Ceneus' deathless name;
'Theseus, endued with more than mortal might,
'Or Polyphemus, like the gods in fight?
'With these of old to toils of battle bred,
'In early youth my hardy days I led;
'Fir'd with the thirst which virtuous envy breeds,
'And smit with love of honourable deeds.
'Strongest of men, they pierced the mountain boar,
'Ranged the wild deserts red with monsters' gore,
'And from their hills the shaggy Centaurs tore.
'Yet these with soft persuasive arts I sway'd;
'When Nestor spoke, they listen'd and obey'd.
'If in my youth, e'en these esteem'd me wise,
'Do you, young warriors, hear my aged advice.
'Atrides, seize not on the beauteous slave;

10

'That prize the Greeks by common suffrage gave:
'Nor thou, Achilles, treat our prince with pride;
'Let kings be just, and sov'reign pow'r preside.
'Thee, the first honours of the war adorn,
'Like gods in strength, and of a goddess born;
'Him, awful majesty exalts above
'The pow'rs of earth, and sceptred sons of Jove.
'Let both unite with well-consenting mind,
'So shall authority with strength be join'd.
'Leave me, O king! to calm Achilles' rage;
'Rule thou thyself, as more advanced in age.
'Forbid it, gods! Achilles should be lost,
'The pride of Greece, and bulwark of our host.'
    This said, he ceas'd: the king of men replies:
'Thy years are awful, and thy words are wise.
'But that imperious, that unconquer'd soul,
'No laws can limit, no respect control;
'Before his pride must his superiors fall,
'His word the law, and he the lord of all?
'Him must our hosts, our chiefs, ourself obey?
'What king can bear a rival in his sway?
'Grant that the gods his matchless force have giv'n;
'Has foul reproach a privilege from heav'n?'
Here on the monarch's speech Achilles broke,
And furious, thus, and interrupting, spoke:
'Tyrant, I well deserv'd thy galling chain,
'To live thy slave, and still to serve in vain,
'Should I submit to each unjust decree;
'Command thy vassals, but command not me.
'Seize on Briseis, whom the Grecians doom'd
'My prize of war, yet tamely see resum'd;
'And seize secure; no more Achilles draws
'His conqu'ring sword in any woman's cause.
'The gods command me to forgive the past;
'But let this first invasion be the last:
'For know, thy blood, when next thou dar'st invade,
'Shall stream in vengeance on my reeking blade.
    At this they ceas'd; the stern debate expir'd:
The chiefs in sullen majesty retir'd.
    Achilles with Patroclus took his way,
Where near his tents his hollow vessels lay.
Mean time Atrides launch'd with numerous oars
A well-rigg'd ship for Chrysa's sacred shores:

11

High on the deck was fair Chryseis plac'd,
And sage Ulysses with the conduct grac'd:
Safe in her sides the hecatomb they stow'd,
Then, swiftly sailing, cut the liquid road.
  The host to expiate, next the king prepares,
With pure lustrations and with solemn pray'rs.
Wash'd by the briny wave, the pious train
Are cleans'd; and cast th'ablutions in the main.
Along the shores whole hecatombs were laid,
And bulls and goats to Phoebus' altars paid.
The sable fumes in curling spires arise,
And waft their grateful odours to the skies.
  The army thus in sacred rites engaged,
Atrides still with deep resentment raged.
To wait his will two sacred heralds stood,
Talthybius and Eurybates the good.
'Haste to the fierce Achilles' tent,' (he cries,)
'Thence bear Briseis as our royal prize:
'Submit he must; or, if they will not part,
'Ourself in arms shall tear her from his heart.'
  Th'unwilling heralds act their lord's commands;
Pensive they walk along the barren sands:
Arriv'd, the hero in his tent they find,
With gloomy aspect, on his arms reclin'd.
At awful distance long they silent stand,
Loth to advance, or speak their hard command;
Decent confusion! This the godlike man
Perceiv'd, and thus with accent mild began:
'With leave and honour enter our abodes,
'Ye sacred ministers of men and gods!
'I know your message; by constraint you came;
'Not you, but your imperious lord, I blame.
'Patroclus, haste, the fair Briseis bring;
'Conduct my captive to the haughty king.
'But witness, heralds, and proclaim my vow,
'Witness to gods above, and men below!
'But first, and loudest, to your prince declare,
'That lawless tyrant whose commands you bear;
'Unmov'd as death Achilles shall remain,
'Though prostrate Greece should bleed at every vein:
'The raging chief in frantic passion lost,
'Blind to himself, and useless to his host,
'Unskill'd to judge the future by the past,

'In blood and slaughter shall repent at last.'
  Patroclus now th'unwilling beauty brought;
She, in soft sorrows, and in pensive thought,
Pass'd silent, as the heralds held her hand,
And oft look'd back, slow-moving o'er the strand.
  Not so his loss the fierce Achilles bore;
But sad retiring to the sounding shore,
O'er the wild margin of the deep he hung,
That kindred deep from whence his mother sprung;
There, bath'd in tears of anger and disdain,
Thus loud lamented to the stormy main:
' O parent goddess! since in early bloom
' Thy son must fall, by too severe a doom;
' Sure, to so short a race of glory born,
' Great Jove in justice should this span adorn.
' Honour and fame at least the Thunderer owed;
' And ill he pays the promise of a god.
' If yon proud monarch thus thy son defies,
' Obscures my glories, and resumes my prize.'
  Far in the deep recesses of the main,
Where aged Ocean holds his watery reign,
The goddess-mother heard. The waves divide;
And like a mist she rose above the tide;
Beheld him mourning on the naked shores,
And thus the sorrows of his soul explores:
' Why grieves my son? thy anguish let me share,
' Reveal the cause, and trust a parent's care.'
  He deeply sighing said: ' To tell my woe,
' Is but to mention what too well you know.
' From Thebè, sacred to Apollo's name,
' (Eëtion's realm,) our conqu'ring army came,
' With treasure loaded and triumphant spoils,
' Whose just division crown'd the soldier's toils;
' But bright Chryseis, heav'nly prize! was led
' By vote selected to the general's bed.
' The priest of Phoebus sought by gifts to gain
' His beauteous daughter from the victor's chain;
' The fleet he reach'd, and, lowly bending down,
' Held forth the sceptre and the laurel crown,
' Entreating all; but chief implor'd for grace
' The brother-kings of Atreus' royal race:
' The gen'rous Greeks their joint consent declare,
' The priest to reverence, and release the fair.

13

'Not so Atrides: he, with wonted pride,
'The sire insulted, and his gifts denied:
'Th'insulted sire (his god's peculiar care)
'To Phoebus pray'd, and Phoebus heard the pray'r:
'A dreadful plague ensues; th'avenging darts
'Incessant fly, and pierce the Grecian hearts.
'A prophet then, inspir'd by heaven, arose,
'And points the crime, and thence derives the woes:
'Myself the first th'assembled chiefs incline
'T'avert the vengeance of the pow'r divine;
'Then, rising in his wrath, the monarch storm'd;
'Incens'd he threaten'd, and his threats perform'd:
'The fair Chryseis to her sire was sent,
'With offer'd gifts to make the god relent;
'But now he seiz'd Briseis' heav'nly charms,
'And of my valour's prize defrauds my arms,
'Defrauds the votes of all the Grecian train;
'And service, faith, and justice, plead in vain.
'But, goddess! thou thy suppliant son attend,
'To high Olympus' shining court ascend,
'Urge all the ties to former service ow'd,
'And sue for vengeance to the thundering god.
'Oft hast thou triumph'd in the glorious boast
'That thou stood'st forth, of all the ethereal host,
'Th'undaunted guard of cloud-compelling Jove.
'When the bright partner of his awful reign,
'When bold rebellion shook the realms above,
'The warlike maid, and monarch of the main,
'Traitor-gods, by mad ambition driv'n,
'Durst threat with chains th'omnipotence of heav'n.
'Then call'd by thee, the monster Titan came;
'(Whom gods Briareus, men Aegeon name;)
'Through wandering skies enormous stalk'd along;
'Not he that shakes the solid earth so strong:
'With giant-pride at Jove's high throne he stands,
'And brandish'd round him all his hundred hands.
'Th'affrighted gods confess'd their awful lord,
'They dropp'd the fetters, trembled and ador'd.
'This, goddess, this to his rememb'rance call,
'Embrace his knees, at his tribunal fall;
'Conjure him far to drive the Grecian train,
'To hurl them headlong to their fleet and main,
'To heap the shores with copious death, and bring

14

'The Greeks to know the curse of such a king:
'Let Agamemnon lift his haughty head
'O'er all his wide dominion of the dead,
'And mourn in blood, that e'er he durst disgrace
'The boldest warrior of the Grecian race.'
'Unhappy son!' (fair Thetis thus replies,
While tears celestial trickle from her eyes,)
'Why have I borne thee with a mother's throes,
'To fates averse, and nurs'd for future woes?
'So short a space the light of heav'n to view!
'So short a space! and fill'd with sorrow too!
'O might a parent's careful wish prevail,
'Far, far from Ilion should thy vessels sail,
'And thou, from camps remote, the danger shun,
'Which now, alas! too nearly threats my son.
'Yet (what I can) to move thy suit I'll go
'To great Olympus crown'd with fleecy snow.
'Meantime, secure within thy ships from far
'Behold the field, nor mingle in the war.
'The sire of gods, and all th'ethereal train,
'On the warm limits of the farthest main,
'Now mix with mortals, nor disdain to grace
'The feasts of Aethiopia's blameless race:
'Twelve days the pow'rs indulge the genial rite,
'Returning with the twelfth revolving light.
'Then will I mount the brazen dome, and move
'The high tribunal of immortal Jove.'
     The goddess spoke: the rolling waves unclose;
Then down the deep she plunged, from whence she rose,
And left him sorrowing on the lonely coast
In wild resentment for the fair he lost.

     In Chrysa's port now sage Ulysses rode;
Beneath the deck the destin'd victims stow'd;
The sails they furl'd, they lash'd the mast aside,
And dropp'd their anchors, and the pinnace tied.
Next on the shore their hecatomb they land,
Chryseis last descending on the strand.
Her, thus returning from the furrow'd main,
Ulysses led to Phoebus' sacred fane;
Where at his solemn altar, as the maid
He gave to Chryses, thus the hero said:
'Hail, reverend priest! to Phoebus' awful dome
'A suppliant I from great Atrides come:

15

'Unransom'd here receive the spotless fair;
'Accept the hecatomb the Greeks prepare;
'And may thy god, who scatters darts around,
'Aton'd by sacrifice, desist to wound.'
　　At this the sire embraced the maid again,
So sadly lost, so lately sought in vain.
Then near the altar of the darting king,
Dispos'd in rank their hecatomb they bring:
With water purify their hands, and take
The sacred offering of the salted cake;
While thus with arms devoutly raised in air,
And solemn voice, the priest directs his prayer:
'God of the silver bow, thy ear incline,
'Whose power encircles Cilla the divine;
'Whose sacred eye thy Tenedos surveys,
'And gilds fair Chrysa with distinguish'd rays.
'If, fir'd to vengeance at thy priest's request,
'Thy direful darts inflict the raging pest;
'Once more attend! avert the wasteful woe,
'And smile propitious, and unbend thy bow.'
　　So Chryses pray'd, Apollo heard his prayer:
And now the Greeks their hecatomb prepare;
Between their horns the salted barley threw,
And with their heads to heaven the victim slew:
The limbs they sever from th'inclosing hide;
The thighs, selected to the gods, divide;
On these, in double cauls involved with art,
The choicest morsels lay from every part.
The priest himself before his altar stands,
And burns the offering with his holy hands,
Pours the black wine, and sees the flame aspire;
The youths with instruments surround the fire:
The thighs thus sacrificed, and entrails drest,
Th'assistants part, transfix, and roast the rest;
Then spread the tables, the repast prepare,
Each takes his seat, and each receives his share.
When now the rage of hunger was repress'd,
With pure libations they conclude the feast;
The youths with wine the copious goblets crown'd,
And, pleas'd, dispense the flowing bowls around.
With hymns divine the joyous banquet ends,
The Paeans lengthen'd till the sun descends:
The Greeks, restor'd, the grateful notes prolong:

Apollo listens, and approves the song.
　　'Twas night; the chiefs beside their vessel lie,
Till rosy morn had purpled o'er the sky:
Then launch, and hoist the mast; indulgent gales
Supplied by Phoebus, fill the swelling sails;
The milk-white canvas bellying as they blow,
The parted ocean foams and roars below:
Above the bounding billows swift they flew,
Till now the Grecian camp appear'd in view.
Far on the beach they haul their barks to land,
(The crooked keel divides the yellow sand,)
Then part, where stretch'd along the winding bay
The ships and tents in mingled prospect lay.
　　But, raging still, amidst his navy sat
The stern Achilles, steadfast in his hate:
Nor mix'd in combat, nor in council join'd;
But wasting cares lay heavy on his mind:
In his black thoughts revenge and slaughter roll,
And scenes of blood rise dreadful in his soul.
　　Twelve days were past, and now the dawning light
The gods had summon'd to th'Olympian height:
Jove, first ascending from the watery bowers,
Leads the long order of ethereal powers.
When like the morning mist, in early day,
Rose from the flood the daughter of the sea;
And to the seats divine her flight address'd.
There, far apart, and high above the rest,
The Thunderer sat; where old Olympus shrouds
His hundred heads in heaven, and props the clouds.
Suppliant the goddess stood: one hand she placed
Beneath his beard, and one his knees embraced.
'If e'er, O father of the gods!' she said,
'My words could please thee, or my actions aid;
'Some marks of honour on thy son bestow,
'And pay in glory what in life you owe.
'Fame is at least by heavenly promise due
'To life so short, and now dishonour'd too.
'Avenge this wrong, oh ever just and wise!
'Let Greece be humbled, and the Trojans rise;
'Till the proud king, and all th'Achaian race
'Shall heap with honours him they now disgrace.'
　　Thus Thetis spoke, but Jove in silence held
The sacred councils of his breast conceal'd.

17

Not so repuls'd, the goddess closer press'd,
Still grasp'd his knees, and urged the dear request.
'O sire of gods and men! thy suppliant hear,
'Refuse or grant; for what has Jove to fear?
'Or, oh! declare, of all the powers above,
'Is wretched Thetis least the care of Jove?'
    She said, and sighing thus the god replies,
Who rolls the thunder o'er the vaulted skies:
'What hast thou ask'd? Ah why should Jove engage
'In foreign contests, and domestic rage,
'The gods' complaints, and Juno's fierce alarms,
'While I, too partial, aid the Trojan arms?
'Go, lest the haughty partner of my sway
'With jealous eyes thy close access survey;
'But part in peace, secure thy prayer is sped:
'Witness the sacred honours of our head,
'The nod that ratifies the will divine,
'The faithful, fix'd, irrevocable sign;
'This seals thy suit, and this fulfils thy vows—'
He spoke, and awful bends his sable brows;
Shakes his ambrosial curls, and gives the nod;
The stamp of fate, and sanction of the god:
High heaven with trembling the dread signal took,
And all Olympus to the centre shook.
    Swift to the seas profound the goddess flies,
Jove to his starry mansion in the skies.
The shining synod of th'immortals wait
The coming god, and from their thrones of state
Arising silent, rapt in holy fear,
Before the majesty of heaven appear.
Trembling they stand, while Jove assumes the throne,
All, but the god's imperious queen alone:
Late had she view'd the silver-footed dame,
And all her passions kindled into flame.
'Say, artful manager of heaven,' (she cries,)
'Who now partakes the secrets of the skies?
'Thy Juno knows not the decrees of fate,
'In vain the partner of imperial state.
'What fav'rite goddess then those cares divides,
'Which Jove in prudence from his consort hides?'
    To this the Thunderer: 'Seek not thou to find
'The sacred counsels of almighty mind:
'Involv'd in darkness lies the great decree,

'Nor can the depths of fate be pierced by thee.
'What fits thy knowledge, thou the first shalt know:
'The first of gods above and men below:
'But thou, nor they, shall search the thoughts that roll
'Deep in the close recesses of my soul.'
　　Full on the sire, the goddess of the skies
Roll'd the large orbs of her majestic eyes,
And thus return'd: 'Austere Saturnius, say,
'From whence this wrath, or who controls thy sway?
'Thy boundless will, for me, remains in force,
'And all thy counsels take the destin'd course.
'But 'tis for Greece I fear: for late was seen
'In close consult the silver-footed queen.
'Jove to his Thetis nothing could deny,
'Nor was the signal vain that shook the sky.
'What fatal favour has the goddess won,
'To grace her fierce inexorable son?
'Perhaps in Grecian blood to drench the plain,
'And glut his vengeance with my people slain.'
　　Then thus the god: 'Oh restless fate of pride,
'That strives to learn what heaven resolves to hide;
'Vain is the search, presumptuous and abhorr'd,
'Anxious to thee, and odious to thy lord.
'Let this suffice: th'immutable decree
'No force can shake: what is, that ought to be.
'Goddess submit, nor dare our will withstand,
'But dread the power of this avenging hand;
'Th'united strength of all the gods above
'In vain resists th'omnipotence of Jove.'
　　The Thunderer spoke, nor durst the queen reply;
A reverend horror silenced all the sky.
The feast disturb'd, with sorrow Vulcan saw
His mother menaced, and the gods in awe;
Peace at his heart, and pleasure his design,
Thus interpos'd the architect divine:
'The wretched quarrels of the mortal state
'Are far unworthy, gods! of your debate:
'Let men their days in senseless strife employ,
'We, in eternal peace, and constant joy.
'Thou, goddess-mother, with our sire comply,
'Nor break the sacred union of the sky:
'Lest, rous'd to rage, he shake the blest abodes,
'Launch the red lightning, and dethrone the gods.

19

'If you submit, the Thunderer stands appeas'd;
'The gracious power is willing to be pleas'd.'
Thus Vulcan spoke; and, rising with a bound,
The double bowl with sparkling nectar crown'd,
Which held to Juno in a cheerful way,
'Goddess,' (he cried,) 'be patient and obey.
'Dear as you are, if Jove his arm extend,
'I can but grieve, unable to defend.
'What god so daring in your aid to move,
'Or lift his hand against the force of Jove?
'Once in your cause I felt his matchless might,
'Hurl'd headlong downward from th' ethereal height;
'Toss'd all the day in rapid circles round;
'Nor, till the sun descended, touch'd the ground:
'Breathless I fell, in giddy motion lost;
'The Sinthians raised me on the Lemnian coast.'
He said, and to her hands the goblet heav'd,
Which, with a smile, the white-arm'd queen receiv'd.
Then to the rest he fill'd; and, in his turn,
Each to his lips applied the nectar'd urn.
Vulcan with awkward grace his office plies,
And unextinguish'd laughter shakes the skies.
Thus the blest gods the genial day prolong,
In feasts ambrosial, and celestial song.
Apollo tun'd the lyre; the muses round
With voice alternate aid the silver sound.
Meantime the radiant sun, to mortal sight
Descending swift, roll'd down the rapid light.
Then to their starry domes the gods depart,
The shining monuments of Vulcan's art:
Jove on his couch reclin'd his awful head,
And Juno slumber'd on the golden bed.

Book XXII — *The Death of Hector*

Hector, son of the Trojan King Priam, is slain by Achilles, whose friend Patroclus had previously been killed by Hector. Hector's death occasions deep lamentation in Troy.

Thus to their bulwarks, smit with panic fear,
The herded Ilians rush like driven deer;
There safe, they wipe the briny drops away,

And drown in bowls the labours of the day.
Close to the walls, advancing o'er the fields,
Beneath one roof of well-compacted shields,
March, bending on, the Greeks' embodied powers,
Far-stretching in the shade of Trojan towers.
Great Hector singly stay'd; chain'd down by fate,
There fix'd he stood before the Scaean gate;
Still his bold arms determin'd to employ,
The guardian still of long-defended Troy.
 Apollo now to tir'd Achilles turns,
'The power confess'd in all his glory burns,
'And what' (he cries) 'has Peleus' son in view,
'With mortal speed a godhead to pursue?
'For not to thee to know the gods is given,
'Unskill'd to trace the latent marks of heaven.
'What boots thee now, that Troy forsook the plain?
'Vain thy past labour, and thy present vain:
'Safe in their walls are now her troops bestow'd,
'While here thy frantic rage attacks a god.'
 The chief incens'd: 'Too partial god of day!
'To check my conquest in the middle way:
'How few in Ilion else had refuge found!
'What gasping numbers now had hit the ground!
'Thou robb'st me of a glory justly mine,
'Powerful of godhead, and of fraud divine:
'Mean fame, alas! for one of heavenly strain,
'To cheat a mortal who repines in vain.'
 Then to the city, terrible and strong,
With high and haughty steps he tower'd along:
So the proud courser, victor of the prize,
To the near goal with double ardour flies.
Him, as he blazing shot across the field,
The careful eyes of Priam first beheld.
Not half so dreadful rises to the sight,
Through the thick gloom of some tempestuous night,
Orion's dog, (the years when autumn weighs,)
And o'er the feebler stars exerts his rays;
Terrific glory! for his burning breath
Taints the red air with fevers, plagues, and death.
So flam'd his fiery mail. Then wept the sage:
He strikes his reverend head, now white with age;
He lifts his wither'd arms; obtests the skies;
He calls his much-lov'd son with feeble cries:

The son, resolv'd Achilles' force to dare,
Full at the Scaean gate expects the war:
While the sad father on the rampart stands,
And thus adjures him with extended hands:
'Ah, stay not, stay not! guardless and alone;
'Hector, my lov'd, my dearest, bravest son!
'Methinks already I behold thee slain,
'And stretch'd beneath that fury of the plain.
'Implacable Achilles! might'st thou be
'To all the gods no dearer than to me!
'Thee, vultures wild should scatter round the shore,
'And bloody dogs grow fiercer from thy gore!
'How many valiant sons I late enjoy'd,
'Valiant in vain! by thy curs'd arm destroy'd:
'Or, worse than slaughter'd, sold in distant isles
'To shameful bondage and unworthy toils.
'Two, while I speak, my eyes in vain explore,
'Two from one mother sprung, my Polydore
'And loved Lycaon; now perhaps no more!
'Oh! if in yonder camp they live,
'What heaps of gold, what treasures would I give!
' (Their grandsire's wealth, by right of birth their own,
'Consign'd his daughter with Lelegia's throne:)
'But if (which heaven forbid) already lost,
'All pale they wander on the Stygian coast,
'What sorrows then must their sad mother know,
'What anguish I! unutterable woe!
'Yet less than anguish, less to her, to me,
'Less to all Troy, if not depriv'd of thee.
'Yet shun Achilles! enter yet the wall;
'And spare thyself, thy father, spare us all!
'Save thy dear life: or if a soul so brave
'Neglect that thought, thy dearer glory save.
'Pity, while yet I live, these silver hairs;
'While yet thy father feels the woes he bears,
'Yet curs'd with sense! a wretch, whom in his rage
' (All trembling on the verge of helpless age)
'Great Jove has placed, sad spectacle of pain!
'The bitter dregs of fortune's cup to drain:
'To fill with scenes of death his closing eyes,
'And number all his days by miseries!
'My heroes slain, my bridal bed o'erturn'd,
'My daughters ravish'd, and my city burn'd,

22

'My bleeding infants dash'd against the floor;
'These I have yet to see, perhaps yet more!
'Perhaps ev'n I, reserv'd by angry fate
'The last sad relic of my ruined state
'(Dire pomp of sovereign wretchedness!) must fall
'And stain the pavement of my regal hall;
'Where famish'd dogs, late guardians of my door,
'Shall lick their mangled master's spatter'd gore.
'Yet for my sons I thank ye, gods! 'twas well:
'Well have they perish'd, for in fight they fell.
'Who dies in youth and vigour, dies the best,
'Struck through with wounds, all honest on the breast.
'But when the fates, in fulness of their rage,
'Spurn the hoar head of unresisting age,
'In dust the reverend lineaments deform,
'And pour to dogs the life-blood scarcely warm;
'This, this is misery! the last, the worst,
'That man can feel: man, fated to be curs'd!'
    He said, and acting what no words could say,
Rent from his head the silver locks away.
With him the mournful mother bears a part:
Yet all their sorrows turn not Hector's heart:
The zone unbraced, her bosom she display'd;
And thus, fast-falling the salt tears, she said:
'Have mercy on me, O my son! revere
'The words of age; attend a parent's prayer!
'If ever thee in these fond arms I press'd,
'Or still'd thy infant clamours at this breast;
'Ah! do not thus our helpless years forego,
'But, by our walls secur'd, repel the foe.
'Against his rage if singly thou proceed,
'Should'st thou, (but heaven avert it!) should'st thou bleed,
'Nor must thy corse lie honour'd on the bier,
'Nor spouse, nor mother, grace thee with a tear;
'Far from our pious rites, those dear remains
'Must feast the vultures on the naked plains.'
So they, while down their cheeks the torrents roll:
But fix'd remains the purpose of his soul;
Resolv'd he stands, and with a fiery glance
Expects the hero's terrible advance.
So, roll'd up his den, the swelling snake
Beholds the traveller approach the brake;
When, fed with noxious herbs, his turgid veins

23

Have gather'd half the poisons of the plains;
He burns, he stiffens with collected ire,
And his red eyeballs glare with living fire.
Beneath a turret, on his shield reclin'd,
He stood, and question'd thus his mighty mind:
'Where lies my way? To enter in the wall?
'Honour and shame th'ungenerous thought recall:
'Shall proud Polydamas before the gate
'Proclaim, his counsels are obey'd too late?
'Which timely follow'd but the former night,
'What numbers had been sav'd by Hector's flight?
'That wise advice rejected with disdain,
'Feel my folly in my people slain.
'Methinks my suffering country's voice I hear,
'But most, her worthless sons insult my ear,
'On my rash courage charge the chance of war,
'And blame those virtues which they cannot share.
'No — if I e'er return, return I must
'Glorious, my country's terror laid in dust:
'Or if I perish, let her see my fall
'In field at least, and fighting for her wall.
'And yet suppose these measures I forego,
'Approach unarm'd, and parley with the foe,
'The warrior-shield, the helm, and lance lay down,
'And treat on terms of peace to save the town:
'The wife withheld, the treasure ill-detain'd,
' (Cause of the war, and grievance of the land,)
'With honourable justice to restore;
'And add half Ilion's yet remaining store,
'Which Troy shall, sworn, produce; that injur'd Greece
'May share our wealth, and leave our walls in peace.
'But why this thought? unarm'd if I should go,
'What hope of mercy from this vengeful foe,
'But woman-like to fall, and fall without a blow?
'We greet not here, as man conversing man,
'Met at an oak, or journeying o'er a plain;
'No season now for calm, familiar talk,
'Like youths and maidens in an evening walk:
'War is our business, but to whom is given
'To die or triumph, that determine heaven!'
     Thus pondering, like a god the Greek drew nigh:
His dreadful plumage nodded from on high;
The Pelian javelin, in his better hand,

Shot trembling rays that glitter'd o'er the land;
And on his breast the beamy splendours shone
Like Jove's own lightning, or the rising sun.
As Hector sees, unusual terrors rise,
Struck by some god, he fears, recedes, and flies:
He leaves the gates, he leaves the walls behind;
Achilles follows like the winged wind.
Thus at the panting dove the falcon flies;
(The swiftest racer of the liquid skies;)
Just when he holds, or thinks he holds, his prey,
Obliquely wheeling through th'aerial way,
With open beak and shrilling cries he springs,
And aims his claws, and shoots upon his wings:
No less fore-right the rapid chase they held,
One urg'd by fury, one by fear impell'd;
Now circling round the walls their course maintain,
Where the high watch-tower overlooks the plain;
Now where the fig-trees spread their umbrage broad,
(A wider compass,) smoke along the road.
Next by Scamander's double source they bound,
Where two fam'd fountains burst the parted ground:
This hot through scorching clefts is seen to rise,
With exhalations steaming to the skies;
That the green banks in summer's heat o'erflows,
Like crystal clear, and cold as winter snows.
Each gushing fount a marble cistern fills,
Whose polish'd bed receives the falling rills;
Where Trojan dames (e'er yet alarm'd by Greece)
Wash'd their fair garments in the days of peace.
By these they pass'd, one chasing, one in flight;
(The mighty fled, pursued by stronger might;)
Swift was the course; no vulgar prize they play,
No vulgar victim must reward the day;
(Such as in races crown the speedy strife;)
The prize contended was great Hector's life.
    As when some hero's funerals are decreed,
In grateful honour of the mighty dead;
Where high rewards the vigorous youth inflame,
(Some golden tripod, or some lovely dame,)
The panting coursers swiftly turn the goal,
And with them turns the rais'd spectator's soul:
Thus three times round the Trojan wall they fly;
The gazing gods lean forward from the sky:

To whom, while eager on the chase they look,
The sire of mortals and immortals spoke:
'Unworthy sight! the man, belov'd of heaven,
'Behold, inglorious round yon city driven!
'My heart partakes the generous Hector's pain;
'Hector, whose zeal whole hecatombs has slain.
'Whose grateful fumes the gods receiv'd with joy,
'From Ida's summits, and the towers of Troy:
'Now see him flying! to his fears resign'd,
'And Fate, and fierce Achilles, close behind.
'Consult, ye powers, ('tis worthy your debate)
'Whether to snatch him from impending fate,
'Or let him bear, by stern Pelides slain,
'(Good as he is,) the lot impos'd on man?'
    Then Pallas thus: 'Shall he whose vengeance forms
'The forky bolt, and blackens heaven with storms,
'Shall he prolong one Trojan's forfeit breath,
'A man, a mortal, pre-ordain'd to death?
'And will no murmurs fill the courts above?
'No gods indignant blame their partial Jove?'
'Go then,' (return'd the sire,) 'without delay;
'Exert thy will: I give the fates their way.'
Swift at the mandate pleas'd Tritonia flies,
And stoops impetuous from the cleaving skies.
    As through the forest, o'er the vale and lawn,
The well-breath'd beagle drives the flying fawn;
In vain he tries the covert of the brakes,
Or deep beneath the trembling thicket shakes:
Sure of the vapour in the tainted dews,
The certain hound his various maze pursues:
Thus step by step, where'er the Trojan wheel'd,
There swift Achilles compass round the field.
Oft as to reach the Dardan gates he bends,
And hopes th'assistance of his pitying friends,
(Whose showering arrows, as he cours'd below,
From the high turrets might oppress the foe,)
So oft Achilles turns him to the plain:
He eyes the city, but he eyes in vain.
As men in slumbers seem with speedy pace
One to pursue, and one to lead the chase,
Their sinking limbs the fancied course forsake,
Nor this can fly, nor that can overtake:
No less the labouring heroes pant and strain;

26

While that but flies, and this pursues, in vain.
What god, O Muse! assisted Hector's force,
With Fate itself so long to hold the course?
Phoebus it was: who, in his latest hour,
Endued his knees with strength, his nerves with power:
And great Achilles, lest some Greek's advance
Should snatch the glory from his lifted lance,
Sign'd to the troops, to yield his foe the way,
And leave untouch'd the honours of the day.
Jove lifts the golden balances, that show
The fates of mortal men, and things below:
Here each contending hero's lot he tries,
And weighs, with equal hand, their destinies.
Low sinks the scale surcharg'd with Hector's fate;
Heavy with death it sinks, and hell receives the weight.
Then Phoebus left him. Fierce Minerva flies
To stern Pelides, and, triumphing, cries:
'O lov'd of Jove! this day our labours cease,
'And conquest blazes with full beams on Greece.
'Great Hector falls; that Hector fam'd so far,
'Drunk with renown, insatiable of war,
'Falls by thy hand, and mine! nor force nor flight
'Shall more avail him, nor his god of light.
'See, where in vain he supplicates above,
'Roll'd at the feet of unrelenting Jove!
'Rest here: myself will lead the Trojan on,
'And urge to meet the fate he cannot shun.'
Her voice divine the chief with joyful mind
Obey'd, and rested, on his lance reclined.
While like Deiphobus the martial dame,
(Her face, her gesture, and her arms, the same,)
In show an aid, by hapless Hector's side
Approach'd, and greets him thus with voice belied:
'Too long, O Hector! have I borne the sight
'Of this distress, and sorrow'd in thy flight:
'It fits us now a noble stand to make,
'And here, as brothers, equal fates partake.'
Then he: 'O prince! allied in blood and fame,
'Dearer than all that own a brother's name;
'Of all that Hecuba to Priam bore,
'Long tried, long lov'd; much lov'd, but honour'd more!
'Since you of all our numerous race alone
'Defend my life, regardless of your own.'

27

Again the goddess: 'Much my father's prayer,
'And much my mother's, press'd me to forbear:
'My friends embraced my knees, adjur'd my stay,
'But stronger love impell'd, and I obey.
'Come then, the glorious conflict let us try,
'Let the steel sparkle and the javelin fly;
'Or let us stretch Achilles on the field,
'Or to his arm our bloody trophies yield.'
    Fraudful she said; then swiftly march'd before;
The Dardan hero shuns his foe no more.
Sternly they met. The silence Hector broke;
His dreadful plumage nodded as he spoke:
'Enough, O son of Peleus! Troy has view'd
'Her walls thrice circled, and her chief pursued.
'But now some god within me bids me try
'Thine, or my fate: I kill thee, or I die.
'Yet on the verge of battle let us stay,
'And for a moment's space suspend the day:
'Let heaven's high powers be call'd to arbitrate
'The just conditions of this stern debate:
'(Eternal witnesses of all below,
'And faithful guardians of the treasur'd vow!)
'To them I swear: if, victor in the strife,
'Jove by these hands shall shed thy noble life,
'No vile dishonour shall thy corse pursue;
'Stripp'd of its arms alone, (the conqueror's due,)
'The rest to Greece uninjur'd I'll restore:
'Now plight thy mutual oath, I ask no more.'
'Talk not of oaths,' (the dreadful chief replies,
While anger flash'd from his disdainful eyes,)
'Detested as thou art, and ought to be,
'Nor oath nor pact Achilles plights with thee;
'Such pacts, as lambs and rabid wolves combine,
'Such leagues, as men and furious lions join,
'To such I call the gods! one constant state
'Of lasting rancour and eternal hate:
'No thought but rage, and never-ceasing strife,
'Till death extinguish rage, and thought, and life.
'Rouse then thy forces this important hour,
'Collect thy soul, and call forth all thy power.
'No farther subterfuge, no farther chance;
''Tis Pallas, Pallas gives thee to my lance.
'Each Grecian ghost by thee depriv'd of breath,

28

'Now hovers round, and calls thee to thy death.'
    He spoke, and launch'd his javelin at the foe;
But Hector shunn'd the meditated blow:
He stoop'd, while o'er his head the flying spear
Sung innocent, and spent its force in air.
Minerva watch'd it falling on the land,
Then drew, and gave to great Achilles' hand,
Unseen of Hector, who, elate with joy,
Now shakes his lance, and braves the dread of Troy:
'The life you boasted to that javelin given,
'Prince! you have miss'd. My fate depends on heaven.
'To thee (presumptuous as thou art) unknown
'Or what must prove my fortune, or thy own.
'Boasting is but an art, our fears to blind,
'And with false terrors sink another's mind.
'But know, whatever fate I am to try,
'By no dishonest wound shall Hector die;
'I shall not fall a fugitive at least,
'My soul shall bravely issue from my breast.
'But first, try thou my arm; and may this dart
'End all my country's woes, deep buried in thy heart!'
    The weapon flew, its course unerring held;
Unerring, but the heavenly shield repell'd
The mortal dart; resulting with a bound
From off the ringing orb, it struck the ground.
Hector beheld his javelin fall in vain,
Nor other lance nor other hope remain;
He calls Deiphobus, demands a spear,
In vain, for no Deiphobus was there.
All comfortless he stands: then, with a sigh,
''Tis so — heaven wills it, and my hour is nigh!
'I deem'd Deiphobus had heard my call,
'But he secure lies guarded in the wall.
'A god deceiv'd me; Pallas, 'twas thy deed:
'Death and black fate approach! 'tis I must bleed:
'No refuge now, no succour from above,
'Great Jove deserts me, and the son of Jove,
'Propitious once, and kind! Then welcome fate!
''Tis true I perish, yet I perish great:
'Yet in a mighty deed I shall expire,
'Let future ages hear it, and admire!'
    Fierce, at the word, his weighty sword he drew,
And, all collected, on Achilles flew.

29

So Jove's bold bird, high balanc'd in the air,
Stoops from the clouds to truss the quivering hare.
Nor less Achilles his fierce soul prepares;
Before his breast the flaming shield he bears,
Refulgent orb! above his fourfold cone
The gilded horse-hair sparkled in the sun,
Nodding at every step, (Vulcanian frame!)
And as he mov'd, his figure seem'd on flame.
As radiant Hesper shines with keener light,
Far beaming o'er the silver host of night,
When all the starry train emblaze the sphere:
So shone the point of great Achilles' spear.
In his right hand he waves the weapon round,
Eyes the whole man, and meditates the wound;
But the rich mail Patroclus lately wore,
Securely cased the warrior's body o'er.
One place at length he spies, to let in fate,
Where 'twixt the neck and throat the jointed plate
Gave entrance: through that penetrable part
Furious he drove the well-directed dart:
Nor pierc'd the windpipe yet, nor took the power
Of speech, unhappy! from thy dying hour.
Prone on the field the bleeding warrior lies,
While thus, triumphing, stern Achilles cries:
'At last is Hector stretch'd upon the plain,
'Who fear'd no vengeance for Patroclus slain:
'Then, prince! you should have fear'd, what now you feel;
'Achilles absent was Achilles still.
'Yet a short space the great avenger stay'd,
'Then low in dust thy strength and glory laid.
'Peaceful he sleeps, with all our rites adorn'd,
'For ever honour'd, and for ever mourn'd:
'While, cast to all the rage of hostile power,
'Thee birds shall mangle, and the dogs devour.'
      Then Hector, fainting at th'approach of death:
'By thy own soul! by those who gave thee breath!
'By all the sacred prevalence of prayer;
'Ah, leave me not for Grecian dogs to tear!
'The common rites of sepulture bestow,
'To soothe a father's and a mother's woe;
'Let their large gifts procure an urn at least,
'And Hector's ashes in his country rest.'
'No, wretch accurs'd;' relentless he replies,

(Flames, as he spoke, shot flashing from his eyes.)
'Not those who gave me breath should bid me spare,
'Nor all the sacred prevalence of prayer.
'Could I myself the bloody banquet join!
'No — to the dogs that carcass I resign.
'Should Troy to bribe me bring forth all her store,
'And, giving thousands, offer thousands more;
'Should Dardan Priam, and his weeping dame,
'Drain their whole realm to buy one funeral flame;
'Their Hector on the pile they should not see,
'Nor rob the vultures of one limb of thee.'
　　Then thus the chief, his dying accents drew:
'Thy rage, implacable! too well I knew:
'The Furies that relentless breast have steel'd,
'And curs'd thee with a heart that cannot yield.
'Yet think, a day will come, when Fate's decree
'And angry gods shall wreak this wrong on thee;
'Phoebus and Paris shall avenge my fate,
'And stretch thee here, before this Scaean gate.'
　　He ceas'd: the fates suppress'd his labouring breath,
And his eyes stiffen'd at the hand of death;
To the dark realm the spirit wings its way,
(The manly body left a load of clay,)
And plaintive glides along the dreary coast,
A naked, wandering, melancholy ghost;
Achilles, musing as he roll'd his eyes
O'er the dead hero, thus (unheard) replies:
'Die thou the first! when Jove and heaven ordain,
'I follow thee.' He said, and stripp'd the slain.
Then, forcing backward from the gaping wound
The reeking javelin, cast it on the ground.
The thronging Greeks behold with wondering eyes,
His manly beauty and superior size:
While some, ignobler, the great dead deface
With wounds ungenerous, or with taunts disgrace.
'How changed that Hector! who, like Jove, of late
'Sent lightning on our fleets and scatter'd fate!'
　　High o'er the slain the great Achilles stands,
Begirt with heroes and surrounding bands;
And thus aloud, while all the host attends:
'Princes and leaders! countrymen and friends!
'Since now at length the powerful will of heaven
'The dire destroyer to our arm has given,

'Is not Troy fall'n already? Haste, ye powers!
'See if already their deserted towers
'Are left unmann'd; or if they yet retain
'The souls of heroes, their great Hector slain?
'But what is Troy, or glory what to me?
'Or why reflects my mind on aught but thee,
'Divine Patroclus! death has seal'd his eyes;
'Unwept, unhonour'd, uninterr'd he lies!
'Can his dear image from my soul depart,
'Long as the vital spirit moves my heart?
'If, in the melancholy shades below,
'The flames of friends and lovers cease to glow,
'Yet mine shall sacred last; mine, undecay'd,
'Burn on through death, and animate my shade.
'Meanwhile, ye sons of Greece, in triumph bring
'The corse of Hector, and your Paeans sing.
'Be this the song, slow moving tow'rd the shore,
'Hector is dead, and Ilion is no more.'
    Then his fell soul a thought of vengeance bred;
(Unworthy of himself, and of the dead;)
The nervous ancles bor'd, his feet he bound
With thongs inserted through the double wound;
These fix'd up high behind the rolling wain,
His graceful head was trail'd along the plain.
Proud on his car th'insulting victor stood,
And bore aloft his arms, distilling blood.
The sudden clouds of circling dust arise.
He smites the steeds; the rapid chariot flies;
Now lost is all that formidable air;
The face divine, and long-descending hair,
Purple the ground, and streak the sable sand;
Deform'd, dishonour'd, in his native land!
Given to the rage of an insulting throng!
And, in his parent's sight, now dragg'd along.
    The mother first beheld with sad survey;
She rent her tresses, venerably grey,
And cast far off the regal veils away.
With piercing shrieks his bitter fate she moans,
While the sad father answers groans with groans;
Tears after tears his mournful cheeks o'erflow,
And the whole city wears one face of woe:
No less than if the rage of hostile fires,
From her foundations curling to her spires,

O'er the proud citadel at length should rise,
And the last blaze send Ilion to the skies.
The wretched monarch of the falling state,
Distracted presses to the Dardan gate:
Scarce the whole people stop his desperate course,
While strong affliction gives the feeble force;
Grief tears his heart, and drives him to and fro,
In all the raging impotence of woe.
At length he roll'd in dust, and thus begun,
Imploring all, and naming one by one:
'Ah! let me, let me go where sorrow calls;
'I, only I, will issue from your walls,
'(Guide or companion, friends! I ask ye none,)
'And bow before the murderer of my son
'My grief perhaps his pity may engage;
'Perhaps at least he may respect my age.
'He has a father too; a man like me;
'One, not exempt from age and misery:
'(Vigorous no more, as when his young embrace
'Begot this pest of me, and all my race.)
'How many valiant sons, in early bloom,
'Has that curs'd hand sent headlong to the tomb!
'Thee, Hector! last; thy loss (divinely brave!)
'Sinks my sad soul with sorrow to the grave.
'Oh had thy gentle spirit pass'd in peace,
'The son expiring in the sire's embrace,
'While both thy parents wept thy fatal hour,
'And, bending o'er thee, mix'd the tender shower!
'Some comfort that had been, some sad relief,
'To melt in full satiety of grief!'
     Thus wail'd the father, groveling on the ground,
And all the eyes of Ilion stream'd around.
     Amidst her matrons Hecuba appears:
(A mourning princess, and a train in tears:)
'Ah! why has heaven prolong'd this hated breath,
'Patient of horrors, to behold thy death?
'O Hector! late thy parents' pride and joy,
'The boast of nations! the defence of Troy!
'To whom her safety and her fame she ow'd,
'Her chief, her hero, and almost her god!
'O fatal change! become in one sad day
'A senseless corse! inanimated clay!'
     But not as yet the fatal news had spread

33

To fair Andromache, of Hector dead;
As yet no messenger had told his fate,
Nor e'en his stay without the Scaean gate.
Far in the close recesses of the dome
Pensive she plied the melancholy loom;
A growing work employ'd her secret hours,
Confus'dly gay with intermingled flowers.
Her fair-hair'd handmaids heat the brazen urn,
The bath preparing for her lord's return:
In vain: alas! her lord returns no more!
Unbathed he lies, and bleeds along the shore!
Now from the walls the clamours reach her ear
And all her members shake with sudden fear;
Forth from her ivory hand the shuttle falls,
As thus, astonish'd, to her maids she calls:
'Ah, follow me!' (she cried;) 'what plaintive noise
'Invades my ear? 'Tis sure my mother's voice.
'My faltering knees their trembling frame desert,
'A pulse unusual flutters at my heart.
'Some strange disaster, some reverse of fate
'(Ye gods avert it!) threats the Trojan state.
'Far be the omen which my thoughts suggest!
'But much I fear my Hector's dauntless breast
'Confronts Achilles; chas'd along the plain,
'Shut from our walls! I fear, I fear him slain!
'Safe in the crowd he ever scorn'd to wait,
'And sought for glory in the jaws of fate:
'Perhaps that noble heat has cost his breath,
'Now quench'd for ever in the arms of death.'
    She spoke; and, furious, with distracted pace,
Fears in her heart, and anguish in her face,
Flies through the dome, (the maids her steps pursue,)
And mounts the walls, and sends around her view.
Too soon her eyes the killing object found,
The godlike Hector dragg'd along the ground.
A sudden darkness shades her swimming eyes:
She faints, she falls; her breath, her colour, flies.
Her hair's fair ornaments, the braids that bound,
The net that held them, and the wreath that crown'd,
The veil and diadem, flew far away;
(The gift of Venus on her bridal day.)
Around, a train of weeping sisters stands,
To raise her sinking with assistant hands.

Scarce from the verge of death recall'd, again
She faints, or but recovers to complain:
'O wretched husband of a wretched wife!
'Born with one fate, to one unhappy life!
'For sure one star its baneful beam display'd
'On Priam's roof, and Hippoplacia's shade.
'From different parents, different climes, we came,
'At different periods, yet our fate the same!
'Why was my birth to great Eëtion ow'd,
'And why was all that tender care bestow'd?
'Would I had never been! — Oh thou, the ghost
'Of my dead husband! miserably lost.'
'Thou to the dismal realms for ever gone!
'And I abandon'd, desolate, alone!
'An only child, once comfort of my pains,
'Sad product now of hapless love, remains!
'No more to smile upon his sire! no friend
'To help him now! no father to defend!
'For should he 'scape the sword, the common doom,
'What wrongs attend him, and what grief to come!
'E'en from his own paternal roof expell'd,
'Some stranger ploughs his patrimonial field.
'The day that to the shades the father sends,
'Robs the sad orphan of his father's friends:
'He, wretched outcast of mankind! appears
'For ever sad, for ever bath'd in tears;
'Amongst the happy, unregarded he
'Hangs on the robe or trembles at the knee;
'While those his father's former bounty fed,
'Nor reach the goblet, nor divide the bread:
'The kindest but his present wants allay,
'To leave him wretched the succeeding day.
'Frugal compassion! Heedless, they who boast
'Both parents still, nor feel what he has lost,
'Shall cry, Begone! thy father feasts not here:
'The wretch obeys, retiring with a tear.
'Thus wretched, thus retiring all in tears,
'To my sad soul Astyanax appears!
'Forced by repeated insults to return,
'And to his widow'd mother vainly mourn.
'He who, with tender delicacy bred,
'With princes sported, and on dainties fed,
'And, when still evening gave him up to rest,

35

'Sunk oft in down upon the nurse's breast,
'Must—ah what must he not? Whom Ilion calls
'Astyanax, from her well-guarded walls,
'Is now that name no more, unhappy boy!
'Since now no more thy father guards his Troy.
'But thou, my Hector! liest expos'd in air,
'Far from thy parents' and thy consort's care,
'Whose hand in vain, directed by her love,
'The martial scarf and robe of triumph wove.
'Now to devouring flames be these a prey,
'Useless to thee, from this accursed day!
'Yet let the sacrifice at least be paid,
'An honour to the living, not the dead!'
　　So spake the mournful dame: her matrons hear,
Sigh back her sighs, and answer tear with tear.

THE ODYSSEY

Book XXII — *The Slaying of the Suitors*

After a succession of misadventures and strange encounters,
Odysseus reaches his home at Ithaca. During his long absence his wife
Penelope has been importuned by a multitude of suitors. Odysseus
slays all but two, as well as the unfaithful members of the household.
The variant name of Odysseus is Ulysses.

Then fierce the hero o'er the threshold strode;
Stripp'd of his rags, he blaz'd out like a god.
Full in their face the lifted bow he bore,
And quiver'd deaths, a formidable store;
Before his feet the rattling shower he threw,
And thus, terrific, to the suitor-crew:
'One venturous game this hand hath won to-day,
'Another, princes! yet remains to play;
'Another mark our arrow must attain.
'Phoebus, assist! nor be the labour vain.'
Swift as the word the parting arrow sings,
And bears thy fate, Antinous, on its wings:
Wretch that he was, of unprophetic soul!
High in his hands he rear'd the golden bowl!
Even then to drain it lengthen'd out his breath;
Changed to the deep, the bitter draught of death:
For fate who fear'd amidst a feastful band?
And fate to numbers, by a single hand?
Full through his throat Ulysses' weapon pass'd,
And pierced his neck. He falls, and breathes his last.
The tumbling goblet the wide floor o'erflows,
A stream of gore burst spouting from his nose;
Grim in convulsive agonies he sprawls:
Before him spurn'd the loaded table falls,
And spreads the pavement with a mingled flood
Of floating meats, and wine, and human blood.

Amaz'd, confounded, as they saw him fall,
Up rose the throngs tumultuous round the hall:
O'er all the dome they cast a haggard eye,
Each look'd for arms: in vain; no arms were nigh;
'Aim'st thou at princes?' (all amaz'd they said;)
'Thy last of games unhappy hast thou play'd;
'Thy erring shaft has made our bravest bleed,
'And death, unlucky guest, attends thy deed.
'Vultures shall tear thee.' Thus incens'd they spoke,
While each to chance ascrib'd the wondrous stroke,
Blind as they were; for death even now invades
His destin'd prey, and wraps them all in shades.
Then, grimly frowning, with a dreadful look,
That wither'd all their hearts, Ulysses spoke:
'Dogs, ye have had your day! ye fear'd no more
'Ulysses vengeful from the Trojan shore;
'While, to your lust and spoil a guardless prey,
'Our house, our wealth, our helpless handmaids lay:
'Not so content, with bolder frenzy fir'd,
'Even to our bed presumptuous you aspir'd:
'Laws or divine or human fail'd to move,
'Or shame of men, or dread of gods above;
'Heedless alike of infamy or praise,
'Or Fame's eternal voice in future days,
'The hour of vengeance, wretches, now is come;
'Impending fate is yours, and instant doom.'
        Thus dreadful he. Confus'd the suitors stood;
From their pale cheeks recedes the flying blood:
Trembling they sought their guilty heads to hide;
Alone the bold Eurymachus replied;
'If, as thy words import,' (he thus began,)
'Ulysses lives, and thou the mighty man,
'Great are thy wrongs, and much hast thou sustain'd
'In thy spoil'd palace, and exhausted land;
'The cause and author of those guilty deeds,
'Lo! at thy feet unjust Antinous bleeds.
'Not love, but wild ambition was his guide;
'To slay thy son, thy kingdoms to divide,
'These were his aims; but juster Jove denied.
'Since cold in death th'offender lies, oh spare
'Thy suppliant people, and receive their prayer!
'Brass, gold, and treasures, shall the spoil defray,
'Two hundred oxen every prince shall pay.

'The waste of years refunded in a day.
'Till then thy wrath is just.' Ulysses burn'd
With high disdain, and sternly thus return'd:
'All, all the treasures that enrich'd our throne
'Before your rapines, join'd with all your own,
'If offer'd, vainly should for mercy call;
''Tis you that offer, and I scorn them all:
'Your blood is my demand, your lives the prize,
'Till pale as yonder wretch each suitor lies.
'Hence with those coward terms; or fight or fly;
'This choice is left you to resist or die;
'And die I trust ye shall.' He sternly spoke:
With guilty fears the pale assembly shook.
Alone Eurymachus exhorts the train:
'Yon archer, comrades, will not shoot in vain;
'But from the threshold shall his darts be sped,
' (Whoe'er he be,) till every prince lie dead?
'Be mindful of yourselves, draw forth your swords,
'And to his shafts obtend these ample boards;
' (So need compels.) Then, all united strive
'The bold invader from his post to drive;
'The city rous'd shall to our rescue haste,
'And this mad archer soon have shot his last.'
       Swift as he spoke, he drew his traitor sword,
And like a lion rush'd against his lord:
The wary chief the rushing foe repress'd,
Who met the point and forced it in his breast:
His falling hand deserts the lifted sword,
And prone he falls extended o'er the board!
Before him wide, in mix'd effusion, roll
Th'untasted viands, and the jovial bowl.
Full through his liver pass'd the mortal wound,
With dying rage his forehead beats the ground;
He spurn'd the seat with fury as he fell,
And the fierce soul to darkness div'd, and hell.
Next bold Amphinomus his arms extends
To force the pass; the godlike man defends.
Thy spear, Telemachus, prevents th'attack;
The brazen weapon, driving through his back,
Thence through his breast its bloody passage tore;
Flat falls he thundering on the marble floor,
And his crush'd forehead marks the stone with gore.
He left his javelin in the dead, for fear

The long encumbrance of the weighty spear
To the fierce foe advantage might afford,
To rush between, and use the shorten'd sword.
With speedy ardour to his sire he flies,
And, 'Arm, great father! arm:' (in haste he cries:)
'Lo hence I run for other arms to wield,
'For missive javelins, and for helm and shield;
'Fast by our side, let either faithful swain
'In arms attend us, and their part sustain.'
'Haste, and return,' (Ulysses made reply,)
'While yet th'auxiliar shafts this hand supply;
'Lest thou alone, encounter'd by an host,
'Driven from the gate, th'important pass be lost.'
    With speed Telemachus obeys, and flies
Where piled in heaps the royal armour lies;
Four brazen helmets, eight refulgent spears,
And four broad bucklers to his sire he bears:
At once in brazen panoply they shone,
At once each servant braced his armour on;
Around their king a faithful guard they stand,
While yet each shaft flew deathful from his hand:
Chief after chief expir'd at every wound,
And swell'd the bleeding mountain on the ground.
Soon as his store of flying fates was spent,
Against the wall he set the bow unbent;
And now his shoulders bear the massy shield,
And now his hands two beamy javelins wield:
He frowns beneath his nodding plume, that play'd
O'er the high crest, and cast a dreadful shade.
    There stood a window near, whence, looking down
From o'er the porch, appear'd the subject town.
A double strength of valves secured the place,
A high and narrow, but the only pass:
The cautious king, with all preventing care,
To guard that outlet, placed Eumaeus there:
When Agelaus thus: 'Has none the sense
'To mount yon window, and alarm from thence
'The neighbour-town? the town shall force the door,
'And this bold archer soon shall shoot no more.'
    Melanthius then: 'That outlet to the gate
'So near adjoins that one may guard the strait.
'But other methods of defence remain;
'Myself with arms can furnish all the train;

'Stores from the royal magazine I bring,
'And their own darts shall pierce the prince and king.'
  He said: and mounting up the lofty stairs,
Twelve shields, twelve lances, and twelve helmets bears:
All arm, and sudden round the hall appears
A blaze of bucklers, and a wood of spears.
  The hero stands oppress'd with mighty woe,
On every side he sees the labour grow:
'Oh curs'd event! and oh unlook'd-for aid.'
'Melanthius or the women have betray'd —
'Oh my dear son!' — The father with a sigh
Then ceas'd; the filial virtue made reply:
'Falsehood is folly, and 'tis just to own
'The fault committed: this was mine alone;
'My haste neglected yonder door to bar,
'And hence the villain has supplied their war.
'Run, good Eumaeus, then, and (what before
'I thoughtless err'd in) well secure the door:
'Learn, if by female fraud this deed were done,
'Or (as my thought misgives) by Dolius' son.'
  While yet they spoke, in quest of arms again
To the high chamber stole the faithless swain,
Not unobserv'd. Eumaeus watchful ey'd,
And thus address'd Ulysses near his side:
'The miscreant we suspected takes that way;
'Him, if this arm be powerful, shall I slay?
'Or drive him hither, to receive the meed
'From thy own hand, of this detested deed?'
'Not so;' (replied Ulysses;) 'leave him there,
'For us sufficient is another care:
'Within the structure of this palace wall
'To keep enclos'd his masters till they fall.
'Go you, and seize the felon; backward bind
'His arms and legs, and fix a plank behind;
'On this his body by strong cords extend,
'And on a column near the roof suspend:
'So studied tortures his vile days shall end.'
  The ready swains obey'd with joyful haste;
Behind the felon unperceiv'd they pass'd.
As round the room in quest of arms he goes;
(The half-shut door conceals his lurking foes;)
One hand sustain'd a helm, and one the shield
Which old Laertes wont in youth to wield,

41

Cover'd with dust, with dryness chapp'd and worn,
The brass corroded, and the leather torn.
Thus laden, o'er the threshold as he stepp'd,
Fierce on the villain from each side they leap'd,
Back by the hair the trembling dastard drew
And down reluctant on the pavement threw.
Active and pleas'd the zealous swains fulfil
At every point their master's rigid will:
First, fast behind, his hands and feet they bound,
Then straiten'd cords involv'd his body round;
So drawn aloft, athwart the column tied,
The howling felon swung from side to side.
  Eumaeus scoffing then with keen disdain:
'There pass thy pleasing night, O gentle swain!
'On that soft pillow, from that envied height,
'First may'st thou see the springing dawn of light;
'So timely rise when morning streaks the east,
'To drive thy victims to the suitors' feast.'
  This said, they left him, tortur'd as he lay,
Secured the door, and hasty strode away:
Each, breathing death, resum'd his dangerous post
Near great Ulysses; four against an host.
When lo! descending to her hero's aid,
Jove's daughter Pallas, War's triumphant maid;
In Mentor's friendly form she join'd his side:
Ulysses saw, and thus with transport cried:
'Come, ever welcome, and thy succour lend;
'O every sacred name in one! my friend!
'Early we lov'd, and long our loves have grown;
'Whate'er through life's whole series I have done,
'Or good, or grateful, now to mind recall,
'And, aiding this one hour, repay it all.'
  Thus he; but pleasing hopes his bosom warm
Of Pallas latent in the friendly form.
The adverse host the phantom-warrior ey'd,
And first, loud-threatening, Agelaus cried:
'Mentor, beware, nor let that tongue persuade
'Thy frantic arm to lend Ulysses aid;
'Our force successful shall our threat make good,
'And with the sire and son's commix thy blood.
'What hop'st thou here? Thee first the sword shall slay,
'Then lop thy whole posterity away;
'Far hence thy banish'd consort shall we send;

'With his thy forfeit lands and treasures blend;
'Thus, and thus only, shalt thou join thy friend.'
　　His barbarous insult even the goddess fires,
Who thus the warrior to revenge inspires:
'Art thou Ulysses? where then shall we find
'The patient body and the constant mind?
'That courage, once the Trojans' daily dread,
'Known nine long years, and felt by heroes dead?
'And where that conduct, which revenged the lust
'Of Priam's race, and laid proud Troy in dust?
'If this, when Helen was the cause, were done;
'What for thy country now, thy queen, thy son?
'Rise then in combat, at my side attend;
'Observe what vigour gratitude can lend,
'And foes how weak, oppos'd against a friend!'
　　She spoke; but willing longer to survey
The sire and son's great acts, withheld the day;
By farther toils decreed the brave to try,
And level pois'd the wings of victory;
Then with a change of form eludes their sight,
Perch'd like a swallow on a rafter's height,
And unperceiv'd enjoys the rising fight.
Damastor's son, bold Agelaus, leads
The guilty war, Eurynomus succeeds;
With these Pisander, great Polyctor's son,
Sage Polybus, and stern Amphimedon,
With Demoptolemus: these six survive;
The best of all the shafts had left alive.
Amidst the carnage, desperate as they stand,
Thus Agelaus rous'd the lagging band:
'The hour is come, when yon fierce man no more
'With bleeding princes shall bestrew the floor;
'Lo! Mentor leaves him with an empty boast;
'The four remain, but four against an host.
'Let each at once discharge the deadly dart.
'One sure of six shall reach Ulysses' heart;
'Thus shall one stroke the glory lost regain:
'The rest must perish, their great leader slain.'
　　Then all at once their mingled lances threw,
And thirsty all of one man's blood they flew;
In vain! Minerva turn'd them with her breath,
And scatter'd short, or wide, the points of death!
With deaden'd sound one on the threshold falls,

One strikes the gate, one rings against the walls:
The storm pass'd innocent. The godlike man
Now loftier trod, and dreadful thus began:
''Tis now (brave friends) our turn, at once to throw
' (So speed them Heaven) our javelins at the foe.
'That impious race to all their past misdeeds
'Would add our blood. Injustice still proceeds.'
    He spoke: at once their fiery lances flew:
Great Demoptolemus Ulysses slew;
Euryades receiv'd the prince's dart;
The goatherd's quiver'd in Pisander's heart;
Fierce Elatus, by thine, Eumaeus, falls;
Their fall in thunder echoes round the walls.
The rest retreat; the victors now advance,
Each from the dead resumes his bloody lance.
Again the foe discharge the steely shower;
Again made frustrate by the virgin-power,
Some, turn'd by Pallas, on the threshold fall,
Some wound the gate, some ring against the wall;
Some weak, or ponderous with the brazen head,
Drop harmless, on the pavement sounding dead.
    Then bold Amphimedon his javelin cast;
Thy hand, Telemachus, it lightly raz'd:
And from Ctesippus' arm the spear elanced
On good Eumaeus' shield and shoulder glanced:
Not lessen'd of their force (so slight the wound)
Each sung along, and dropp'd upon the ground.
Fate doom'd thee next, Eurydamas, to bear
Thy death, ennobled by Ulysses' spear.
By the bold son Amphimedon was slain,
And Polybus renown'd, the faithful swain.
Pierced through the breast the rude Ctesippus bled,
And thus Philaetius gloried o'er the dead:
'There end thy pompous vaunts, and high disdain;
'O sharp in scandal, voluble, and vain!
'How weak is mortal pride! To Heaven alone
'Th'event of actions and our fates are known:
'Scoffer, behold what gratitude we bear:
'The victim's heel is answer'd with this spear.'
    Ulysses brandish'd high his vengeful steel,
And Damastorides that instant fell;
Fast by, Leocritus expiring lay;
The prince's javelin tore its bloody way

Through all his bowels: down he tumbles prone,
His batter'd front and brains besmear the stone.
  Now Pallas shines confess'd; aloft she spread
The arm of vengeance o'er their guilty heads;
The dreadful aegis blazes in their eye:
Amaz'd they see, they tremble, and they fly:
Confus'd, distracted, through the rooms they fling:
Like oxen madden'd by the breese's sting,
When sultry days, and long, succeed the gentle spring.
Not half so keen fierce vultures of the chase
Stoop from the mountains on the feather'd race,
When the wide field extended snares beset;
With conscious dread they shun the quivering net:
No help, no flight; but, wounded every way,
Headlong they drop; the fowlers seize the prey.
On all sides thus they double wound on wound,
In prostrate heaps the wretches beat the ground,
Unmanly shrieks precede each dying groan,
And a red deluge floats the reeking stone.
  Leiodes first before the victor falls:
The wretched augur thus for mercy calls:
'Oh gracious hear, nor let thy suppliant bleed:
'Still undishonour'd, or by word or deed,
'Thy house, for me, remains; by me repress'd
'Full oft was check'd th'injustice of the rest:
'Averse they heard me when I counsell'd well,
'Their hearts were harden'd, and they justly fell.
'Oh, spare an augur's consecrated head,
'Nor add the blameless to the guilty dead.
'Priest as thou art! for that detested band
'Thy lying prophecies deceived the land:
'Against Ulysses have thy vows been made;
'For them thy daily orisons were paid:
'Yet more, even to our bed thy pride aspires:
'One common crime one common fate requires.'
  Thus speaking, from the ground the sword he took
Which Agelaus' dying hand forsook:
Full through his neck the weighty falchion sped:
Along the pavement roll'd the muttering head.
  Phemius alone the hand of vengeance spar'd,
Phemius the sweet, the heaven-instructed bard.
Beside the gate the reverend minstrel stands;
The lyre, now silent, trembling in his hands;

45

Dubious to supplicate the chief, or fly
To Jove's inviolable altar nigh,
Where oft Laertes holy vows had paid,
And oft Ulysses smoking victims laid.
His honour'd harp with care he first set down,
Between the laver and the silver throne;
Then, prostrate stretch'd before the dreadful man,
Persuasive thus, with accent soft began:
'O king! to mercy be thy soul inclin'd,
'And spare the poet's ever-gentle kind.
'A deed like this thy future fame would wrong,
'For dear to gods and man is sacred song.
'Self-taught I sing; by Heaven, and Heaven alone,
'The genuine seeds of poesy are sown:
'And (what the gods bestow) the lofty lay
'To gods alone and godlike worth we pay.
'Save then the poet, and thyself reward;
''Tis thine to merit, mine is to record.
'That here I sung, was force, and not desire
'This hand reluctant touch'd the warbling wire;
'And, let thy son attest, nor sordid pay,
'Nor servile flattery, stain'd the moral lay.'
      The moving words Telemachus attends,
His sire approaches, and the bard defends.
'O mix not, father, with those impious dead
'The man divine; forbear that sacred head:
'Medon, the herald, too, our arms may spare,
'Medon, who made my infancy his care;
'If yet he breathes, permit thy son to give
'Thus much to gratitude, and bid him live.'
      Beneath a table, trembling with dismay,
Couch'd close to earth, unhappy Medon lay,
Wrapp'd in a new-slain ox's ample hide;
Swift at the word he cast his screen aside,
Sprung to the prince, embraced his knee with tears,
And thus with grateful voice address'd his ears:
'O prince! O friend! lo here thy Medon stands:
'Ah stop the hero's unresisted hands,
'Incens'd too justly by that impious brood,
'Whose guilty glories now are set in blood.'
      To whom Ulysses with a pleasing eye:
'Be bold, on friendship and my son rely;
'Live, an example for the world to read,

46

'How much more safe the good than evil deed:
'Thou, with the heaven-taught bard, in peace resort
'From blood and carnage to yon open court:
'Me other work requires.'—With timorous awe
From the dire scene th'exempted two withdraw,
Scarce sure of life, look round, and trembling move
To the bright altars of Protector Jove.
　　　Meanwhile Ulysses search'd the dome, to find
If yet there live of all th'offending kind.
Not one! complete the bloody tale he found.
All steep'd in blood, all gasping on the ground.
So, when by hollow shores the fisher-train
Sweep with their arching nets the hoary main,
And scarce the meshy toils the copious draught contain,
All naked of their element, and bare,
The fishes pant, and gasp in thinner air;
Wide o'er the sands are spread the stiffening prey,
Till the warm sun exhales their soul away.
　　　And now the king commands his son to call
Old Euryclea to the deathful hall:
The son observant not a moment stays;
The aged governess with speed obeys;
The sounding portals instant they display;
The matron moves, the prince directs the way.
On heaps of death the stern Ulysses stood,
All black with dust, and cover'd thick with blood.
So the grim lion from the slaughter comes,
Dreadful he glares, and terribly he foams,
His breast with marks of carnage painted o'er,
His jaws all dropping with the bull's black gore.
　　　Soon as her eyes the welcome object met,
The guilty fall'n, the mighty deed complete;
A scream of joy her feeble voice essay'd:
The hero check'd her, and compos'dly said:
'Woman, experienc'd as thou art, control
'Indecent joy, and feast thy secret soul.
'T'insult the dead is cruel and unjust;
'Fate and their crime have sunk them to the dust.
'Nor heeded these the censure of mankind,
'The good and bad were equal in their mind.
'Justly the price of worthlessness they paid,
'And each now wails an unlamented shade.
'But thou sincere! O Euryclea, say,

47

'What maids dishonour us, and what obey?'
    Then she: 'In these thy kingly walls remain
' (My son) full fifty of the handmaid train,
'Taught, by my care, to cull the fleece or weave,
'And servitude with pleasing tasks deceive;
'Of these, twice six pursue their wicked way,
'Nor me, nor chaste Penelope obey;
'Nor fits it that Telemachus command
' (Young as he is) his mother's female band.
'Hence to the upper chambers let me fly,
'Where slumbers soft now close the royal eye;
'There wake her with the news'—the matron cried.
'Not so, (Ulysses, more sedate, replied,)
'Bring first the crew who wrought these guilty deeds.'
    In haste the matron parts; the king proceeds.
'Now to dispose the dead, the care remains
'To you, my son, and you, my faithful swains;
'Th'offending females to that task we doom,
'To wash, to scent, and purify the room:
'These (every table cleans'd, and every throne,
'And all the melancholy labour done,)
'Drive to yon court, without the palace-wall,
'There the revenging sword shall smite them all;
'So with the suitors let them mix in dust,
'Stretch'd in a long oblivion of their lust.'
    He said: the lamentable train appear,
Each vents a groan, and drops a tender tear:
Each heav'd her mournful burden and beneath
The porch depos'd the ghastly heap of death.
The chief severe, compelling each to move,
Urged the dire task imperious from above:
With thirsty sponge they rub the tables o'er;
(The swains unite their toil;) the walls, the floor,
Wash'd with th'effusive wave, are purged of gore.
Once more the palace set in fair array,
To the base court the females take their way:
There compass'd close between the dome and wall,
(Their life's last scene,) they trembling wait their fall.
    Then thus the prince: 'To these shall we afford
'A fate so pure, as by the martial sword?
'To these, the nightly prostitutes to shame,
'And base revilers of our house and name?'
    Thus speaking, on the circling wall he strung

48

A ship's tough cable, from a column hung;
Near the high top he strain'd it strongly round,
Whence no contending foot could reach the ground.
Their heads above connected in a row,
They beat the air with quivering feet below:
Thus on some tree hung struggling in the snare,
The doves or thrushes flap their wings in air.
Soon fled the soul impure, and left behind
The empty corse to waver with the wind.

Then forth they led Melanthius, and began
Their bloody work; they lopp'd away the man,
Morsel for dogs! then trimm'd with brazen shears
The wretch, and shorten'd of his nose and ears;
His hands and feet last felt the cruel steel;
He roar'd, and torments gave his soul to hell.
They wash, and to Ulysses take their way,
So ends the bloody business of the day.

To Euryclea then address'd the king:
'Bring hither fire, and hither sulphur bring,
'To purge the palace: then the queen attend,
'And let her with her matron-train descend;
'The matron-train, with all the virgin-band,
'Assemble here, to learn their lord's command.'

Then Euryclea: 'Joyful I obey,
'But cast those mean dishonest rags away;
'Permit me first the royal robes to bring:
'Ill suits this garb the shoulders of a king.'
'Bring sulphur straight, and fire,' (the monarch cries.)
She hears, and at the word obedient flies.
With fire and sulphur, cure of noxious fumes,
He purged the walls, and blood-polluted rooms.
Again the matron springs with eager pace,
And spreads her lord's return from place to place.
They hear, rush forth, and instant round him stand,
A gazing throng, a torch in every hand.
They saw, they knew him, and with fond embrace
Each humbly kiss'd his knee, or hand, or face;
He knows them all: in all such truth appears,
Even he indulges the sweet joy of tears.

Alexander Pope

HESIOD

HESIOD, who flourished in the ninth century B. C., was himself a tiller of the soil. His didactic epic, *Works and Days,* a poetic handbook for farmers, glorifies labor as a means of escape from the evil that pervades the universe. Another work, the *Theogony,* relates tales of the ancient deities.

THE SPREAD OF EVIL

With succeeding ages, evil becomes more dominant, and man correspondingly deteriorates.

When gods alike and mortals rose to birth,
A golden race th'immortals formed on earth
Of many languaged men: they lived of old
When Saturn reigned in heaven, an age of gold.
Like gods they lived, with calm untroubled mind,
Free from the toil and anguish of our kind:
Nor e'er decrepid age misshaped their frame,
The hand's, the foot's proportions still the same.
Strangers to ill, their lives in feasts flowed by:
Wealthy in flocks; dear to the blest on high:
Dying they sank in sleep, nor seemed to die.
Theirs was each good; the life-sustaining soil
Yielded its copious fruits, unbribed by toil:
They with abundant goods midst quiet lands
All willing shared the gatherings of their hands.
When earth's dark womb had closed this race around,
High Jove as daemons raised them from the ground.
Earth-wandering spirits they their charge began,
The ministers of good, and guards of man.
Mantled with mist of darkling air they glide,
And compass earth, and pass on every side:
And mark with earnest vigilance of eyes
Where just deeds live, or crooked wrongs arise —
Kingly their state; and, delegate from heaven,
By their vicarious hands the wealth of fields is given.

The gods then formed a second race of man,
Degenerate far; and silver years began.
Unlike the mortals of a golden kind:
Unlike in frame of limbs and mould of mind.
Yet still a hundred years beheld the boy
Beneath the mother's roof, her infant joy,
All tender and unformed: but when the flower
Of manhood bloomed, it withered in a hour.
Their frantic follies wrought them pain and woe:
Nor mutual outrage could their hands forego:
Nor would they serve the gods: nor altars raise
That in just cities shed their holy blaze.
Them angry Jove ingulfed, who dared refuse
The gods their glory and their sacred dues:
Yet named the second-blest in earth they lie,
And second honours grace their memory.
    The Sire of heaven and earth created then
A race, the third of many-languaged men.
Unlike the silver they: of brazen mould:
With ashen war-spears terrible and bold:
Their thoughts were bent on violence alone,
The deeds of battle and the dying groan.
Bloody their feasts, with wheaten food unblest:
Of adamant was each unyielding breast.
Huge, nerved with strength each hardy giant stands,
And mocks approach with unresisted hands:
Their mansions, implements, and armour shine
In brass; dark iron slept within the mine.
They by each other's hands inglorious fell,
In freezing darkness plunged, the house of hell:
Fierce though they were, their mortal course was run;
Death gloomy seized and snatched them from the sun.
    Them when th'abyss had covered from the skies,
Lo! the fourth age on nurturing earth arise:
Jove formed the race a better, juster line;
A race of heroes and of stamp divine:
Lights of the age that rose before our own;
As demi-gods o'er earth's wide regions known.
Yet these dread battle hurried to their end:
Some where the seven-fold gates of Thebes ascend —
The Cadmian realm, where they with fatal might
Strove for the flocks of Oedipus in fight.
Some war in navies led to Troy's far shore;

O'er the great space of sea their course they bore,
For sake of Helen with the beauteous hair:
And death for Helen's sake o'erwhelmed them there.
Them on earth's utmost verge the god assigned
A life, a seat, distinct from human kind:
Beside the deepening whirlpools of the main,
In those blest isles where Saturn holds his reign,
Apart from Heaven's immortals: calm they share
A rest unsullied by the clouds of care:
And yearly thrice with sweet luxuriance crowned
Springs the ripe harvest from the teeming ground.
    Oh would that nature had denied me birth
Midst this fifth race, this iron age of earth:
That long before within the grave I lay,
Or long hereafter could behold the day!
Corrupt the race, with toils and griefs opprest,
Nor day nor night can yield a pause of rest.
Still do the gods a weight of care bestow,
Though still some good is mingled with the woe.
Jove on this race of many-languaged man,
Speeds the swift ruin which but slow began;
For scarcely spring they to the light of day
Ere age untimely strews their temples gray.
No fathers in the sons their features trace:
The sons reflect no more the father's face:
The host with kindness greets his guest no more,
And friends and brethren love not as of yore.
Reckless of heaven's revenge, the sons behold
The hoary parents wax too swiftly old,
And, impious, point the keen dishonouring tongue
With hard reproofs and bitter mockeries hung:
Nor grateful in declining age repay
The nurturing fondness of their better day.
Now man's right hand is law: for spoil they wait
And lay their mutual cities desolate:
Unhonoured he, by whom his oath is feared,
Nor are the good beloved, the just revered.
With favour graced the evil-doer stands,
Nor curbs with shame nor equity his hands:
With crooked slanders wounds the virtuous man,
And stamps with perjury what hate began.
Lo! ill-rejoicing Envy, winged with lies,
Scattering calumnious rumours as she flies,

The steps of miserable men pursue
With haggard aspect, blasting to the view,
Till those fair forms in snowy raiment bright
Leave the broad earth and heaven-ward soar from sight:
Justice and Modesty from mortals driven,
Rise to th'immortal family of heaven:
Dread sorrows to forsaken man remain;
No cure of ills: no remedy of pain.

C. A. Elton

ADVICE TO FARMERS

In poetic form, the following lines constitute a series of agricultural precepts.

Plough naked still, and naked sow the soil,
And naked reap, if kindly to thy toil
Thou hope to gather all that Ceres yields,
And view thy crops in season crown the fields;
Lest thou to strangers' gates penurious rove,
And every needy effort fruitless prove:
E'en as to me thou cam'st: but hope no more
That I shall give or lend thee of my store.
Oh foolish Perses! be the labours thine
Which the good gods to earthly man assign;
Lest with thy spouse, thy babes, thou vagrant ply,
And sorrowing crave those alms which all deny.
Twice may thy plaints benignant favour gain,
And haply thrice may not be poured in vain;
If still persisting plead thy wearying prayer,
Thy words are nought, thy eloquence is air.
Did exhortation move, the thought should be,
From debt releasement, days from hunger free.
A house, a woman, and a steer provide,
Thy slave to tend the cows, but not thy bride.
Within let all fit implements abound,
Lest with refused entreaty wandering round,
Thy wants still press, the season glides away,
And thou with scanted labour mourn the day.
Thy task defer not till the morn arise,
Or the third sun th'unfinished work surprise.
The idler never shall his garners fill,

Nor he that still defers and lingers still.
Lo! diligence can prosper every toil;
The loiterer strives with loss and execrates the soil.
　　When rest the keen strength of th' o'erpowering sun
From heat that made the pores in rivers run;
When rushes in fresh rains autumnal Jove,
And man's unburthened limbs now lighter move;
(For now the star of day with transient light
Rolls o'er our heads and joys in longer night;)
When from the worm the forest boles are sound,
Trees bud no more, but earthward cast around
Their withering foliage, then remember well
The timely labour, and thy timber fell.
Hew from the wood a timber of three feet;
Three cubits may the pestle's length complete;
Seven feet the fittest axle-tree extends;
If eight the log, the eighth a mallet lends.
Cleave many curved blocks thy wheel to round,
And let three spans its outmost orbit bound,
Whereon slow-rolling thy suspended wain,
Ten spans in breadth, may traverse firm the plain.
　　If hill or field supply a holm-oak bough
Of bending figure like the downward plough,
Bear it away: this durable remains
While the strong steers in ridges cleave the plains:
If with fine nails thy artist join the whole,
Affix the share-beam, and adapt the pole.
　　Two ploughs provide, on household works intent,
This art-compacted, that of native bent:
A prudent fore-thought: one may crashing fail,
The other, instant yoked, shall prompt avail.
Of elm or bay the draught-pole firm endures,
The plough-tail holm, the share-beam oak secures.
　　Two males procure: be nine their sum of years:
Then hale and strong for toil the sturdy steers:
Nor shall they head-strong-struggling spurn the soil,
And snap the plough and mar th'unfinished toil.
In forty's prime thy ploughman: one with bread
Of four-squared loaf in double portions fed.
He steadily shall cut the furrow true,
Nor towards his fellows glance a rambling view,
Still on his task intent: a stripling throws
Heedless the seed, and in one furrow strows

54

The lavish handful twice: while wistful stray
His longing thoughts to comrades far away.
    Mark yearly when among the clouds on high
Thou hear'st the shrill crane's migratory cry,
Of ploughing time the sign and wintry rains:
Care gnaws his heart who destitute remains
Of the fit yoke: for then the season falls
To feed thy horned steers within their stalls.
Easy to speak the word, "beseech thee friend!
Thy wagon and thy yoke of oxen lend:"
Easy the prompt refusal; "nay, but I
Have need of oxen, and their work is nigh."
Rich in his own conceit, he then too late
May think to rear the waggon's timbered weight:
Fool! nor yet knows the complicated frame
A hundred seasoned blocks may fitly claim:
These let thy timely care provide before,
And pile beneath thy roof the ready store.
    Improve the season: to the plough apply
Both thou and thine; and toil in wet and dry:
Haste to the field with break of glimmering morn,
That so thy grounds may wave with thickening corn.
    In spring upturn the glebe: and break again
With summer tilth the iterated plain.
It shall not mock thy hopes: be last thy toil,
Raised in light ridge, to sow the fallowed soil:
The fallowed soil bids execration fly,
And brightens with content the infant's eye.
    Jove subterrene, chaste Ceres claim thy vow,
When, grasping first the handle of the plough,
O'er thy broad oxen's backs thy quickening hand
With lifted stroke lets fall the goading wand,
Whilst yoked and harnessed by the fastening thong,
They slowly drag the draught-pole's length along.
So shall the sacred gifts of earth appear,
And ripe luxuriance clothe the plenteous ear.
    A boy should tread thy steps: with rake o'erlay
The buried seed, and scare the birds away:
(Good is the apt economy of things,
While evil management its mischief brings:)
Thus, if aerial Jove thy cares befriend,
And crown thy tillage with a prosperous end,
Shall the rich ear in fulness of its grain

Nod on the stalk and bend it to the plain.
So shalt thou sweep the spider's films away,
That round thy hollow bins lie hid from day:
I ween, rejoicing in the foodful stores
Obtained at length, and laid within thy doors:
For plenteousness shall glad thee through the year
Till the white blossoms of the spring appear:
Nor thou on others' heaps a gazer be,
But others owe their borrowed store to thee.

C. A. Elton

TYRTAEUS

TYRTAEUS was a seventh century B. C. elegiac poet. He was traditionally believed to have been a lame Athenian schoolmaster. Author of inspiring martial poems.

HOMAGE TO MARTIAL YOUTH

Yet are ye Hercules' unconquer'd race —
    Remand, heroic tribe, your spirit lost!
Nor yet all-seeing Jove averts his face;
    Then meet without a fear the thronging host.

Each to the foe his steady shield oppose,
    Accoutred to resign his hateful breath:
The friendly sun a mild effulgence throws
    On valour's grave, though dark the frown of death.

Yes! ye have known the ruthless work of war!
    Yes! ye have known its tears — its heavy woe;
When, scattering in pale flight, ye rush'd afar,
    Or chas'd the routed squadrons of the foe.

Of those who dare, a strong compacted band,
    Firm for the fight their warrior-spirits link,
And grapple with the foeman, hand to hand,
    How few, through deadly wounds expiring, sink.

They, foremost in the ranks of battle, guard
    Th'inglorious multitude that march behind;
While shrinking fears the coward's step retard,
    And dies each virtue in the feeble mind.

But 'tis not in the force of words to paint
    What varied ills attend th'ignoble troop,
Who trembling on the scene of glory faint,
    Or wound the fugitives that breathless droop.

Basely the soldier stabs, with hurried thrust,
   The unresisting wretch, that shieldless flies!
At his last gasp dishonour'd in the dust
   (His back transfix'd with spears) the dastard lies!

Thus then, bold youth, the rules of valour learn:
   Stand firm, and fix on earth thy rooted feet:
Bite with thy teeth thy eager lips; and stern
   In conscious strength, the rushing onset meet:

And shelter with thy broad and bossy shield
   Thighs and shins, thy shoulders and thy breast;
The long spear ponderous in thy right-hand wield,
   And on thy head high nod the dreadful crest.

Mark well the lessons of the warlike art,
   That teach thee, if the shield with ample round,
Protect thy bosom, to approach the dart,
   Nor choose with timid care the distant ground.

But, for close combat with the fronting foe,
   Elate in valorous attitude draw near;
And aiming, hand to hand, the fateful blow,
   Brandish thy temper'd blade or massy spear.

Yes! for the rage of stubborn grapple steel'd,
   Grasp the sword's hilt, and couch the long-beat lance;
Foot to the foeman's foot, and shield to shield,
   Crest ev'n to crest, and helm to helm, advance.

But ye, light arm'd who, trembling in the rear,
   Bear smaller targets, at a distance, throw
The hissing stone, or hurl the polish'd spear,
   (Plac'd nigh your panoply) to mar the foe.

Richard Polwhele

THEOGNIS

THEOGNIS, who flourished in the sixth century B. C., was an aristocrat who went into exile. He is the author of many elegiac poems largely directed as emphasis on good manners and morals.

MORALITY AND MANNERS

To rear a child is easy, but to teach
Morals and manners is beyond our reach;
To make the foolish wise, the wicked good,
That science never yet was understood.
The sons of Esculapius, if their art
Could remedy a perverse and a wicked heart,
Might earn enormous wages! But, in fact,
The mind is not compounded and compact
Of precept and example; human art
In human nature has no share or part.
Hatred of vice, the fear of shame and sin,
Are things of native growth, not grafted in:
Else wise and worthy parents might correct
In children's hearts each error and defect:
Whereas we see them disappointed still,
No scheme nor artifice of human skill
Can rectify the passions or the will.

Our commonwealth preserves its former frame,
Our common people are no more the same:
They that in skins and hides were rudely dress'd
Nor dream't of law, nor sought to be redress'd
By rules of right, but in the days of old
Flock'd to the town, like cattle to the fold,
Are now the brave and wise; and we, the rest,
(Their betters nominally, once the best)
Degenerate, debased, timid, mean!
Who can endure to witness such a scene?

59

Their easy courtesies, the ready smile,
Prompt to deride, to flatter, and beguile!
Their utter disregard of right or wrong,
Of truth or honour! — Out of such a throng
(For any difficulties, any need,
For any bold design or manly deed)
Never imagine you can choose a just
Or steady friend, or faithful in his trust.
But change your habits! let them go their way!
Be condescending, affable, and gay!

I walk by rule and measure, and incline
To neither side, but take an even line;
Fix'd in a single purpose and design.
With learning's happy gifts to celebrate,
To civilize and dignify the state:
Not leaguing with the discontented crew,
Nor with the proud and arbitrary few.

The generous and the brave, in common fame,
From time to time encounter praise or blame;
The vulgar pass unheeded; none escape
Scandal or insult in some form or shape.
Most fortunate are those, alive or dead,

Of whom the least is thought, the least is said.
Court not a tyrant's favour, nor combine
To further his iniquitous design;
But, if your faith is pledg'd, though late and loth,
If convenants have pass'd between you both,
Never assassinate him! keep your oath!
But should he still misuse his lawless power
To trample on the people, and devour,
Depose or overturn him; anyhow!
Your oath permits it, and the gods allow.

The sovereign single person — what cares he
For love or hate, for friend or enemy? —
His single purpose is utility.

If popular distrust and hate prevail,
If saucy mutineers insult and rail,
Fret not your eager spirit, — take a line
Just, sober, and discreet, the same as mine.

60

Let no persuasive art tempt you to place
Your confidence in crafty minds and base; —
How can it answer? Will their help avail
When danger presses, and your foes assail?
The blessing which the gods in bounty send,
Will they consent to share it with a friend?
No! — To bestrew the waves with scatter'd grain,
To cultivate the surface of the main,
Is not a task more absolutely vain

Than cultivating such allies as these, —
Fickle and unproductive as the seas.
Such are all baser minds, never at rest,
With new demands importunately press'd,
A new pretension or a new request;
Till, foil'd with a refusal of the last,
They disavow their obligations past.
But brave and gallant hearts are cheaply gain'd,
Faithful adherents, easily retain'd;
Men that will never disavow the debt
Of gratitude, or cancel or forget.

Waste not your efforts, struggle not, my friend,
Idle and old abuses to defend:
Take heed! the very measures that you press
May bring repentance with their own success.

Rash angry words, and spoken out of season,
When passion has usurp'd the throne of reason,
Have ruin'd many. — Passion is unjust,
And, for an idle transitory gust
Of gratified revenge, dooms us to pay
With long repentance at a later day.

The gods send Insolence to lead astray
The man whom Fortune and the Fates betray;
Predestin'd to precipitate decay.
Wealth nurses Insolence, and wealth, we find,
When coupled with a poor and paltry mind,
Is evermore with insolence combin'd.
Never in anger with the meaner sort
Be mov'd to a contemptuous retort,
Deriding their distresses; nor despise

61

In hasty speech their wants and miseries.
Jove holds the balance, and the gods dispense
For all mankind riches and indigence.

Join with the world; adopt with every man
His party views, his temper, and his plan;
Strive to avoid offence, study to please,
Like the sagacious inmate of the seas,
That an accommodating colour brings,
Conforming to the rock to which he clings;
With every change of place changing his hue;
The model for a statesman such as you.

Let not a base calumnious pretence,
Exaggerating a minute offence,
Move you to wrong a friend; if, every time,
Faults in a friend were treated as a crime,
Here upon earth no friendship could have place.
But we, the creatures of a faulty race
Amongst ourselves, offend and are forgiven:
Vengeance is the prerogative of heaven.

Schemes unadvisable and out of reason
Are best adjourn'd — wait for a proper season!
Time and a fair conjuncture govern all.
Hasty ambition hurries to a fall;
A fall predestin'd and ordain'd by heaven:
By a judicial madness madly driven,
Mistaking and confounding good and evil,
Men lose their senses, as they leave their level.

A trusty partisan, faithful and bold,
Is worth his weight in silver or in gold,
For times of trouble. — But the race is rare;
Steady determin'd men, ready to share
Good or ill fortune! —, such, if such there are,
Could you survey the world, and search it round,
And bring together all that could be found,
The largest company you could enroll,
A single vessel could embark the whole! —
So few there are! the noble manly minds
Faithful and firm, the men that honour binds;
Impregnable to danger and to pain
And low seduction in the shape of gain.

62

From many a friend you must withhold your plans;
No man is safe with many partisans,
No secret! — With a party, sure but small,
Of bold adherents, trusty men withal,
You may succeed: else ruin must ensue,
Inevitable, for your friends and you.
An exile has no friends! no partisan
Is firm or faithful to the banish'd man;
A disappointment and a punishment,
Harder to bear, and worse than banishment.

Happy the man, with worldly wealth and ease,
Who, dying in good time, departs in peace.
Nor yet reduc'd to wander as a stranger
In exile and distress and daily danger;
To fawn upon his foes, to risk the trial
Of a friend's faith, and suffer a denial!

No mean or coward heart will I commend
In an old comrade or a party friend:
Nor with ungenerous, hasty zeal decry
A noble-minded gallant enemy.
And lapt beneath a load of earth to lie!
Not to be born — never to see the sun —
No worldly blessing is a greater one!
And the next best is speedily to die,

You, great Apollo, with its walls and towers
Fenc'd and adorn'd of old this town of ours!
Such favour in thy sight Alcathous won,
Of Pelops old the fair and manly son.
Now, therefore, in the clemency divine,
Protect these very walls, our own and thine!
Guide and assist us, turn aside the boast
Of the destroying haughty Persian host!
So shall thy people each returning spring
Slay fatted hecatombs, and gladly bring
Fair gifts, with chaunted hymns and lively song,
Dances and feasts, and happy shouts among;
Before thy altar, glorifying thee,
In peace and health and wealth, cheerful and free.

Yet much I fear the faction and the strife,
Throughout our Grecian cities, raging rife,

And their wild councils. But do thou defend
This town of ours, our founder and our friend!
Wide have I wander'd, far beyond the sea,
Even to the distant shores of Sicily,
To broad Euboea's plentiful domain,
With the rich vineyards in its planted plain;
And to the sunny wave and winding edge
Of fair Eurotas, with its reedy sedge;
Where Sparta stands in simple majesty,
Among her manly rulers, there was I!
Greeted and welcom'd (there and everywhere)
With courteous entertainment, kind and fair;
Yet still my weary spirit would repine,
Longing again to view this land of mine.

Henceforward no design nor interest
Shall ever move me, but the first and best,
With learning's happy gift to celebrate,
To adorn and dignify my native state.
The song, the dance, music and verse agreeing,
Will occupy my life, and fill my being:
Pursuits of elegance and learned skill
(With good repute and kindness and good will,
Among the wiser sort) will pass my time
Without an enemy, without a crime;
Harmless and just with every rank of men,
Both the free native and the denizen.

J. H. Frere

SAPPHO

SAPPHO was a poetess who flourished in the seventh century B. C. She is associated with Mytilene, the chief city of Lesbos, where she conducted a school of poetry. Her themes were largely amatory.

SAPPHO DEAD

Thou liest dead, and there will be no memory left
    behind
Of thee or thine in all the earth, for never didst
    thou bind
The roses of Pierian streams upon thy brow; thy
    doom
Is writ to flit with unknown ghosts in cold and
    nameless gloom.

Edwin Arnold

EVENING LULLABY
Hesperus brings all things back
Which the daylight made us lack,
Brings the sheep and goats to rest,
Brings the baby to the breast.

Edwin Arnold

THOUGHTS ON LOVE

Oh, my sweet mother, 'tis in vain,
    I cannot weave as once I wove,
So wildered is my heart and brain
    With thinking of that youth I love.

Thomas Moore

65

SWEET APPLE

Like the sweet apple which reddens upon the
    topmost bough,
A-top on the topmost twig, — which the pluckers
    forgot, somehow, —
Forgot it not, nay, but got it not, for none could
    get it till now.

Dante G. Rossetti

FLOWERS

Of foliage and flowers love-laden
    Twine wreaths for thy flowing hair,
With thine own soft fingers, maiden,
    Weave garlands of parsley fair;
For flowers are sweet, and the Graces
    On suppliants wreathed with the may
Look down from their heavenly places,
    But turn from the crownless away.

John Addington Symonds

HYMN TO APHRODITE

Star-throned, incorruptible Aphrodite,
Child of Zeus, wile-weaving, I supplicate thee,
Tame me not with pangs of the heart, dread mistress,
    Nay, nor with anguish.

But come thou, if erst in the days departed
Thou didst lend thine ear to my lamentation,
And from far, the house of thy sire deserting,
    Camest with golden

Car yoked: thee thy beautiful sparrows hurried
Swift with multitudinous pinions fluttering
O'er black earth, adown from the height of heaven
    Through middle ether:

Quickly journeyed they; and, O thou, blest Lady,
Smiled at me with brow of undying lustre,
Asked me what new grief at my heart lay, wherefore
     Now I had called thee,

What I fain would have to assuage the torment
Of my frenzied soul. "And whom now, to please thee,
Must persuasion lure to thy love, and who now,
     Sappho, hath wronged thee?

Yea, for though she flies, she shall quickly chase thee;
Yea, though gifts she spurns, she shall soon bestow them;
Yea, though now she loves not, she soon shall love thee,
     Yea, though she will not!"

Come, come now too! Come, and from heavy heart-ache
Free my soul, and all that my longing yearns to
Have done, do thou; be thou for me thyself too
     Help in the battle!

John Addington Symonds

ANACREON

ANACREON was a lyric poet of the sixth century B. C. His main themes were sensual and sympotic.

YOUTH DECAYS

Golden hues of youth are fled;
Hoary locks deform my head.
Bloomy graces, dalliance gay,
All the flowers of life decay.
Withering age begins to trace
Sad memorials o'er my face:
Time has shed its sweetest bloom,
All the future must be gloom!
This awakes my hourly sighing;
Dreary is the thought of dying!
Pluto's is a dark abode,
Sad the journey, sad the road:
And, the gloomy travel o'er,
Ah! we can return no more!

Thomas Moore

TAKE THE CASH, AND LET THE CREDIT GO

Rich in bliss, I proudly scorn
The stream of Amalthea's horn!
Nor should I ask to call the throne
Of the Tartessian prince my own;
To totter through his train of years,
The victim of declining fears.
One little hour of joy for me
Is worthy a dull eternity.

Thomas Moore

PINDAR

PINDAR (518-438 B. C.) was a lyric poet. Of distinguished family, he traveled extensively. Of his odes in seventeen books, three books, together with fragments, have survived. Their subjects are largely athletic victories, but these poems are also pervaded by religious implications.

GLORIFICATION OF THEOXENOS

O soul, 'tis thine in season meet,
To pluck of love the blossom sweet,
    When hearts are young:
But he who sees the blazing beams,
The light that from that forehead streams,
    And is not stung; —
Who is not storm-tost with desire, —
Lo! he, I ween, with frozen fire,
Of adamant or stubborn steel,
Is forged in his cold heart that cannot feel.

Disowned, dishonoured, and denied
By Aphrodite, glittering-eyed,
    He either toils
All day for gold, a sordid gain,
Or bent beneath a woman's reign,
    In petty broils,
Endures her insolence, a drudge,
Compelled the common path to trudge;
But I, apart from this disease,
Wasting away like wax of holy bees,
Which the sun's splendor wounds, do pine,
Whene'er I see the young-limbed bloom divine
Of boys. Lo! look you well; for here in Tenedos,
Grace and Persuasion dwell in young Theoxenos.

John Addington Symonds

ELYSIAN BLISS

For them the night all through
In that broad realm below,
The splendor of the sun spreads endless light;
'Mid rosy meadows bright,
Their city of the tombs with incense-trees,
And golden chalices
Of flowers, and fruitage fair,
Scenting the breezy air,
Is laden. There with horses and with play,
With games and lyres, they while the hours away

On every side around
Pure happiness is found,
With all the blooming beauty of the world;
There fragrant smoke, uncurled
From altars where the blazing fire is dense
With perfumed frankincense,
Burned unto gods in heaven,
Through all the land is driven,
Making its pleasant places odorous
With scented gales and sweet airs amorous.

John Addington Symonds

THEOCRITUS

THEOCRITUS of Syracuse (c. 310-250 B. C.) is the author of poetic sketches or Idylls, descriptive of rustic life in his native Sicily. He has been the model, for Latin and other poets in succeeding centuries, of pastoral vignettes.

DAPHNIS

In a shady spot at noonday, shepherds challenge each other to song.

THYRSIS:

Sweet are the whispers of yon pine that makes
Low music o'er the spring, and, Goatherd, sweet
Thy piping; second thou to Pan alone.
Is his the horned ram? then thine the goat.
Is his the goat? to thee shall fall the kid;
And toothsome is the flesh of unmilked kids.

GOATHERD:

Shepherd, thy lay is as the noise of streams
Falling and falling aye from yon tall crag.
If for their meed the Muses claim the ewe,
Be thine the stall-fed lamb; or if they choose
The lamb, take thou the scarce less-valued ewe.

THYRSIS:

Pray, by the Nymphs, pray, Goatherd, seat thee here
Against this hill-slope in the tamarisk shade,
And pipe me somewhat, while I guard thy goats.

GOATHERD:

I durst not, Shepherd, O I durst not pipe
At noontide; fearing Pan, who at that hour
Rests from the toils of hunting. Harsh is he;
Wrath at his nostrils aye sits sentinel.
But, Thyrsis, thou canst sing of Daphnis' woes;

71

High is thy name for woodland minstrelsy:
Then rest we in the shadow of the elm
Fronting Priapus and the Fountain-nymphs.
There, where the oaks are and the Shepherd's seat,
Sing as thou sang'st erewhile, when matched with him
Of Libya, Chromis; and I'll give thee, first,
To milk, ay thrice, a goat — she suckles twins,
Yet ne'ertheless can fill two milkpails full; —
Next, a deep drinking-cup, with sweet wax scoured,
Two-handled, newly-carven, smacking yet
O' the chisel. Ivy reaches up and climbs
About its lip, gilt here and there with sprays
Of woodbine, that enwreathed about it flaunts
Her saffron fruitage. Framed therein appears
A damsel ('tis a miracle of art)
In robe and snood: and suitors at her side
With locks fair-flowing, on her right and left,
Battle with words, that fail to reach her heart.
She, laughing, glances now on this, flings now
Her chance regards on that: they, all for love
Wearied and eye-swoln, find their labour lost.
Carven elsewhere an ancient fisher stands
On the rough rocks: thereto the old man with pains
Drags his great casting-net, as one that toils
Full stoutly: every fibre of his frame
Seems fishing; so about the gray-beard's neck
(In might a youngster yet) the sinews swell.
Hard by the wave-beat sire a vineyard bends
Beneath its graceful load of burnished grapes;
A boy sits on the rude fence watching them.
Near him two foxes; down the rows of grapes
One hanging steals the ripest; one assails
With wiles the poor lad's scrip, to leave him soon
Stranded and supperless. He plaits meanwhile
With ears of corn a right fine cricket-trap,
And fits it on a rush: for vines, for scrip,
Little he cares, enamoured of his toy.
The cup is hung all round with lissom briar,
Triumph of Aeolian art, a wondrous sight.
It was a ferryman's of Calydon:
A goat it cost me, and a great white cheese.
Ne'er yet my lips came near it, virgin still
It stands. And welcome to such boon art thou,

If for my sake thou'lt sing that lay of lays.
I jest not: up, lad, sing: no songs thou'lt own
In the dim land where all things are forgot.

THYRSIS:

> Begin, sweet Maids, begin the woodland song.
> The voice of Thyrsis. Aetna's Thyrsis I.
> Where were ye, Nymphs, oh where, while Daphnis pined?
> In fair Peneus' or in Pindus' glens?
> For great Anapus' stream was not your haunt,
> Nor Aetna's cliff, nor Acis' sacred rill.
> Begin, sweet Maids, begin the woodland song.
> O'er him the wolves, the jackals howled o'er him;
> The lion in the oak-copse mourned his death.
> Begin, sweet Maids, begin the woodland song.
> The kine and oxen stood around his feet,
> The heifers and the calves wailed all for him.
> Begin, sweet Maids, begin the woodland song.
> First from the mountain Hermes came, and said,
> "Daphnis, who frets thee? Lad, whom lov'st thou so?"
> Begin, sweet Maids, begin the woodland song.
> Came herdsmen, shepherds came, and goatherds came;
> All asked what ailed the lad. Priapus came
> And said, "Why pine, poor Daphnis? while the maid
> Foots it round every pool and every grove.
> Begin, sweet Maids, begin the woodland song.
> "O lack-love and perverse, in quest of thee;
> Herdsman in name, but goatherd rightlier called.
> With eyes that yearn the goatherd marks his kids
> Run riot, for he fain would frisk as they:
> Begin, sweet Maids, begin the woodland song.
> "With eyes that yearn dost thou too mark the laugh
> Of maidens, for thou may'st not share their glee."
> Still naught the herdsman said: he drained alone
> His bitter portion, till the fatal end.
> Begin, sweet Maids, begin the woodland song.
> Came Aphrodite, smiles on her sweet face,
> False smiles, for heavy was her heart, and spake:
> "So, Daphnis, thou must try a fall with Love!
> But stalwart Love hath won the fall of thee."
> Begin, sweet Maids, begin the woodland song.
> Then "Ruthless Aphrodite," Daphnis said,
> "Accursed Aphrodite, foe to man!

Say'st thou mine hour is come, my sun hath set?
Dead as alive, shall Daphnis work Love woe.
Begin, sweet Maids, begin the woodland song.
"Fly to Mount Ida, where the swain (men say)
And Aphrodite — to Anchises fly:
There are oak-forests; here but galingale,
And bees that make a music round the hives.
Begin, sweet Maids, begin the woodland song.
"Adonis owed his bloom to tending flocks
And smiting hares, and bringing wild beasts down.
Begin, sweet Maids, begin the woodland song.
"Face once more Diomed: tell him I have slain
The herdsman Daphnis! now I challenge thee!
Begin, sweet Maids, begin the woodland song.
"Farewell, wolf, jackal, mountain-prisoned bear!
Ye'll see no more by grove or glade or glen
Your herdsman Daphnis! Arethuse, farewell,
And the bright streams that pour down Thymbris' side.
Begin, sweet Maids, begin the woodland song.
"I am that Daphnis, who lead here my kine,
Bring here to drink my oxen and my calves.
Begin, sweet Maids, begin the woodland song.
"Pan, Pan, oh whether great Lyceum's crags
Thou haunt'st to-day, or mightier Maenalus,
Come to the Sicel isle! Abandon now
Rhium and Helice, and the mountain-cairn
(That e'en gods cherish) of Lycaeon's son!
Forget, sweet Maids, forget your woodland song.
"Come, king of song o'er this my pipe, compact
With wax and honey-breathing, arch thy lip:
For surely I am torn from life by Love.
Forget, sweet Maids, forget your woodland song.
"From thicket now and thorn let violets spring,
Now let white lilies drape the juniper,
And pines grow figs, and nature all go wrong:
For Daphnis dies. Let deer pursue the hounds,
And mountain-owls outsing the nightingale."
Forget, sweet Maids, forget your woodland song.
So spake he, and he never spake again.
Fain Aphrodite would have raised his head;
But all his thread was spun. So down the stream
Went Daphnis: closed the waters o'er a head
Dear to the Nine, of nymphs not unbeloved.

74

Forget, sweet Maids, forget your woodland song.
Now give me goat and cup; that I may milk
The one, and pour the other to the Muse.
Fare ye well, Muses, o'er and o'er farewell!
I'll sing strains lovelier yet in days to be.

GOATHERD:

Thyrsis, let honey and the honeycomb
Fill thy sweet mouth, and figs of Aegilus:
For ne'er cicala trilled so sweet a song.
Here is the cup: mark, friend, how sweet it smells:
The Hours, thou'lt say, have washed it in their well.
Hither, Cissaetha! Thou, go milk her! Kids,
Be steady, or your pranks will rouse the ram.

C. S. Calverley

A CURE FOR LOVE

Nicias, poet and physician, is love-sick. Song, then, is the only remedy: just as Polyphemus, the Cyclops, by song, eased his love for the sea-nymph Galatea.

There is none other medicine, Nicias, against Love, neither unguent, methinks, nor salve to sprinkle, — none, save the Muses of Pieria! Now a delicate thing is their minstrelsy in man's life, and a sweet, but hard to procure. Methinks thou know'st this well, who art thyself a leech, and beyond all men art plainly dear to the Muses nine.

'Twas surely thus the Cyclops fleeted his life most easily, he that dwelt among us, — Polyphemus of old time, — when the beard was yet young on his cheek and chin; and he loved Galatea. He loved, not with apples, not roses, nor locks of hair, but with fatal frenzy, and all things else he held but trifles by the way. Many a time from the green pastures would his ewes stray back, self-shepherded, to the fold. But he was singing of Galatea, and pining in his place he sat by the sea-weed of the beach, from the dawn of day, with the direst hurt beneath his breast of mighty Cypris's sending, — the wound of her arrow in his heart!

Yet this remedy he found, and sitting on the crest of the tall cliff, and looking to the deep, 'twas thus he would sing: —

SONG OF THE CYCLOPS

O milk-white Galatea, why cast off him that loves thee? More white than is pressed milk to look upon, more delicate than the lamb

75

art thou, than the young calf wantoner, more sleek than the unripened grape! Here dost thou resort, even so, when sweet sleep possesses me, and home straightway dost thou depart when sweet sleep lets me go, fleeing me like an ewe that has seen the grey wolf.

I fell in love with thee, maiden, I, on the day when first thou camest, with my mother, and didst wish to pluck the hyacinths from the hill, and I was thy guide on the way. But to leave loving thee, when once I had seen thee, neither afterward, nor now at all, have I the strength, even from that hour. But to thee all this is as nothing, by Zeus, nay, nothing at all!

I know, thou gracious maiden, why it is that thou dost shun me. It is all for the shaggy brow that spans all my forehead, from this to the other ear, one long unbroken eyebrow. And but one eye is on my forehead, and broad is the nose that overhangs my lip. Yet I (even such as thou seest me) feed a thousand cattle, and from these I draw and drink the best milk in the world. And cheese I never lack, in summer time or autumn, nay, nor in the dead of winter, but my baskets are always overladen.

Also I am skilled in piping, as none other of the Cyclops here, and of thee, my love, my sweet-apple, and of myself too I sing, many a time, deep in the night. And for thee I tend eleven fawns, all crescent-browed, and four young whelps of the bear.

Nay, come thou to me, and thou shalt lack nothing that now thou hast. Leave the grey sea to roll against the land; more sweetly, in this cavern, shalt thou fleet the night with me! Thereby the laurels grow, and there the slender cypresses, there is the ivy dun, and the sweet clustered grapes; there is chill water, that for me deep-wooded Etna sends down from the white snow, a draught divine! Ah who, in place of these, would choose the sea to dwell in, or the waves of the sea?

But if thou dost refuse because my body seems shaggy and rough, well, I have faggots of oakwood, and beneath the ashes is fire unwearied, and I would endure to let thee burn my very soul, and this my one eye, the dearest thing that is mine.

Ah me, that my mother bore me not a finny thing, so would I have gone down to thee, and kissed thy hand, if thy lips thou wouldst not suffer me to kiss! And I would have brought thee either white lilies, or the soft poppy with its scarlet petals. Nay, these are summer's flowers, and those are flowers of winter, so I could not have brought thee them all at one time.

Now, verily, maiden, now and here will I learn to swim, if perchance some stranger come hither, sailing with his ship, that I may see why it is so dear to thee, to have thy dwelling in the deep.

Come forth, Galatea, and forget as thou comest, even as I that sit

76

here have forgotten, the homeward way! Nay, choose with me to go shepherding, with me to milk the flocks, and to pour the sharp rennet in, and to fix the cheeses.

There is none that wrongs me but that mother of mine, and her do I blame. Never, nay, never once has she spoken a kind word for me to thee, and that though day by day she beholds me wasting. I will tell her that my head, and both my feet are throbbing, that she may somewhat suffer, since I too am suffering.

O Cyclops, Cyclops, whither are thy wits wandering? Ah that thou wouldst go, and weave thy wicker-work, and gather broken boughs to carry thy lambs: in faith, if thou didst this, far wiser wouldst thou be!

Milk the ewe that thou hast, why pursue the thing that shuns thee? Thou wilt find, perchance, another, and a fairer Galatea. Many be the girls that bid me play with them through the night, and softly they all laugh, if perchance I answer them. On land it is plain that I too seem to be somebody!

Lo, thus Polyphemus still shepherded his love with song, and lived lighter than if he had given gold for ease.

Andrew Lang

BION

BION, who flourished in the second century B. C., produced a number of bucolic idylls, of which seventeen fragments are extant.

LAMENT FOR ADONIS

A wedding-song and a threnody were the features of the festival of Adonis.

I mourn for Adonis — Adonis is dead,
    Fair Adonis is dead and the Loves are lamenting.
Sleep, Cypris, no more on thy purple-strewed bed:
    Arise, wretch stoled in black; beat thy breast
        unrelenting,
And shriek to the worlds, "Fair Adonis is dead!"

I mourn for Adonis — the Loves are lamenting.
    He lies on the hills in his beauty and death;
The white tusk of a boar has transpierced his white
        thigh.
    Cytherea grows mad at his thin gasping breath,
While the black blood drips down on the pale ivory,
    And his eyeballs lie quenched with the weight of
        his brows;
The rose fades from his lips, and upon them just
        parted
The kiss dies the goddess consents not to lose,
Though the kiss of the Dead cannot make her glad
        hearted:
He knows not who kisses him dead in the dews.

I mourn for Adonis — the Loves are lamenting.
    Deep, deep in the thigh is Adonis's wound,
But a deeper is Cypris's bosom presenting.
    The youth lieth dead while his dogs howl around,
And the nymphs weep aloud from the mists of the
        hills,
And the poor Aphrodite, with tresses unbound,

All dishevelled, unsandaled, shrieks mournful and
      shrill
Through the dusk of the groves. The thorns
      tearing his feet,
Gather up the red flower of her blood which is holy,
    Each footstep she takes; and the valleys repeat
The sharp cry she utters and draw it out slowly.
    She calls on her spouse, her Assyrian, on him
Her own youth, while the dark blood spreads over
      his body,
The chest taking hue from the gash in the limb,
And the bosom, once ivory, turning to ruddy.

Ah, ah, Cytherea! the Loves are lamenting.
    She lost her fair spouse and so lost her fair smile:
When he lived she was fair, by the whole world's
      consenting,
    Whose fairness is dead with him: woe worth the
      while!
All the mountains above and the oaklands below
    Murmur, ah, ah, Adonis! the streams overflow
Aphrodite's deep wail; river-fountains in pity
    Weep soft in the hills, and the flowers as they
      blow
Redden outward with sorrow, while all hear her go
    With the song of her sadness through mountain
      and city.

Ah, ah, Cytherea! Adonis is dead.
    Fair Adonis is dead — Echo answers, Adonis!
Who weeps not for Cypris, when bowing her head
    She stares at the wound where it gapes and
      astonies?
— When, ah, ah! — she saw how the blood ran away
    And empurpled the thigh, and, with wild hands
      flung out,
Said with sobs: "Stay, Adonis! unhappy one, stay,
    Let me feel thee once more, let me ring thee
      about
With the clasp of my arms, and press kiss into kiss!
    Wait a little, Adonis, and kiss me again,
For the last time, beloved, — and but so much of this
    That the kiss may learn life from the warmth of
      the strain!

—Till thy breath shall exude from the soul to my
      mouth,
    To my heart, and, the love-charm I once more
      receiving,
May drink thy love in it and keep of a truth
    That one kiss in the place of Adonis the living.

Thou fliest me, mournful one, fliest me far,
    My Adonis, and seekest the Acheron portal, —
To Hell's cruel King goest down with a scar,
    While I weep and live on like a wretched
      immortal,
And follow no step! O Persephone, take him,
    My husband — thou'rt better and brighter than I,
So all beauty flows down to thee: I cannot make him
    Look up at my grief; there's despair in my cry.
Since I wail for Adonis who died to me — died to
    me —
    Then, I fear *thee!* — Art thou dead, my Adored?
Passion ends like a dream in the sleep that's denied
    to me.
    Cypris is widowed, the Loves seek their lord
All the house through in vain. Charm of cestus has
    ceased
    With thy clasp! O too bold in the hunt past pre-
      venting,
Ay, mad, thou so fair, to have strife with a beast!"
    Thus the goddess wailed on — and the Loves are
    lamenting.

Ah, ah, Cytherea! Adonis is dead.
She wept tear after tear with the blood which was shed,
And both turned into flowers for earth's garden-close,
Her tear to the wind-flower; his blood to the rose.

I mourn for Adonis — Adonis is dead.
    Weep no more in the woods, Cytherea, thy
      lover!
So, well: make a place for his corse in thy bed,
    With the purples thou sleepest in, under and
      over.
He's fair though a corse — a fair corse, like a
    sleeper.
    Lay him soft in the silks he had pleasure to fold

When, beside thee at night, holy dreams deep and
      deeper
    Enclosed his young life on the couch made of
      gold.
Love him still, poor Adonis; cast on him together
    The crowns and the flowers: since he died from
      The place,
Why, let all die with him; let blossoms go wither,
    Rain myrtles and olive-buds down on his face.
Rain the myrrh down, let all that is best fall
      a-pining,
    Since the myrrh of his life from thy keeping is
      swept.
Pale he lay, thine Adonis, in purples reclining;
    The Loves raised their voices around him and wept.
They have shorn their bright curls off to cast on
      Adonis;
One treads on his bow, — on his arrows, another, —
One breaks up a well-feathered quiver, and one is
    Bent low at a sandal, untying the strings,
    And one carries the vases of gold from the springs,
While one washes the wound, — and behind them
      a brother
Fans down on the body sweet air with his wings.

Cytherea herself now the Loves are lamenting.
    Each torch at the door Hymenaeus blew out;
And, the marriage-wreath dropping its leaves as
      repenting,
    No more "Hymen, Hymen," is chanted about,
But the *ai ai* instead — "ai alas!" is begun
    For Adonis, and then follows "Ai Hymenaeus!"
The Graces are weeping for Cinyris' son,
    Sobbing low each to each, "His fair eyes cannot
      see us!"
Their wail strikes more shrill than the sadder Dione's.
The Fates mourn aloud for Adonis, Adonis,
Deep chanting; he hears not a word that they say:
    He *would* hear, but Persephone has him in
      keeping.
— Cease moan, Cytherea! leave pomps for to-day,
And weep new when a new year refits thee for
      weeping.

                Elizabeth Barrett Browning

MOSCHUS

MOSCHUS of Syracuse was a bucolic poet who flourished in the second century B. C. Eight poems and some fragments are extant.

BION IS DEAD!

Mourn, Dorian stream, departed Bion mourn!
Pour the hoarse murmur from pallid urn!
Sigh, groves and lawns! ye plants, in sorrow wave;
Ye flowers, breathe sickly sweets o'er Bion's grave!
Anemones and roses, blush your grief;
Expand, pale hyacinth, thy letter'd leaf!
Thy marks of anguish more distinctly show —
Ah! well the tuneful herdsman claims your woe!

Begin, and in the tenderest notes complain!
Sicilian Muse, begin the mournful strain!
Ye nightingales, that soothe the shadowy vale,
Warble to Arethusa's streams the tale
Of Bion dead. Lamenting Nature's pride,
He sunk! ah, then the Dorian music died!

Begin, and in the tenderest notes complain!
Sicilian Muse, begin the mournful strain!
Ye swans of Strymon, bid so sweet a note
As Bion breathed along your green banks, float
O'er the still wave! and tell Bistonia's maids,
That Doric Orpheus charms no more the glades.

Begin, and in the tenderest notes complain!
Sicilian Muse, begin the mournful strain!
Dear to the Muse, alas! no more he sings
By yon lone oak that shades the plashy springs.
He roams a spectre through the glooms of fear,
And chants the oblivious verse to Pluto's ear.
O'er the hushed hills his pensive heifers rove,
Refuse their pasture, and forget their love!

Begin, and in the tenderest notes complain!
Sicilian Muse, begin the mournful strain!
Thee — thee, O Bion, snatch'd from earth away,
The Satyrs wail'd and e'en the god of day!
Pan for thy numbers heaved his sighing breast,
And sad Priapus mourn'd in sable vest.
The Naiads in despairing anguish stood,
And swell'd with briny tears their fountain-flood.
Mute Echo, as her mimic music dies,
Amidst her dreary rocks lamenting lies.
The trees resigned their fruitage at thy death,
And all the faded flowers, their scented breath.
The ewes no milk — the hives no honey gave;
But what avail'd it the rich stores to save?
What, that the bee no balmy floweret sips,
Extinct the sweeter honey of thy lips?

Begin, and in the tenderest notes complain!
Sicilian Muse, begin the mournful strain!
Not with such grief the Dolphin fill'd the seas,
Or Philomela's plaint the woodland breeze,
Or Progne's bitter woe the mountains hoar,
Or wild Alcyone the fatal shore;
Or faithful Cerylus the cave, where lies
His mate, still breathing fondness as she dies;
Or Memnon's screaming birds his orient tomb,
As now they utter, at their Bion's doom!
Begin, and in the tenderest notes complain!

Sicilian Muse, begin the mournful strain!
The lovelorn nightingales that learn'd his song,
The swallows twittering shrill, the boughs among,
Join their sad notes; the vocal groves reply —
"Sigh too, ye turtles, for your Bion sigh!"

Begin, and in the tenderest notes complain!
Sicilian Muse, begin the mournful strain!
Who now, regretted swain, thy pipe shall play;
Touch the fair stops, or trill the melting lay?
Faint from thy lips still breathe the mellow reeds;
Still on their dying sweetness Echo feeds:
To bear those melodies to Pan be mine;
Though he may fear to risk his fame with mine!
Begin, and in the tenderest notes complain!

83

Sicilian Muse, begin the mournful strain!
And Galatea too bewails thy fate —
Fair nymph, who oft upon the seashore sate
Sooth'd by thy songs, and fled the Cyclops' arms —
Far other strains are thine! far other charms!
Now on the sand she sits — forgets the sea —
Yet feeds thy herds, and still remembers thee!

Begin, and in the tenderest notes complain!
Sicilian Muse, begin the mournful strain!
With thee, O swain, expired the Muses' bliss —
The roseate bloom of youth, the roseate kiss!
The fluttering Cupids round thy ashes cry,
And fond — fond Venus mixes many a sigh!
She loves thee as Adonis' parting breath —
As his last kisses so endear'd by death!
Here — here, O Meles, musical in woe,
Sad for another son thy tide shall flow!
For thy first poet mourn'd thy plaintive wave;
Each murmur deepen'd at thy Homer's grave:
Another grief (melodious stream) appears!
Alas! another poet claims thy tears!
Dear to the fountains which inspire the Muse,
That drank of Helicon — this Arethuse!
That bard his harp to beauteous Helen strung!
And the dire anger of Pelides sung:
This — in his softer lay no wars display'd,
But chanted Pan all peaceful in the shade!
He framed his reeds, or milk'd his kine, or led
His herds to pasture, singing as they fed!
And oft, so dear to Venus, he caress'd
The little Cupid in his panting breast.

Begin, and in the tenderest notes complain!
Sicilian Muse, begin the mournful strain!
The cities and the towns thy death deplore —
Than her own Hesiod Ascra mourns thee more!
Not thus her Pindar Hylae's grief bemoans —
Not Lesbos thus Alcaeus' manly tones!
Not Ceos, Paros, thus regret their bards —
And Mitylene yet thy reed regards
Beyond her Sappho's lyre; and every swain
Pipes thee, O Bion, on his native plain.
The Samian's gentle notes thy memory greet —

84

Philetas too — and Lycidas of Crete!
Now, breathing heavy sighs, each heart despairs,
Though erst full many a jocund revel theirs.
Thee too, dear bard, Theocritus bewails,
The sweetest warbler of Sicilia's dales!
And I, who suit to sorrow's melting tone
The Ausonian verse, but mimic music own;
If e'er the charms of melody I knew,
'Tis to thy forming skill the praise is due.
Others may claim thy gold — the gold be theirs!
Ours be the Doric Muse, thy wealthier heirs.

Begin, and in the tenderest notes complain!
Sicilian Muse, begin the mournful strain!
Though fade crisp anise, and the parsley's green,
And vivid mallows from the garden scene;
The balmy breath of spring their life renews,
And bids them flourish in their former hues!
But we, the great, the valiant, and the wise,
When once the seal of death hath closed our eyes,
Lost in the hollow tomb obscure and deep,
Slumber, to wake no more, one long unbroken sleep!
Thou too, while many a scrannel reed I hear
Grating eternal harshness on my ear —
Thou too, thy charm of melting music o'er,
Shut in the silent earth, shalt rise no more!

Begin, and in the tenderest notes complain!
Sicilian Muse, begin the mournful strain!
'Twas poison gave thee to the grasp of death —
Ah! could not poison sweeten at thy breath?
Who for those lips of melody could dare
The venom'd chalice (murderous wretch) prepare?
Such wretches rove with vengeance at their heels;
While now at this drear hour my bosom feels
The bursting sigh! like Orpheus could I go,
Or wise Ulysses, to the shades below,
To Pluto's home my steps should straight repair,
To hear what numbers thou art chanting there.
But sing, as in the genial realms of light,
Some sweet bucolic to the queen of night:
She once amid those golden meadows play'd,

And sung the Dorian song in Aetna's shade.
Thy music shall ascend with all the fire —
With all the strong effect of Orpheus' lyre!
Fair Proserpine shall listen to thy strain,
And, pitying, send thee to thy hills again.
O that, as Orpheus' lyre reclaim'd his wife,
My pipe had power to bring thy shade to life!

Richard Polwhele

DRAMA

Aeschylus

Sophocles

Euripides

Aristophanes

AESCHYLUS

AESCHYLUS (525/4-456 B. C.) is one of the greatest universal dramatists. H
witnessed the culmination of Athenian democratic government: fought at Mara
thon in 490, where the Greeks gained their first victory over the Persians, an
twice visited the court in Sicily. He died at Gela, in Sicily, in 456 B. C.

The dramas of Aeschylus gained him thirteen first prizes. In all, he produce
some ninety plays, of which seven are extant.

THE PERSIANS

This play, produced in 472 B. C. in Athens, celebrates the Gree
victory over the Persians at Salamis in 480 B. C. Although his dram
stresses the defeat of the Persians, the poet is compassionate and ex
tends the significance of the catastrophe into cosmic implications tha
are applicable to all humanity.

CHARACTERS IN THE PLAY

ATOSSA, widow of Darius and mother of Xerxes
MESSENGER
GHOST OF DARIUS
XERXES
CHORUS OF PERSIAN ELDERS, who compose the Persian Council of Sta

(SCENE: — Before the Council-Hall of the Persian Kings at Susa. Th
tomb of Darius the Great is visible. The time is 480 B. C., shortl
after the battle of Salamis. The play opens with the Choru
of Persian Elders singing a choral lyric.)

CHORUS: While o'er the fields of Greece the embattled troops
Of Persia march with delegated sway,

88

We o'er their rich and gold-abounding seats
Hold faithful our firm guard; to this high charge
Xerxes, our royal lord, the imperial son
Of great Darius, chose our honour'd age.
But for the king's return, and his arm'd host
Blazing with gold, my soul presaging ill
Swells in my tortured breast: for all her force
Hath Asia sent, and for her youth I sigh.
Nor messenger arrives, nor horseman spurs
With tidings to this seat of Persia's kings.
The gates of Susa and Ecbatana
Pour'd forth their martial trains; and Cissia sees
Her ancient towers forsaken, while her youth,
Some on the bounding steed, the tall bark some
Ascending, some with painful march on foot,
Haste on, to arrange the deep'ning files of war.
Amistres, Artaphernes, and the might
Of great Astaspes, Megabazes bold,
Chieftains of Persia, kings, that, to the power
Of the great king obedient, march with these
Leading their martial thousands; their proud steeds
Prance under them; steel bows and shafts their arms,
Dreadful to see, and terrible in fight,
Deliberate valour breathing in their souls.
Artembares, that in his fiery horse
Delights; Masistres; and Imaeus bold,
Bending with manly strength his stubborn bow;
Pharandaces, and Sosthanes, that drives
With military pomp his rapid steeds.
Others the vast prolific Nile hath sent;
Pegastagon, that from Aegyptus draws
His high birth; Susicanes; and the chief
That reigns o'er sacred Memphis, great Arsames;
And Ariomardus, that o'er ancient Thebes
Bears the supreme dominion; and with these,
Drawn from their watery marshes, numbers train'd
To the stout oar. Next these the Lycian troops,
Soft sons of luxury; and those that dwell
Amid the inland forests, from the sea
Far distant; these Metragathes commands,
And virtuous Arceus, royal chiefs, that shine
In burnish'd gold, and many a whirling car
Drawn by six generous steeds from Sardis lead,

A glorious and a dreadful spectacle.
And from the foot of Tmolus, sacred mount,
Eager to bind on Greece the servile yoke,
Mardon and Tharybis the massy spear
Grasp with unwearied vigour; the light lance
The Mysians shake. A mingled multitude
Swept from her wide dominions skill'd to draw
The unerring bow, in ships Euphrates sends
From golden Babylon. With falchions arm'd
From all the extent of Asia move the hosts
Obedient to their monarch's stern command.
Thus march'd the flower of Persia, whose loved youth
The world of Asia nourish'd, and with sighs
Laments their absence; many an anxious look
Their wives, their parents send, count the slow days,
And tremble at the long-protracted time.

    Already o'er the adverse strand
In arms the monarch's martial squadrons spread;
    The threat'ning ruin shakes the land,
And each tall city bows its tower'd head.
      Bark bound to bark, their wondrous way
      They bridge across the indignant sea;
The narrow Hellespont's vex'd waves disdain,
His proud neck taught to wear the chain.
Now has the peopled Asia's warlike lord,
      By land, by sea, with foot, with horse,
      Resistless in his rapid course,
O'er all their realms his warring thousands pour'd;
      Now his intrepid chiefs surveys,
And glitt'ring like a god his radiant state displays.

    Fierce as the dragon scaled in gold
Through the deep files he darts his glowing eye;
    And pleased their order to behold,
His gorgeous standard blazing to the sky,
      Rolls onward his Assyrian car,
      Directs the thunder of the war,
Bids the wing'd arrows' iron storm advance
      Against the slow and cumbrous lance.
What shall withstand the torrent of his sway
      When dreadful o'er the yielding shores
      The impetuous tide of battle roars,

And sweeps the weak opposing mounds away?
    So Persia, with resistless might,
Rolls her unnumber'd hosts of heroes to the fight.

    For when misfortune's fraudful hand
Prepares to pour the vengeance of the sky,
What mortal shall her force withstand?
What rapid speed the impending fury fly?
    Gentle at first with flatt'ring smiles
    She spreads her soft enchanting wiles,
So to her toils allures her destined prey,
    Whence man ne'er breaks unhurt away.
For thus from ancient times the Fates ordain
    That Persia's sons should greatly dare,
    Unequall'd in the works of war;
Shake with their thund'ring steeds the ensanguined plain,
    Dreadful the hostile walls surround,
And lay their rampired towers in ruins on the ground.

    Taught to behold with fearless eyes
The whitening billows foam beneath the gale,
    They bid the naval forests rise,
Mount the slight bark, unfurl the flying sail,
    And o'er the angry ocean bear
    To distant realms the storm of war.
For this with many a sad and gloomy thought
    My tortured breast is fraught:
Ah me! for Persia's absent sons I sigh;
    For while in foreign fields they fight,
    Our towns exposed to wild affright
An easy prey to the invader lie:
    Where, mighty Susa, where thy powers,
To wield the warrior's arms, and guard thy regal towers?

    Crush'd beneath the assailing foe
    Her golden head must Cissia bend;
While her pale virgins, frantic with despair,
Through all her streets awake the voice of wo;
    And flying with their bosoms bare,
    Their purfled stoles in anguish rend:
    For all her youth in martial pride,
    Like bees that, clust'ring round their king,
    Their dark imbodied squadrons bring,

Attend their sceptred monarch's side,
And stretch across the watery way
From shore to shore their long array.
The Persian dames, with many a tender fear,
In grief's sad vigils keep the midnight hour;
Shed on the widow'd couch the streaming tear,
And the long absence of their loves deplore.
Each lonely matron feels her pensive breast
Throb with desire, with aching fondness glow,
Since in bright arms her daring warrior dress'd
Left her to languish in her love-lorn wo.

Now, ye grave Persians, that your honour'd seats
Hold in this ancient house, with prudent care
And deep deliberation, so the state
Requires, consult we, pond'ring the event
Of this great war, which our imperial lord,
The mighty Xerxes from Darius sprung,
The stream of whose rich blood flows in our veins,
Leads against Greece; whether his arrowy shower
Shot from the strong-braced bow, or the huge spear
High brandish'd, in the deathful field prevails.
But see, the monarch's mother: like the gods
Her lustre blazes on our eyes: my queen,
Prostrate I fall before her: all advance
With reverence, and in duteous phrase address her.

(Atossa *enters with her retinue. The Elders do their obeisance to her.*)

LEADER OF THE CHORUS: Hail, queen, of Persia's high-zoned dames
    Age-honour'd mother of the potent Xerxes,   [supreme,
    Imperial consort of Darius, hail!
    The wife, the mother of the Persians' god,
    If yet our former glories fade not from us.
ATOSSA: And therefore am I come, leaving my house
    That shines with gorgeous ornaments and gold,
    Where in past days Darius held with me
    His royal residence. With anxious care
    My heart is tortured: I will tell you, friends,
    My thoughts, not otherwise devoid of fear,
    Lest mighty wealth with haughty foot o'erturn
    And trample in the dust that happiness,
    Which, not unbless'd by Heaven, Darius raised.
    For this with double force unquiet thoughts

Past utterance fill my soul; that neither wealth
With all its golden stores, where men are wanting,
Claims reverence; nor the light, that beams from power,
Shines on the man whom wealth disdains to grace.
The golden stores of wealth indeed are ours;
But for the light (such in the house I deem
The presence of its lord) there I have fears.
Advise me then, you whose experienced age
Supports the state of Persia: prudence guides
Your councils, always kind and faithful to me.

LEADER: Speak, royal lady, what thy will, assured
We want no second bidding, where our power
In word or deed waits on our zeal: our hearts
In this with honest duty shall obey thee.

ATOSSA: Oft, since my son hath march'd his mighty host
Against the Ionians, warring to subdue
Their country, have my slumbers been disturb'd
With dreams of dread portent; but most last night,
With marks of plainest proof. I'll tell thee then:
Methought two women stood before my eyes
Gorgeously vested, one in Persian robes
Adorn'd, the other in the Doric garb.
With more than mortal majesty they moved,
Of peerless beauty; sisters too they seem'd,
Though distant each from each they chanced to dwell,
In Greece the one, on the barbaric coast
The other. 'Twixt them soon dissension rose:
My son then hasted to compose their strife,
Soothed them to fair accord, beneath his car
Yokes them, and reins their harness'd necks. The one,
Exulting in her rich array, with pride
Arching her stately neck, obey'd the reins;
The other with indignant fury spurn'd
The car, and dash'd it piecemeal, rent the reins,
And tore the yoke asunder; down my son
Fell from the seat, and instant at his side
His father stands, Darius, at his fall
Impress'd with pity: him when Xerxes saw,
Glowing with grief and shame he rends his robes.
This was the dreadful vision of the night.
When I arose, in the sweet-flowing stream
I bathed my hands, and on the incensed altars
Presenting my oblations to the gods

To avert these ills, an eagle I beheld
Fly to the altar of the sun; aghast
I stood, my friends, and speechless; when a hawk
With eager speed runs thither, furious cuffs
The eagle with his wings, and with his talons
Unplumes his head; meantime the imperial bird
Cowers to the blows defenceless. Dreadful this
To me that saw it, and to you that hear.
My son, let conquest crown his arms, would shine
With dazzling glory; but should Fortune frown,
The state indeed presumes not to arraign
His sovereignty; yet how, his honour lost,
How shall he sway the sceptre of this land?

LEADER: We would not, royal lady, sink thy soul
With fear in the excess, nor raise it high
With confidence. Go then, address the gods;
If thou hast seen aught ill, entreat their power
To avert that ill, and perfect ev'ry good
To thee, thy sons, the state, and all thy friends.
Then to the earth, and to the mighty dead
Behooves thee pour libations; gently call
Him that was once thy husband, whom thou saw'st
In visions of the night; entreat his shade
From the deep realms beneath to send to light
Triumph to thee and to thy son; whate'er
Bears other import, to inwrap, to hide it
Close in the covering earth's profoundest gloom.
This, in the presage of my thoughts that flow
Benevolent to thee, have I proposed;
And all, we trust, shall be successful to thee.

ATOSSA: Thy friendly judgment first hath placed these dreams
In a fair light, confirming the event
Benevolent to my son and to my house.
May all the good be ratified! These rites
Shall, at thy bidding, to the powers of heaven,
And to the manes of our friends, be paid
In order meet, when I return; meanwhile
Indulge me, friends, who wish to be inform'd
Where, in what clime, the towers of Athens rise.

LEADER: Far in the west, where sets the imperial sun.

ATOSSA: Yet my son will'd the conquest of this town.

LEADER: May Greece through all her states bend to his power!

ATOSSA: Send they embattled numbers to the field?

94

LEADER: A force that to the Medes hath wrought much wo.
ATOSSA: Have they sufficient treasures in their houses?
LEADER: Their rich earth yields a copious fount of silver.
ATOSSA: From the strong bow wing they the barbed shaft?
LEADER: They grasp the stout spear, and the massy shield.
ATOSSA: What monarch reigns, whose power commands their ranks?
LEADER: Slaves to no lord, they own no kingly power.
ATOSSA: How can they then resist the invading foe?
LEADER: As to spread havoc through the numerous host,
That round Darius form'd their glitt'ring files.
ATOSSA: Thy words strike deep, and wound the parent's breast
Whose sons are march'd to such a dangerous field.
LEADER: But, if I judge aright, thou soon shalt hear
Each circumstance; for this way, mark him, speeds
A Persian messenger; he bears, be sure,
Tidings of high import, or good or ill.

(A Messenger *enters.)*

MESSENGER: Wo to the towns through Asia's peopled realms!
Wo to the land of Persia, once the port
Of boundless wealth, how is thy glorious state
Vanish'd at once, and all thy spreading honours
Fall'n, lost! Ah me! unhappy is his task
That bears unhappy tidings: but constraint
Compels me to relate this tale of wo.
Persians, the whole barbaric host is fall'n.
CHORUS *(chanting)*: O horror, horror! What a baleful train
Of recent ills! Ah, Persians, as he speaks
Of ruin, let your tears stream to the earth.
MESSENGER: It is ev'n so, all ruin; and myself,
Beyond all hope returning, view this light.
CHORUS *(chanting)*: How tedious and oppressive is the weight
Of age, reserved to hear these hopeless ills!
MESSENGER: I speak not from report; but these mine eyes
Beheld the ruin which my tongue would utter.
CHORUS *(chanting)*: Wo, wo is me! Then has the iron storm,
That darken'd from the realms of Asia, pour'd
In vain its arrowy shower on sacred Greece.
MESSENGER: In heaps the unhappy dead lie on the strand
Of Salamis, and all the neighbouring shores.
CHORUS *(chanting)*: Unhappy friends, sunk, perish'd in the sea;
Their bodies, mid the wreck of shatter'd ships,
Mangled, and rolling on the encumber'd waves!

95

MESSENGER: Naught did their bows avail, but all the troops
    In the first conflict of the ships were lost.
CHORUS *(chanting)*: Raise the funeral cry, with dismal notes
    Wailing the wretch'd Persians. O, how ill
    They plann'd their measures, all their army perish'd!
MESSENGER: O Salamis, how hateful is thy name!
    And groans burst from me when I think of Athens.
CHORUS *(chanting)*: How dreadful to her foes! Call to remembrance
    How many Persian dames, wedded in vain,
    Hath Athens of their noble husbands widow'd?
ATOSSA: Astonied with these ills, my voice thus long
    Hath wanted utterance: griefs like these exceed
    The power of speech or question: yet ev'n such,
    Inflicted by the gods, must mortal man
    Constrain'd by hard necessity endure.
    But tell me all, without distraction tell me,
    All this calamity, though many a groan
    Burst from thy labouring heart. Who is not fallen?
    What leader must we wail? What sceptred chief
    Dying hath left his troops without a lord?
MESSENGER: Xerxes himself lives, and beholds the light.
ATOSSA: That word beams comfort on my house, a ray
    That brightens through the melancholy gloom.
MESSENGER: Artembares, the potent chief that led
    Ten thousand horse, lies slaughtered on the rocks
    Of rough Sileniae. The great Dadaces,
    Beneath whose standard march'd a thousand horse,
    Pierced by a spear, fell headlong from the ship.
    Tenagon, bravest of the Bactrians, lies
    Roll'd on the wave-worn beach of Ajax' isle.
    Lilaeus, Arsames, Argestes, dash
    With violence in death against the rocks
    Where nest the silver doves. Arcteus, that dwelt
    Near to the fountains of the Egyptian Nile,
    Adeues, and Pheresba, and Pharnuchus
    Fell from one ship. Matallus, Chrysa's chief,
    That led his dark'ning squadrons, thrice ten thousand,
    On jet-black steeds, with purple gore distain'd
    The yellow of his thick and shaggy beard.
    The Magian Arabus, and Artames
    From Bactra, mould'ring on the dreary shore
    Lie low. Amistris, and Amphistreus there
    Grasps his war-wearied spear; there prostrate lies

The illustrious Ariomardus; long his loss
Shall Sardis weep: thy Mysian Sisames,
And Tharybis, that o'er the burden'd deep
Led five times fifty vessels; Lerna gave
The hero birth, and manly grace adorn'd
His pleasing form, but low in death he lies
Unhappy in his fate. Syennesis,
Cilicia's warlike chief, who dared to front
The foremost dangers, singly to the foes
A terror, there too found a glorious death.
These chieftains to my sad remembrance rise,
Relating but a few of many ills.

ATOSSA: This is the height of ill, ah me! and shame
To Persia, grief, and lamentation loud.
But tell me this, afresh renew thy tale:
What was the number of the Grecian fleet,
That in fierce conflict their bold barks should dare
Rush to encounter with the Persian hosts.

MESSENGER: Know then, in numbers the barbaric fleet
Was far superior: in ten squadrons each
Of thirty ships, Greece plough'd the deep; of these
One held a distant station. Xerxes led
A thousand ships; their number well I know;
Two hundred more, and seven, that swept the seas
With speediest sail: this was their full amount.
And in the engagement seem'd we not secure
Of victory? But unequal fortune sunk
Our scale in fight, discomfiting our host.

ATOSSA: The gods preserve the city of Minerva.

MESSENGER: The walls of Athens are impregnable,
Their firmest bulwarks her heroic sons.

ATOSSA: Which nay first advanced to the attack?
Who led to the onset, tell me; the bold Greeks,
Or, glorying in his numerous fleet, my son?

MESSENGER: Our evil genius, lady, or some god
Hostile to Persia, led to ev'ry ill.
Forth from the troops of Athens came a Greek,
And thus address'd thy son, the imperial Xerxes: —
"Soon as the shades of night descend, the Grecians
Shall quit their station; rushing to their oars
They mean to separate, and in secret flight
Seek safety." At these words, the royal chief,
Little conceiving of the wiles of Greece

And gods averse, to all the naval leaders
Gave his high charge: — "Soon as yon sun shall cease
To dart his radiant beams, and dark'ning night
Ascends the temple of the sky, arrange
In three divisions your well-ordered ships,
And guard each pass, each outlet of the seas:
Others enring around this rocky isle
Of Salamis. Should Greece escape her fate,
And work her way by secret flight, your heads
Shall answer the neglect." This harsh command
He gave, exulting in his mind, nor knew
What Fate design'd. With martial discipline
And prompt obedience, snatching a repast,
Each mariner fix'd well his ready oar.
Soon as the golden sun was set, and night
Advanced, each train'd to ply the dashing oar,
Assumed his seat; in arms each warrior stood,
Troop cheering troop through all the ships of war.
Each to the appointed station steers his course;
And through the night his naval force each chief
Fix'd to secure the passes. Night advanced,
But not by secret flight did Greece attempt
To escape. The morn, all beauteous to behold,
Drawn by white steeds bounds o'er the enlighten'd earth;
At once from ev'ry Greek with glad acclaim
Burst forth the song of war, whose lofty notes
The echo of the island rocks return'd,
Spreading dismay through Persia's hosts, thus fallen
From their high hopes; no flight this solemn strain
Portended, but deliberate valour bent
On daring battle; while the trumpet's sound
Kindled the flames of war. But when their oars
The paean ended, with impetuous force
Dash'd the resounding surges, instant all
Rush'd on in view: in orderly array
The squadron on the right first led, behind
Rode their whole fleet; and now distinct we heard
From ev'ry part this voice of exhortation: —
"Advance, ye sons of Greece, from thraldom save
Your country, save your wives, your children save,
The temples of your gods, the sacred tomb
Where rest your honour'd ancestors; this day
The common cause of all demands your valour."

Meantime from Persia's hosts the deep'ning shout
Answer'd their shout; no time for cold delay;
But ship 'gainst ship its brazen beak impell'd.
First to the charge a Grecian galley rush'd;
Ill the Phoenician bore the rough attack,
Its sculptured prow all shatter'd. Each advanced
Daring an opposite. The deep array
Of Persia at the first sustain'd the encounter;
But their throng'd numbers, in the narrow seas
Confined, want room for action; and, deprived
Of mutual aid, beaks clash with beaks, and each
Breaks all the other's oars: with skill disposed
The Grecian navy circled them around
With fierce assault; and rushing from its height
The inverted vessel sinks: the sea no more
Wears its accustomed aspect, with foul wrecks
And blood disfigured; floating carcasses
Roll on the rocky shores: the poor remains
Of the barbaric armament to flight
Ply every oar inglorious: onward rush
The Greeks amid the ruins of the fleet,
As through a shoal of fish caught in the net,
Spreading destruction: the wide ocean o'er
Wailings are heard, and loud laments, till night
With darkness on her brow brought grateful truce.
Should I recount each circumstance of wo,
Ten times on my unfinished tale the sun
Would set; for be assured that not one day
Could close the ruin of so vast a host.

ATOSSA: Ah, what a boundless sea of wo hath burst
On Persia, and the whole barbaric race!

MESSENGER: These are not half, not half our ills; on these
Came an assemblage of calamities,
That sunk us with a double weight of wo.

ATOSSA: What fortune can be more unfriendly to us
Than this? Say on, what dread calamity
Sunk Persia's host with greater weight of wo.

MESSENGER: Whoe'er of Persia's warriors flow'd in prime
Of vig'rous youth, or felt their generous souls
Expand with courage, or for noble birth
Shone with distinguish'd lustre, or excell'd
In firm and duteous loyalty, all these
Are fall'n, ignobly, miserably fall'n.

ATOSSA: Alas, their ruthless fate, unhappy friends!
　　　But in what manner, tell me, did they perish?
MESSENGER: Full against Salamis an isle arises,
　　　Of small circumference, to the anchor's bark
　　　Unfaithful; on the promontory's brow,
　　　That overlooks the sea, Pan loves to lead
　　　The dance: to this the monarch sends these chiefs,
　　　That when the Grecians from their shatter'd ships
　　　Should here seek shelter, these might hew them down
　　　An easy conquest, and secure the strand
　　　To their sea-wearied friends; ill judging what
　　　The event: but when the fav'ring god to Greece
　　　Gave the proud glory of this naval fight,
　　　Instant in all their glitt'ring arms they leap'd
　　　From their light ships, and all the island round
　　　Encompass'd, that our bravest stood dismay'd;
　　　While broken rocks, whirl'd with tempestuous force,
　　　And storms of arrows crush'd them; the Greeks
　　　Rush to the attack at once, and furious spread
　　　The carnage, till each mangled Persian fell.
　　　Deep were the groans of Xerxes when he saw
　　　This havoc; for his seat, a lofty mound
　　　Commanding the wide sea, oerlook'd his hosts.
　　　With rueful cries he rent his royal robes,
　　　And through his troops embattled on the shore
　　　Gave signal of retreat; then started wild,
　　　And fled disorder'd. To the former ills
　　　These are fresh miseries to awake thy sighs.
ATOSSA: Invidious Fortune, how thy baleful power
　　　Hath sunk the hopes of Persia! Bitter fruit
　　　My son hath tasted from his purposed vengeance
　　　On Athens, famed for arms; the fatal field
　　　Of Marathon, red with barbaric blood,
　　　Sufficed not; that defeat he thought to avenge,
　　　And pull'd this hideous ruin on his head.
　　　But tell me, if thou canst, where didst thou leave
　　　The ships that happily escaped the wreck?
MESSENGER: The poor remains of Persia's scatter'd fleet
　　　Spread ev'ry sail for flight, as the wind drives,
　　　In wild disorder; and on land no less
　　　The ruin'd army; in Boeotia some,
　　　With thirst oppress'd, at Crene's cheerful rills
　　　Were lost; forespent with breathless speed some pass

The fields of Phocis, some the Doric plain,
And near the gulf of Melia, the rich vale
Through which Sperchius rolls his friendly stream.
Achaea thence and the Thessalian state
Received our famish'd train; the greater part
Through thirst and hunger perish'd there, oppress'd
At once by both: but we our painful steps
Held onwards to Magnesia, and the land
Of Macedonia, o'er the ford of Axius,
And Bolbe's sedgy marshes, and the heights
Of steep Pangaeos, to the realms of Thrace.
That night, ere yet the season, breathing frore,
Rush'd winter, and with ice incrusted o'er
The flood of sacred Strymon: such as own'd
No god till now, awe-struck, with many a prayer
Adored the earth and sky. When now the troops
Had ceased their invocations to the gods,
O'er the stream's solid crystal they began
Their march; and we, who took our early way,
Ere the sun darted his warm beams, pass'd safe:
But when his burning orb with fiery rays
Unbound the middle current, down they sunk
Each over other; happiest he who found
The speediest death: the poor remains, that 'scaped,
With pain through Thrace dragg'd on their toilsome march,
A feeble few, and reach'd their native soil;
That Persia sighs through all her states, and mourns
Her dearest youth. This is no feigned tale:
But many of the ills, that burst upon us
In dreadful vengeance, I refrain to utter.

(The Messenger *withdraws.)*

LEADER OF THE CHORUS: O Fortune, heavy with affliction's load,
    How hath thy foot crush'd all the Persian race!
ATOSSA: Ah me, what sorrows for our ruin'd host
    Oppress my soul! Ye visions of the night
    Haunting my dreams, how plainly did you show
    These ills! — You set them in too fair a light.
    Yet, since your bidding hath in this prevail'd,
    First to the gods wish I to pour my prayers,
    Then to the mighty dead present my off'rings,
    Bringing libations from my house too late,
    I know, to change the past; yet for the future,

If haply better fortune may await it,
Behooves you, on this sad event, to guide
Your friends with faithful counsels. Should my son
Return ere I have finish'd let your voice
Speak comfort to him; friendly to his house
Attend him, nor let sorrow rise on sorrows.

(Atossa *and her retinue go out.*)

CHORUS *(singing)*: Awful sovereign of the skies,
             When now o'er Persia's numerous host
Thou badest the storm with ruin rise,
             All her proud vaunts of glory lost,
             Ecbatana's imperial head
By thee was wrapp'd in sorrow's dark'ning shade;
             Through Susa's palaces with loud lament,
             By their soft hands their veils all rent,
             The copious tear the virgins pour,
             That trickles their bare bosoms o'er.
From her sweet couch up starts the widow's bride,
             Her lord's loved image rushing on her soul,
Throws the rich ornaments of youth aside,
             And gives her griefs to flow without control:
Her griefs not causeless; for the mighty slain
Our melting tears demand, and sorrow-soften'd strain.
Now her wailings wide despair
             Pours these exhausted regions o'er:
Xerxes, ill-fated, led the war;
             Xerxes, ill-fated, leads no more;
Xerxes sent forth the unwise command,
The crowded ships, unpeopled all the land;
             That land, o'er which Darius held his reign,
             Courting the arts of peace, in vain,
             O'er all his grateful realms adored,
             The stately Susa's gentle lord.
Black o'er the waves his burden'd vessels sweep,
             For Greece elate the warlike squadrons fly;
Now crush'd, and whelm'd beneath the indignant deep
             The shatter'd wrecks and lifeless heroes lie:
While, from the arms of Greece escaped, with toil
The unshelter'd monarch roams o'er Thracia's dreary soil.

             The first in battle slain
             By Cychrea's craggy shore
Through sad constraint, ah me! forsaken lie,

102

All pale and smear'd with gore: —
Raise high the mournful strain,
And let the voice of anguish pierce the sky: —
Or roll beneath the roaring tide,
By monsters rent of touch abhorr'd;
While through the widow'd mansion echoing wide
Sounds the deep groan, and wails its slaughter'd lord:
Pale with his fears the helpless orphan there
Gives the full stream of plaintive grief to flow;
While age its hoary head in deep despair
Bends, list'ning to the shrieks of wo.
With sacred awe
The Persian law
No more shall Asia's realms revere;
To their lord's hand
At his command,
No more the exacted tribute bear.
Who now falls prostrate at the monarch's throne?
His regal greatness is no more.
Now no restraint the wanton tongue shall own,
Free from the golden curb of power;
For on the rocks, wash'd by the beating flood,
His awe commanding nobles lie in blood.

(Atossa *returns, clad in the garb of mourning;
she carries offerings for the tomb of Darius.*)

ATOSSA: Whoe'er, my friends, in the rough stream of life
Hath struggled with affliction, thence is taught
That, when the flood begins to swell, the heart
Fondly fears all things when the fav'ring gale
Of Fortune smooths the current, it expands
With unsuspecting confidence, and deems
That gale shall always breathe. So to my eyes
All things now wear a formidable shape,
And threaten from the gods: my ears are pierced
With sounds far other than of song. Such ills
Dismay my sick'ning soul: hence from my house
Nor glitt'ring car attends me, nor the train
Of wonted state, while I return, and bear
Libations soothing to the father's shade
In the son's cause: delicious milk, that foams
White from the sacred heifer; liquid honey,
Extract of flowers; and from its virgin fount

The running crystal; this pure draught, that flow'd
From the ancient vine, of power to bathe the spirits
In joy; the yellow olive's fragrant fruit,
That glories in its leaves, unfading verdure;
With flowers of various hues, earth's fairest offspring
Inwreathed. But you, my friends, amid these rites
Raise high your solemn warblings, and invoke
Your lord, divine Darius; I meanwhile
Will pour these off'rings to the infernal gods.

CHORUS *(chanting)*: Yes, royal lady, Persia's honour'd grace,
To earth's dark chambers pour thy off'rings: we
With choral hymns will supplicate the powers
That guide the dead, to be propitious to us.
And you, that o'er the realms of night extend
Your sacred sway, thee mighty earth, and thee
Hermes; thee chief, tremendous king, whose throne
Awes with supreme dominion, I adjure:
Send, from your gloomy regions, send his shade
Once more to visit this ethereal light;
That he alone, if aught of dread event
He sees yet threat'ning Persia, may disclose
To us poor mortals Fate's extreme decree.

  Hears the honour'd godlike king?
  These barbaric notes of wo,
Taught in descant sad to ring,
  Hears he in the shades below?
  Thou, O Earth, and you, that lead
  Through your sable realms the dead,
  Guide him as he takes his way,
And give him to the ethereal light of day!

  Let the illustrious shade arise
  Glorious in his radiant state,
  More than blazed before our eyes,
  Ere sad Susa mourn'd his fate.
  Dear he lived, his tomb is dear,
  Shrining virtues we revere:
  Send them, monarch of the dead,
Such as Darius was, Darius' shade.
  He in realm-unpeopling war
  Wasted not his subjects' blood,
  Godlike in his will to spare,
  In his councils wise and good.

104

Rise then, sovereign lord, to light;
On this mound's sepulchral height
Lift thy sock in saffron died,
And rear thy rich tiara's regal pride!

Great and good, Darius, rise:
Lord of Persia's lord, appear:
Thus involved with thrilling cries
Come, our tale of sorrow hear!
War her Stygian pennons spreads,
Brooding darkness o'er our heads;
For stretch'd along the dreary shore
The flow'r of Asia lies distain'd with gore.
Rise, Darius, awful power;
Long for thee our tears shall flow.
Why thy ruin'd empire o'er
Swells this double flood of wo?
Sweeping o'er the azure tide
Rode thy navy's gallant pride:
Navy now no more, for all
Beneath the whelming wave—

(While the Chorus *sings,* Atossa *performs her ritual by the tomb. As the song concludes the* Ghost of Darius *appears from the tomb.)*

GHOST OF DARIUS: Ye faithful Persians, honour'd now in age,
Once the companions of my youth, what ills
Afflict the state? The firm earth groans, it opes,
Disclosing its vast deeps; and near my tomb
I see my wife: this shakes my troubled soul
With fearful apprehensions; yet her off'rings
Pleased I receive. And you around my tomb
Chanting the lofty strain, whose solemn air
Draws forth the dead, with grief-attemper'd notes
Mournfully call me: not with ease the way
Leads to this upper air; and the stern gods,
Prompt to admit, yield not a passage back
But with reluctance: much with them my power
Availing, with no tardy step I come.
Say then, with what new ill doth Persia groan?
CHORUS *(chanting)*: My wonted awe o'ercomes me; in thy presence
I dare not raise my eyes, I dare not speak.
GHOST OF DARIUS: Since from the realms below, by the sad strains,

105

Adjured, I come, speak; let thy words be brief;
Say whence thy grief, tell me unawed by fear.
CHORUS *(chanting)*: I dread to forge a flattering tale, I dread
To grieve thee with a harsh offensive truth.
GHOST OF DARIUS: Since fear hath chained his tongue, high-
honour'd dame,
Once my imperial consort, check thy tears,
Thy griefs, and speak distinctly. Mortal man
Must bear his lot of wo; afflictions rise
Many from sea, many from land, if life
Be haply measured through a lengthen'd course.
ATOSSA: O thou that graced with Fortune's choicest gifts
Surpassing mortals, while thine eyes beheld
Yon sun's ethereal rays, livedst like a god
Bless'd amid thy Persians; bless'd I deem thee now
In death, ere sunk in this abyss of ills,
Darius, hear at once our sum of wo;
Ruin through all her states hath crush'd thy Persia.
GHOST OF DARIUS: By pestilence, or faction's furious storms?
ATOSSA: Not so; near Athens perish'd all our troops.
GHOST OF DARIUS: Say, of my sons, which led the forces thither?
ATOSSA: The impetuous Xerxes, thinning all the land.
GHOST OF DARIUS: By sea or land dared he this rash attempt?
ATOSSA: By both; a double front the war presented.
GHOST OF DARIUS: A host so vast what march conducted o'er?
ATOSSA: From shore he bridged the Hellespont.
GHOST OF DARIUS: What! could he chain the mighty Bosphorus?
ATOSSA: Ev'n so, some god assisting his design.
GHOST OF DARIUS: Some god of power to cloud his better sense.
ATOSSA: The event now shows what mischiefs he achieved.
GHOST OF DARIUS: What suffer'd they, for whom your sorrows flow?
ATOSSA: His navy sunk spreads ruin through the camp.
GHOST OF DARIUS: Fell all his host beneath the slaught'ring spear?
ATOSSA: Susa, through all her streets, mourns her lost sons.
GHOST OF DARIUS: How vain the succour, the defence of arms?
ATOSSA: In Bactra age and grief are only left.
GHOST OF DARIUS: Ah, what a train of warlike youth is lost!
ATOSSA: Xerxes, astonished, desolate, alone —
GHOST OF DARIUS: How will this end? Nay, pause not. Is he safe?
ATOSSA: Fled o'er the bridge, that join'd the adverse strands.
GHOST OF DARIUS: And reach'd this shore in safety? Is this true?
ATOSSA: True are thy words, and not to be gainsay'd.
GHOST OF DARIUS: With what a winged course the oracles

Haste their completion! With the lightning's speed
Jove on my son hath hurled his threaten'd vengeance:
Yet I implored the gods that it might fall
In time's late process: but when rashness drives
Impetuous on, the scourge of Heaven upraised
Lashes the Fury forward; hence these ills
Pour headlong on my friends. Not weighing this,
My son, with all the fiery pride of youth,
Hath quickened their arrival, while he hoped
To bind the sacred Hellespont, to hold
The raging Bosphorus, like a slave, in chains,
And dared the advent'rous passage, bridging firm
With links of solid iron his wondrous way,
To lead his numerous host; and swell'd with thoughts
Presumptuous, deem'd vain mortal! that his power
Should rise above the gods' and Neptune's might.
And was not his the phrensy of the soul?
But much I fear lest all my treasured wealth
Fall to some daring hand an easy prey.

ATOSSA: This from too frequent converse with bad men
The impetuous Xerxes learn'd; these caught his ear
With thy great deeds, as winning for the sons
Vast riches with thy conquering spear, while he
Tim'rous and slothful, never, save in sport,
Lifted his lance, nor added to the wealth
Won by his noble fathers. This reproach
Oft by bad men repeated, urged his soul
To attempt this war, and lead his troops to Greece.

GHOST OF DARIUS: Great deeds have they achieved, and memorable
For ages never hath this wasted state
Suffer'd such ruin, since heaven's awful king
Gave to one lord Asia's extended plains
White with innumerous flocks, and to his hands
Consign'd the imperial sceptre. Her brave hosts
A Mede first led; the virtues of his son
Fix'd firm the empire, for his temperate soul
Breathed prudence, Cyrus next, by fortune graced,
Adorn'd the throne, and bless'd his grateful friends
With peace: he to his mighty monarchy
Join'd Lydia, and the Phrygians; to his power
Ionia bent reluctant; but the gods
With victory his gentle virtues crown'd.
His son then wore the regal diadem.

107

Next to disgrace his country, and to stain
The splendid glories of this ancient throne,
Rose Mardus: him, with righteous vengeance fired
Artaphernes, and his confederate chiefs
Crush'd in his palace Maraphis assumed
The sceptre: After him Artaphernes.
Me next to this exalted eminence,
Crowning my great ambition, Fortune raised.
In many a glorious field my glittering spear
Flamed in the van of Persia's numerous hosts;
But never wrought such ruin to the state.
Xerxes, my son, in all the pride of youth
Listens to youthful counsels, my commands
No more remember'd; hence, my hoary friends,
Not the whole line of Persia's sceptred lords,
You know it well, so wasted her brave sons.

LEADER OF THE CHORUS: Why this? To what fair end are these
        thy words
Directed? Sovereign lord, instruct thy Persians
How, mid this ruin, best to guide their state.

GHOST OF DARIUS: No more 'gainst Greece lead your embattled hosts;
Not though your deep'ning phalanx spreads the field
Outnumb'ring theirs, their very earth fights for them.

LEADER: What may thy words import? How fight for them?

GHOST OF DARIUS: With famine it destroys your cumbrous train.

LEADER: Choice levies, prompt for action, will we send.

GHOST OF DARIUS: Those, in the fields of Greece that now remain,
Shall not revisit safe the Persian shore.

LEADER: What! shall not all the host of Persia pass
Again from Europe o'er the Hellespont?

GHOST OF DARIUS: Of all their numbers few, if aught avails
The faith of heaven-sent oracles to him
That weighs the past, in their accomplishment
Not partial: hence he left, in faithless hope
Confiding, his selected train of heroes.
These have their station where Asopus flows
Wat'ring the plain, whose grateful currents roll
Diffusing plenty through Boeotia's fields.
There misery waits to crush them with the load
Of heaviest ills, in vengeance for their proud
And impious daring; for where'er they held
Through Greece their march, they fear'd not to profane
The statues of the gods; their hallow'd shrines

Emblazed, o'erturn'd their altars, and in ruins,
Rent from their firm foundations, to the ground
Levell'd their temples; such their frantic deeds,
Nor less their suff'rings; greater still awaits them;
For Vengeance hath not wasted all her stores;
The heap yet swells; for in Plataea's plains
Beneath the Doric spear the clotted mass
Of carnage shall arise, that the high mounds,
Piled o'er the dead, to late posterity
Shall give this silent record to men's eyes,
That proud aspiring thoughts but ill beseem
Weak mortals: for oppression, when it springs,
Puts forth the blade of vengeance, and its fruit
Yields a ripe harvest of repentant wo.
Behold this vengeance, and remember Greece,
Remember Athens: henceforth let not pride,
Her present state disdaining, strive to grasp
Another's, and her treasured happiness
Shed on the ground: such insolent attempts
Awake the vengeance of offended Jove.
But you, whose age demands more temperate thoughts,
With words of well-placed counsel teach his youth
To curb that pride, which from the gods calls down
Destruction on his head. *(To* Atossa*)* And thou, whose age
The miseries of thy Xerxes sink with sorrow,
Go to thy house, thence choose the richest robe,
And meet thy son; for through the rage of grief
His gorgeous vestments from his royal limbs
Are foully rent. With gentlest courtesy
Soothe his affliction; for his duteous ear,
I know, will listen to thy voice alone.
Now to the realms of darkness I descend.
My ancient friends, farewell, and mid these ills
Each day in pleasure bathe your drooping spirits,
For treasured riches naught avail the dead.

(The Ghost of Darius *vanishes into the tomb.)*

LEADER: These many present, many future ills
    Denounced on Persia, sink my soul with grief.
ATOSSA: Unhappy fortune, what a tide of ills
    Bursts o'er me! Chief this foul disgrace, which shows
    My son divested of his rich attire,

His royal robes all rent, distracts my thoughts.
But I will go, choose the most gorgeous vest,
And haste to meet my son. Ne'er in his woes
Will I forsake whom my soul holds most dear.

(Atossa *departs as the* Chorus *begins its song.)*

CHORUS: Ye powers that rule the skies,
    Memory recalls our great, our happy fate,
      Our well-appointed state,
    The scenes of glory opening to our eyes,
      When this vast empire o'er
    The good Darius, with each virtue bless'd
      That forms a monarch's breast,
    Shielding his subjects with a father's care,
      Invincible in war,
    Extended like a god his awful power,
      Then spread our arms their glory wide,
      Guarding to peace her golden reign:
      Each tower 'd city saw with pride
    Safe from the toils of war her homeward-marching train.
      Nor Haly's shallow strand
    He pass'd, nor from his palace moved his state;
      He spoke; his word was Fate.
    What strong-based cities could his might withstand?
      Not those that lift their heads
    Where to the sea the floods of Strymon pass,
      Leaving the huts of Thrace;
    Nor those, that far the extended ocean o'er
      Stand girt with many a tower;
    Nor where the Hellespont his broad wave spreads;
      Nor the firm bastions' rampired might,
      Whose foot the deep Propontis laves;
      Nor those, that glorying in their height
    Frown o'er the Pontic sea, and shade his darken'd waves.

      Each sea-girt isle around
    Bow'd to this monarch: humbled Lesbos bow'd;
      Paros, of its marble proud;
    Naxos with vines, with olives Samos crown'd:
      Him Myconos adored;
    Chios, the seat of beauty; Andros steep,
      That stretches o'er the deep

To meet the wat'ry Tenos; him each bay
        Bound by the Icarian sea,
Him Melos, Gnidus, Rhodes confess'd their lord;
        O'er Cyprus stretch'd his sceptred hand:
        Paphos and Solos own'd his power,
        And Salamis, whose hostile strand,
The cause of all our wo, is red with Persian gore.
        Ev'n the proud towns, that rear'd
Sublime along the Ionian coast their towers,
        Where wealth her treasure pours,
Peopled from Greece, his prudent reign revered.
        With such unconquer'd might
His hardy warriors shook the embattled fields,
        Heroes that Persia yields,
And those from distant realms that took their way,
        And wedged in close array
Beneath his glitt'ring banners claim'd the fight.
        But now these glories are no more:
        Farewell the big war's plumed pride:
        The gods have crush'd this trophied power;
Sunk are our vanquish'd arms beneath the indignant tide.

(Xerxes *enters with a few followers. His royal raiment
is torn. The entire closing scene is sung or chanted.*)

XERXES: Ah me, how sudden have the storms of Fate,
        Beyond all thought, all apprehension, burst
        On my devoted head! O Fortune, Fortune!
        With what relentless fury hath thy hand
        Hurl'd desolation on the Persian race
        Wo unsupportable! The torturing thought
        Of our lost youth comes rushing on my mind,
        And sinks me to the ground. O Jove, that I
        Had died with those brave men that died in fight!
CHORUS: O thou afflicted monarch, once the lord
        Of marshall'd armies, of the lustre beam'd
        From glory's ray o'er Persia, of her sons
        The pride, the grace, whom ruin now hath sunk
        In blood! The unpeopled land laments her youth
        By Xerxes led to slaughter, till the realms
        Of death are gorged with Persians; for the flower
        Of all the realm, thousands, whose dreadful bows
        With arrowy shower annoy'd the foe, are fall'n.

111

XERXES: Your fall, heroic youths, distracts my soul.
CHORUS: And Asia sinking on her knee, O king,
    Oppress'd with griefs oppress'd bends to the earth.
XERXES: And I, wretched fortune, I was born
    To crush, to desolate my ruin'd country!
CHORUS: I have no voice, no swelling harmony,
    No descant, save these notes of wo,
    Harsh, and responsive to the sullen sigh,
    Rude strains, that unmelodious flow,
    To welcome thy return.
XERXES: Then bid them flow, bid the wild measures flow
    Hollow, unmusical, the notes of grief;
    They suit my fortune, and dejected state.
CHORUS: Yes, at thy royal bidding shall the strain
    Pour the deep sorrows of my soul;
    The suff'rings of my bleeding country plain,
    And bid the mournful measures roll.
    Again the voice of wild despair
    With thrilling shrieks shall pierce the air;
    For high the god of war his flaming crest
    Raised, with the fleet of Greece surrounded,
    The haughty arms of Greece with conquest bless'd,
    And Persia's wither'd force confounded,
    Dash'd on the dreary beach her heroes slain,
    Or whelm'd them in the darken'd main.
XERXES: To swell thy griefs ask ev'ry circumstance.
CHORUS: Where are thy valiant friends, thy chieftains where?
    Pharnaces, Susas, and the might
    Of Pelagon, and Dotamas? The spear
    Of Agabates bold in fight?
    Psammis in mailed cuirass dress'd,
    And Susiscanes' glitt'ring crest?
XERXES: Dash'd from the Tyrian vessel on the rocks
    Of Salamis they sunk, and smear'd with gore
    The heroes on the dreary strand are stretch'd.
CHORUS: Where is Pharnuchus? Ariomardus where,
    With ev'ry gentle virtue graced?
    Lilaeus, that from chiefs renown'd in war
    His high-descended lineage traced?
    Where rears Sebalces his crown-circled head:
    Where Tharybis to battles bred,
    Artembares, Hystaechmes bold,
    Memphis, Masistres sheath'd in gold?

XERXES: Wretch that I am! These on the abhorred town
    Ogygian Athens, roll'd their glowing eyes
    Indignant; but at once in the fierce shock
    Of battle fell, dash'd breathless on the ground.
CHORUS: There does the son of Batanochus lie,
    Through whose rich veins the unsullied blood
    Of Susamus, down from the lineage high
    Of noble Mygabatas flow'd:
    Alpistus, who with faithful care
    Number'd the deep'ning files of war,
    The monarch's eye; on the ensanguined plain
    Low is the mighty warrior laid?
Is great Aebares 'mong the heroes slain,
    And Partheus number'd with the dead? —
Ah me! those bursting groans, deep-charged with wo,
    The fate of Persia's princes show.
XERXES: To my grieved memory thy mournful voice,
    Tuned to the saddest notes of wo, recalls
    My brave friends lost; and my rent heart returns
    In dreadful symphony the sorrowing strain.
CHORUS: Yet once more shall I ask thee, yet once more,
    Where is the Mardian Xanthes' might,
    The daring chief, that from the Pontiac shore
    Led his strong phalanx to the fight?
    Anchares where, whose high-raised shield
    Flamed foremost in the embattled field?
Where the high leaders of thy mail-clad horse,
    Daixis and Arsaces where?
Where Cigdadatas and Lythinmas' force,
    Waving untired his purple spear?
XERXES: Entomb'd, I saw them in the earth entomb'd;
    Nor did the rolling car with solemn state
    Attend their rites: I follow'd: low they lie
    (Ah me, the once great leaders of my host!),
    Low in the earth, without their honours lie.
CHORUS: O wo, wo, wo! Unutterable wo
    The demons of revenge have spread;
    And Ate from her drear abode below
    Rises to view the horrid deed.
XERXES: Dismay, and rout, and ruin, ills that wait
    On man's afflicted fortune, sink us down.
CHORUS: Dismay, and rout, and ruin on us wait,
    And all the vengeful storms of Fate:

Ill flows on ill, on sorrows sorrows rise;
Misfortune leads her baleful train;
    Before the Ionian squadrons Persia flies,
Or sinks ingulf'd beneath the main.
Fall'n, fall'n is her imperial power,
And conquest on her banners waits no more.

XERXES: At such a fall, such troops of heroes lost,
    How can my soul but sink in deep despair?
    Cease thy sad strain.

CHORUS: Is all thy glory lost?

XERXES: Seest thou these poor remains of my rent robes?

CHORUS: I see, I see.

XERXES: And this ill-furnish'd quiver?

CHORUS: Wherefore preserved?

XERXES: To store my treasured arrows.

CHORUS: Few, very few.

XERXES: And few my friendly aids.

CHORUS: I thought these Grecians shrunk appall'd at arms.

XERXES: No: they are bold and daring: these sad eyes
    Beheld their violent and deathful deeds.

CHORUS: The ruin, sayst thou, of thy shattered fleet?

XERXES: And in the anguish of my soul I rent
    My royal robes.

CHORUS: Wo, wo!

XERXES: And more than wo!

CHORUS: Redoubled, threefold wo!

XERXES: Disgrace to me,
    But triumph to the foe.

CHORUS: Are all thy powers
    In ruin crush'd?

XERXES: No satrap guards me now.

CHORUS: Thy faithful friends sunk in the roaring main.

XERXES: Weep, weep their loss, and lead me to my house;
    Answer my grief with grief, an ill return
    Of ills for ills. Yet once more raise that strain
    Lamenting my misfortune; beat thy breast,
    Strike, heave the groan; awake the Mysian strain
    To notes of loudest wo; rend thy rich robes,
    Pluck up thy beard, tear off thy hoary locks,
    And bathe thine eyes in tears: thus through the streets
    Solemn and slow with sorrow lead my steps;
    Lead to my house, and wail the fate of Persia.

CHORUS: Yes, once more at thy bidding shall the strain

Pour the deep sorrows of my soul;
The suff'rings of my bleeding country plain,
And bid the Mysian measures roll.
Again the voice of wild despair
With thrilling shrieks shall pierce the air;
For high the god of war his flaming crest
Raised, with the fleet of Greece surrounded,
The haughty arms of Greece with conquest bless'd,
And Persia's withered force confounded,
Dash'd on the dreary beach her heroes slain,
Or whelm'd them in the darken'd main.

Robert Potter

SOPHOCLES

SOPHOCLES (C. 496-406 B. C.) is one of the greatest tragic poets in all literary history. Born at Colonus, near Athens, in an aristocratic environment, he was trained in dancing and music, participated in Athenian civic duties, and attained distinctive official positions, including a priesthood.

123 plays are attributed to him, of which seven are extant. What is of primary interest to Sophocles is the working out of human motives. The tragic doom of his characters is an element in human life, and man suffers in conflict with great crises.

ELECTRA

The date of this drama falls between 418 and 410 B. C. Orestes, placed by his sister Electra as a child under the care of King Strophius, returns to avenge the murder of his father Agamemnon. Clytemnestra, wife of Agamemnon, and her loved Aegisthus are the guilty pair. The motif of the drama is vengeance, directed by Electra herself.

CHARACTERS IN THE PLAY

ORESTES, son of Agamemnon and Clytemnestra
ELECTRA
CHRYSOTHEMIS } sisters of Orestes
An OLD MAN, formerly the Paedagogus or Attendant of Orestes
CLYTEMNESTRA
AEGISTHUS
CHORUS OF WOMEN OF MYCENAE

MUTE PERSONS

PYLADES, son of Strophius, King of Crisa, the friend of Orestes
A HANDMAID of Clytemnestra
Two ATTENDANTS of Orestes

116

(SCENE: — *At Mycenae, before the palace of the Pelopidae. It is morning and the new-risen sun is bright. The* PAEDAGOGUS *enters on the left of the spectators, accompanied by the two youths,* ORESTES *and* PYLADES.)

PAEDAGOGUS: Son of him who led our hosts at Troy of old, son of Agamemnon! — now thou mayest behold with thine eyes all that thy soul hath desired so long. There is the ancient Argos of thy yearning, — that hallowed scene whence the gad-fly drove the daughter of Inachus; and there, Orestes, is the Lycean Agora, named from the wolf-slaying god; there, on the left, Hera's famous temple; and in this place to which we have come, deem that thou seest Mycenae rich in gold, with the house of the Pelopidae there, so often stained with bloodshed; whence I carried thee of yore, from the slaying of thy father, as thy kinswoman, thy sister, charged me; and saved thee, and reared thee up to manhood, to be the avenger of thy murdered sire.

Now, therefore, Orestes, and thou, best of friends, Pylades, our plans must be laid quickly; for lo, already the sun's bright ray is waking the songs of the birds into clearness, and the dark night of stars is spent. Before, then, anyone comes forth from the house, take counsel; seeing that the time allows not of delay, but is full ripe for deeds.

ORESTES: True friend and follower, how well dost thou prove thy loyalty to our house! As a steed of generous race, though old, loses not courage in danger, but pricks his ear, even so thou urgest us forward, and art foremost in our support. I will tell thee, then, what I have determined; listen closely to my words, and correct me, if I miss the mark in aught.

When I went to the Pythian oracle, to learn how I might avenge my father on his murderers, Phoebus gave me the response which thou art now to hear: — that alone, and by stealth, without aid of arms or numbers, I should snatch the righteous vengeance of my hand. Since, then, the god spake to us on this wise, thou must go into yonder house, when opportunity gives the entrance, and learn all that is passing there, so that thou mayest report to us from sure knowledge. Thine age, and the lapse of time will prevent them from recognising thee; they will never suspect who thou art, with that silvered hair. Let thy tale be that thou art a Phocian stranger, sent by Phanoteus; for he is the greatest of their allies. Tell them, and confirm it with thine oath, that Orestes hath perished by a fatal chance, — hurled at the Pythian games from his rapid chariot; be that the substance of thy story.

117

We, meanwhile, will first crown my father's tomb, as the god enjoined, with drink-offerings and the luxuriant tribute of severed hair; then come back, bearing in our hands an urn of shapely bronze, — now hidden in the brushwood, as I think thou knowest, — so to gladden them with the false tidings that this my body is no more, but has been consumed with fire and turned to ashes. Why should the omen trouble me, when by a feigned death I find life indeed, and win renown? I trow, no word is ill-omened, if fraught with gain. Often ere now have I seen wise men die in vain report; then, when they return home, they are held in more abiding honour: as I trust that from this rumour I also shall emerge in radiant life, and yet shine like a star upon my foes.

O my fatherland, and ye gods of the land, receive me with good fortune in this journey, — and ye also, halls of my fathers, for I come with a divine mandate to cleanse you righteously; send me not dishonoured from the land, but grant that I may rule over my possessions, and restore my house!

Enough; — be it now thy care, old man, to go and heed thy task; and we twain will go forth; for so occasion bids, chief ruler of every enterprise for men.

ELECTRA *(within)*: Ah me, ah me!

PAEDAGOGUS: Hark, my son, — from the doors, methought, came the sound of some handmaid moaning within.

ORESTES: Can it be the hapless Electra? Shall we stay here, and listen to her laments?

PAEDAGOGUS: No, no: before all else, let us seek to obey the command of Loxias, and thence make a fair beginning, by pouring libations to thy sire; that brings victory within our grasp, and gives us the mastery in all that we do.

(Exeunt Paedagogus *on the spectators' left,* Orestes *and* Pylades *on the right. — Enter* Electra, *from the house. She is meanly clad.)*

ELECTRA *(chanting)*: O thou pure sunlight, and thou air, earth's canopy, how often have ye heard the strains of my lament, the wild blows against this bleeding breast, when dark night fails! And my wretched couch in yonder house of woe knows well, ere now, how I keep the watches of the night, — how often I bewail my hapless sire; to whom deadly Ares gave not of his gifts in a strange land, but my mother, and her mate Aegisthus, cleft his head with murderous axe, as woodmen fell an oak. And for this no plaint bursts from any lip save mine, when thou, my father, hath died a death so cruel and so piteous!

But never will I cease from dirge and sore lament, while I look on the trembling rays of the bright stars, or on this light of day; but like the nightingale, slayer of her offspring, I will wail without ceasing, and cry aloud to all, here, at the doors of my father.

O home of Hades and Persephone! O Hermes of the shades! O potent Curse, and ye, dread daughters of the gods, Erinyes, — ye who behold when a life is reft by violence, when a bed is dishonoured by stealth, — come, help me, avenge the murder of my sire, — and send to me my brother; for I have no more the strength to bear up alone against the load of grief that weighs me down.

(As Electra *finishes her lament, the* Chorus of Women of Mycenae *enter. The following lines between* Electra *and the* Chorus *are chanted responsively.)*

CHORUS: Ah, Electra, child of a wretched mother, why art thou ever pining thus in ceaseless lament for Agamemnon, who long ago was wickedly ensnared by thy false mother's wiles, and betrayed to death by a dastardly hand? Perish the author of that deed, if I may utter such a prayer!

ELECTRA: Ah, noble-hearted maidens, ye have come to soothe my woes. I know and feel it, it escapes me not; but I cannot leave this task undone, or cease from mourning for my hapless sire. Ah, friends whose love responds to mine in every mood, leave me to rave thus, — oh leave me, I entreat you!

CHORUS: But never by laments or prayers shalt thou recall thy sire from that lake of Hades to which all must pass. Nay, thine is a fatal course of grief, passing ever from due bounds into a cureless sorrow; wherein there is no deliverance from evils. Say, wherefore art thou enamoured of misery?

ELECTRA: Foolish is the child who forgets a parent's piteous death. No, dear to my soul is the mourner that laments for Itys, Itys, evermore, that bird distraught with grief, the messenger of Zeus. Ah, queen of sorrow, Niobe, thee I deem divine, — thee, who evermore weepest in thy rocky tomb!

CHORUS: Not to thee alone of mortals, my daughter, hath come any sorrow which thou bearest less calmly than those within, thy kinswomen and sisters, Chrysothemis and Iphianassa, who still live, — as he, too, lives, sorrowing in a secluded youth, yet happy in that this famous realm of Mycenae shall one day welcome him to his heritage, when the kindly guidance of Zeus shall have brought him to this land, — Orestes.

119

ELECTRA: Yes, I wait for him with unwearied longing, as I move on my sad path from day to day, unwed and childless, bathed in tears, bearing that endless doom of woe; but he forgets all that he has suffered and heard. What message comes to me, that is not belied? He is ever yearning to be with us, but, though he yearns, he never resolves.

CHORUS: Courage, my daughter; great still in heaven is Zeus, who sees and governs all: leave thy bitter quarrel to him; forget not thy foe, but refrain from excess of wrath against them; for Time is a god who makes rough ways smooth. Not heedless is the son of Agamemnon, who dwells by Crisa's pastoral shore; not heedless is the god who reigns by Acheron.

ELECTRA: Nay, the best part of life hath passed away from me in hopelessness, and I have no strength left it; I, who am pining away without children,— whom no loving champion shields,— but, like some despised alien, I serve in the halls of my father, clad in this mean garb, and standing at a meagre board.

CHORUS: Piteous was the voice heard at his return, and piteous, as thy sire lay on the festal couch, when the straight, swift blow was dealt him with the blade of bronze. Guile was the plotter, Lust the slayer, dread parents of a dreadful shape; whether it was mortal that wrought therein, or god.

ELECTRA: O that bitter day, bitter beyond all that have come to me; O that night. O the horrors of that unutterable feast, the ruthless death-strokes that my father saw from the hands of twain, who took my life captive by treachery, who doomed me to woe! May the great god of Olympus give them sufferings in requital, and never may their splendour bring them joy, who have done such deeds!

CHORUS: Be advised to say no more; canst thou not see what conduct it is which already plunges thee so cruelly in self-made miseries? Thou hast greatly aggravated thy troubles, ever breeding wars with thy sullen soul; but such strife should not be pushed to a conflict with the strong.

ELECTRA: I have been forced to it,— forced by dread causes; I know my own passion, it escapes me not; but, seeing that the causes are so dire, I will never curb these frenzied plaints, while life is in me. Who indeed, ye kindly sisterhood, who that think aright, would deem that any word of solace could avail me? Forbear, forbear, my comforters! Such ills must be numbered with those which have no cure; I can never know a respite from my sorrows, or a limit to this wailing.

CHORUS: At least it is in love, like a true-hearted mother, that I dissuade thee from adding misery to miseries.

ELECTRA: But what measure is there in my wretchedness? Say, how can it be right to neglect the dead? Was that impiety ever born in mortal? Never may I have praise of such: never, when my lot is cast in pleasant places, may I cling to selfish ease, or dishonour my sire by restraining the wings of shrill lamentation!

For if the hapless dead is to lie in dust and nothingness, while the slayers pay not with blood for blood, all regard for man, all fear of heaven, will vanish from the earth.

LEADER OF THE CHORUS: I come, my child, in zeal for thy welfare no less than for mine own; but if I speak not well, then be it as thou wilt; for we will follow thee.

ELECTRA: I am ashamed, my friends, if ye deem me too impatient for my oft complaining; but, since a hard constraint forces me to this, bear with me. How indeed could any woman of noble nature refrain, who saw the calamities of a father's house, as I see them by day and night continually, not fading, but in the summer of their strength? I, who, first, from the mother that bore me have found bitter enmity; next, in mine own home I dwell with my father's murderers; they rule over me, and with them it rests to give or to withhold what I need.

And then think what manner of days I pass, when I see Aegisthus sitting on my father's throne, wearing the robes which he wore, and pouring libations at the hearth where he slew my sire; and when I see the outrage that crowns all, the murderer in our father's bed at our wretched mother's side, if mother she should be called, who is his wife; but so hardened is she that she lives with that accursed one, fearing no Erinys; nay, as if exulting in her deeds, having found the day on which she treacherously slew my father of old, she keeps it with dance and song, and month by month sacrifices sheep to the gods who have wrought her deliverance.

But I, hapless one, beholding it, weep and pine in the house, and bewail the unholy feast named after my sire, — weep to myself alone; since I may not even indulge my grief to the full measure of my yearning. For this woman, in professions so noble, loudly upbraids me with such taunts as these: 'Impious and hateful girl, hast thou alone lost a father, and is there no other mourner in the world? An evil doom be thine, and may the gods infernal give thee no riddance from thy present laments.'

Thus she insults; save when any one brings her word that Orestes is coming; then, infuriated, she comes up to me, and

121

cries; — 'Hast not thou brought this upon me? Is not this deed thine, who didst steal Orestes from my hands, and privily convey him forth? Yet be sure that thou shalt have thy due reward.' So she shrieks; and aiding her, the renowned spouse at her side is vehement in the same strain, — that abject dastard, that utter pest, who fights his battles with the help of women. But I, looking ever for Orestes to come and end these woes, languish in my misery. Always intending to strike a blow, he has worn out every hope that I could conceive. In such a case, then, friends, there is no room for moderation or for reverence; in sooth, the stress of ills leaves no choice but to follow evil ways.

LEADER: Say, is Aegisthus near while thou speakest thus, or absent from home?

ELECTRA: Absent, certainly; do not think that I should have come to the doors, if he had been near; but just now he is afield.

LEADER: Might I converse with thee more freely, if this is so?

ELECTRA: He is not here, so put thy question; what wouldst thou?

LEADER: I ask thee, then, what sayest thou of thy brother? Will he come soon, or is he delaying? I fain would know.

ELECTRA: He promises to come; but he never fulfils the promise.

LEADER: Yea, a man will pause on the verge of a great work.

ELECTRA: And yet I saved him without pausing.

LEADER: Courage; he is too noble to fail his friends.

ELECTRA: I believe it; or I should not have lived so long.

LEADER: Say no more now; for I see thy sister coming from the house, Chrysothemis, daughter of the same sire and mother, with sepulchral gifts in her hands, such as are given to those in the world below.

(Chrysothemis *enters from the palace. She is richly dressed.*)

CHRYSOTHEMIS: Why, sister, hast thou come forth once more to declaim thus at the public doors? Why wilt thou not learn with any lapse of time to desist from vain indulgence of idle wrath? Yet this I know, — that I myself am grieved at our plight; indeed, could I find the strength, I would show what love I bear them. But now, in these troubled waters, 'tis best, methinks, to shorten sail; I care not to seem active, without the power to hurt. And would that thine own conduct were the same! Nevertheless, right is on the side of thy choice, not of that which I advise; but if I am to live in freedom, our rulers must be obeyed in all things.

ELECTRA: Strange indeed, that thou, the daughter of such a sire as thine, shouldst forget him, and think only of thy mother; All thy admonitions to me have been taught by her; no word is thine own. Then take thy choice, — to be imprudent; or prudent, but forgetful of thy friends: thou, who has just said that, couldst thou find the strength, thou wouldst show thy hatred of them; yet, when I am doing my utmost to avenge my sire, thou givest no aid, but seekest to turn thy sister from her deed.

Does not this crown our miseries with cowardice? For tell me, — or let me tell thee, — what I should gain by ceasing from these laments? Do I not live? — miserably, I know, yet well enough for me. And I vex them, thus rendering honour to the dead, if pleasure can' be felt in that world. But thou, who tellest me of thy hatred, hatest in word alone, while in deeds thou art with the slayers of thy sire. I, then, would never yield to them, though I were promised the gifts which now make thee proud; thine be the richly-spread table and the life of luxury. For me, be it food enough that I do not wound mine own conscience; I covet not such privilege as thine, — nor wouldst thou, wert thou wise. But now, when thou mightest be called daughter of the noblest father among men, be called the child of thy mother; so shall thy baseness be most widely seen, in betrayal of thy dead sire and of thy kindred.

LEADER: No angry word, I entreat! For both of you there is good in what is urged, — if thou, Electra, wouldst learn to profit by her counsel, and she, again, by thine.

CHRYSOTHEMIS: For my part, friends, I am not wholly unused to her discourse; nor should I have touched upon this theme, had I not heard that she was threatened with a dread doom, which shall restrain her from her long-drawn laments.

ELECTRA: Come, declare it then, this terror! If thou canst tell me of aught worse than my present lot, I will resist no more.

CHRYSOTHEMIS: Indeed, I will tell thee all that I know. They purpose, if thou wilt not cease from these laments, to send thee where thou shalt never look upon the sunlight, but pass thy days in a dungeon beyond the borders of this land, there to chant thy dreary strain. Bethink thee, then, and do not blame me hereafter, when the blow hath fallen; now is the time to be wise.

ELECTRA: Have they indeed resolved to treat me thus?

CHRYSOTHEMIS: Assuredly, whenever Aegisthus comes home.

ELECTRA: If that be all, then may he arrive with speed!

CHRYSOTHEMIS: Misguided one! what dire prayer is this?

ELECTRA: That he may come, if he hath any such intent.

CHRYSOTHEMIS: That thou mayst suffer — what? Where are thy wits?

ELECTRA: That I may fly as far as may be from you all.

123

CHRYSOTHEMIS: But hast thou no care for thy present life?

ELECTRA: Aye, my life is marvellously fair.

CHRYSOTHEMIS: It might be, couldst thou only learn prudence.

ELECTRA: Do not teach me to betray my friends.

CHRYSOTHEMIS: I do not, — but to bend before the strong.

ELECTRA: Thine be such flattery: those are not my ways.

CHRYSOTHEMIS: 'Tis well, however, not to fall by folly.

ELECTRA: I will fall, if need be, in the cause of my sire.

CHRYSOTHEMIS: But our father, I know, pardons me for this.

ELECTRA: It is for cowards to find peace in such maxims.

CHRYSOTHEMIS: So thou wilt not hearken, and take my counsel?

ELECTRA: No, verily; long may be it before I am so foolish.

CHRYSOTHEMIS: Then I will go forth upon mine errand.

ELECTRA: And whither goest thou? To whom bearest thou these offerings?

CHRYSOTHEMIS: Our mother sends me with funeral libations for our sire.

ELECTRA: How sayest thou? For her deadliest foe?

CHRYSOTHEMIS: Slain by her own hand — so thou wouldest say.

ELECTRA: What friend hath persuaded her? Whose wish was this?

CHRYSOTHEMIS: The cause, I think, was some dread vision of the night.

ELECTRA: Gods of our house! be ye with me — now at last!

CHRYSOTHEMIS: Dost thou find any encouragement in this terror?

ELECTRA: If thou wouldst tell me the vision, then I could answer.

CHRYSOTHEMIS: Nay, I can tell but little of the story.

ELECTRA: Tell what thou canst; a little word hath often marred, or made, men's fortunes.

CHRYSOTHEMIS: 'Tis said that she beheld our sire, restored to the sunlight, at her side once more; then he took the sceptre, — once his own, but now borne by Aegisthus, — and planted it at the hearth; and thence a fruitful bough sprang upward, wherewith the whole land of Mycenae was overshadowed. Such was the tale that I heard told by one who was present when she declared her dream to the Sun-god. More than this I know not, — save that she sent me by reason of that fear. So by the gods of our house I beseech thee, hearken to me, and be not ruined by folly. For if thou repel me now, thou wilt come back to seek me in thy trouble.

ELECTRA: Nay, dear sister, let none of these things in thy hands touch the tomb; nor neither custom nor piety allows thee to dedicate gifts or bring libations to our sire from a hateful wife. No — to the winds with them! or bury them deep in the earth, where none of them shall ever come near his place of rest; but, when she dies, let her find these treasures laid up for her below.

And were she not the most hardened of all women, she

124

would never have sought to pour these offerings of enmity on the grave of him whom she slew. Think now if it is likely that the dead in the tomb should take these honours kindly at her hand, who ruthlessly slew him, like a foeman, and mangled him, and, for ablution, wiped off the blood-stains on his head? Canst thou believe that these things which thou bringest will absolve her of the murder?

It is not possible. No, cast these things aside; give him rather a lock cut from thine own tresses, and on my part, hapless that I am, — scant gifts these, but my best, — this hair, not glossy with unguents, and this girdle, decked with no rich ornament. Then fall down and pray that he himself may come in kindness from the world below, to aid us against our foes; and that the young Orestes may live to set his foot upon his foes in victorious might, that henceforth we may crown our father's tomb with wealthier hands than those which grace it now.

I think, indeed, I think that he also had some part in sending her these appalling dreams; still, sister, do this service, to help thyself, and me, and him, that most beloved of all men, who rests in the realm of Hades, thy sire and mine.

LEADER: The maiden counsels piously; and thou, friend, wilt do her bidding, if thou art wise.

CHRYSOTHEMIS: I will. When a duty is clear, reason forbids that two voices should contend, and claims the hastening of the deed. Only, when I attempt this task, aid me with your silence, I entreat you, my friends; for, should my mother hear of it, methinks I shall yet have cause to rue my venture.

(Chrysothemis *departs, to take the offerings to Agamemnon's grave.*)

CHORUS *(singing):* If I am not an erring seer and one who fails in wisdom, Justice, that hath sent the presage, will come triumphant in her righteous strength, — will come ere long, my child, to avenge. There is courage in my heart, through those new tidings of the dream that breathes comfort. Not forgetful is thy sire, the lord of Hellas; not forgetful is the two-edged axe of bronze that struck the blow of old, and slew him with foul cruelty.

The Erinys of untiring feet, who is lurking in her dread ambush, will come, as with the march and with the might of a great host. For wicked ones have been fired with passion that hurried them to a forbidden bed, to accursed bridals, to a marriage stained with guilt of blood. Therefore am I sure that the portent will not fail to bring woe upon the partners in crime.

125

Verily mortals cannot read the future in fearful dreams or oracles, if this vision of the night find not due fulfilment.

O chariot-race of Pelops long ago, source of many a sorrow, what weary troubles hast thou brought upon this land! For since Myrtilus sank to rest beneath the waves, when a fatal and cruel hand hurled him to destruction out of the golden car, this house was never yet free from misery and violence.

(Clytemnestra *enters from the palace.*)

CLYTEMNESTRA: At large once more, it seems, thou rangest, — for Aegisthus is not here, who always kept thee at least from passing the gates, to shame thy friends. But now, since he is absent, thou takest no heed of me; though thou hast said of me oft-times, and to many, that I am a bold and lawless tyrant, who insults thee and thine. I am guilty of no insolence; I do but return the taunts that I often hear from thee.

Thy father — this is thy constant pretext — was slain by me. Yes, by me — I know it well; it admits of no denial; for Justice slew him, and not I alone, — Justice, who it became thee to support hadst thou been right-minded; seeing that this father of thine, whom thou art ever lamenting, was the one man of the Greeks who had the heart to sacrifice thy sister to the gods — he, the father, who had not shared the mother's pangs.

Come, tell me now, wherefore, or to please whom, did he sacrifice her? To please the Argives, thou wilt say? Nay, they had no right to slay my daughter. Or if, forsooth, it was to screen his brother Menelaus that he slew my child, was he not to pay me the penalty for that? Had not Menelaus two children, who should in fairness have been taken before my daughter, as sprung from the sire and mother who had caused that voyage? Or had Hades some strange desire to feast on my offspring, rather than on hers? Or had that accursed father lost all tenderness for the children of my womb, while he was tender to the children of Menelaus? Was not that the part of a callous and perverse parent? I think so, though I differ from thy judgment; and so would say the dead, if she could speak. For myself, then, I view the past without dismay; but if thou deemest me perverse, see that thine own judgment is just, before thou blame thy neighbour.

ELECTRA: This time thou canst not say that I have done anything to provoke such words from thee. But, if thou wilt give me leave, I fain would declare the truth, in the cause alike of my dead sire and of my sister.

CLYTEMNESTRA: Indeed, thou hast my leave; and didst thou always address me in such a tone, thou wouldst be heard without pain.

ELECTRA: Then I will speak. Thou sayest that thou hast slain my father. What word could bring thee deeper shame than that, whether the deed was just or not? But I must tell thee that thy deed was not just: no, thou wert drawn on to it by the wooing of the base man who is now thy spouse.

Ask the huntress Artemis what sin she punished when she stayed the frequent winds at Aulis; or I will tell thee; for we may not learn from her. My father — so I have heard — was once disporting himself in the grove of the goddess, when his footfall startled a dappled and antlered stag; he shot it, and chanced to utter a certain boast concerning its slaughter. Wroth thereat, the daughter of Leto detained the Greeks, that, in quittance for the wild creature's life, my father should yield up the life of his own child. Thus it befell that she was sacrificed; since the fleet had no other release, homeward or to Troy; and for that cause, under sore constraint and with sore reluctance, at last he slew her — not for the sake of Menelaus.

But grant — for I will take thine own plea — grant that the motive of his dead was to benefit his brother; — was that a reason for his dying by thy hand? Under what law? See that, in making such a law for men, thou make not trouble and remorse for thyself; for, if we are to take blood for blood, thou wouldst be the first to die, didst thou meet with thy desert.

But look if thy pretext is not false. For tell me, if thou wilt, wherefore thou art now doing the most shameless deeds of all, — dwelling as wife with that blood-guilty one, who first helped thee to slay my sire, and bearing children to him, while thou hast cast out the earlier-born, the stainless offspring of a stainless marriage. How can I praise these things? Or wilt thou say that this, too, is thy vengeance for thy daughter? Nay, a shameful plea, if so thou plead; 'tis not well to wed an enemy for a daughter's sake.

But indeed I may not even counsel thee, — who shriekest that I revile my mother; and truly I think that to me thou art less a mother than a mistress; so wretched is the life that I live, ever beset with miseries by thee and by thy partner. And that other, who scarce escaped thy hand, the hapless Orestes, is wearing out his ill-starred days in exile. Often hast thou charged me with rearing him to punish thy crime; and I would have done so, if I could, thou mayst be sure: — for that matter, denounce me to all, as disloyal, if thou wilt, or petulant, or impudent; for if

I am accomplished in such ways, methinks I am no unworthy child of thee.

LEADER OF THE CHORUS: I see that she breathes forth anger; but whether justice be with her, for this she seems to care no longer.

CLYTEMNESTRA (*to the* Chorus): And what manner of care do I need to use against her, who hath thus insulted a mother, and this at her ripe age? Thinkest thou not that she would go forward to any deed, without shame?

ELECTRA: Now be assured that I do feel shame for this, though thou believe it not; I know that my behavior is unseemly, and becomes me ill. But then the enmity on thy part, and thy treatment, compel me in mine own despite to do thus; for base deeds are taught by base.

CLYTEMNESTRA: Thou brazen one! Truly I and my sayings and my deeds give thee too much matter for words.

ELECTRA: The words are thine, not mine; for thine is the action; and the acts find the utterance.

CLYTEMNESTRA: Now by our lady Artemis, thou shalt not fail to pay for this boldness, so soon as Aegisthus returns.

ELECTRA: Lo, thou art transported by anger, after granting me free speech, and hast no patience to listen.

CLYTEMNESTRA: Now wilt thou not hush thy clamour, or even suffer me to sacrifice, when I have permitted thee to speak unchecked?

ELECTRA: I hinder not, — begin thy rites, I pray thee; and blame not my voice, for I shall say no more.

CLYTEMNESTRA: Raise then, my handmaid, the offerings of many fruits, that I may uplift my prayers to this our king, for deliverance from my present fears. Lend now a gracious ear, O Phoebus our defender, to my words, though they be dark; for I speak not among friends, nor is it meet to unfold my whole thought to the light, while she stands near me, lest with her malice and her garrulous cry she spread some rash rumour throughout the town: but hear me thus, since on this wise I must speak.

That vision which I saw last night in doubtful dreams — if it hath come for my good, grant, Lycean king, that it be fulfilled; but if for harm, then let it recoil upon my foes. And if any are plotting to hurl me by treachery from the high estate which now is mine, permit them not; rather vouchsafe that, still living thus unscathed, I may bear sway over the house of the Atreidae and this realm, sharing prosperous days with the friends who share them now, and with those of my children from whom no enmity or bitterness pursues me.

O Lycean Apollo, graciously hear these prayers, and grant

them to us all, even as we ask! For the rest, though I be silent, I deem that thou, a god, must know it; all things, surely, are seen by the sons of Zeus.

(The Paedagogus *enters.)*

PAEDAGOGUS: Ladies, might a stranger crave to know if this be the palace of the king Aegisthus?

LEADER: It is, sir; thou thyself hast guessed aright.

PAEDAGOGUS: And am I right in surmising that this lady is his consort? She is of queenly aspect.

LEADER: Assuredly; thou art in the presence of the queen.

PAEDAGOGUS: Hail, royal lady! I bring glad tidings to thee and to Aegisthus, from a friend.

CLYTEMNESTRA: I welcome the omen; but I would fain know from thee, first, who may have sent thee.

PAEDAGOGUS: Phanoteus the Phocian, on a weighty mission.

CLYTEMNESTRA: What is it, sir? Tell me; coming from a friend, then wilt bring, I know, a kindly message.

PAEDAGOGUS: Orestes is dead; that is the sum.

ELECTRA: Oh, miserable that I am! I am lost this day!

CLYTEMNESTRA: What sayest thou, friend, what sayest thou?—listen not to her!

PAEDAGOGUS: I said, and say again—Orestes is dead.

ELECTRA: I am lost, hapless one, I am undone!

CLYTEMNESTRA (*to* Electra): See thou to thine own concerns.—But do thou, sir, tell me exactly,—how did he perish?

PAEDAGOGUS: I was sent for that purpose, and will tell thee all. Having gone to the renowned festival, the pride of Greece, for the Delphian games, when he heard the loud summons to the foot-race which was first to be decided, he entered the lists, a brilliant form, a wonder in the eyes of all there; and, having finished his course at the point where it began, he went out with the glorious meed of victory. To speak briefly, where there is much to tell, I know not the man whose deeds and triumphs have matched his; but one thing thou must know; in all the contests that the judges announced, he bore away the prize; and men deemed him happy, as oft as the herald proclaimed him an Argive, by name Orestes, son of Agamemnon, who once gathered the famous armament of Greece.

Thus far, 'twas well; but, when a god sends harm, not even the strong man can escape. For on another day, when chariots were to try their speed at sunrise, he entered, with many charioteers. One was an Achaean, one from Sparta, two masters of yoked cars were Libyans; Orestes, driving Thessalian mares, came fifth among them; the sixth from Aetolia, with chestnut colts; a Magnesian was the seventh; the eighth, with white horses, was of Aenian stock; the ninth, from Athens, built of gods; there was a Boeotian too, making the tenth chariot.

They took their stations where the appointed umpires placed them by lot and ranged the cars; then, at the sound of the brazen trump, they started. All shouted to their horses, and shook the reins in their hands; the whole course was filled with the noise of rattling chariots; the dust flew upward; and all, in a confused throng, plied their goads unsparingly, each of them striving to pass the wheels and the snorting steeds of his rivals; for alike at their backs and at their rolling wheels the breath of the horses foamed and smote.

Orestes, driving close to the pillar at either end of the course, almost grazed it with his wheel each time, and, giving rein to the trace-horse on the right, checked the horse on the inner side. Hitherto, all the chariots had escaped overthrow; but presently the Aenian's hard-mouthed colts ran away, and, swerving, as they passed from the sixth into the seventh round, dashed their foreheads against the team of the Barcaean. Other mishaps followed the first, shock on shock and crash on crash, till the whole race-ground of Crisa was strewn with the wreck of the chariots.

Seeing this, the wary charioteer from Athens drew aside and paused, allowing the billow of chariots, surging in mid course, to go by. Orestes was driving last, keeping his horses behind, — for his trust was in the end; but when he saw that the Athenian was alone left in, he sent a shrill cry ringing through the ears of his swift colts, and gave chase. Team was brought level with team, and so they raced, — first one man, then the other, showing his head in front of the chariots.

Hitherto the ill-fated Orestes had passed safely through every round, steadfast in his steadfast car; at last, slackening his left rein while the horse was turning, unawares he struck the edge of the pillar; he broke the axle-box in twain; he was thrown over the chariot-rail; he was caught in the shapely reins; and, as he fell on the ground, his colts were scattered into the middle of the course.

But when the people saw him fallen from the car, a cry of pity went up for the youth, who had done such deeds and was meeting such a doom, — now dashed to earth, now tossed feet uppermost to the sky, — till the charioteers, with difficulty checking the career of his horses, loosed him, so covered with blood that no friend who saw it would have known the hapless corpse. Straightway they burned it on a pyre; and chosen men of Phocis are bringing in a small urn of bronze the sad dust of that mighty form, to find due burial in his fatherland.

Such is my story, — grievous to hear, if words can grieve; but for us, who beheld, the greatest of sorrows that these eyes have seen.

LEADER: Alas, alas! Now, methinks, the stock of our ancient masters hath utterly perished, root and branch.

CLYTEMNESTRA: O Zeus, what shall I call these tidings, — glad tidings? Or dire, but gainful? 'Tis a bitter lot, when mine own calamities make the safety of my life.

PAEDAGOGUS: Why art thou so downcast, lady, at this news?

CLYTEMNESTRA: There is a strange power in motherhood; a mother may be wronged, but she never learns to hate her child.

PAEDAGOGUS: Then it seems that we have come in vain.

CLYTEMNESTRA: Nay, not in vain; how canst thou say 'in vain,' when thou hast brought me sure proofs of his death? — His, who sprang from mine own life, yet, forsaking me who had suckled and reared him, became an exile and an alien; and, after he went out of this land, he saw me no more; but, charging me with the murder of his sire, he uttered dread threats against me; so that neither by night nor by day could sweet sleep cover mine eyes, but from moment to moment I lived in fear of death. Now, however — since this day I am rid of terror from him, and from this girl, — that worse plague who shared my home, while still she drained my very life-blood, — now, methinks, for aught that she can threaten, I shall pass my days in peace.

ELECTRA: Ah, woe is me! Now, indeed, Orestes, thy fortune may be lamented, when it is thus with thee, and thou art mocked by this thy mother! Is it not well?

CLYTEMNESTRA: Not with thee; but his state is well.

ELECTRA: Hear, Nemesis of him who hath lately died!

CLYTEMNESTRA: She hath heard who should be heard, and hath ordained well.

ELECTRA: Insult us, for this is the time of thy triumph.

CLYTEMNESTRA: Then will not Orestes and thou silence me?

ELECTRA: We are silenced; much less should we silence thee.

CLYTEMNESTRA: Thy coming, sir, would deserve larger recompense, if thou hast hushed her clamorous tongue.

PAEDAGOGUS: Then I may take my leave, if all is well.

CLYTEMNESTRA: Not so; thy welcome would then be unworthy of me,

131

and of the ally who sent thee. Nay, come thou in; and leave her without, to make loud lament for herself and for her friends.

(Clytemnestra *and the* Paedagogus *enter the palace.*)

ELECTRA: How think ye? Was there not grief and anguish there, wondrous weeping and wailing of that miserable mother, for the son who perished by such a fate? Nay, she left us with a laugh! Ah, woe is me! Dearest Orestes, how is my life quenched by thy death? Thou hast torn away with thee from my heart the only hopes which still were mine, — that thou wouldst live to return some day, an avenger of thy sire, and of me unhappy. But now — whither shall I turn? I am alone, bereft of thee, as of my father.

Henceforth I must be a slave again among those whom most I hate, my father's murderers. Is it not well with me? But never, at least, henceforward, will I enter the house to dwell with them: nay, at these gates I will lay me down, and here, without a friend, my days shall wither. Therefore, if any in the house be wroth, let them slay me; for 'tis a grace, if I die, but if I live, a pain; I desire life no more.

(The following lines between Electra *and the* Chorus *are chanted responsively.)*

CHORUS: Where are the thunderbolts of Zeus, or where is the bright Sun, if they look upon these things, and brand them not, but rest?
ELECTRA: Woe, woe, ah me, ah me!
CHORUS: O daughter, why weepest thou?
ELECTRA *(with hands outstretched to heaven)*: Alas!
CHORUS: Utter no rash cry!
ELECTRA: Thou wilt break my heart!
CHORUS: How meanest thou?
ELECTRA: If thou suggest a hope concerning those who have surely passed to the realm below, thou wilt trample yet more upon my misery.
CHORUS: Nay, I know how, ensnared by a woman for a chain of gold, the prince Amphiaraus found a grave; and now beneath the earth —
ELECTRA: Ah me, ah me!
CHORUS: — he reigns in fulness of force.
ELECTRA: Alas!
CHORUS: Alas indeed! for the murderess —

132

ELECTRA: Was slain.

CHORUS: Yea.

ELECTRA: I know it, I know it; for a champion arose to avenge the mourning dead; but to me no champion remains; for he who yet was left hath been snatched away.

CHORUS: Hapless art thou, and hapless is thy lot!

ELECTRA: Well know I that, too well, — I, whose life is a torrent of woes dread and dark, a torrent that surges through all the months!

CHORUS: We have seen the course of thy sorrow.

ELECTRA: Cease, then, to divert me from it, when no more —

CHORUS: How sayest thou?

ELECTRA: — when no more can I have the comfort of hope from a brother, the seed of the same noble sire.

CHORUS: For all men it is appointed to die.

ELECTRA: What, to die as that ill-starred one died, amid the tramp of racing steeds, entangled in the reins that dragged him?

CHORUS: Cruel was his doom, beyond thought!

ELECTRA: Yea, surely; when in foreign soil, without ministry of my hands —

CHORUS: Alas!

ELECTRA: — he is buried, ungraced by me with sepulture or with tears.

(Chrysothemis *enters in excitement.*)

CHRYSOTHEMIS: Joy wings my feet, dear sister, not careful of seemliness, if I come with speed; for I bring joyful news, to relieve thy long sufferings and sorrows.

ELECTRA: And whence couldst thou find help for my woes, whereof no cure can be imagined?

CHRYSOTHEMIS: Orestes is with us, — know this from my lips, — in living presence, as surely as thou seest me here.

ELECTRA: What, art thou mad, poor girl? Art thou laughing at my sorrows, and thine own?

CHRYSOTHEMIS: Nay, by our father's hearth, I speak not in mockery; I tell thee that he is with us indeed.

ELECTRA: Ah, woe is me! And from whom has thou heard this tale, which thou believest so lightly?

CHRYSOTHEMIS: I believe it on mine own knowledge, not on hearsay; I have seen clear proofs.

ELECTRA: What hast thou seen, poor girl, to warrant thy belief? Whither, I wonder hast thou turned thine eyes, that thou art fevered with this baneful fire?

CHRYSOTHEMIS: Then, for the gods' love, listen, that thou mayest know my story, before deciding whether I am sane or foolish.

133

ELECTRA: Speak on, then, if thou findest pleasure in speaking.

CHRYSOTHEMIS: Well, thou shalt hear all that I have seen. When I came to our father's ancient tomb, I saw that streams of milk had lately flowed from the top of the mound, and that his sepulchre was encircled with garlands of all flowers that blow. I was astonished at the sight, and peered about, lest haply some one should be close to my side. But when I perceived that all the place was in stillness, I crept nearer to the tomb; and on the mound's edge I saw a lock of hair, freshly severed.

And the moment that I saw it, ah me, a familiar image rushed upon my soul, telling me that there I beheld a token of him whom most I love, Orestes. Then I took it in my hands, and uttered no ill-omened word, but the tears of joy straightway filled mine eyes. And I know well, as I knew then, that this fair tribute has come from none but him. Whose part else was that, save mine and thine? And I did it not, I know, — nor thou; how shouldst thou? — when thou canst not leave this house, even to worship the gods, but at thy peril. Nor, again, does our mother's heart incline to do such deeds, nor could she have so done without our knowledge.

No, these offerings are from Orestes! Come, dear sister, courage! No mortal life is attended by a changeless fortune. Ours was once gloomy; but this day, perchance, will seal the promise of much good.

ELECTRA: Alas for this folly! How I have been pitying thee!

CHRYSOTHEMIS: What, are not my tidings welcome?

ELECTRA: Thou knowest not whither or into what dreams thou wanderest.

CHRYSOTHEMIS: Should I not know what mine own eyes have seen?

ELECTRA: He is dead, poor girl; and thy hopes in that deliverer are gone; look not to him.

CHRYSOTHEMIS: Woe, woe is me! From whom hast thou heard this?

ELECTRA: From the man who was present when he perished.

CHRYSOTHEMIS: And where is he? Wonder steals over my mind.

ELECTRA: He is within, a guest not unpleasing to our mother.

CHRYSOTHEMIS: Ah, woe is me! Whose, then, can have been those ample offerings to our father's tomb?

ELECTRA: Most likely, I think, some one brought those gifts in memory of the dead Orestes.

CHRYSOTHEMIS: O, hapless that I am! And I was bringing such news in joyous haste, ignorant, it seems, how dire was our plight; but now that I have come, I find fresh sorrows added to the old!

ELECTRA: So stands thy case; yet, if thou wilt hearken to me, thou wilt lighten the load of our present trouble.

CHRYSOTHEMIS: Can I ever raise the dead to life?

ELECTRA: I meant not that; I am not so foolish.

CHRYSOTHEMIS: What biddest thou, then, for which my strength avails?

ELECTRA: That thou be brave in doing what I enjoin.

CHRYSOTHEMIS: Nay, if any good can be done, I will not refuse.

ELECTRA: Remember, nothing succeeds without toil.

CHRYSOTHEMIS: I know it, and will share thy burden with all my power.

ELECTRA: Hear, then, how I am resolved to act. As for the support of friends, thou thyself must know that we have none; Hades hath taken our friends away, and we two are left alone. I, so long as I heard that my brother still lived and prospered, had hopes that he would yet come to avenge the murder of our sire. But now that he is no more, I look next to thee, not to flinch from aiding me thy sister to slay our father's murderer, Aegisthus: — I must have no secret from thee more.

How long art thou to wait inactive? What hope is left standing, to which thine eyes can turn? Thou hast to complain that thou art robbed of thy father's heritage; thou hast to mourn that thus far thy life is fading without nuptial song or wedded love. Nay, and do not hope that such joys will ever be thine; Aegisthus is not so ill-advised as ever to permit that children should spring from thee or me for his own sure destruction. But if thou wilt follow my counsels, first thou wilt win praise of piety from our dead sire below, and from our brother too; next, thou shalt be called free henceforth, as thou wert born, and shalt find worthy bridals; for noble natures draw the gaze of all.

Then seest thou not what fair fame thou wilt win for thyself and for me, by hearkening to my word? What citizen or stranger, when he sees us, will not greet us with praises such as these? — 'Behold these two sisters, my friends, who saved their father's house; who, when their foes were firmly planted of yore, took their lives in their hands and stood forth as avengers of blood! Worthy of love are these twain, worthy of reverence from all; at festivals, and wherever the folk are assembled, let these be honoured of all men for their prowess.' Thus will every one speak of us, so that in life and in death our glory shall not fail.

Come, dear sister, hearken! Work with thy sire, share the burden of thy brother, win rest from woes for me and for thyself, — mindful of this, that an ignoble life brings shame upon the noble.

LEADER OF THE CHORUS: In such case as this, forethought is helpful for those who speak and those who hear.

CHRYSOTHEMIS: Yes, and before she spake, my friends, were she blest with a sound mind, she would have remembered caution, as she doth not remember it.

Now whither canst thou have turned thine eyes, that thou art arming thyself with such rashness, and calling me to aid thee? Seest thou not, thou art a woman, not a man, and no match for thine adversaries in strength? And their fortune prospers day by day, while ours is ebbing and coming to nought. Who, then, plotting to vanquish foe so strong, shall escape without suffering deadly scathe? See that we change not our evil plight to worse, if any one hears these words. It brings us no relief of benefit, if, after winning fair fame, we die an ignominious death; for mere death is not the bitterest, but rather when one who wants to die cannot obtain even that boon.

Nay, I beseech thee, before we are utterly destroyed, and leave our house desolate, restrain thy rage! I will take care that thy words remain secret and harmless; and learn thou the prudence, at last though late, of yielding, when so helpless, to thy rulers.

LEADER: Hearken; there is no better gain for mortals to win than foresight and a prudent mind.

ELECTRA: Thou hast said nothing unlooked-for; I well knew that thou wouldst reject what I proffered. Well! I must do this deed with mine own hand, and alone; for assuredly I will not leave it void.

CHRYSOTHEMIS: Alas! Would thou hadst been so purposed on the day of our father's death! What mightst thou not have wrought?

ELECTRA: My nature was the same then, but my mind less ripe.

CHRYSOTHEMIS: Strive to keep such a mind through all thy life.

ELECTRA: These counsels mean that thou wilt not share my deed.

CHRYSOTHEMIS: No; for the venture is likely to bring disaster.

ELECTRA: I admire thy prudence; thy cowardice I hate.

CHRYSOTHEMIS: I will listen not less calmly when thou praise me.

ELECTRA: Never fear to suffer that from me.

CHRYSOTHEMIS: Time enough in the future to decide that.

ELECTRA: Begone; there is no power to help in thee.

CHRYSOTHEMIS: Not so; but in thee, no mind to learn.

ELECTRA: Go, declare all this to thy mother!

CHRYSOTHEMIS: But, again, I do not hate thee with such a hate.

ELECTRA: Yet know at least to what dishonour thou bringest me.

CHRYSOTHEMIS: Dishonour, no! I am only thinking of thy good.

ELECTRA: Am I bound, then, to follow thy rule of right?

CHRYSOTHEMIS: When thou art wise, then thou shalt be our guide.

ELECTRA: Sad, that one who speaks so well should speak amiss!

CHRYSOTHEMIS: Thou hast well described the fault to which thou cleavest.

ELECTRA: How? Dost thou not think that I speak with justice?

CHRYSOTHEMIS: But sometimes justice itself is fraught with harm.

ELECTRA: I care not to live by such a law.

CHRYSOTHEMIS: Well, if thou must do this, thou wilt praise me yet.

ELECTRA: And do it I will, no whit dismayed by thee.

CHRYSOTHEMIS: Is this so indeed? Wilt thou not change thy counsels?

ELECTRA: No, for nothing is more hateful than bad counsel.

CHRYSOTHEMIS: Thou seemest to agree with nothing that I urge.

ELECTRA: My resolve is not new, but long since fixed.

CHRYSOTHEMIS: Then I will go; thou canst not be brought to approve my words, nor I to commend thy conduct.

ELECTRA: Nay, go within; never will I follow thee, however much thou mayst desire it; it were great folly even to attempt an idle quest.

CHRYSOTHEMIS: Nay, if thou art wise in thine own eyes, be such wisdom thine; by and by, when thou standest in evil plight, thou wilt praise my words.

(Chrysothemis *goes into the palace.*)

CHORUS *(singing):* When we see the birds of the air, with sure instinct, careful to nourish those who give them life and nurture, why do not we pay these debts in like measure? Nay, by the lightning-flash of Zeus, by Themis throned in heaven, it is not long till sin brings sorrow.

Voice that comest to the dead beneath the earth, send piteous cry, I pray thee, to the son of Atreus in that world, a joyless message of dishonour; tell him that the fortunes of his house are now distempered; while, among his children, strife of sister with sister hath broken the harmony of loving days. Electra, forsaken, braves the storm alone; she bewails alway, hapless one, her father's fate, like the nightingale unwearied in lament; she recks not of death, but is ready to leave the sunlight, could she but quell the two Furies of her house. Who shall match such noble child of noble sire?

No generous soul designs, by a base life, to cloud a fair repute, and leave a name inglorious; as thou, too, O my daughter, hast chosen to mourn all thy days with those that mourn, and hast spurned dishonour, that thou mightest win at once a twofold praise, as wise, and as the best of daughters.

May I yet see thy life raised in might and wealth above thy foes, even as now it is humbled beneath their hand! For I have found thee in no prosperous estate; and yet, for observance of

137

nature's highest laws, winning the noblest renown, by thy piety towards Zeus.

(Orestes *enters, with* Pylades *and two attendants, one of them carrying a funeral urn.*)

ORESTES: Ladies, have we been directed aright, and are we on the right path to our goal?

LEADER OF THE CHORUS: And what seekest thou? With what desire hast thou come?

ORESTES: I have been searching for the home of Aegisthus.

LEADER: Well, thou hast found it; and thy guide is blameless.

ORESTES: Which of you, then, will tell those within that our company, long desired, hath arrived?

LEADER: This maiden,—if the nearest should announce it.

ORESTES: I pray thee, mistress, make it known in the house that certain men of Phocis seek Aegisthus.

ELECTRA: Ah, woe is me! Surely ye are not bringing the visible proofs of that rumour which we heard?

ORESTES: I know nothing of thy 'rumour'; but the aged Strophius charged me with tidings of Orestes.

ELECTRA: What are they, sir? Ah, how I thrill with fear!

ORESTES: He is dead; and in a small urn, as thou seest, we bring the scanty relics home.

ELECTRA: Ah me unhappy! There, at last, before mine eyes, I see that woful burden in your hands!

ORESTES: If thy tears are for aught which Orestes hath suffered, know that yonder vessel holds his dust.

ELECTRA: Ah, sir, allow me, then, I implore thee, if this urn indeed contains him, to take it in my hands,—that I may weep and wail, not for these ashes alone, but for myself and for all our house therewith!

ORESTES (*to the attendants*): Bring it and give it her, whoe'er she be; for she who begs this boon must be one who wished him no evil, but a friend, or haply a kinswoman in blood.

(*The urn is placed in* Electra's *hands.*)

ELECTRA: Ah, memorial of him whom I loved best on earth! Ah, Orestes, whose life hath no relic left save this,—how far from the hopes with which I sent thee forth is the manner in which I receive thee back! Now I carry thy poor dust in my hands; but thou wert radiant, my child, when I sped thee forth from home! Would that I had yielded up my breath, ere, with these hands, I stole thee away, and sent thee to a strange land, and rescued thee from death; that so thou mightest have been stricken down on that self-same day, and had thy portion in the tomb of thy sire!

But now, an exile from home and fatherland, thou hast perished miserably, far from thy sister; woe is me, these loving hands have not washed or decked thy corpse, not taken up, as was meet, their sad burden from the flaming pyre. No! at the hands of strangers, hapless one, thou hast had those rites, and so art come to us, a little dust in a narrow urn.

Ah, woe is me for my nursing long ago, so vain, that I oft bestowed on thee with loving toil! For thou wast never thy mother's darling so much as mine; nor was any in the house thy nurse but I; and by thee I was ever called 'sister.' But now all this hath vanished in a day, with thy death; like a whirlwind, thou hast swept all away with thee. Our father is gone; I am dead in regard to thee; thou thyself hast perished: our foes exult; that mother, who is none, is mad with joy, — she of whom thou didst oft send me secret messages, thy heralds, saying that thou thyself wouldst appear as an avenger. But our evil fortune, thine and mine, hath reft all that away, and hath sent thee forth unto me thus, — no more the form that I loved so well, but ashes and an idle shade.

Ah me, ah me! O piteous dust! Alas, thou dear one, sent on a dire journey, how hast undone me, —undone me indeed, O brother mine!

Therefore take me to this thy home, me who am as nothing, to thy nothingness, that I may dwell with thee henceforth below; for when thou wert on earth, we shared alike; and now I fain would die, that I may not be parted from thee in the grave. For I see that the dead have rest from pain.

LEADER: Bethink thee, Electra, thou art the child of mortal sire, and mortal was Orestes; therefore grieve not too much. This is a debt which all of us must pay.

ORESTES: Alas, what shall I say? What words can serve me at this pass? I can restrain my lips no longer!

ELECTRA: What hath troubled thee? Why didst thou say that?

ORESTES: Is this the form of the illustrious Electra that I behold?

ELECTRA: It is; and very grievous is her plight.

ORESTES: Alas, then, for this miserable fortune!

ELECTRA: Surely, sir, thy lament is not for me?

ORESTES: O form cruelly, godlessly misused!

ELECTRA: Those ill-omened words, sir, fit no one better than me.

ORESTES: Alas for thy life, unwedded and all unblest!

ELECTRA: Why this steadfast gaze, stranger, and these laments?
ORESTES: How ignorant was I, then, of mine own sorrows!
ELECTRA: By what that hath been said hast thou perceived this?
ORESTES: By seeing thy sufferings, so many and so great.
ELECTRA: And yet thou seest but a few of my woes.
ORESTES: Could any be more painful to behold?
ELECTRA: This, that I share the dwelling of the murderers.
ORESTES: Whose murderers? Where lies the guilt at which thou hintest?
ELECTRA: My father's; — and then I am their slave perforce.
ORESTES: Who is it that subjects thee to this constraint?
ELECTRA: A mother, — in name, but no mother in her deeds.
ORESTES: How doth she oppress thee? With violence or with hardship?
ELECTRA: With violence, and hardships, and all manner of ill.
ORESTES: And is there none to succour, or to hinder?
ELECTRA: None. I had one; and thou hast shown me his ashes.
ORESTES: Hapless girl, how this sight hath stirred my pity!
ELECTRA: Know, then, that thou art the first who ever pitied me.
ORESTES: No other visitor hath ever shared thy pain.
ELECTRA: Surely thou art not some unknown kinsman?
ORESTES: I would answer, if these were friends who hear us.
ELECTRA: Oh, they are friends; thou canst speak without mistrust.
ORESTES: Give up this urn, then, and thou shalt be told all.
ELECTRA: Nay, I beseech thee be not so cruel to me, sir!
ORESTES: Do as I say, and never fear to do amiss.
ELECTRA: I conjure thee, rob me not of my chief treasure!
ORESTES: Thou must not keep it.
ELECTRA: Ah woe is me for thee, Orestes, if I am not to give thee burial!
ORESTES: Hush! — no such word! — Thou hast no right to lament.
ELECTRA: No right to lament for my dead brother?
ORESTES: It is not meet for thee to speak of him thus.
ELECTRA: Am I so dishonoured of the dead?
ORESTES: Dishonoured of none: — but this is not thy part.
ELECTRA: Yes, if these are the ashes of Orestes that I hold.
ORESTES: They are not; a fiction clothed them with his name.

(He gently takes the urn from her.)

ELECTRA: And where is that unhappy one's tomb?
ORESTES: There is none; the living have no tomb.
ELECTRA: What sayest thou, boy?
ORESTES: Nothing that is not true.
ELECTRA: The man is alive?
ORESTES: If there be life in me.
ELECTRA: What? Art thou he?

140

ORESTES: Look at this signet, once our father's, and judge if I speak truth.

ELECTRA: O blissful day!

ORESTES: Blissful, in very deed!

ELECTRA: Is this thy voice?

ORESTES: Let no other voice reply.

ELECTRA: Do I hold thee in my arms?

ORESTES: As mayest thou hold me always!

ELECTRA: Ah, dear friends and fellow-citizens, behold Orestes here, who was feigned dead, by that feigning hath come safely home!

LEADER: We see him, daughter; and for this happy fortune a tear of joy trickles from our eyes.

(The following lines between Orestes *and* Electra *are chanted responsively.)*

ELECTRA: Offspring of him whom I loved best, thou hast come even now, thou hast come, and found and seen her whom thy heart desired.

ORESTES: I am with thee; — but keep silence for a while.

ELECTRA: What meanest thou?

ORESTES: 'Tis better to be silent, lest someone within should hear.

ELECTRA: Nay, by ever-virgin Artemis, I will never stoop to fear women, stay-at-homes, vain burdens of the ground!

ORESTES: Yet remember that in women, too, dwells the spirit of battle; thou hast had good proof of that, I ween.

ELECTRA: Alas! Ah me! Thou hast reminded me of my sorrow, one which, from its nature, cannot be veiled, cannot be done away with, cannot forget!

ORESTES: I know this also; but when occasion prompts, then will be the moment to recall those deeds.

ELECTRA: Each moment of all time, as it comes, would be meet occasion for these my just complaints; scarcely now have I had my lips set free.

ORESTES: I grant it; therefore guard thy freedom.

ELECTRA: What must I do?

ORESTES: When the season serves not, do not wish to speak too much.

ELECTRA: Nay, who could fitly exchange speech for such silence, when thou hast appeared? For now I have seen thy face, beyond all thought and hope!

ORESTES: Thou sawest it, when the gods moved me to come . . .

ELECTRA: Thou hast told me of a grace above the first, if a god hath indeed brought thee to our house; I acknowledge therein the work of heaven.

ORESTES: I am loth, indeed, to curb thy gladness, but yet this excess of joy moves my fear.

ELECTRA: O thou who, after many a year, hast deigned thus to gladden mine eyes by thy return, do not, now that thou hast seen me in all my woe ——

ORESTES: What is thy prayer?

ELECTRA: —— do not rob me of the comfort of thy face; do not force me to forego it!

ORESTES: I should be wroth, indeed, if I saw another attempt it.

ELECTRA: My prayer is granted?

ORESTES: Canst thou doubt?

ELECTRA: Ah, friends, I heard a voice I could never have hoped to hear; nor could I have restrained my emotion in silence, and without a cry, when I heard it.

Ah me! But now I have thee; thou art come to me with the light of that dear countenance, which never, even in sorrow, could I forget.

(The chant is concluded.)

ORESTES: Spare all superfluous words; tell me not of our mother's wickedness, or how Aegisthus drains the wealth of our father's house by lavish luxury or aimless waste; for the story would not suffer thee to keep due limit. Tell me rather that which will serve our present need, — where we must show ourselves, or wait in ambush, that this our coming may confound the triumph of our foes.

And look that our mother read not thy secret in thy radiant face, when we twain have advanced into the house, but make lament, as for the feigned disaster; for when we have prospered, then there will be leisure to rejoice and exult in freedom.

ELECTRA: Nay, brother, as it pleases thee, so shall be my conduct also; for all my joy is a gift from thee, and not mine own. Nor would I consent to win a great good for myself at the cost of the least pain to thee; for so should I ill serve the divine power that befriends us now.

But thou knowest how matters stand here, I doubt not: thou must have heard that Aegisthus is from home, but our mother within; — and fear not that she will ever see my face lit up with smiles; for mine old hatred of her hath sunk into my heart; and, since I have beheld thee, for very joy I shall never cease to weep. How indeed should I cease, who have seen thee come home this day, first as dead, and then in life?

142

Strangely hast thou wrought on me; so that, if my father should return alive, I should no longer doubt my senses, but should believe that I saw him. Now, therefore, that thou hast come to me so wondrously, command me as thou wilt; for, had I been alone, I should have achieved one of two things, — a noble deliverance, or a noble death.

ORESTES: Thou hadst best be silent; for I hear some one within preparing to go forth.

ELECTRA (*to* Orestes *and* Pylades): Enter, sirs; especially as ye bring that which no one could repulse from these doors, though he receive it without joy.

(The Paedagogus *enters from the palace.)*

PAEDAGOGUS: Foolish and senseless children! Are ye weary of your lives, or was there no wit born in you, that ye see not how ye stand, not on the brink, but in the very midst of deadly perils? Nay, had I not kept watch this long while at these doors, your plans would have been in the house before yourselves; but, as it is, my care shielded you from that. Now have done with this long discourse, these insatiate cries of joy, and pass within; for in such deeds delay is evil, and 'tis well to make an end.

ORESTES: What, then, will be my prospects when I enter?

PAEDAGOGUS: Good; for thou art secured from recognition.

ORESTES: Thou hast reported me, I presume, as dead?

PAEDAGOGUS: Know that here thou art numbered with the shades.

ORESTES: Do they rejoice, then, at these tidings? Or what say they?

PAEDAGOGUS: I will tell thee at the end; meanwhile, all is well for us on their part, — even that which is not well.

ELECTRA: Who is this brother? I pray thee, tell me.

ORESTES: Dost thou not perceive?

ELECTRA: I cannot guess.

ORESTES: Knowest thou not the man to whose hands thou gavest me once?

ELECTRA: What man? How sayest thou?

ORESTES: By whose hands, through thy forethought, I was secretly conveyed forth to Phocian soil.

ELECTRA: Is this he in whom, alone of many, I found a true ally of old, when our sire was slain?

ORESTES: 'Tis he; question me no further.

ELECTRA: O joyous day! O sole preserver of Agamemnon's house, how hast thou come? Art thou he indeed, who didst save my brother and myself from many sorrows? O dearest hands; O

143

messenger whose feet were kindly servants! How couldst thou be with me so long, and remain unknown, nor give a ray of light, but afflict me by fables, while possessed of truths most sweet? Hail, father, — for 'tis a father that I seem to behold! All hail, — and know that I have hated thee, and loved thee, in one day, as never man before!

PAEDAGOGUS: Enough, methinks; as for the story of the past, many are the circling nights, and days as many, which shall show it thee, Electra, in its fulness. (*To* Orestes *and* Pylades.) But this is my counsel to you twain, who stand there — now is the time to act; now Clytemnestra is alone, — no man is now within; but, if ye pause, consider that ye will have to fight, not with the inmates alone, but with other foes more numerous and better skilled.

ORESTES: Pylades, this our task seems no longer to crave many words, but rather that we should enter the house forthwith, — first adoring the shrines of my father's gods, who keep these gates.

(Orestes *and* Pylades *enter the palace, followed by the* Paedagogus. — Electra *remains outside*.)

ELECTRA: O King Apollo! graciously hear them, and hear me besides, who so oft have come before thine altar with such gifts as my devout hand could bring! And now, O Lycean Apollo, with such vows as I can make, I pray thee. I supplicate, I implore, grant us thy benignant aid in these designs, and show me how impiety is rewarded by the gods!

(Electra *enters the palace*.)

CHORUS (*singing*): Behold how Ares moves onward, breathing deadly vengeance, against which none may strive!

Even now the pursuers of dark guilt have passed beneath your roof, the hounds which none may flee. Therefore the vision of my soul shall not long tarry in suspense.

The champion of the spirits infernal is ushered with stealthy feet into the house, the ancestral palace of his sire, bearing keen-edged death in his hands; and Hermes, son of Maia, who hath shrouded the guile in darkness, leads him forward, even to the end, and delays no more.

(Electra *enters from the palace*.)

ELECTRA: Ah, dearest friends, in a moment the men will do the deed; — but wait in silence.

CHORUS: How is it? — what do they now?

ELECTRA: She is decking the urn for burial, and those two stand close to her.

CHORUS: And why hast thou sped forth?

ELECTRA: To guard against Aegisthus entering before we are aware.

CLYTEMNESTRA (within): Alas! Woe for the house forsaken of friends and filled with murderers!

ELECTRA: A cry goes up within: — hear ye not, friends?

CHORUS: I heard, ah me, sounds dire to hear, and shuddered!

CLYTEMNESTRA (within): O hapless that I am! — Aegisthus, where, where art thou?

ELECTRA: Hark, once more a voice resounds!

CLYTEMNESTRA (within): My son, my son, have pity on thy mother!

ELECTRA: Thou hadst none for him, nor for the father that begat him.

CHORUS: Ill-fated realm and race, now the fate that hath pursued thee day by day is dying, — is dying!

CLYTEMNESTRA (within): Oh, I am smitten!

ELECTRA: Smite, if thou canst, once more!

CLYTEMNESTRA (within): Ah, woe is me again!

ELECTRA: Would that the woe were for Aegisthus too!

CHORUS: The curses are at work; the buried live; blood flows for blood, drained from the slayers by those who died of yore.

(Orestes *and* Pylades *enter from the palace.*)

Behold, they come! That red hand reeks with sacrifice to Ares; nor can I blame the deed.

ELECTRA: Orestes, how fare ye?

ORESTES: All is well within the house, if Apollo's oracle spake well.

ELECTRA: The guilty one is dead?

ORESTES: Fear no more that thy proud mother will ever put thee to dishonour.

CHORUS: Cease; for I see Aegisthus full in view.

ELECTRA: Rash boys, back, back!

ORESTES: Where see ye the man?

ELECTRA: Yonder, at our mercy, he advances from the suburb, full of joy.

CHORUS: Make with all speed for the vestibule; that, as your first task prospered, so this again may prosper now.

ORESTES: Fear not, — we will perform it.

ELECTRA: Haste, then, whither thou wouldst.

ORESTES: See, I am gone.

ELECTRA: I will look to matters here.

(Orestes and Pylades *go back into the palace.)*

CHORUS: 'Twere well to soothe his ear with some few words of seeming gentleness, that he may rush blindly upon the struggle with his doom.

(Aegisthus enters.)

AEGISTHUS: Which of you can tell me, where are those Phocian strangers, who, 'tis said, have brought us tidings of Orestes slain in the wreck of his chariot? Thee, thee I ask, yes, thee, in former days so bold, — for methinks it touches thee most nearly; thou best must know, and best canst tell.

ELECTRA: I know assuredly; else were I a stranger to the fortune of my nearest kinsfolk.

AEGISTHUS: Where then may be the strangers? Tell me.

ELECTRA: Within; they have found a way to the heart of their hostess.

AEGISTHUS: Have they in truth reported him dead?

ELECTRA: Nay, not reported only; they have shown him.

AEGISTHUS: Can I, then, see the corpse with mine own eyes?

ELECTRA: Thou canst, indeed; and 'tis no enviable sight.

AEGISTHUS: Indeed, thou hast given me a joyful meeting, beyond thy wont.

ELECTRA: Joy be thine, if in these things thou findest joy.

AEGISTHUS: Silence, I say, and throw wide the gates, for all Mycenaeans and Argives to behold; that, if any of them were once buoyed on empty hopes from this man, now seeing him dead, they may receive my curb, instead of waiting till my chastisement make them wise perforce!

ELECTRA: No loyalty is lacking on my part; time hath taught me the prudence of concord with the stronger.

(The central doors of the palace are thrown open and a shrouded corpse is disclosed. Orestes *and* Pylades *stand near it.)*

AEGISTHUS: O Zeus, I behold that which hath not fallen save by the doom of jealous Heaven; but, if Nemesis attend that word, be it unsaid!

Take all the covering from the face, that kinship, at least, may receive the tribute of lament from me also.

ORESTES: Lift the veil thyself; not my part this, but thine, to look upon these relics, and to greet them kindly.

AEGISTHUS: 'Tis good counsel, and I will follow it. — *(To* Electra*)* But thou — call me Clytemnestra, if she is within.

ORESTES: Lo, she is near thee: turn not thine eyes elsewhere.

(Aegisthus *removes the face-cloth from the corpse*.)

AEGISTHUS: O, what sight is this!

ORESTES: Why so scared? Is the face so strange?

AEGISTHUS: Who are the men into whose mid toils I have fallen, hapless that I am?

ORESTES: Nay, hast thou not discovered ere now that the dead, as thou miscallest them, are living?

AEGISTHUS: Alas, I read the riddle: this can be none but Orestes who speaks to me!

ORESTES: And, though so good a prophet, thou wast deceived so long?

AEGISTHUS: Oh lost, undone! yet suffer me to say one word . . .

ELECTRA: In heaven's name, my brother, suffer him not to speak further, or to plead at length! When mortals are in the meshes of fate, how can such respite avail one who is to die? No, — slay him forthwith, and cast his corpse to the creatures from whom such as he should have burial, far from our sight! To me, nothing but this can make amends for the woes of the past.

ORESTES *(to* Aegisthus*)*: Go in, and quickly; the issue here is not of words, but of thy life.

AEGISTHUS: Why take me into the house? If this deed be fair, what need of darkness? Why is thy hand not prompt to strike?

ORESTES: Dictate not, but go where thou didst slay my father, that in the same place thou mayest die.

AEGISTHUS: Is this dwelling doomed to see all woes of Pelops' line, now, and in time to come?

ORESTES: Thine, at least; trust my prophetic skill so far.

AEGISTHUS: The skill thou vauntest belonged not to thy sire.

ORESTES: Thou bandiest words, and our going is delayed. Move forward!

AEGISTHUS: Lead thou.

ORESTES: Thou must go first.

AEGISTHUS: Lest I escape thee?

ORESTES: No, but that thou mayest not choose how to die; I must not spare thee any bitterness of death. And well it were if this judgment came straightway upon all who dealt in lawless deeds, even the judgment of the sword; so should not wickedness abound.

(Orestes *and* Pylades *drive* Aegisthus *into the palace*.)

CHORUS *(singing)*: O house of Atreus, through how many sufferings hast thou come forth at last in freedom, crowned with good by this day's enterprise!

R. C. Jebb

EURIPIDES

EURIPIDES (c. 485-c. 400 B. C.) was one of the trio of great dramatists that includes Aeschylus and Sophocles. Nineteen of his plays are extant, out of the ninety-two that he composed. His themes are human relationships and their moral impacts and implications. In particular, Euripides is interested in portraying the emotional and psychological reactions of women, and in rationalizing legend and the omnipotence of the gods.

IPHIGENIA IN TAURIS

In this drama, which was produced between 413 and 408 B. C. Agamemnon has brought his daughter Iphigenia to Aulis as a sacrifice to Artemis or Diana. But with the aid of the goddess Iphigenia is taken to Tauris, where she serves as a priestess. A religious rite requires that visiting strangers be slain sacrificially. Iphigenia's brother Orestes and his friend Pylades arrive on the scene, potential victims. But in an episode of dramatic tension Iphigenia and the two friends make their escape

CHARACTERS IN THE PLAY

IPHIGENIA, daughter of Agamemnon
ORESTES, brother of Iphigenia
PYLADES, friend of Orestes
THOAS, King of the Taurians
HERDSMAN
MESSENGER
MINERVA
CHORUS of Greek Women, captives, attendants on Iphigenia in the temple

(SCENE: — Before the great temple of Diana of the Taurians. A blood-stained altar is prominently in view. Iphigenia, clad as a priestess, enters from the temple.)

IPHIGENIA: To Pisa, by the fleetest coursers borne,
Comes Pelops, son of Tantalus, and weds

148

The virgin daughter of Oenomaus:
From her sprung Atreus; Menelaus from him,
And Agamemnon; I from him derive
My birth, his Iphigenia, by his queen,
Daughter of Tyndarus. Where frequent winds
Swell the vex'd Euripus with eddying blasts,
And roll the darkening waves, my father slew me,
A victim to Diana, so he thought,
For Helen's sake, its bay where Aulis winds,
To fame well known, for there his thousand ships,
The armament of Greece, the imperial chief
Convened, desirous that his Greeks should snatch
The glorious crown of victory from Troy,
And punish the base insult to the bed
Of Helen, vengeance grateful to the soul
Of Menelaus. But 'gainst his ships at sea
Long barr'd, and not one favouring breeze to swell
His flagging sails, the hallow'd flames the chief
Consults, and Calchas thus disclosed the fates: —
"Imperial leader of the Grecian host,
Hence shalt thou not unmoor thy vessels, ere
Diana as a victim shall receive
Thy daughter Iphigenia: what the year
Most beauteous should produce, thou to the queen
Dispensing light didst vow to sacrifice:
A daughter Clytemnestra in thy house
Then bore (the peerless grace of beauty thus
To me assigning); her must thou devote
The victim." Then Ulysses by his arts,
Me, to Achilles as design'd a bride,
Won from my mother. My unhappy fate
To Aulis brought me; on the altar there
High was I placed, and o'er me gleam'd the sword,
Aiming the fatal wound: but from the stroke
Diana snatch'd me, in exchange a hind
Giving the Grecians; through the lucid air
Me she conveyed to Tauris, here to dwell,
Where o'er barbarians a barbaric king
Holds his rude sway, named Thoas, whose swift foot
Equals the rapid wing: me he appoints
The priestess of this temple, where such rites
Are pleasing to Diana, that the name
Alone claims honour; for I sacrifice

(Such, ere I came, the custom of the state)
Whatever Grecian to this savage shore
Is driven: the previous rites are mine; the deed
Of blood, too horrid to be told, devolves
On others in the temple: but the rest,
In reverence to the goddess, I forbear.
But the strange visions which the night now past
Brought with it, to the air, if that may soothe
My troubled thought, I will relate. I seem'd,
As I lay sleeping, from this land removed,
To dwell at Argos, resting on my couch
Mid the apartments of the virgin train.
Sudden the firm earth shook: I fled, and stood
Without; the battlements I saw, and all
The rocking roof fall from its lofty height
In ruins to the ground: of all the house,
My father's house, one pillar, as I thought,
Alone was left, which from its cornice waved
A length of auburn locks, and human voice
Assumed: the bloody office, which is mine
To strangers here, respecting, I to death,
Sprinkling the lustral drops, devoted it
With many tears. My dream I thus expound: —
Orestes, whom I hallow'd by my rites,
Is dead: for sons are pillars of the house;
They, whom my lustral lavers sprinkle die.
I cannot to my friends apply my dream,
For Strophius, when I perish'd, had no son.
Now, to my brother, absent though he be,
Libations will I offer: this, at least,
With the attendants given me by the king,
Virgins of Greece, I can: but what the cause
They yet attend me not within the house,
The temple of the goddess, where I dwell?

(She goes into the temple. Orestes
and Pylades *enter cautiously.)*

ORESTES: Keep careful watch, lest some one come this way.
PYLADES: I watch, and turn mine eye to every part.
ORESTES: And dost thou, Pylades, imagine this
        The temple of the goddess, which we seek,
        Our sails from Argos sweeping o'er the main?

150

PYLADES: Orestes, such my thought, and must be thine.
ORESTES: And this the altar wet with Grecian blood?
PYLADES: Crimson'd with gore behold its sculptured wreaths.
ORESTES: See, from the battlements what trophies hang!
PYLADES: The spoils of strangers that have here been slain.
ORESTES: Behooves us then to watch with careful eye.
    O Phoebus, by thy oracles again
    Why hast thou led me to these toils? E'er since,
    In vengeance for my father's blood, I slew
    My mother, ceaseless by the Furies driven,
    Vagrant, an outcast, many a bending course
    My feet have trod: to thee I came, of thee
    Inquired this whirling frenzy by what means,
    And by what means my labours I might end.
    Thy voice commanded me to speed my course
    To this wild coast of Tauris, where a shrine
    Thy sister hath, Diana; thence to take
    The statue of the goddess, which from heaven
    (So say the natives) to this temple fell:
    This image, or by fraud or fortune won,
    The dangerous toil achieved, to place the prize
    In the Athenian land: no more was said;
    But that, performing this, I should obtain
    Rest from my toils. Obedient to thy words,
    On this unknown, inhospitable coast
    Am I arrived. Now Pylades (for thou
    Art my associate in this dangerous task),
    Of thee I ask, What shall we do? for high
    The walls, thou seest, which fence the temple round.
    Shall we ascend their height? But how escape
    Observing eyes? Or burst the brazen bars?
    Of these we nothing know: in the attempt
    To force the gates, or meditating means
    To enter, if detected, we shall die.
    Shall we then, ere we die, by flight regain
    The ship in which we hither plough'd the sea?
PYLADES: Of flight we brook no thought, nor such hath been
    Our wont; nor may the god's commanding voice
    Be disobey'd; but from the temple now
    Retiring, in some cave, which the black sea
    Beats with its billows, we may lie conceal'd
    At distance from our bark, lest some, whose eyes
    May note it, bear the tidings to the king,

And we be seized by force. But when the eye
Of night comes darkling on, then must we dare,
And take the polish'd image from the shrine,
Attempting all things: and the vacant space
Between the triglyphs (mark it well) enough
Is open to admit us; by that way
Attempt we to descend: in toils the brave
Are daring; of no worth the abject soul.

ORESTES: This length of sea we plough'd not, from this coast,
Nothing effected, to return: but well
Hast thou advised; the god must be obey'd.
Retire we then where we may lie conceal'd;
For never from the god will come the cause,
That what his sacred voice commands should fall
Effectless. We must dare. No toil to youth
Excuse, which justifies inaction, brings.

(They go out. Iphigenia and the Chorus
enter from the temple.)

IPHIGENIA (singing): You, who your savage dwellings hold
    Nigh this inhospitable main,
  'Gainst clashing rocks with fury roll'd,
    From all but hallow'd words abstain.

Virgin queen, Latona's grace,
Joying in the mountain chase,
To thy court, thy rich domain,
To thy beauteous-pillar'd fane
Where our wondering eyes behold
Battlements that blaze with gold,
Thus my virgin steps I bend,
Holy, the holy to attend;
Servant, virgin, queen, to thee;
Power, who bear'st life's golden key,
Far from Greece for steeds renown'd,
From her walls with towers crown'd,
From the beauteous-planted meads
Where his train Eurotas leads,
Visiting the loved retreats,
Once my father's royal seats.

CHORUS (singing): I come. What cares disturb thy rest?
    Why hast thou brought me to the shrine?

Doth some fresh grief afflict thy breast?
    Why bring me to this seat divine?
Thou daughter of that chief, whose powers
    Plough'd with a thousand keels the strand,
And ranged in arms shook Troy's proud towers
    Beneath the Atreidae's great command?

IPHIGENIA *(singing)*: O ye attendant train,
How is my heart oppress'd with wo!
What notes, save notes of grief, can flow,
    A harsh and unmelodious strain?
My soul domestic ills oppress with dread,
And bid me mourn a brother dead.
What visions did my sleeping sense appal
    In the past dark and midnight hour!
    'Tis ruin, ruin all.
    My father's house, — it is no more:
No more is his illustrious line.
    What dreadful deeds hath Argos known!
One only brother, Fate, was mine;
    And dost thou rend him from me? Is he gone
To Pluto's dreary realms below?
    For him, as dead, with pious care
    This goblet I prepare;
And on the bosom of the earth shall flow
Streams from the heifer mountain-bred,
    The grape's rich juice, and, mix'd with these,
    The labour of the yellow bees,
Libations soothing to the dead.
Give me the oblation: let me hold
The foaming goblet's hallow'd gold.
O thou, the earth beneath,
    Who didst from Agamemnon spring;
To thee, deprived of vital breath,
    I these libations bring.
Accept them: to thy honour'd tomb,
Never, ah! never shall I come;
Never these golden tresses bear,
To place them there, there shed the tear;
For from my country far, a hind
There deem'd as slain, my wild abode I find.

CHORUS *(singing)*: To thee thy faithful train
    The Asiatic hymn will raise,
A doleful, a barbaric strain,

Responsive to thy lays,
And steep in tears the mournful song, —
Notes, which to the dead belong;
Dismal notes, attuned to woe
By Pluto in the realms below:
No sprightly air shall we employ
To cheer the soul, and wake the sense of joy.

IPHIGENIA *(singing)*: The Atreidae are no more;
Extinct their sceptre's golden light;
My father's house from its proud height
    Is fallen: its ruins I deplore.
Who of her kings at Argos holds his reign,
Her kings once bless'd? But Sorrow's train
Rolls on impetuous for the rapid steeds
    Which o'er the strand with Pelops fly.
From what atrocious deeds
Starts the sun back, his sacred eye
Of brightness, loathing, turn'd aside?
    And fatal to their house arose,
From the rich ram, Thessalia's golden pride,
    Slaughter on slaughter, woes on woes:
Thence, from the dead ages past,
    Vengeance came rushing on its prey,
    And swept the race of Tantalus away.
Fatal to thee its ruthless haste;
    To me too fatal, from the hour
My mother wedded, from the night
She gave me to life's opening light,
    Nursed by affliction's cruel power.
Early to me, the Fates unkind,
To know what sorrow is assign'd:
Me Leda's daughter, hapless dame,
    First blooming offspring of her bed
(A father's conduct here I blame),
    A joyless victim bred;
    When o'er the strand of Aulis, in the pride
Of beauty kindling flames of love,
High on my splendid car I move,
    Betrothed to Thetis' son a bride:
Ah, hapless bride, to all the train
Of Grecian fair preferr'd in vain!
But now, a stranger on the strand,
    'Gainst which the wild waves beat,

154

I hold my dreary, joyless seat,
Far distant from my native land,
Nor nuptial bed is mine, nor child, nor friend.
     At Argos now no more I raise
     The festal song in Juno's praise;
Nor o'er the loom sweet-sounding bend,

As the creative shuttle flies;
Give forms of Titans fierce to rise;
And, dreadful with her purple spear,
     Image Athenian Pallas there;
But on this barbarous shore
     The unhappy stranger's fate I moan,
The ruthless altar stain'd with gore,
     His deep and dying groan;
And, for each tear that weeps his woes,
From me a tear of pity flows.
Of these the sad remembrance now must sleep:
A brother dead, ah me! I weep:
At Argos him, by fate oppress'd,
I left an infant at the breast,
A beauteous bud, whose opening charm
Then blossom'd in his mother's arms;
Orestes, born to high command,
The imperial sceptre of the Argive land.

LEADER OF THE CHORUS: Leaving the sea-wash'd shore a herdsman
     Speeding, with some fresh tidings to thee fraught.   [comes

(A Herdsman *enters.)*

HERDSMAN: Daughter of Agamemnon, and bright gem
     Of Clytemnestra, hear strange things from me.
IPHIGENIA: And what of terror doth thy tale import?
HERDSMAN: Two youths, swift-rowing 'twixt the clashing rocks
     Of our wild sea, are landed on the beach,
     A grateful offering at Diana's shrine,
     And victims to the goddess. Haste, prepare
     The sacred lavers, and the previous rites.
IPHIGENIA: Whence are the strangers? from what country named?
HERDSMAN: From Greece: this only, nothing more, I know.
IPHIGENIA: Didst thou not hear what names the strangers bear?
HERDSMAN: One by the other was call'd Pylades.
IPHIGENIA: How is the stranger, his companion, named?

155

HERDSMAN: This none of us can tell: we heard it not.
IPHIGENIA: How saw you them? how seized them? by what chance?
HERDSMAN: Mid the rude cliffs that o'er the Euxine hang —
IPHIGENIA: And what concern have herdsmen with the sea?
HERDSMAN: To wash our herds in the salt wave we came.
IPHIGENIA: To what I ask'd return: how seized you them?
    Tell me the manner; this I wish to know:
    For slow the victims come, nor hath some while
    The altar of the goddess, as was wont,
    Been crimson'd with the streams of Grecian blood.
HERDSMAN: Our herds, which in the forest feed, we drove
    Amid the tide that rushes to the shore,
    'Twixt the Symplegades: it was the place,
    Where in the rifted rock the chafing surge
    Hath hallow'd a rude cave, the haunt of those
    Whose quest is purple. Of our number there
    A herdsman saw two youths, and back return'd
    With soft and silent step; then pointing, said,
    "Do you not see them? These are deities
    That sit there." One, who with religious awe
    Revered the gods, with hands uplifted pray'd,
    His eyes fix'd on them, — "Son of the sea-nymph
    Leucothoe, guardian of the labouring bark,
    Our lord Palaemon, be propitious to us!
    Or sit you on our shores, bright sons of Jove,
    Castor and Pollux? Or the glorious boast
    Of Nereus, father of the noble choir
    Of fifty Nereids?" One, whose untaught mind
    Audacious folly harden'd 'gainst the sense
    Of holy awe, scoff'd at his prayers, and said, —
    "These are wreck'd mariners, that take their seat
    In the cleft rock through fear, as they have heard
    Our prescribed rite, that here we sacrifice
    The stranger." To the greater part he seem'd
    Well to have spoken, and we judged it meet
    To seize the victims, by our country's law
    Due to the goddess. Of the stranger youths,
    One at this instant started from the rock:
    Awhile he stood, and wildly toss'd his head,
    And groan'd, his loose arms trembling all their length,
    Convulsed with madness; and a hunter loud
    Then cried, — "Dost thou behold her, Pylades?
    Dost thou not see this dragon fierce from hell

Rushing to kill me, and against me rousing
Her horrid vipers? See this other here,
Emitting fire and slaughter from her vests,
Sails on her wings, my mother in her arms
Bearing, to hurl this mass of rock upon me!
Ah, she will kill me! Whither shall I fly?"
His visage might we see no more the same,
And his voice varied; now the roar of bulls,
The howl of dogs now uttering, mimic sounds
Sent by the maddening Furies, as they say.
Together thronging, as of death assured,
We sit in silence; but drew his sword,
And, like a lion rushing mid our herds,
Plunged in their sides the weapon, weening thus
To drive the Furies, till the briny wave
Foam'd with their blood. But when among our herds
We saw this havoc made, we all 'gan rouse
To arms, and blew our sounding shells to alarm
The neighbouring peasants; for we thought in fight
Rude herdsmen to these youthful strangers, train'd
To arms, ill match'd; and forthwith to our aid
Flock'd numbers. But, his frenzy of its force
Abating on the earth the stranger falls,
Foam bursting from his mouth: but when he saw
The advantage, each adventured on and hurl'd
What might annoy him fallen: the other youth
Wiped off the foam, took of his person care,
His fine-wrought robe spread over him; with heed
The flying stones observing, warded off
The wounds, and each kind office to his friend
Attentively perform'd. His sense return'd;
The stranger started up, and soon perceived
The tide of foes that roll'd impetuous on,
The danger and distress that closed them round.
He heaved a sigh; an unremitting storm
Of stones we pour'd, and each incited each:
Then we his dreadful exhortation heard: —
"Pylades, we shall die; but let us die
With glory; draw thy sword, and follow me."
But when we saw the enemies advance
With brandish'd swords, the steep heights crown'd with wood
We fell in flight: but others, if one flies,
Press on them; if again they drive these back,

What before fled turns, with a storm of stones
Assaulting them; but, what exceeds belief,
Hurl'd by a thousand hands, not one could hit
The victims of the goddess: scarce at length,
Not by brave daring seized we them, but round
We closed upon them, and their swords with stones
Beat, wily, from their hands; for on their knees
They through fatigue had sunk upon the ground:
We bare them to the monarch of this land:
He view'd them, and without delay to thee
Sent them devoted to the cleansing vase,
And to the altar. Victims such as these,
O virgin, wish to find; for if such youths
Thou offer, for thy slaughter Greece will pay,
Her wrongs to thee at Aulis well avenged.

LEADER: These things are wonderful, which thou hast told
Of him, whoe'er he be, the youth from Greece
Arrived on this inhospitable shore.

IPHIGENIA: 'Tis well: go thou, and bring the strangers hither:
What here is to be done shall be our care.

(The Herdsman *departs.)*

O my unhappy heart! before this hour
To strangers thou wast gentle, always touch'd
With pity, and with tears their tears repaid,
When Grecians, natives of my country, came
Into my hands: but from the dreams, which prompt
To deeds ungentle, showing that no more
Orestes views the sun's fair light, who'er
Ye are that hither come, me will you find
Relentless now. This is the truth, my friends:
My heart is rent; and never will the wretch,
Who feels affliction's cruel tortures, bear
Good-will to those that are more fortunate.
Never came gale from Jove, nor flying bark,
Which 'twixt the dangerous rocks of the Euxine sea
Brought Helen hither, who my ruin wrought,
Nor Menelaus; that on them my foul wrongs
I might repay, and with an Aulis here
Requite the Aulis there, where I was seized,
And, as a heifer, by the Grecians slain:
My father too, who gave me birth, was priest.
Ah me! the sad remembrance of those ills

Yet lives: how often did I stroke thy cheek,
And, hanging on thy kness, address thee thus: —
"Alas, my father! I by thee am led
A bride to bridal rites unbless'd and base:
Them, while by thee I bleed, my mother hymns,
And the Argive dames, with hymeneal strains,
And with the jocund pipe the house resounds:
But at the altar I by thee am slain;
For Pluto was the Achilles, not the son
Of Peleus, whom to me thou didst announce
The affianced bridegroom, and by guile didst bring
To bloody nuptials in the rolling car."
But, o'er mine eyes the veil's fine texture spread,
This brother in my hands who now is lost,
I clasp'd not, though his sister; did not press
My lips to his, through virgin modesty,
As going to the house of Peleus: then
Each fond embrace I to another time
Deferr'd, as soon to Argos to return.
If, O unhappy brother, thou art dead,
From what a state, thy father's envied height
Of glory, loved Orestes, art thou torn! —
These false rules of the goddess much I blame:
Whoe'er of mortals is with slaughter stain'd,
Or hath at childbirth given assisting hands,
Or chanced to touch aught dead, she as impure
Drives from her altars; yet herself delights
In human victims bleeding at her shrine.
Ne'er did Latona from the embrace of Jove
Bring forth such inconsistence: I then deem
The feast of Tantalus, where gods were guests,
Unworthy of belief, as that they fed
On his son's flesh delighted: and I think
These people, who themselves have a wild joy
In shedding human blood, their saving guilt
Charge on the goddess: for this truth I hold;
None of the gods is evil, or doth wrong.

(She enters the temple.)

CHORUS *(singing)*: Ye rocks, ye clashing rocks, whose brow
Frowns o'er the darken'd deeps below;
Whose wild, inhospitable wave,
From Argos flying and her native spring,

The virgin once was known to brave,
Tormented with the brize's maddening sting,
    From Europe when the rude sea o'er
    She pass'd to Asia's adverse shore;
Who are these hapless youths, that dare to land,
    Leaving those soft, irriguous meads,
    Where, his green margin fringed with reeds,
    Eurotas rolls his ample tide,
    Or Dirce's hallow'd waters glide,
And touch this barbarous, stranger-hating strand,
    The altars where a virgin dews,
    And blood the pillar'd shrine imbrues?

    Did they with oars impetuous sweep
    (Rank answering rank) the foamy deep,
    And wing their bark with flying sails,
To raise their humble fortune their desire;
    Eager to catch the rising gales,
Their bosoms with the love of gain on fire?
    For sweet is hope to man's fond breast;
    The hope of gain, insatiate guest,
Though on her oft attends Misfortune's train;
    For daring man she tempts to brave
    The dangers of the boisterous wave,
    And leads him heedless of his fate
    Through many a distant barbarous state.
Vain his opinions, his pursuits are vain!
    Boundless o'er some her power is shown,
    But some her temperate influence own.

    How did they pass the dangerous rocks
    Clashing with rude, tremendous shocks?
    How pass the savage-howling shore,
Where once the unhappy Phineus held his reign,
    And sleep affrighted flies its roar,
Steering their rough course o'er this boisterous main,
    Form'd in a ring, beneath whose waves
    The Nereid train in high arch'd caves
Weave the light dance, and raise the sprightly song,
    While, whispering in their swelling sails,
    Soft Zephyrs breathe, or southern gales
    Piping amid their tackling play,
    As their bark ploughs its watery way
Those hoary cliffs, the haunts of birds, along,

To that wild strand, the rapid race
Where once Achilles deign'd to grace?

O that from Troy some chance would bear
Leda's loved daughter, fatal fair!
(The royal virgin's vows are mine)
That her bright tresses roll'd in crimson dew,
Her warm blood flowing at this shrine
The altar of the goddess might imbrue;
And Vengeance, righteous to repay
Her former mischiefs, seize her prey!
But with what rapture should I hear his voice,
If one this shore should reach from Greece,
And bid the toils of slavery cease!
Or might I in the hour of rest
With pleasing dreams of Greece be bless'd;
So in my house, my native land rejoice;
In sleep enjoy the pleasing strain
For happiness restored again!

(Iphigenia *enters from the temple.*)

IPHIGENIA: But the two youths, their hands fast bound in chains,
The late-seized victims to the goddess, come.
Silence, my friends; for, destined at the shrine
To bleed, the Grecian strangers near approach;
And no false tidings did the herdsman bring.
LEADER OF THE CHORUS: Goddess revered, if grateful to thy soul
This state presents such sacrifice, accept
The victims, which the custom of this land
Gives thee, but deem'd unholy by the Greeks.

(Guards lead in Orestes *and* Pylades, *bound.)*

IPHIGENIA: No more; that to the goddess each due rite
Be well perform'd shall be my care. Unchain
The strangers' hands; that, hallow'd as they are,
They may no more be bound.

(The guards release Orestes *and* Pylades.*)*

    Go, prepare
Within the temple what the rites require.
Unhappy youths, what mother brought you forth,
Your father who? Your sister, if perchance
Ye have a sister, of what youths deprived?

For brother she shall have no more. Who knows
Whom such misfortunes may attend? For dark
What the gods will creeps on; and none can tell
The ills to come: this fortune from the sight
Obscures. But, O unhappy strangers, say,
Whence came you? Sail'd you long since for this land?
But long will be your absence from your homes,
For ever, in the dreary realms below.

ORESTES: Lady, whoe'er thou art, why for these things
Dost thou lament? why mourn for ills, which soon
Will fall on us? Him I esteem unwise,
Who, when he sees death near, tries to o'ercome
Its terrors with bewailings, without hope
Of safety: ill he adds to ill, and makes
His folly known, yet dies. We must give way
To fortune; therefore mourn not thou for us:
We know, we are acquainted with your rites.

IPHIGENIA: Which of you by the name of Pylades
Is call'd? This first it is my wish to know.

ORESTES: If aught of pleasure that may give thee, he.

IPHIGENIA: A native of what Grecian state, declare.

ORESTES: What profit knowing this wouldst thou obtain?

IPHIGENIA: And are you brothers, of one mother born?

ORESTES: Brother, by friendship, lady, not by birth.

IPHIGENIA: To thee what name was by thy father given?

ORESTES: With just cause I Unhappy might be call'd.

IPHIGENIA: I ask not that; to fortune that ascribe.

ORESTES: Dying unknown, rude scoffs I shall avoid.

IPHIGENIA: Wilt thou refuse? Why are thy thoughts so high?

ORESTES: My body thou mayst kill, but not my name.

IPHIGENIA: Wilt thou not say a native of what state?

ORESTES: The question naught avails, since I must die.

IPHIGENIA: What hinders thee from granting me this grace?

ORESTES: The illustrious Argos I my country boast.

IPHIGENIA: By the gods, stranger, is thy birth from thence?

ORESTES: My birth is from Mycenae, once the bless'd.

IPHIGENIA: Dost thou an exile fly, or by what fate?

ORESTES: Of my free will, in part not free, I fly.

IPHIGENIA: Wilt thou then tell me what I wish to know?

ORESTES: Whate'er is foreign to my private griefs.

IPHIGENIA: To my dear wish from Argos thou art come.

ORESTES: Not to my wish; but if to thine, enjoy it.

IPHIGENIA: Troy, whose fame spreads so wide, perchance thou know'st.

IPHIGENIA: False dreams, farewell; for nothing you import.
ORESTES: O that I ne'er had known her, ev'n in dreams!
IPHIGENIA: They say she is no more, by way destroy'd.
ORESTES: It is so: you have heard no false reports.
IPHIGENIA: Is Helena with Menelaus return'd?
ORESTES: She is; and one I love her coming rues.
IPHIGENIA: Where is she? Me too she of old hath wrong'd.
ORESTES: At Sparta with her former lord she dwells.
IPHIGENIA: By Greece, and not by me alone abhorr'd!
ORESTES: I from her nuptials have my share of grief.
IPHIGENIA: And are the Greeks, as Fame reports, return'd?
ORESTES: How briefly all things dost thou ask at once!
IPHIGENIA: This favour, ere thou die, I wish to obtain.
ORESTES: Ask, then: since such thy wish, I will inform thee.
IPHIGENIA: Calchas, the prophet, — came he back from Troy?
ORESTES: He perish'd: at Mycenae such the fame.
IPHIGENIA: Goddess revered! But doth Ulysses live?
ORESTES: He lives, they say, but is not yet return'd.
IPHIGENIA: Perish the wretch, nor see his country more!
ORESTES: Wish him not ill, for all with him is ill.
IPHIGENIA: But doth the son of sea-born Thetis live?
ORESTES: He lives not: vain his nuptial rites at Aulis.
IPHIGENIA: That all was fraud, as those who felt it say.
ORESTES: But who art thou, inquiring thus of Greece?
IPHIGENIA: I am from thence, in early youth undone.
ORESTES: Thou hast a right to inquire what there hath pass'd.
IPHIGENIA: What know'st thou of the chief, men call the bless'd?
ORESTES: Who? Of the bless'd was not the chief I knew.
IPHIGENIA: The royal Agamemnon, son of Atreus.
ORESTES: Of him I know not, lady; cease to ask.
IPHIGENIA: Nay, by the gods, tell me, and cheer my soul.
ORESTES: He's dead, the unhappy chief: no single ill.
IPHIGENIA: Dead! by what adverse fate? O wretched me!
ORESTES: Why mourn for this? How doth it touch thy breast?
IPHIGENIA: The glories of his former state I mourn.
ORESTES: Dreadfully murdered by a woman's hand.
IPHIGENIA: How wretched she that slew him, he thus slain!
ORESTES: Now then forbear: of him inquire no more.
IPHIGENIA: This only: lives the unhappy monarch's wife?
ORESTES: She, lady, is no more, slain by her son.
IPHIGENIA: Alas, the ruin'd house! What his intent?
ORESTES: To avenge on her his noble father slain.
IPHIGENIA: An ill, but righteous deed, how justly done!

ORESTES: Though righteous, by the gods he is not bless'd.
IPHIGENIA: Hath Agamemnon other offspring left?
ORESTES: He left one virgin daughter, named Electra.
IPHIGENIA: Of her that died a victim is aught said?
ORESTES: This only, dead, she sees the light no more.
IPHIGENIA: Unhappy she! the father too who slew her!
ORESTES: For a bad woman she unseemly died.
IPHIGENIA: At Argos lives the murdered father's son?
ORESTES: Nowhere he lives, poor wretch! and everywhere.
ORESTES: Nor are those gods, that have the name of wise,
  Less false than fleeting dreams. In things divine,
  And in things human, great confusion reigns.
  One thing is left; that, not unwise of soul,
  Obedient to the prophet's voice he perish'd;
  For that he perish'd, they who know report.
LEADER: What shall we know, what of our parents know?
  If yet they live or not, who can inform us?
IPHIGENIA: Hear me: this converse prompts a thought, which gives
  Promise of good, ye youths of Greece, to you,
  To these, and me: thus may it well be done,
  If, willing to my purpose, all assent.
  Wilt thou, if I shall save thee, go for me
  A messenger to Argos, to my friend
  Charged with a letter, which a captive wrote,
  Who pitied me, nor murderous thought my hand,
  But that he died beneath the law, these rites
  The goddess deeming just? for from that hour
  I have not found who might to Argos bear
  Himself my message, back with life return'd,
  Or send to any of my friends my letter.
  Thou, therefore, since it seems thou dost not bear
  Ill-will to me, and dost Mycenae know,
  And those I wish to address, be safe, and live,
  No base reward for a light letter, life
  Receiving; and let him, since thus the state
  Requires, without thee to the goddess bleed.
ORESTES: Virgin unknown, well hast thou said in all
  Save this, that to the goddess he should bleed
  A victim; that were heavy grief indeed.
  I steer'd the vessel to these ills; he sail'd
  Attendant on my toils: to gain thy grace
  By his destruction, and withdraw myself
  From sufferings, were unjust: thus let it be:

Give him the letter; to fulfil thy wish,
To Argos he will bear it: me let him
Who claims that office, slay: base is his soul,
Who in calamities involves his friends,
And saves himself; this is a friend, whose life,
Dear to me as my own, I would preserve.
IPHIGENIA: Excellent spirit! from some noble root
It shows thee sprung, and to thy friends a friend
Sincere; of those that share my blood if one
Remains, such may he be! for I am not
Without a brother, strangers, from my sight
Though distant now. Since then thy wish is such,
Him will I send to Argos; he shall bear
My letter; thou shalt die; for this desire
Hath strong possession of thy noble soul.
ORESTES: Who then shall do the dreadful deed, and slay me?
IPHIGENIA: I: to atone the goddess is my charge.
ORESTES: A charge unenvied, virgin, and unbless'd.
IPHIGENIA: Necessity constrains: I must obey.
ORESTES: Wilt thou, a woman, plunge the sword in men?
IPHIGENIA: No: but thy locks to sprinkle round is mine.
ORESTES: Whose then, if I may ask, the bloody deed?
IPHIGENIA: To some within the temple this belongs.
ORESTES: What tomb is destined to receive my corse?
IPHIGENIA: The hallow'd fire within, and a dark cave.
ORESTES: O, that a sister's hand might wrap these limbs!
IPHIGENIA: Vain wish, unhappy youth, whoe'er thou art,
Hast thou conceived; for from this barbarous land
Far is her dwelling. Yet, of what my power
Permits (since thou from Argos draw'st thy birth),
No grace will I omit: for in the tomb
I will place much of ornament, and pour
The dulcet labour of the yellow bee,
From mountain flowers extracted, on thy pyre.
But I will go, and from the temple bring
The letter; yet 'gainst me no hostile thought
Conceive. You, that attend here, guard them well,
But without chains. To one, whom most I love
Of all my friends, to Argos I shall send
Tidings perchance unlook'd for; and this letter,
Declaring those whom he thought dead alive,
Shall bear him an assured and solid joy.

(She enters the temple.)

CHORUS *(chanting)*: Thee, o'er whose limbs the bloody drops shall soon
 Be from the lavers sprinkled, I lament.
ORESTES: This asks no pity, strangers: but farewell.
CHORUS *(chanting)*: Thee for thy happy fate we reverence, youth
 Who to thy country shall again return.
PYLADES: To friends unwish'd, who leave their friends to die.
CHORUS *(chanting)*: Painful dismission! Which shall I esteem
 Most lost, alas, alas! which most undone?
 For doubts my wavering judgment yet divide,
 If chief for thee my sighs should swell, or thee.
ORESTES: By the gods, Pylades, is thy mind touch'd
 In manner like as mine?
PYLADES: I cannot tell;
 Nor to thy question have I to reply.
ORESTES: Who is this virgin? With what zeal for Greece
 Made she inquiries of us what the toils
 At Troy, if yet the Grecians were return'd,
 And Calchas, from the flight of birds who form'd
 Presages of the future. And she named
 Achilles: with what tenderness bewail'd
 The unhappy Agamemnon! Of his wife
 She ask'd me, — of his children: thence her race
 This unknown virgin draws, an Argive; else
 Ne'er would she send this letter, nor have wish'd
 To know these things, as if she bore a share
 (If Argos flourish) in its prosperous state.
PYLADES: Such were my thoughts (but thou hast given them words,
 Preventing me) of every circumstance,
 Save one: the fate of kings all know, whose state
 Holds aught of rank. But pass to other thoughts.
ORESTES: What? Share them; so thou best mayst be inform'd.
PYLADES: That thou shouldst die, and I behold this light,
 Were base: with thee I sail'd, with thee to die
 Becomes me; else shall I obtain the name
 Of a vile coward through the Argive state,
 And the deep vales of Phocis. Most will think
 (For most think ill) that by betraying thee
 I saved myself, home to return alone;
 Or haply that I slew thee, and thy death
 Contrived, that in the ruin of thy house
 Thy empire I might grasp, to me devolved
 As wedded to thy sister, now sole heir.
 These things I fear, and hold them infamous.

166

Behooves me then with thee to die, with thee
To bleed a victim, on the pyre with thine
To give my body to the flames; for this
Becomes me as thy friend, who dreads reproach.
ORESTES: Speak more auspicious words: 'tis mine to bear
Ills that are mine; and single when the wo,
I would not bear it double. What thou sayst
Is vile and infamous, would light on me,
Should I cause thee to die, who in my toils
Hast borne a share: to me, who from the gods
Suffer afflictions which I suffer, death
Is not unwelcome: thou art happy, thine
An unpolluted and a prosperous house;
Mine impious and unbless'd: if thou art saved,
And from my sister (whom I gave to thee,
Betroth'd thy bride) art bless'd with sons, my name
May yet remain, nor all my father's house
In total ruin sink. Go then, and live:
Dwell in the mansion of thy ancestors:
And when thou comest to Greece, to Argos famed
For warrior-steeds, by this right hand I charge thee
Raise a sepulchral mound, and on it place
A monument to me; and to my tomb
Her tears, her tresses let my sister give;
And say, that by an Argive woman's hand
I perish'd, to the altar's bloody rites
A hallow'd victim. Never let thy soul
Betray my sister, for thou seest her state,
Of friends how destitute, her father's house
How desolate. Farewell. Of all my friends,
Thee have I found most friendly, from my youth
Train'd up with me, in all my sylvan sports
Thou dear associate, and through many toils
Thou faithful partner of my miseries.
Me Phoebus, though a prophet, hath deceived,
And, meditating guile, hath driven me far
From Greece, of former oracles ashamed;
To him resign'd, obedient to his words,
I slew my mother, and my meed is death.
PYLADES: Yes, I will raise thy tomb: thy sister's bed
I never will betray, unhappy youth,
For I will hold thee dearer when thou art dead,
Than while thou livest; nor hath yet the voice

167

Of Phoebus quite destroy'd thee, though thou stand
To slaughter nigh; but sometimes mighty woes
Yield mighty changes, so when Fortune wills.
ORESTES: Forbear: the words of Phoebus naught avail me;
For, passing from the shrine, the virgin comes.

(Iphigenia *enters from the temple. She is carrying a letter.*)

IPHIGENIA *(to the guards)*: Go you away, and in the shrine prepare
What those, who o'er the rites preside, require.

(The guards go into the temple.)

Here, strangers, is the letter folded close:
What I would further, hear. The mind of man
In dangers, and again, from fear relieved,
Of safety when assured, is not the same:
I therefore fear lest he, who should convey
To Argos this epistle, when return'd
Safe to his native country, will neglect
My letter, as a thing of little worth.
ORESTES: What wouldst thou then? What is thy anxious thought?
IPHIGENIA: This: let him give an oath that he will bear
To Argos this epistle to those friends,
To whom it is my ardent wish to send it.
ORESTES: And wilt thou in return give him thy oath?
IPHIGENIA: That I will do, or will not do, say what.
ORESTES: To send him from this barbarous shore alive.
IPHIGENIA: That's just: how should he bear my letter else?
ORESTES: But will the monarch to these things assent?
IPHIGENIA: By me induced. Him I will see embark'd.
ORESTES: Swear then; and thou propose the righteous oath.
IPHIGENIA: This, let him say, he to my friends will give.
PYLADES: Well, to thy friends this letter I will give.
IPHIGENIA: Thee will I send safe through the darkening rocks.
PYLADES: What god dost thou invoke to attest thy oath?
IPHIGENIA: Diana, at whose shrine high charge I hold.
PYLADES: And I heaven's potent king, the awful Jove.
IPHIGENIA: But if thou slight thy oath, and do me wrong?
PYLADES: Never may I return. But if thou fail,
And save me not?
IPHIGENIA: Then never, while I live,
May I revisit my loved Argos more!
PYLADES: One thing, not mention'd, thy attention claims.

168

IPHIGENIA: If honour owes it, this will touch us both.
PYLADES: Let me in this be pardon'd, if the bark
    Be lost, and with it in the surging waves
    Thy letter perish, and I naked gain
    The shore; no longer binding be the oath.
IPHIGENIA: Know'st thou what I will do? For various ills
    Arise to those that plough the dangerous deep.
    What in this letter is contain'd, what here
    Is written, all I will repeat to thee,
    That thou mayst bear my message to my friends.
    'Gainst danger thus I guard: if thou preserve
    The letter, that though silent will declare
    My purport; if it perish in the sea,
    Saving thyself, my words too thou wilt save.
PYLADES: Well hast thou said touching the gods and me.
    Say then to whom at Argos shall I bear
    This letter? What relate as heard from thee?
IPHIGENIA *(reading)*: This message to Orestes, to the son
    Of Agamemnon, bear: — She, who was slain
    At Aulis, Iphigenia, sends thee this:
    She lives, but not to those who then were there.
ORESTES: Where is she? From the dead return'd to life?
IPHIGENIA: She whom thou seest: but interrupt me not.
    To Argos, O my brother, ere I die,
    Bear me from this barbaric land, and far
    Remove me from this altar's bloody rites,
    At which to slay the stranger is my charge. —
ORESTES: What shall I say? Where are we, Pylades?
IPHIGENIA: Or on thy house for vengeance will I call,
    Orestes. Twice repeated, learn the name.
ORESTES: Ye gods!
IPHIGENIA: In my cause why invoke the gods?
ORESTES: Nothing: proceed: my thoughts were wandering wide:
    Strange things of thee unask'd I soon shall learn.
IPHIGENIA: Tell him the goddess saved me, in exchange
    A hind presenting, which my father slew
    A victim, deeming that he plunged his sword
    Deep in my breast: me in this land she placed.
    Thou hast my charge: and this my letter speaks.
PYLADES: O thou hast bound me with an easy oath:
    What I have sworn with honest purpose, long
    Defer I not, but thus discharge mine oath.

To thee a letter from thy sister, lo,
I bear, Orestes; and I give it thee.

(Pylades *hands the letter to* Orestes.)

ORESTES: I do receive it, but forbear to unclose
Its foldings, greater pleasure first to enjoy
Than words can give. My sister, O most dear,
Astonish'd ev'n to disbelief, I throw
Mine arms around thee with a fond embrace,
In transport at the wondrous things I hear.

LEADER OF THE CHORUS: Stranger, thou dost not well with hands profane
Thus to pollute the priestess of the shrine,
Grasping her garments hallow'd from the touch.

ORESTES: My sister, my dear sister, from one sire,
From Agamemnon sprung, turn not away,
Holding thy brother thus beyond all hope.

IPHIGENIA: My brother! Thou my brother! Wilt thou not
Unsay these words? At Argos far he dwells.

ORESTES: Thy brother, O unhappy! is not there.

IPHIGENIA: Thee did the Spartan Tyndarus bring forth?

ORESTES: And from the son of Pelops' son I sprung.

IPHIGENIA: What say'st thou? Canst thou give me proof of this?

ORESTES: I can: ask something of my father's house.

IPHIGENIA: Nay, it is thine to speak, mine to attend.

ORESTES: First let me mention things which I have heard
Electra speak to thee is known the strife
Which fierce 'twixt Atreus and Thyestes rose.

IPHIGENIA: Yes, I have heard it; for the golden ram, —

ORESTES: In the rich texture didst thou not inweave it?

IPHIGENIA: O thou most dear! Thou windest near my heart.

ORESTES: And image in the web the averted sun?

IPHIGENIA: In the fine threads that figure did I work.

ORESTES: For Aulis did thy mother bathe thy limbs?

IPHIGENIA: I know it, to unlucky spousals led.

ORESTES: Why to thy mother didst thou send thy locks?

IPHIGENIA: Devoted for my body to the tomb.

ORESTES: What I myself have seen I now as proofs
Will mention. In thy father's house, hung high
Within thy virgin chambers, the old spear
Of Pelops, which he brandish'd when he slew
Oenomaus, and won his beauteous bride,
The virgin Hippodamia, Pisa's boast.

IPHIGENIA: O thou most dear (for thou art he), most dear

170

Acknowledged, thee. Orestes, do I hold,
From Argos, from thy country distant far?
ORESTES: And hold I thee, my sister, long deem'd dead?
Grief mix'd with joy, and tears, not taught by woe
To rise, stand melting in thy eyes and mine.
IPHIGENIA: Thee yet and infant in thy nurse's arms
I left, a babe I left thee in the house.
Thou art more happy, O my soul, than speech
Knows to express. What shall I say? 'tis all
Surpassing wonder and the power of words.
ORESTES: May we together from this hour be bless'd!
IPHIGENIA: An unexpected pleasure, O my friends,
Have I received; yet fear I from my hands
Lest to the air it fly. O sacred hearths
Raised by the Cyclops! O my country, loved
Mycenae! Now that thou didst give me birth,
I thank thee; now I thank thee, that my youth
Thou trainedst, since my brother thou has train'd,
A beam of light, the glory of his house.
ORESTES: We in our race are happy; but our life,
My sister, by misfortunes is unhappy.
IPHIGENIA: I was, I know, unhappy, when the sword
My father, frantic, pointed at my neck.
ORESTES: Ah me! methinks ev'n now I see thee there.
IPHIGENIA: When to Achilles, brother, not a bride,
I to the sacrifice by guile was led,
And tears and groans the altar compass'd round.
ORESTES: Alas, the lavers there!
IPHIGENIA: I mourn'd the deed
My father dared; unlike a father's love, to me.
Cruel, unlike a father's love, to me.
ORESTES: Ill deeds succeed to ill: if thou hadst slain
Thy brother, by some god impell'd, what griefs
Must have been thine at such a dreadful deed!
IPHIGENIA (chanting): Dreadful, my brother, O how dreadful! scarce
Hast thou escaped a foul, unhallow'd death,
Slain by my hands. But how will these things end?
What Fortune will assist me? What safe means
Shall I devise to send thee from this state,
From slaughter, to thy native land, to Argos,
Ere with thy blood the cruel sword be stain'd?
This to devise, O my unhappy soul!
This to devise is thine. Wilt thou by land,

171

Thy bark deserted, speed thy flight on foot?
Perils await thee mid these barbarous tribes,
Through pathless wilds; and 'twixt the clashing rocks,
Narrow the passage for the flying bark,
And long, Unhappy, ah, unhappy me!
What god, what mortal, what unlook'd-for chance
Will expedite our dangerous way, and show
Two sprung from Atreus a release from ills?

LEADER: What having seen and heard I shall relate,
Is marvellous, and passes fabling tales.

PYLADES: When after absence long, Orestes, friend
Meets friend, embraces will express their joy.
Behooves us now, bidding farewell to grief,
And heedful to obtain the glorious name
Of safety, from this barbarous land to fly.
The wise, of fortune not regardless, seize
The occasion, and to happiness advance.

ORESTES: Well hast thou said; and Fortune here, I ween,
Will aid us; to the firm and strenuous mind
More potent works the influence divine.

IPHIGENIA: Nothing shall check, nothing restrain my speech:
First will I question thee what fortune waits
Electra: this to know would yield me joy.

ORESTES: With him *(pointing to* Pylades*)* she dwells, and happy is her life.

IPHIGENIA: Whence then is he? and from what father sprung?

ORESTES: From Phocis: Strophius is his father named.

IPHIGENIA: By Atreus' daughter to my blood allied?

ORESTES: Nearly allied: my only faithful friend.

IPHIGENIA: He was not then, me when my father slew.

ORESTES: Childless was Strophius for some length of time.

IPHIGENIA: O thou, the husband of my sister, hail!

ORESTES: More than relation, my preserver too.

IPHIGENIA: But to thy mother why that dreadful deed?

ORESTES: Of that no more: to avenge my father's death.

IPHIGENIA: But for what cause did she her husband slay?

ORESTES: Of her inquire not: thou wouldst blush to hear.

IPHIGENIA: The eyes of Argos now are raised to thee.

ORESTES: There Menelaus is lord; I, outcast, fly.

IPHIGENIA: Hath he then wrong'd his brother's ruin'd house?

ORESTES: Not so: the Furies fright me from the land.

IPHIGENIA: The madness this, which seized thee on the shore?

ORESTES: I was not first beheld unhappy there.

IPHIGENIA: Stern powers! they haunt thee for thy mother's blood.

ORESTES: And ruthless make me champ the bloody bit.
IPHIGENIA: Why to this region has thou steer'd thy course?
ORESTES: Commanded by Apollo's voice, I come.
IPHIGENIA: With what intent? if that may be disclosed.
ORESTES: I will inform thee, though to length of speech
This leads. When vengeance from my hands o'ertook
My mother's deeds — foul deeds, which let me pass
In silence — by the Furies' fierce assaults
To flight I was impell'd: to Athens then
Apollo sent me, that, my cause there heard,
I might appease the vengeful powers, whose names
May not be utter'd: the tribunal there
Is holy, which for Mars, when stain'd with blood,
Jove in old times establish'd. There arrived,
None willingly received me, by the gods
As one abhorr'd and they, who felt the touch
Of shame, the hospitable board alone
Yielded; and though one common roof beneath,
Their silence showing they disdain'd to hold
Converse with me, I took from them apart
Alone repast; to each was placed a bowl
Of the same measure; this they filled with wine,
And bathed their spirits in delight. Unmeet
I deem'd it to express offence at those
Who entertain'd me, but in silence grieved,
Showing a cheer as though I mark'd it not,
And sigh'd for that I shed my mother's blood.
A feast, I hear, at Athens is ordain'd
From this my evil plight, ev'n yet observed,
In which the equal-measured bowl then used
Is by that people held in honour high.
But when to the tribunal on the mount
Of Mars I came, one stand I took, and one
The eldest of the Furies opposite:
The cause was heard touching my mother's blood,
And Phoebus saved me by his evidence:
Equal, by Pallas number'd, were the votes,
And I from doom of blood victorious freed.
Such of the Furies as there sat, appeased
By the just sentence, nigh the court resolved
To fix their seat; but others, whom the law
Appeased not, with relentless tortures still
Pursued me, till I reach'd the hallow'd soil

Of Phoebus: stretch'd before his shrine, I swore
Foodless to waste my wretched life away,
Unless the god, by whom I was undone,
Would save me: from the golden tripod burst
The voice divine, and sent me to this shore,
Commanding me to bear the image hence,
Which fell from Jove, and in the Athenian land
To fix it. What the oracular voice assign'd
My safety, do thou aid: if we obtain
The statue of the goddess, I no more
With madness shall be tortured, but this arm
Shall place thee in my bark, which ploughs the waves
With many an oar, and to Mycenae safe
Bear thee again. Show then a sister's love,
O thou most dear; preserve thy father's house,
Preserve me too; for me destruction waits,
And all the race of Pelops, if we bear not
This heaven-descended image from the shrine.

LEADER: The anger of the gods hath raged severe,
And plunged the race of Tantalus in woes.

IPHIGENIA: Ere thy arrival here, a fond desire
To be again at Argos, and to see
Thee, my loved brother, fill'd my soul. Thy wish
Is my warm wish, to free thee from thy toils,
And from its ruins raise my father's house;
Nor harbour I 'gainst him, that slew me, thought
Of harsh resentment: from thy blood my hands
Would I keep pure, thy house I would preserve.
But from the goddess how may this be hid?
The tyrant too I fear, when he shall find
The statue on its marble base no more.
What then from death will save me? What excuse
Shall I devise? Yet by one daring deed
Might these things be achieved: couldst thou bear hence
The image, me too in thy gallant bark
Placing secure, how glorious were the attempt!
Me if thou join not with thee, I am lost
Indeed; but thou, with prudent measures form'd,
Return. I fly no danger, not ev'n death,
Be death required, to save thee: no: the man
Dying is mourn'd, as to his house a loss;
But woman's weakness is of light esteem.

ORESTES: I would not be the murderer of my brother,

174

And of thee too; sufficient is her blood.
No; I will share thy fortune, live with thee,
Or with thee die: to Argos I will lead thee,
If here I perish not; or dying, here
Remain with thee. But what my mind suggests,
Hear: If Diana were averse to this,
How could the voice of Phoebus from his shrine
Declare that to the state of Pallas hence
The statue of the goddess I should bear,
And see thy face? All this, together weigh'd,
Gives hope of fair success, and our return.

IPHIGENIA: But how effect it, that we neither die,
And what we wish achieve? For our return
On this depends: this claims deliberate thought.
ORESTES: Have we not means to work the tyrant's death?
IPHIGENIA: For strangers full of peril were the attempt.
ORESTES: Thee would it save and me, it must be dared.
IPHIGENIA: I could not: yet thy promptness I approve.
ORESTES: What if thou lodge me in the shrine conceal'd?
IPHIGENIA: That in the shades of night we may escape?
ORESTES: Night is a friend to frauds, the light to truth.
IPHIGENIA: Within are sacred guards; we 'scape not them.
ORESTES: Ruin then waits us: how can we be saved?
IPHIGENIA: I think I have some new and safe device.
ORESTES: What is it? Let me know: impart thy thought.
IPHIGENIA: Thy sufferings for my purpose I will use,—
ORESTES: To form devices quick is woman's wit.
IPHIGENIA: And say, thy mother slain, thou fled'st from Argos.
ORESTES: If to aught good, avail thee of my ills.
IPHIGENIA: Unmeet then at this shrine to offer thee.
ORESTES: What cause alleged? I reach not thine intent.
IPHIGENIA: As now impure: when hallow'd, I will slay thee.
ORESTES: How is the image thus more promptly gain'd?
IPHIGENIA: Thee I will hallow in the ocean waves.
ORESTES: The statue we would gain is in the temple.
IPHIGENIA: That, by thy touch polluted, I would cleanse.
ORESTES: Where? On the watery margin of the main?
IPHIGENIA: Where thy tall bark secured with cables rides.
ORESTES: And who shall bear the image in his hands?
IPHIGENIA: Myself; profaned by any touch but mine.
ORESTES: What of this blood shall on my friend be charged?
IPHIGENIA: His hands, it shall be said, like thine are stain'd.
ORESTES: In secret this, or to the king disclosed?

IPHIGENIA: With his assent; I cannot hide it from him.
ORESTES: My bark with ready oars attends thee near.
IPHIGENIA: That all be well appointed, be thy charge.
ORESTES: One thing alone remains; that these conceal
    Our purpose: but address them, teach thy tongue
    Persuasive words: a woman hath the power
    To melt the heart to pity: thus perchance
    All things may to our warmest wish succeed.
IPHIGENIA: Ye train of females, to my soul most dear,
    On you mine eyes are turn'd, on you depends
    My fate; with prosperous fortune to be bless'd,
    Or to be nothing, to my country lost,
    Of a dear kinsman and a much-loved brother
    Deprived. This plea I first would urge, that we
    Are women, and have hearts by nature form'd
    To love each other, of our mutual trusts
    Most firm preservers. Touching our design,
    Be silent, and assist our flight: naught claims
    More honour than the faithful tongue. You see
    How the same fortune links us three, most dear
    Each to other, to revisit safe
    Our country, or to die. If I am saved,
    That thou mayst share my fortune, I to Greece
    Will bring thee safe: but thee by this right hand,
    Thee I conjure, and thee; by this loved cheek
    Thee, by thy knees, by all that in your house
    Is dearest to you, father, mother, child,
    If you have children. What do you reply?
    Which of you speaks assent? Or which dissents?
    But be you all assenting: for my plea
    If you approve not, ruin falls on me,
    And my unhappy brother too must die.
LEADER: Be confident, loved lady and consult
    Only thy safety: all thou givest in charge,
    Be witness, mighty Jove, I will conceal.
IPHIGENIA: O, for this generous promise be you bless'd.

(To Orestes *and* Pylades.*)*

To enter now the temple be thy part,
And thine: for soon the monarch of the land
Will come, inquiring if the strangers yet
Have bow'd their necks as victims at the shrine.
Goddess revered, who in the dreadful bay

Of Aulis from my father's slaughtering hand
Didst save me; save me now, and these: through thee,
Else will the voice of Phoebus be no more
Held true by mortals. From this barbarous land
To Athens go propitious: here to dwell
Beseems thee not; thine be a polish'd state!

(Orestes, Pylades *and* Iphigenia *enter the temple.*)

CHORUS *(singing)*: O bird, that round each craggy height
    Projecting o'er the sea below,
Wheelest thy melancholy flight,
    Thy song attuned to notes of woe;
The wise thy tender sorrows own,
Which thy lost lord unceasing moan;
Like thine, sad halcyon, be my strain,
    A bird, that have no wings to fly:
    With fond desire for Greece I sigh,
And for my much-loved social train;
Sigh for Diana, pitying maid,
    Who joys to rove o'er Cynthus' heights.
Or in the branching laurel's shade,
    Or in the soft-hair'd palm delights,
Or the hoar olive's sacred boughs,
Lenient of sad Latona's woes;
Or in the lake, that rolls its wave
Where swans their plumage love to lave;
Then, to the Muses soaring high,
The homage pay of melody.

Ye tears, what frequent-falling showers
    Roll'd down these cheeks in streams of woe.
When in the dust my country's towers
    Lay levell'd by the conquering foe;
And, to their spears a prey, their oars
Brought me to these barbaric shores!
For gold exchanged, a traffic base,
    No vulgar slave, the task is mine,
    Here at Diana's awful shrine,
Who loves the woodland hind to chase,
The virgin priestess to attend,
    Daughter of rich Mycenae's lord;
At other shrines her wish to bend,
    Where bleeds the victim less abhorr'd:

No respite to her griefs she knows;
Not so the heart inured to woes,
As train'd to sorrow's rigid lore:
Now comes a change; it mourns no more:
But to long bliss when ill succeeds,
The anguish'd heart for ever bleeds.
Thee, loved virgin, freed from fear
Home the Argive bark shall bear:
Mountain Pan, with thrilling strain,
To the oars that dash the main
In just cadence well agreed,
Shall accord his wax-join'd reed:
Phoebus, with a prophet's fire
Sweeping o'er his seven-string'd lyre,
And his voice attuning high
To the swelling harmony,
Thee shall guide the wild waves o'er
To the soft Athenian shore.
Leaving me, thy oars shall sweep
Eager o'er the foaming deep:
Thou shalt catch the rising gales
Swelling in thy firm-bound sails;
And thy bark in gallant pride
Light shall o'er the billows glide.

Might I through the lucid air
Fly where rolls yon flaming car,
O'er those loved and modest bowers,
Where I pass'd my youthful hours,
I would stay my weary flight,
Wave no more my pennons light.
But, amid the virgin band,
Once my loved companions, stand:
Once mid them my charms could move,
Blooming then, the flames of love;
When the mazy dance I trod,
While with joy my mother glow'd;
When to vie in grace was mine,
And in splendid robes to shine;
For, with radiant tints impress'd,
Glow'd for me the gorgeous vest;
And these tresses gave new grace,
As their ringlets shade my face.

(Thoas *and his retinue enter.*)

THOAS: Where is the Grecian lady, to whose charge
This temple is committed? Have her rites
Hallow'd the strangers? Do their bodies burn
In the recesses of the sacred shrine?
LEADER OF THE CHORUS: She comes, and will inform thee, king, of all.

(Iphigenia *comes out of the temple. She is carrying the sacred statue of* Diana.)

THOAS: Daughter of Agamemnon, what means this?
The statue of the goddess in thine arms
Why dost thou bear, from its firm base removed?
IPHIGENIA: There in the portal, monarch, stay thy step.
THOAS: What of strange import in the shrine hath chanced?
IPHIGENIA: Things ominous: that word I, holy, speak.
THOAS: To what is tuned thy proem? Plainly speak.
IPHIGENIA: Not pure the victims, king, you lately seized.
THOAS: What show'd thee this? Or speak'st thou but thy thought?
IPHIGENIA: Back turn'd the sacred image on its base.
THOAS: Spontaneous turn'd, or by an earthquake moved?
IPHIGENIA: Spontaneous, and, averted, closed its eyes.
THOAS: What was the cause? The blood-stain'd stranger's guilt?
IPHIGENIA: That, and naught else; for horrible their deeds.
THOAS: What, have they slain some Scythian on the shore?
IPHIGENIA: They came polluted with domestic blood.
THOAS: What blood? I have a strong desire to know.
IPHIGENIA: They slew their mother with confederate swords.
THOAS: O Phoebus! This hath no barbarian dared.
IPHIGENIA: All Greece indignant chased them from her realms.
THOAS: Bear'st thou for this the image from the shrine?
IPHIGENIA: To the pure air, from stain of blood removed.
THOAS: By what means didst thou know the stranger's guilt?
IPHIGENIA: I learn'd it as the statue started back.
THOAS: Greece train'd thee wise: this well hast thou discern'd.
IPHIGENIA: Now with sweet blandishments they soothe my soul.
THOAS: Some glozing tale from Argos telling thee?
IPHIGENIA: I have one brother: he, they say, lives happy, —
THOAS: That thou mayst save them for their pleasing news?
IPHIGENIA: And that my father lives, by fortune bless'd.
THOAS: But on the goddess well thy thoughts are turn'd.
IPHIGENIA: I hate all Greece; for it hath ruin'd me.
THOAS: What with the strangers, say then, should be done?

179

IPHIGENIA: The law ordain'd in reverence we must hold.
THOAS: Are then thy lavers ready, and the sword?
IPHIGENIA: First I would cleanse them with ablutions pure.
THOAS: In fountain waters, or the ocean wave?
IPHIGENIA: All man's pollutions doth the salt sea cleanse.
THOAS: More holy to the goddess will they bleed.
IPHIGENIA: And better what I have in charge advance.
THOAS: Doth not the wave ev'n 'gainst the temple beat?
IPHIGENIA: This requires solitude: more must I do.
THOAS: Lead where thou wilt: on secret rite I pry not.
IPHIGENIA: The image of the goddess I must cleanse.
THOAS: If it be stain'd with touch of mother's blood.
IPHIGENIA: I could not else have borne it from its base.
THOAS: Just is thy provident and pious thought;
          For this by all the state thou art revered.
IPHIGENIA: Know'st thou what next I would?
THOAS: 'Tis thine thy will to signify.
IPHIGENIA: Give for these strangers chains.
THOAS: To what place can they fly?
IPHIGENIA: A Grecian knows naught faithful.
THOAS: Of my train go some for chains.

(Some attendants go out.)

IPHIGENIA: Let them lead forth the strangers.
THOAS: Be it so.
IPHIGENIA: And veil their faces.
THOAS: From the sun's bright beams?
IPHIGENIA: Some of thy train send with me.
THOAS: These shall go, attending thee.
IPHIGENIA: One to the city send.
THOAS: With what instructions charged?
IPHIGENIA: That all remain within their houses.
THOAS: That the stain of blood they meet not?
IPHIGENIA: These things have pollution in them.
THOAS: Go thou, and bear the instructions.

(An attendant departs.)

IPHIGENIA: That none come in sight.
THOAS: How wisely careful for the city!
IPHIGENIA: Warn our friends most.
THOAS: This speaks thy care for me.
IPHIGENIA: Stay thou before the shrine.
THOAS: To what intent?

IPHIGENIA: Cleanse it with lustral fires.
THOAS: That thy return may find it pure?
IPHIGENIA: But when the strangers come
    Forth from the temple, —
THOAS: What must I then do?
IPHIGENIA: Spread o'er thine eyes a veil.
THOAS: That I receive not pollution?
IPHIGENIA: Tedious if my stay appear, —
THOAS: What bounds may be assign'd?
IPHIGENIA: Deem it not strange.
THOAS: At leisure what the rites require perform.
IPHIGENIA: May this lustration as I wish succeed!
THOAS: Thy wish is mine.

(Orestes *and* Pylades, *bound, are led from the temple in a solemn procession by the guards.* Thoas *and his retinue veil their heads as it slowly moves past.*)

IPHIGENIA *(chanting)*: But from the temple, see,
    The strangers come, the sacred ornaments,
    The hallow'd lambs — for I with blood must wash
    This execrable blood away, — the light
    Of torches, and what else my rites require
    To purify these strangers to the goddess.
    But to the natives of this land my voice
    Proclaims, from this pollution far remove,
    Art thou attendant at the shrine, who liftest
    Pure to the gods thy hands, or nuptial rites
    Dost thou prepare, or pregnant matron; hence,
    Begone, that this defilement none may touch.
    Thou, daughter of Latona and high Jove,
    O royal virgin, if I cleanse the stain
    Of these, and where I ought with holy rites
    Address thee, thou shalt hold thy residence
    In a pure mansion; we too shall be bless'd.
    More though I speak not, goddess, unexpress'd,
    All things to thee and to the gods are known.

(Iphigenia, *carrying the statue, joins the procession as it goes out.* Thoas *and his retinue enter the temple.*)

CHORUS *(singing)*: Latona's glorious offspring claims the song,
    Born the hallow'd shades among,
    Where fruitful Delos winds her valleys low;
        Bright-hair'd Phoebus, skill'd to inspire

181

Raptures, as he sweeps the lyre,
And she that glories in the unerring bow.
From the rocky ridges steep,
At whose feet the hush'd waves sleep,
Left their far-famed native shore,
Them the exulting mother bore
To Parnassus, on whose heights
Bacchus shouting holds his rites;
Glittering in the burnish'd shade,
By the laurel's branches made,
Where the enormous dragon lies,
Brass his scales, and flame his eyes,
Earth-born monster, that around
Rolling guards the oracular ground;
Him, while yet a sportive child,
In his mother's arms that smiled,
Phoebus slew, and seized the shrine
Whence proceeds the voice divine:
On the golden tripod placed,
Throne by falsehood ne'er disgraced,
Where Castalia's pure stream flows,
He the fates to mortal shows.
But when Themis, whom of yore
Earth, her fruitful mother, bore,
From her hallow'd seat he drove,
Earth to avenge her daughter strove,
Forming visions of the night,
Which, in rapt dreams hovering light,
All that Time's dark volumes hold
Might to mortal sense unfold,
When in midnight's sable shades
Sleep the silent couch invades:
Thus did Earth her vengeance boast.
His prophetic honours lost,
Royal Phoebus speeds his flight
To Olympus, on whose height
At the throne of Jove he stands,
Stretching forth his little hands,
Suppliant that the Pythian shrine
Feel no more the wrath divine;
That the goddess he appease;
That her nightly visions cease.
Jove with smiles beheld his son

Early thus address his throne,
Suing with ambitious pride
O'er the rich shrine to preside;
He, assenting, bow'd his head.
Straight the nightly visions fled;
And prophetic dreams no more
Hover'd slumbering mortals o'er:
Now to Phoebus given again,
All his honours pure remain;
Votaries distant regions send
His frequented throne to attend:
And the firm decrees of fate
On his faithful voice await.

(A Messenger *enters.)*

MESSENGER: Say you, that keep the temple, and attend
    The altar, where is Thoas, Scythia's king?
    Open these strong-compacted gates, and call
    Forth from the shrine the monarch of the land.
LEADER OF THE CHORUS: Wherefore? at thy command if I must speak.
MESSENGER: The two young men are gone, through the device
    Of Agamemnon's daughter: from this land
    They fly; and, in their Grecian galley placed,
    The sacred image of the goddess bear.
LEADER: Incredible thy tale: but whom thou seek'st,
    The monarch, from the temple went in haste.
MESSENGER: Whither? for what is doing he should know.
LEADER: We know not: but go thou, and seek for him:
    Where'er thou find him, thou wilt tell him this.
MESSENGER: See, what a faithless race you women are!
    In all that hath been done you have a part.
LEADER: Sure thou art mad! what with the strangers' flight
    Have we to do? But wilt thou not, with all
    The speed thou mayst, go to the monarch's house?
MESSENGER: Not till I first am well inform'd, if here
    Within the temple be the king, or not.

(Shouting.)

Unbar the gates (to you within I speak);
And tell your lord that at the portal here
I stand, and bring him tidings of fresh ills.
    (Thoas *and his attendants enter from the temple.)*
THOAS: Who at the temple of the goddess dares

183

This clamour raise, and thundering at the gates,
Strikes terror through the ample space within?
MESSENGER: With falsehoods would these women drive me hence,
Without to seek thee: thou wast in the shrine.
THOAS: With what intent? or what advantage sought?
MESSENGER: Of these hereafter; what more urgent now
Imports thee, hear: the virgin, in this place
Presiding at the altars, from this land
Is with the strangers fled, and bears with her
The sacred image of the goddess; all
Of her ablutions but a false pretence.
THOAS: How say'st thou? What is her accursed design?
MESSENGER: To save Orestes: this too will amaze thee.
THOAS: Whom? What Orestes? Clytemnestra's son?
MESSENGER: Him at the altar hallow'd now to bleed.
THOAS: Portentous! for what less can it be call'd?
MESSENGER: Think not on that, but hear me; with deep thought
Reflect: weigh well what thou shalt hear; devise
By what pursuit to reach and seize the strangers.
THOAS: Speak: thou advisest well: the sea though nigh,
They fly not so as to escape my spear.
MESSENGER: When to the shore we came, where station's rode
The galley of Orestes, by the rocks
Conceal'd to us, whom thou hadst sent with her
To hold the strangers' chains, the royal maid
Made signs that we retire, and stand aloof,
As if with secret rites she would perform
The purposed expiation: on she went,
In her own hands holding the strangers' chains
Behind them: not without suspicion this,
Yet by thy servants, king, allow'd. At length,
That we might deem her in some purpose high
Employ'd, she raised her voice, and chanted loud
Barbaric strains, as if with mystic rites
She cleansed the stain of blood. When we had sat
A tedious while, it came into our thought,
That from their chains unloosed, the stranger youths
Might kill her, and escape by flight: yet fear
Of seeing what we ought not, kept us still
In silence; but at length we all resolved
To go, though not permitted, where they were.
There we behold the Grecian bark with oars
Well furnish'd, wing'd for flight; and at their seats,

Grasping their oars, were fifty rowers; free
From chains beside the stern the two youths stood.
Some from the prow relieved the keel with poles;
Some weigh'd the anchors up; the climbing ropes
Some hasten'd, through their hands the cables drew,
Launch'd the light bark, and gave her to the main.
But when we saw their treacherous wiles, we rush'd
Heedless of danger, seized the priestess, seized
The halsers, hung upon the helm, and strove
To rend the rudder-bands away. Debate
Now rose: — "What mean you, sailing o'er the seas,
The statue and the priestess from the land
By stealth conveying? Whence art thou, and who,
That bear'st her, like a purchased slave, away?"
He said, "I am her brother; be of this
Inform'd; Orestes, son of Agamemnon:
My sister, so long lost, I bear away,
Recover'd here." But naught the less for that
Held we the priestess, and by force would lead
Again to thee: hence dreadful on our cheeks
The blows; for in their hands no sword they held,
Nor we; but many a rattling stroke the youths
Dealt with their fists, against our sides and breasts
Their arms fierce darting, till our batter'd limbs
Were all disabled: now with dreadful marks
Disfigured, up the precipice we fly,
Some bearing on their heads, some in their eyes
The bloody bruises: standing on the heights,
Our fight was safer, and we hurl'd at them
Fragments of rocks; but, standing on the stern,
The archers with their arrows drove us thence;
And now a swelling wave roll'd in, which drove
The galley towards the land. The sailors fear'd
The sudden swell: on his left arm sustain'd,
Orestes bore his sister through the tide,
Mounted the bark's tall side, and on the deck
Safe placed her, and Diana's holy image,
Which fell from heaven; from the midship his voice
He sent aloud: — "Ye youths, that in this bark
From Argos plough'd the deep, now ply your oars,
And dash the billows till they foam: those things
Are ours, for which we swept the Euxine sea,
And steer'd our course within its clashing rocks."

They gave a cheerful shout, and with their oars
Dash'd the salt wave. The galley, while it rode
Within the harbour, work'd its easy way;
But having pass'd its mouth, the swelling flood
Roll'd on it, and with sudden force the wind
Impetuous rising drove it back: their oars
They slack'd not, stoutly struggling 'gainst the wave;
But towards the land the refluent flood impell'd
The galley; then the royal virgin stood,
And pray'd: — "O daughter of Latona, save me,
Thy priestess save; from this barbaric land
To Greece restore me, and forgive my thefts:
For thou, O goddess, dost thy brother love,
Deem then that I love those allied to me."
The mariners responsive to her prayer
Shouted loud paeans, and their naked arms,
Each cheering each, to their stout oars apply.
But nearer and yet nearer to the rock
The galley drove: some rush'd into the sea,
Some strain'd the ropes that bind the loosen'd sails.
Straight was I hither sent to thee, O king,
To inform thee of these accidents. But haste,
Take chains and gyves with thee; for if the flood
Subside not to a calm, there is no hope
Of safety to the strangers. Be assured,
That Neptune, awful monarch of the main,
Remembers Troy; and hostile to the race
Of Pelops, will deliver to thy hands,
And to thy people, as is meet, the son
Of Agamemnon; and bring back to thee
His sister, who the goddess hath betray'd,
Unmindful of the blood at Aulis shed.
LEADER: Unhappy Iphigenia, thou must die,
　　　　Thy brother too must die, if thou again,
　　　　Seized in thy flight, to thy lord's hands shalt come.
THOAS: Inhabitants of this barbaric land,
　　　　Will you not rein your steeds, will you not fly
　　　　Along the shore, to seize whate'er this skiff
　　　　Of Greece casts forth; and, for your goddess roused,
　　　　Hunt down these impious men? Will you not launch
　　　　Instant your swift-oar'd barks, by sea, by land
　　　　To catch them, from the rugged rock to hurl
　　　　Their bodies, or impale them on the stake?

186

But for you, women, in these dark designs
Accomplices, hereafter, as I find
Convenient leisure, I will punish you.
The occasion urges now, and gives no pause.

(Minerva *appears above.*)

MINERVA: Whither, O royal Thoas, dost thou lead
This vengeful chase? Attend: Minerva speaks.
Cease thy pursuit, and stop this rushing flood
Of arms; for hither, by the fateful voice
Of Phoebus, came Orestes, warn'd to fly
The anger of the Furies, to convey
His sister to her native Argos back,
And to my land the sacred image bear.
Thoas, I speak to thee: him, whom thy rage
Would kill, Orestes, on the wild waves seized,
Neptune, to do me grace, already wafts
On the smooth sea, the swelling surges calm'd.
And thou, Orestes (for my voice thou hear'st,
Though distant far), to my commands attend:
Go, with the sacred image, which thou bear'st,
And with thy sister: but when thou shalt come
To Athens built by gods, there is a place
On the extreme borders of the Attic land,
Close neighbouring to Carystia's craggy height,
Sacred; my people call it Alae: there
A temple raise, and fix the statue there,
Which from the Tauric goddess shall receive
Its name, and from thy toils, which thou, through **Greece**
Driven by the Furies' maddening stings, hast borne;
And mortals shall in future times with hymns
The Tauric goddess there, Diana, hail.
And be this law establish'd; when the feast
For thy deliverance from this shrine is held,
To a man's throat that they apply the sword,
And draw the blood, in memory of these rites,
That of her honours naught the goddess lose.
Thou, Iphigenia, on the hallow'd heights
Of Brauron on this goddess shalt attend
Her priestess, dying shalt be there interr'd,
Graced with the honours of the gorgeous vests
Of finest texture, in their houses left
By matrons who in childbed pangs expired.

These Grecian dames back to their country lead,
I charge thee; justice this return demands,
For I saved thee, when on the mount of Mars
The votes were equal; and from that decree
The shells in number equal still absolve.
But, son of Agamemnon, from this land
Thy sister bear; nor, Thoas, be thou angry.

THOAS: Royal Minerva, he that hears the gods
Commanding, and obeys not, is unwise.
My anger 'gainst Orestes flames no more,
Gone though he be, and bears with him away
The statue of the goddess, and his sister.
Have mortals glory 'gainst the powerful gods
Contending? Let them go, and to thy land
The sacred image bear, and fix it there;
Good fortune go with them. To favour Greece,
These dames, at thy high bidding, I will send.
My arms will I restrain, which I had raised
Against the strangers, and my swift-oar'd barks,
Since, potent goddess, this is pleasing to thee.

MINERVA: I praise thy resolution; for the power
Of Fate o'er thee and o'er the gods prevails.
Breathe soft, ye favouring gales, to Athens bear
These sprung from Agamemnon; on their course
Attending, I will go, and heedful save
My sister's sacred image. You too go *(to the* Chorus*)*
Prosperous, and in the fate that guards you bless'd.

(Minerva *vanishes.*)

CHORUS *(chanting)*: O thou, among the immortal gods revered
And mortal men, Minerva, we will do
As thou commandest; for with transport high,
Exceeding hope, our ears receive thy words.

O Victory, I revere thy awful power:
Guard thou my life, nor ever cease to crown me!

Robert Potter

188

ARISTOPHANES

Apart from the vital dates of Aristophanes (C. 450-C. 385 B. C.) little is known of the personal life of this comic poet. He lived through the apogee of Athenian democracy and the period of the Peloponnesian War. Aristophanes composed some forty plays, of which eleven are extant. These comedies, rich in wit, in fantastic situations, and also in obscenities, consistently contain, as an undercurrent of the comic atmosphere, grave political or moral motifs.

THE BIRDS

The Birds, the longest of Aristophanes' plays, was produced in 414 B. C. at the festival of the Great Dionysia, and gained a second prize. The play is a political fantasy, in which the supreme cosmic power falls into the hands of birds.

CHARACTERS IN THE PLAY

EUELPIDES
PITHETAERUS
TROCHILUS, Servant to Epops
EPOPS (the Hoopoe)
A BIRD
A HERALD
A PRIEST
A POET
An ORACLE-MONGER
METON, a Geometrician
An INSPECTOR
A DEALER IN DECREES
IRIS
A PARRICIDE
CINESIAS, A Dithyrambic Poet
An INFORMER
PROMETHEUS
POSIDON

TRIBALLUS
HERACLES
SLAVES OF PITHETAERUS
MESSENGERS
CHORUS OF BIRDS

(SCENE: — A wild and desolate region; only thickets, rocks, and a single tree are seen. Euelpides and Pithetaerus enter, each with a bird in his hand.)

EUELPIDES *(to his jay)*: Do you think I should walk straight for yon tree?

PITHETAERUS *(to his crow)*: Cursed beast, what are you croaking to me? . . . to retrace my steps?

EUELPIDES: Why, you wretch, we are wandering at random, we are exerting ourselves only to return to the same spot; we're wasting our time.

PITHETAERUS: To think that I should trust to this crow, which has made me cover more than a thousand furlongs!

EUELPIDES: And that I, in obedience to this jay, should have worn my shoes down to the nails!

PITHETAERUS: If only I knew where we were . . .

EUELPIDES: Could you find your country again from here?

PITHETAERUS: No, I feel quite sure I could not, any more than could Execestides find his.

EUELPIDES: Alas!

PITHETAERUS: Aye, aye, my friend, it's surely the road of "Alases" we are following.

EUELPIDES: That Philocrates, the bird-seller, played us a scurvy trick, when he pretended these two guides could help us to find Tereus, the Epops, who is a bird, without being born of one. He has indeed sold us this jay, a true son of Tharrhelides, for an obolus, and this crow for three, but what can they do? Why, nothing whatever but bite and scratch! *(To his jay)* What's the matter with you then, that you keep opening your beak? Do you want us to fling ourselves headlong down these rocks? There is no road that way.

PITHETAERUS: Not even the vestige of a trail in any direction.

EUELPIDES: And what does the crow say about the road to follow?

PITHETAERUS: By Zeus, it no longer croaks the same thing it did.

EUELPIDES: And which way does it tell us to go now?

PITHETAERUS: It says that, by dint of gnawing, it will devour my fingers.

EUELPIDES: What misfortune is ours! we strain every nerve to get to the crows, do everything we can to that end, and we cannot find our way! Yes, spectators, our madness is quite different from that of Sacas. He is not a citizen, and would fain be one at any cost; we, on the contrary, born of an honourable tribe and family and living in the midst of our fellow-citizens, we have fled from our country as hard as ever we could go. It's not that we hate it; we recognize it to be great and rich, likewise that everyone has the right to ruin himself paying taxes; but the crickets only chirrup among the fig-trees for a month or two, whereas the Athenians spend their whole lives in chanting forth judgments from their law-courts. That is why we started off with a basket, a stew-pot and some myrtle boughs and have come to seek a quiet country in which to settle. We are going to Tereus, the Epops, to learn from him, whether, in his aerial flights, he has noticed some town of this kind.

PITHETAERUS: Here! Look!

EUELPIDES: What's the matter?

PITHETAERUS: Why, the crow has been directing me to something up there for some time now.

EUELPIDES: And the jay is also opening its beak and craning its neck to show me I know not what. Clearly, there are some birds about here. We shall soon know, if we kick up a noise to start them.

PITHETAERUS: Do you know what to do? Knock your leg against this rock.

EUELPIDES: And you your head to double the noise.

PITHETAERUS: Well then use a stone instead; take one and hammer with it.

EUELPIDES: Good idea! *(He does so.)* Ho there, within! Slave! slave!

PITHETAERUS: What's that, friend? You say, "slave," to summon Epops? It would be much better to shout, "Epops, Epops."

EUELPIDES: Well then, Epops! Must I knock again? Epops!

TROCHILUS *(rushing out of a thicket)*: Who's there? Who calls my master?

PITHETAERUS *(in terror)*: Apollo the Deliverer! what an enormous beak!

(He defecates. In the confusion both the jay and the crow fly away.)

TROCHILUS *(equally frightened)*: Good god! they are bird-catchers.

EUELPIDES *(reassuring himself)*: But is it so terrible? Wouldn't it be better to explain things?

TROCHILUS *(also reassuring himself)*: You're done for.

EUELPIDES: But we are not men.

TROCHILUS: What are you, then?

EUELPIDES *(defecating also)*: I am the Fearling, an African bird.

TROCHILUS: You talk nonsense.

EUELPIDES: Well, then, just ask it of my feet.

TROCHILUS: And this other one, what bird is it? *(To* Pithetaerus*)* Speak up!

PITHETAERUS *(weakly)*: I? I am a Crapple, from the land of the pheasants.

EUELPIDES: But you yourself, in the name of the gods! what animal are you?

TROCHILUS: Why, I am a slave-bird.

EUELPIDES: Why, have you been conquered by a cock?

TROCHILUS: No, but when my master was turned into a hoopoe, he begged me to become a bird also, to follow and to serve him.

EUELPIDES: Does a bird need a servant, then?

TROCHILUS: That's no doubt because he was once a man. At times he wants to eat a dish of sardines from Phalerum; I seize my dish and fly to fetch him some. Again he wants some pea-soup; I seize a ladle and a pot and run to get it.

EUELPIDES: This is, then, truly a running-bird. Come, Trochilus, do us the kindness to call your master.

TROCHILUS: Why, he has just fallen asleep after a feed of myrtle-berries and a few grubs.

EUELPIDES: Never mind; wake him up.

TROCHILUS: I am certain he will be angry. However, I will wake him to please you.

(He goes back into the thicket.)

PITHETAERUS *(as soon as* Trochilus *is out of sight)*: You cursed brute! why, I am almost dead with terror!

EUELPIDES: Oh! my god! it was sheer fear that made me lose my jay.

PITHETAERUS: Ah! you big coward! were you so frightened that you let go your jay?

EUELPIDES: And did you not lose your crow, when you fell sprawling on the ground? Tell me that.

PITHETAERUS: Not at all.

EUELPIDES: Where is it, then?

PITHETAERUS: It flew away.

EUELPIDES: And you did not let it go? Oh! you brave fellow!

EPOPS *(from within)*: Open the thicket, that I may go out!

(He comes out of the thicket.)

EUELPIDES: By Heracles! what a creature! what plumage! what means this triple crest?

192

EPOPS: Who wants me?

EUELPIDES *(banteringly)*: The twelve great gods used you ill, it seems.

EPOPS: Are you twitting me about my feathers? I have been a man, strangers.

EUELPIDES: It's not you we are jeering at.

EPOPS: At what, then?

EUELPIDES: Why, it's your beak that looks so ridiculous to us.

EPOPS: This is how Sophocles outrages me in his tragedies. Know, I once was Tereus.

EUELPIDES: You were Tereus, and what are you now? a bird or a peacock?

EPOPS: I am a bird.

EUELPIDES: Then where are your feathers? I don't see any.

EPOPS: They have fallen off.

EUELPIDES: Through illness?

EPOPS: No. All birds moult their feathers, you know, every winter, and others grow in their place. But tell me, who are you?

EUELPIDES: We? We are mortals.

EPOPS: From what country?

EUELPIDES: From the land of the beautiful galleys.

EPOPS: Are you dicasts?

EUELPIDES: No, if anything, we are anti-dicasts.

EPOPS: Is that kind of seed sown among you?

EUELPIDES: You have to look hard to find even a little in our fields.

EPOPS: What brings you here?

EUELPIDES: We wish to pay you a visit.

EPOPS: What for?

EUELPIDES: Because you formerly were a man, like we are, formerly you had debts, as we have, formerly you did not want to pay them, like ourselves; furthermore, being turned into a bird, you have when flying seen all lands and seas. Thus you have all human knowledge as well as that of birds. And hence we have come to you to beg you to direct us to some cosy town, in which one can repose as if on thick coverlets.

EPOPS: And are you looking for a greater city than Athens?

EUELPIDES: No, not a greater, but one more pleasant to live in.

EPOPS: Then you are looking for an aristocratic country.

EUELPIDES: I? Not at all! I hold the son of Scellias in horror.

EPOPS: But, after all, what sort of city would please you best?

EUELPIDES: A place where the following would be the most important business transacted. — Some friend would come knocking at the door quite early in the morning saying, "By Olympian Zeus, be at my house early, as soon as you have bathed, and bring

193

your children too. I am giving a nuptial feast, so don't fail, or else don't cross my threshold when I am in distress."

EPOPS: Ah! that's what may be called being fond of hardships! *(To Pithetaerus)* And what say you?

PITHETAERUS: My tastes are similar.

EPOPS: And they are?

PITHETAERUS: I want a town where the father of a handsome lad will stop in the street and say to me reproachfully as if I had failed him, "Ah! Is this well done, Stilbonides? You met my son coming from the bath after the gymnasium and you neither spoke to him, nor kissed him, nor took him with you, nor even felt his balls. Would anyone call you an old friend of mine?"

EPOPS: Ah! wag, I see you are fond of suffering. But there is a city of delights such as you want. It's on the Red Sea.

EUELPIDES: Oh, no. Not a sea-port, where some fine morning the Salaminian galley can appear, bringing a process-server along. Have you no Greek town you can propose to us?

EPOPS: Why not choose Lepreum in Elis for your settlement?

EUELPIDES: By Zeus! I could not look at Lepreum without disgust, because of Melanthius.

EPOPS: Then, again, there is the Opuntian Locris, where you could live.

EUELPIDES: I would not be Opuntian for a talent. But come, what is it like to live with the birds? You should know pretty well.

EPOPS: Why, it's not a disagreeable life. In the first place, one has no purse.

EUELPIDES: That does away with a lot of roguery.

EPOPS: For food the gardens yield us white sesame, myrtle-berries, poppies and mint.

EUELPIDES: Why, 'tis the life of the newly-wed indeed.

PITHETAERUS: Ha! I am beginning to see a great plan, which will transfer the supreme power to the birds, if you will but take my advice.

EPOPS: Take your advice? In what way?

PITHETAERUS: In what way? Well, firstly, do not fly in all directions with open beak; it is not dignified. Among us, when we see a thoughtless man, we ask, "What sort of bird is this?" and Teleas answers, "It's a man who has no brain, a bird that has lost his head, a creature you cannot catch, for it never remains in any one place."

EPOPS: By Zeus himself! your jest hits the mark. What then is to be done?

PITHETAERUS: Found a city.

EPOPS: We birds? But what sort of city should we build?

PITHETAERUS: Oh, really, really! you talk like such a fool! Look down.
EPOPS: I am looking.
PITHETAERUS: Now look up.
EPOPS: I am looking.
PITHETAERUS: Turn your head round.
EPOPS: Ah! it will be pleasant for me if I end in twisting my neck off!
PITHETAERUS: What have you seen?
EPOPS: The clouds and the sky.
PITHETAERUS: Very well! is not this the pole of the birds then?
EPOPS: How their pole?
PITHETAERUS: Or, if you like it, their place. And since it turns and passes through the whole universe, it is called 'pole.' If you build and fortify it, you will turn your pole into a city. In this way you will reign over mankind as you do over the grasshoppers and you will cause the gods to die of rabid hunger.
EPOPS: How so?
PITHETAERUS: The air is between earth and heaven. When we want to go to Delphi, we ask the Boeotians for leave of passage; in the same way, when men sacrifice to the gods, unless the latter pay you tribute, you exercise the right of every nation towards strangers and don't allow the smoke of the sacrifices to pass through your city and territory.
EPOPS: By earth! by snares! by network! by cages! I never heard of anything more cleverly conceived; and, if the other birds approve, I am going to build the city along with you.
PITHETAERUS: Who will explain the matter to them?
EPOPS: You must yourself. Before I came they were quite ignorant, but since I have lived with them I have taught them to speak.
PITHETAERUS: But how can they be gathered together?
EPOPS: Easily. I will hasten down to the thicket to waken my dear Procné and as soon as they hear our voices, they will come to us hot wing.
PITHETAERUS: My dear bird, lose no time, please! Fly at once into the thicket and awaken Procné.

(Epops *rushes into the thicket.*)

EPOPS *(from within; singing)*: Chase off drowsy sleep, dear companion. Let the sacred hymn gush from thy divine throat in melodious strains; roll forth in soft cadence your refreshing melodies to bewail the fate of Itys, which has been the cause of so many tears to us both. Your pure notes rise through the thick leaves of the yew-tree right up to the throne of Zeus, where Phoebus

195

listens to you, Phoebus with his golden hair. And his ivory lyre responds to your plaintive accents; he gathers the choir of the gods and from their immortal lips pours forth a sacred chant of blessed voices.

(The flute is played behind the scene, imitating the song of the nightingale.)

PITHETAERUS: Oh! by Zeus! what a throat that little bird possesses! he has filled the whole thicket with honey-sweet melody!

EUELPIDES: Hush!

PITHETAERUS: What's the matter?

EUELPIDES: Be still!

PITHETAERUS: What for?

EUELPIDES: Epops is going to sing again.

EPOPS *(in the thicket, singing)*: *Epopopoi popoi popopopoi,* here, quick, quick, quick, my comrades in the air; all you who pillage the fertile lands of the husbandmen, the numberless tribes who gather and devour the barley seeds, the swift flying race that sings so sweetly. And you whose gentle twitter resounds through the fields with the little cry of *tiotiotiotiotiotiotiotio*; and you who hop about the branches of the ivy in the gardens; the mountain birds, who feed on the wild olive-berries or the arbutus, hurry to come at my call, *trioto, trioto, totobrix*; you also, who snap up the sharp-stinging gnats in the marshy vales, and you, the francolin with speckled wings; you too, the halcyons, who flit over the swelling waves of the sea, come hither to hear the tidings; let all the tribes of long-necked birds assemble here; know that a clever old man has come to us, bringing an entirely new idea and proposing great reforms. Let all come to the debate here, here, here, here. *Torotorotorotorotix, kikkabau, kikkabau, torotorotorolililix.*

PITHETAERUS: Can you see any bird?

EUELPIDES: By Phoebus, no! and yet I am straining my eyesight to scan the sky.

PITHETAERUS: It was hardly worth Epops' while to go and bury himself in the thicket like a hatching plover.

A BIRD *(entering)*: *Torotix torotix.*

PITHETAERUS: Wait, friend, there's a bird.

EUELPIDES: By Zeus, it is a bird, but what kind? Isn't it a peacock?

PITHETAERUS *(as* Epops *comes out of the thicket)*: Epops will tell us. What is this bird?

EPOPS: It's not one of those you are used to seeing; it's a bird from the marshes.

EUELPIDES: Oh! oh! but he is very handsome with his wings as crimson as flame.

EPOPS: Undoubtedly; indeed he is called flamingo.

EUELPIDES (excitedly): Hi! I say! You!

PITHETAERUS: What are you shouting for?

EUELPIDES: Why, here's another bird.

PITHETAERUS: Aye, indeed; this one's a foreign bird too. (To Epops) What is this bird from beyond the mountains with a look as solemn as it is stupid?

EPOPS: He is called the Mede.

EUELPIDES: The Mede! But, by Heracles, how, if a Mede, has he flown here without a camel?

PITHETAERUS: Here's another bird with a crest.

(From here on, the numerous birds that make up the Chorus keep rushing in.)

EUELPIDES: Ah! that's curious. I say, Epops, you are not the only one of your kind then?

EPOPS: This bird is the son of Philocles, who is the son of Epops; so that, you see, I am his grandfather; just as one might say, Hipponicus, the son of Callias, who is the son of Hipponicus.

EUELPIDES: Then this bird is Callias! Why, what a lot of his feathers he has lost!

EPOPS: That's because he is honest; so the informers set about him and the women too pluck out his feathers.

EUELPIDES: By Posidon, do you see that many-coloured bird? What is his name?

EPOPS: This one? That's the glutton.

EUELPIDES: Is there another glutton besides Cleonymus? But why, if he is Cleonymus, has he not thrown away his crest? But what is the meaning of all these crests? Have these birds come to contend for the double stadium prize?

EPOPS: They are like the Carians, who cling to the crests of their mountains for greater safety.

PITHETAERUS: Oh, Posidon! look what awful swarms of birds are gathering here!

EUELPIDES: By Phoebus! what a cloud! The entrance to the stage is no longer visible so closely do they fly together.

PITHETAERUS: Here is the partridge.

EUELPIDES: Why, there is the francolin.

PITHETAERUS: There is the poachard.

EUELPIDES: Here is the kingfisher. *(To* Epops*)* What's that bird behind the kingfisher?

EPOPS: That's the barber.

EUELPIDES: What? a bird a barber?

PITHETAERUS: Why, Sporgilus is one.

EPOPS: Here comes the owl.

EUELPIDES: And who is it brings an owl to Athens?

EPOPS *(pointing to the various species)*: Here is the magpie, the turtle-dove, the swallow, the horned-owl, the buzzard, the pigeon, the falcon, the ring-dove, the cuckoo, the red-foot, the red-cap, the kestrel, the diver, the ousel, the osprey, the woodpecker . . .

PITHETAERUS: Oh! what a lot of birds!

EUELPIDES: Oh! what a lot of blackbirds!

PITHETAERUS: How they scold, how they come rushing up! What a noise! what a noise!

EUELPIDES: Can they be bearing us ill-will?

PITHETAERUS: Oh! there! there! they are opening their beaks and staring at us.

EUELPIDES: Why, so they are.

LEADER OF THE CHORUS: *Popopopopopo.* Where is he who called me? Where am I to find him?

EPOPS: I have been waiting for you a long while! I never fail in my word to my friends.

LEADER OF THE CHORUS: *Tititititititi.* What good news have you for me?

EPOPS: Something that concerns our common safety, and that is just as pleasant as it is to the point. Two men, who are subtle reasoners, have come here to seek me.

LEADER OF THE CHORUS: Where? How? What are you saying?

EPOPS: I say, two old men have come from the abode of humans to propose a vast and splendid scheme to us.

LEADER OF THE CHORUS: Oh! it's a horrible, unheard-of crime! What are you saying?

EPOPS: Never let my words scare you.

LEADER OF THE CHORUS: What have you done to me?

EPOPS: I have welcomed two men, who wish to live with us.

LEADER OF THE CHORUS: And you have dared to do that!

EPOPS: Yes, and I am delighted at having done so.

LEADER OF THE CHORUS: And are they already with us?

EPOPS: Just as much as I am.

CHORUS *(singing)*: Ah! ah! we are betrayed; 'tis sacrilege! Our friend, he who picked up corn-seeds in the same plains as ourselves, has violated our ancient laws; he has broken the oaths that bind

198

all birds; he has laid a snare for me, he has handed us over to the attacks of that impious race which, throughout all time, has never ceased to war against us.

LEADER OF THE CHORUS: As for this traitorous bird, we will decide his case later, but the two old men shall be punished forthwith; we are going to tear them to pieces.

PITHETAERUS: It's all over with us.

EUELPIDES: You are the sole cause of all our trouble. Why did you bring me from down yonder?

PITHETAERUS: To have you with me.

EUELPIDES: Say rather to have me melt into tears.

PITHETAERUS: Go on! you are talking nonsense. How will you weep with your eyes pecked out?

CHORUS (singing): Io! io! forward to the attack, throw yourselves upon the foe, spill his blood; take to your wings and surround them on all sides. Woe to them! let us get to work with our beaks, let us devour them. Nothing can save them from our wrath, neither the mountain forests, nor the clouds that float in the sky, nor the foaming deep.

LEADER OF THE CHORUS: Come, peck, tear to ribbons. Where is the chief of the cohort? Let him engage the right wing.

(They rush at the two Athenians.)

EUELPIDES: This is the fatal moment. Where shall I fly to, unfortunate wretch that I am?

PITHETAERUS: Wait! Stay here!

EUELPIDES: That they may tear me to pieces?

PITHETAERUS: And how do you think to escape them?

EUELPIDES: I don't know at all.

PITHETAERUS: Come, I will tell you. We must stop and fight them. Let us arm ourselves with these stew-pots.

EUELPIDES: Why with stew-pots?

PITHETAERUS: The owl will not attack us then.

EUELPIDES: But do you see all those hooked claws?

PITHETAERUS: Take the spit and pierce the foe on your side.

EUELPIDES: And how about my eyes?

PITHETAERUS: Protect them with this dish or this vinegar-pot.

EUELPIDES: Oh! what cleverness! what inventive genius! You are a great general, even greater than Nicias, where stratagem is concerned.

LEADER OF THE CHORUS: Forward, forward, charge with your beaks!

Come, no delay. Tear, pluck, strike, flay them, and first of all smash the stew-pot.

EPOPS (*stepping in front of the Chorus*): Oh, most cruel of all animals, why tear these two men to pieces, why kill them? What have they done to you? They belong to the same tribe, to the same family as my wife.

LEADER OF THE CHORUS: Are wolves to be spared? Are they not our most mortal foes? So let us punish them.

EPOPS: If they are your foes by nature, they are your friends in heart, and they come here to give you useful advice.

LEADER OF THE CHORUS: Advice or a useful word from their lips, from them, the enemies of my forbears?

EPOPS: The wise can often profit by the lessons of a foe, for caution is the mother of safety. It is just such a thing as one will not learn from a friend and which an enemy compels you to know. To begin with, it's the foe and not the friend that taught cities to build high walls, to equip long vessels of war; and it's this knowledge that protects our children, our slaves and our wealth.

LEADER OF THE CHORUS: Well then, I agree, let us first hear them, for that is best; one can even learn something in an enemy's school.

PITHETAERUS (*To Euelpides*): Their wrath seems to cool. Draw back a little.

EPOPS: It's only justice, and you will thank me later.

LEADER OF THE CHORUS: Never have we opposed your advice up to now.

PITHETAERUS: They are in a more peaceful mood; put down your stew-pot and your two dishes; spit in hand, doing duty for a spear, let us mount guard inside the camp close to the pot and watch in our arsenal closely; for we must not fly.

EUELPIDES: You are right. But where shall we be buried, if we die?

PITHETAERUS: In the Ceramicus; for, to get a public funeral, we shall tell the Strategi that we fell at Orneae, fighting the country's foes.

LEADER OF THE CHORUS: Return to your ranks and lay down your courage beside your wrath as the hoplites do. Then let us ask these men who they are, whence they come, and with what intent. Here, Epops, answer me.

EPOPS: Are you calling me? What do you want of me?

LEADER OF THE CHORUS: Who are they? From what country?

EPOPS: Strangers, who have come from Greece, the land of the wise.

LEADER OF THE CHORUS: And what fate has led them hither to the land of the birds?

EPOPS: Their love for you and their wish to share your kind of life; to dwell and remain with you always.

LEADER OF THE CHORUS: Indeed, and what are their plans?

EPOPS: They are wonderful, incredible, unheard of.

LEADER OF THE CHORUS: Why, do you think to see some advantage that determines them to settle here? Are they hoping with our help to triumph over their foes or to be useful to their friends?

EPOPS: They speak of benefits so great it is impossible either to describe or conceive them; all shall be yours, all that we see here, there, above and below us; this they vouch for.

LEADER OF THE CHORUS: Are they mad?

EPOPS: They are the sanest people in the world.

LEADER OF THE CHORUS: Clever men?

EPOPS: The slyest of foxes, cleverness its very self, men of the world, cunning, the cream of knowing folk.

LEADER OF THE CHORUS: Tell them to speak and speak quickly; why, as I listen to you, I am beside myself with delight.

EPOPS *(to two attendants)*: Here, you there, take all these weapons and hang them up inside close to the fire, near the figure of the god who presides there and under his protection; *(to* Pithetaerus*)* as for you, address the birds, tell them why I have gathered them together.

PITHETAERUS: Not I, by Apollo, unless they agree with me as the little ape of an armourer agreed with his wife, not to bite me, nor pull me by the balls, nor shove things into my . . .

EUELPIDES *(bending over and pointing his finger at his anus)*: Do you mean this?

PITHETAERUS: No, I mean my eyes.

LEADER OF THE CHORUS: Agreed.

PITHETAERUS: Swear it.

LEADER OF THE CHORUS: I swear it and, if I keep my promise, let judges and spectators give me the victory unanimously.

PITHETAERUS: It is a bargain.

LEADER OF THE CHORUS: And if I break my word, may I succeed by one vote only.

EPOPS *(as* Herald*)*: Hearken, ye people! Hoplites, pick up your weapons and return to your firesides; do not fail to read the decrees of dismissal we have posted.

CHORUS *(singing)*: Man is a truly cunning creature, but nevertheless explain. Perhaps you are going to show me some good way to extend my power, some way that I have not had the wit to find out and which you have discovered. Speak! 'tis to your own interest as well as to mine, for if you secure me some advantage, I will surely share it with you.

LEADER OF THE CHORUS: But what object can have induced you to come among us? Speak boldly, for I shall not break the truce, —until you have told us all.

PITHETAERUS: I am bursting with desire to speak; I have already mixed the dough of my address and nothing prevents me from kneading it ... Slave! bring the chaplet and water, which you must pour over my hands. Be quick!

EUELPIDES: Is it a question of feasting? What does it all mean?

PITHETAERUS: By Zeus, no! but I am hunting for fine, tasty words to break down the hardness of their hearts. *(To the* Chorus*)* I grieve so much for you who at one time were kings ...

LEADER OF THE CHORUS: We kings? Over whom?

PITHETAERUS: ... of all that exists, firstly of me and of this man, even of Zeus himself. Your race is older than Saturn, the Titans and the Earth.

LEADER OF THE CHORUS: What, older than the Earth!

PITHETAERUS: By Phoebus, yes.

LEADER OF THE CHORUS: By Zeus, but I never knew that before!

PITHETAERUS: That's because you are ignorant and heedless, and have never read your Aesop. He is the one who tells us that the lark was born before all other creatures, indeed before the Earth; his father died of sickness, but the Earth did not exist then; he remained unburied for five days, when the bird in its dilemma decided, for want of a better place, to entomb its father in its own head.

EUELPIDES: So that the lark's father is buried at Cephalae.

PITHETAERUS: Hence, if they existed before the Earth, before the gods, the kingship belongs to them by right of priority.

EUELPIDES: Undoubtedly, but sharpen your beak well: Zeus won't be in a hurry to hand over his sceptre to the woodpecker.

PITHETAERUS: It was not the gods, but the birds, who were formerly the masters and kings over men; of this I have a thousand proofs. First of all, I will point you to the cock who governed the Persians before all other monarchs, before Darius and Megabazus. It's in memory of his reign that he is called the Persian bird.

EUELPIDES: For this reason also, even to-day, he alone of all the birds wears his tiara straight on his head, like the Great King.

PITHETAERUS: He was so strong, so great, so feared, that even now, on account of his ancient power, everyone jumps out of bed as soon as ever he crows at daybreak. Blacksmiths, potters, tanners, shoemakers, bathmen, corndealers, lyre-makers and armourers, all put on their shoes and go to work before it is daylight.

EUELPIDES: I can tell you something about that. It was the cock's fault that I lost a splendid tunic of Phrygian wool. I was at a feast in town, given to celebrate the birth of a child; I had drunk pretty freely and had just fallen asleep, when a cock, I suppose in a greater hurry than the rest, began to crow. I thought it was dawn and set out for Halimus. I had hardly got beyond the walls, when a footpad struck me in the back with his bludgeon; down I went and wanted to shout, but he had already made off with my mantle.

PITHETAERUS: Formerly also the kite was ruler and king over the Greeks.

LEADER OF THE CHORUS: The Greeks?

PITHETAERUS: And when he was king, he was the one who first taught them to fall on their knees before the kites.

EUELPIDES: By Zeus! that's what I did myself one day on seeing a kite; but at the moment I was on my knees, and leaning backwards with mouth agape, I bolted an obolus and was forced to carry my meal-sack home empty.

PITHETAERUS: The cuckoo was king of Egypt and of the whole of Phoenicia. When he called out "cuckoo," all the Phoenicians hurried to the fields to reap their wheat and their barley.

EUELPIDES: Hence no doubt the proverb, "Cuckoo! cuckoo! go to the fields, ye circumcised."

PITHETAERUS: So powerful were the birds that the kings of Grecian cities, Agamemnon, Menelaus, for instance, carried a bird on the tip of their sceptres, who had his share of all presents.

EUELPIDES: That I didn't know and was much astonished when I saw Priam come upon the stage in the tragedies with a bird, which kept watching Lysicrates to see if he got any present.

PITHETAERUS: But the strongest proof of all is that Zeus, who now reigns, is represented as standing with an eagle on his head as a symbol of his royalty; his daughter has an owl, and Phoebus, as his servant, has a hawk.

EUELPIDES: By Demeter, the point is well taken. But what are all these birds doing in heaven?

PITHETAERUS: When anyone sacrifices and, according to the rite, offers the entrails to the gods, these birds take their share before Zeus. Formerly men always swore by the birds and never by the gods.

EUELPIDES: And even now Lampon swears by the goose whenever he wishes to deceive someone.

PITHETAERUS: Thus it is clear that you were once great and sacred, but now you are looked upon as slaves, as fools, as Maneses; stones are thrown at you as at raving madmen, even in holy places. A crowd of bird-catchers sets snares, traps, limed twigs and nets of all sorts for you; you are caught, you are sold in heaps and the buyers finger you over to be certain you are fat. Again, if they would but serve you up simply roasted; but they rasp cheese into a mixture of oil, vinegar and laserwort, to which another sweet and greasy sauce is added, and the whole is poured scalding hot over your back, for all the world as if you were diseased meat.

CHORUS (*singing*): Man, your words have made my heart bleed; I have groaned over the treachery of our fathers, who knew not how to transmit to us the high rank they held from their fore-fathers. But 'tis a benevolent Genius, a happy Fate, that sends you to us; you shall be our deliverer and I place the destiny of my little ones and my own in your hands with every confidence.

LEADER OF THE CHORUS: But hasten to tell me what must be done; we should not be worthy to live, if we did not seek to regain our royalty by every possible means.

PITHETAERUS: First I advise that the birds gather together in one city and that they build a wall of great bricks, like that at Babylon, round the plains of the air and the whole region of space that divides earth from heaven.

EPOPS: Oh, Cebriones! oh, Porphyrion! what a terribly strong place!

PITHETAERUS: Then, when this has been well done and completed, you demand back the empire from Zeus; if he will not agree, if he refuses and does not at once confess himself beaten, you declare a sacred war against him and forbid the gods henceforward to pass through your country with their tools up, as hitherto, for the purpose of laying their Alcmenas, their Alopés, or their Semelés! if they try to pass through, you put rings on their tools so that they can't make love any longer. You send another messenger to mankind, who will proclaim to them that the birds are kings, that for the future they must first of all sacrifice to them, and only afterwards to the gods; that it is fitting to appoint to each deity the bird that has most in common with it. For instance, are they sacrificing to Aphrodite, let them at the same time offer barley to the coot; are they immolating a sheep to Posidon, let them consecrate wheat in honour of the duck; if a steer is being offered to Heracles, let honey-cakes be dedicated to the gull; if a goat is being slain for King Zeus, there is a King-Bird, the wren, to whom the sacrifice of a male gnat is due before Zeus himself even.

EUELPIDES: This notion of an immolated gnat delights me! And now let the great Zeus thunder!

LEADER OF THE CHORUS: But how will mankind recognize us as gods and not as jays? Us, who have wings and fly?

PITHETAERUS: You talk rubbish! Hermes is a god and has wings and flies, and so do many other gods. First of all, Victory flies with golden wings, Eros is undoubtedly winged too, and Iris is compared by Homer to a timorous dove.

EUELPIDES: But will not Zeus thunder and send his winged bolts against us?

LEADER OF THE CHORUS: If men in their blindness do not recognize us as gods and so continue to worship the dwellers in Olympus?

PITHETAERUS: Then a cloud of sparrows greedy for corn must descend upon their fields and eat up all their seeds; we shall see then if Demeter will mete them out any wheat.

EUELPIDES: By Zeus, she'll take good care she does not, and you will see her inventing a thousand excuses.

PITHETAERUS: The crows too will prove your divinity to them by pecking out the eyes of their flocks and of their draught-oxen; and then let Apollo cure them, since he is a physician and is paid for the purpose.

EUELPIDES: Oh! don't do that! Wait first until I have sold my two young bullocks.

PITHETAERUS: If on the other hand they recognize that you are God, the principle of life, that you are Earth, Saturn, Posidon, they shall be loaded with benefits.

LEADER OF THE CHORUS: Name me one of these then.

PITHETAERUS: Firstly, the locusts shall not eat up their vine-blossoms; a legion of owls and kestrels will devour them. Moreover, the gnats and the gall-bugs shall no longer ravage the figs; a flock of thrushes shall swallow the whole host down to the very last.

LEADER OF THE CHORUS: And how shall we give wealth to mankind? This is their strongest passion.

PITHETAERUS: When they consult the omens, you will point them to the richest mines, you will reveal the paying ventures to the diviner, and not another shipwreck will happen or sailor perish.

LEADER OF THE CHORUS: No more shall perish? How is that?

PITHETAERUS: When the auguries are examined before starting on a voyage, some bird will not fail to say, "Don't start! there will be a storm," or else, "Go! you will make a most profitable venture."

EUELPIDES: I shall buy a trading-vessel and go to sea. I will not stay with you.

PITHETAERUS: You will discover treasures to them, which were buried in former times, for you know them. Do not all men say, "None knows where my treasure lies, unless perchance it be some bird."

EUELPIDES: I shall send my boat and buy a spade to unearth the vessels.

LEADER OF THE CHORUS: And how are we to give them health, which belongs to the gods?

PITHETAERUS: If they are happy, is not that the chief thing towards health? The miserable man is never well.

LEADER OF THE CHORUS: Old Age also dwells in Olympus. How will they get at it? Must they die in early youth?

PITHETAERUS: Why, the birds, by Zeus, will add three hundred years to their life.

LEADER OF THE CHORUS: From whom will they take them?

PITHETAERUS: From whom? Why, from themselves. Don't you know the cawing crow lives five times as long as a man?

EUELPIDES: Ah! ah! these are far better kings for us than Zeus!

PITHETAERUS (solemnly): Far better, are they not? And firstly, we shall not have to build them temples of hewn stone, closed with gates of gold; they will dwell amongst the bushes and in the thickets of green oak; the most venerated of birds will have no other temple than the foliage of the olive tree; we shall not go to Delphi or to Ammon to sacrifice; but standing erect in the midst of arbutus and wild olives and holding forth our hands filled with wheat and barley, we shall pray them to admit us to a share of the blessings they enjoy and shall at once obtain them for a few grains of wheat.

LEADER OF THE CHORUS: Old man, whom I detested, you are now to me the dearest of all; never shall I, if I can help it, fail to follow your advice.

CHORUS (singing): Inspirited by your words, I threaten my rivals the gods, and I swear that if you march in alliance with me against the gods and are faithful to our just, loyal and sacred bond, we shall soon have shattered their sceptre.

LEADER OF THE CHORUS: We shall charge ourselves with the performance of everything that requires force; that which demands thought and deliberation shall be yours to supply.

EPOPS: By Zeus! it's no longer the time to delay and loiter like Nicias; let us act as promptly as possible . . . In the first place, come, enter, my nest built of brushwood and blades of straw, and tell me your names.

PITHETAERUS: That is soon done; my name is Pithetaerus, and his, Euelpides, of the deme Crioa.

EPOPS: Good! and good luck to you.

PITHETAERUS: We accept the omen.

EPOPS: Come in here.

PITHETAERUS: Very well, you are the one who must lead us and introduce us.

EPOPS: Come then.

(He starts to fly away.)

PITHETAERUS (*Stopping himself*): Oh! my god! do come back here. Hi! tell us how we are to follow you. You can fly, but we cannot.

EPOPS: Well, well.

PITHETAERUS: Remember Aesop's fables. It is told there that the fox fared very badly, because he had made an alliance with the eagle.

EPOPS: Be at ease. You shall eat a certain root and wings will grow on your shoulders.

PITHETAERUS: Then let us enter. Xanthias and Manodorus, pick up our baggage.

LEADER OF THE CHORUS: Hi! Epops! do you hear me?

EPOPS: What's the matter?

LEADER OF THE CHORUS: Take them off to dine well and call your mate, the melodius Procné, whose songs are worthy of the Muses; she will delight our leisure moments.

PITHETAERUS: Oh! I conjure you, accede to their wish; for this delightful bird will leave her rushes at the sound of your voice; for the sake of the gods, let her come here, so that we may contemplate the nightingale.

EPOPS: Let it be as you desire. Come forth, Procné, show yourself to these strangers.

(Procné appears; she resembles a young flute-girl.)

PITHETAERUS: Oh! great Zeus! what a beautiful little bird! what a dainty form! what brilliant plumage! Do you know how dearly I should like to get between her thighs?

EUELPIDES: She is dazzling all over with gold, like a young girl. Oh! how I should like to kiss her!

PITHETAERUS: Why, wretched man, she has two little sharp points on her beak!

EUELPIDES: I would treat her like an egg, the shell of which we remove before eating it; I would take off her mask and then kiss her pretty face.

EPOPS: Let us go in.

PITHETAERUS: Lead the way, and may success attend us.

(Epops *goes into the thicket, followed by*
Pithetaerus *and* Euelpides.)

CHORUS (*singing*): Lovable golden bird, whom I cherish above all others, you, whom I associate with all my songs, nightingale, you have come, you have come, to show yourself to me and to charm me with your notes. Come, you, who play spring melodies upon the harmonious flute, lead off our anapests.

207

(The Chorus turns and faces the audience.)

LEADER OF THE CHORUS: Weak mortals, chained to the earth, creatures of clay as frail as the foliage of the woods, you unfortunate race, whose life is but darkness, as unreal as a shadow, the illusion of a dream, hearken to us, who are immortal beings, ethereal, ever young and occupied with eternal thoughts, for we shall teach you about all celestial matters; you shall know thoroughly what is the nature of the birds, what the origin of the gods, of the rivers, of Erebus, and Chaos; thanks to us, even Prodicus will envy you your knowledge.

At the beginning there was only Chaos, Night, dark Erebus, and deep Tartarus. Earth, the air and heaven had no existence. Firstly, black-winged Night laid a germless egg in the bosom of the infinite deeps of Erebus, and from this, after the revolution of long ages, sprang the graceful Eros with his glittering golden wings, swift as the whirlwinds of the tempest. He mated in deep Tartarus with dark Chaos, winged like himself, and thus hatched forth our race, which was the first to see the light. That of the Immortals did not exist until Eros had brought together all the ingredients of the world, and from their marriage Heaven, Ocean, Earth and the imperishable race of blessed gods sprang into being. Thus our origin is very much older than that of the dwellers in Olympus. We are the offspring of Eros; there are a thousand proofs to show it. We have wings and we lend assistance to lovers. How many handsome youths, who had sworn to remain insensible, have opened their thighs because of our power and have yielded themselves to their lovers when almost at the end of their youth being led away by the gift of a quail, a waterfowl, a goose, or a cock.

And what important services do not the birds render to mortals! First of all, they mark the seasons for them, springtime, winter, and autumn. Does the screaming crane migrate to Libya, —it warns the husbandman to sow, the pilot to take his ease beside his tiller hung up in his dwelling, and Orestes to weave a tunic, so that the rigorous cold may not drive him any more to strip other folk. When the kite reappears, he tells of the return of spring and of the period when the fleece of the sheep must be clipped. Is the swallow in sight? All hasten to sell their warm tunic and to buy some light clothing. We are your Ammon, Delphi, Dodona, your Phoebus Apollo. Before undertaking anything, whether a business transaction, a marriage, or the purchase of food, you consult the birds by reading the omens, and you give

208

this name of omen to all signs that tell of the future. With you a word is an omen, you call a sneeze an omen, a meeting an omen, an unknown sound an omen, a slave or an ass an omen. Is it not clear that we are a prophetic Apollo to you? *(More and more rapidly from here on.)* If you recognize us as gods, we shall be your divining Muses, through us you will know the winds and the seasons, summer, winter, and the temperate months. We shall not withdraw ourselves to the highest clouds like Zeus, but shall be among you and shall give to you and to your children and the children of your children, health and wealth, long life, peace, youth, laughter, songs and feasts; in short, you will all be so well off, that you will be weary and cloyed with enjoyment.

FIRST SEMI-CHORUS *(singing)*: Oh, rustic Muse of such varied note, *tiotiotiotiotiotinx,* I sing with you in the groves and on the mountain tops, *tiotiotiotinx.* I poured forth sacred strains from my golden throat in honour of the god Pan, *tiotiotiotinx,* from the top of the thickly leaved ash, and my voice mingles with the mighty choirs who extol Cybelé on the mountain tops, *totototototototototinx.* 'Tis to our concerts that Phrynichus comes to pillage like a bee the ambrosia of his songs, the sweetness of which so charms the ear, *tiotiotiotinx.*

LEADER OF FIRST SEMI-CHORUS: If there is one of you spectators who wishes to spend the rest of his life quietly among the birds, let him come to us. All that is disgraceful and forbidden by law on earth is on the contrary honourable among us, the birds. For instance, among you it's a crime to beat your father, but with us it's an estimable deed; it's considered fine to run straight at your father and hit him, saying, "Come, lift your spur if you want to fight." The runaway slave, whom you brand, is only a spotted francolin with us. Are you Phrygian like Spintharus? Among us you would be the Phrygian bird, the goldfinch, of the race of Philemon. Are you a slave and a Carian like Execestides? Among us you can create yourself forefathers; you can always find relations. Does the son of Pisias want to betray the gates of the city to the foe? Let him become a partridge, the fitting offspring of his father; among us there is no shame in escaping as cleverly as a partridge.

SECOND SEMI-CHORUS *(singing)*: So the swans on the banks of the Hebrus, *tiotiotiotiotiotinx,* mingle their voices to serenade Apollo, *tiotiotiotinx,* flapping wings the while, *tiotiotiotinx;* their notes reach beyond the clouds of heaven; they startle the various tribes of the beasts; a windless sky calms the waves, *totototototototototinx;* all Olympus resounds, and astonishment seizes its rulers; the Olympian graves and Muses cry aloud the strain, *tiotiotiotinx.*

LEADER OF SECOND SEMI-CHORUS: There is nothing more useful nor more pleasant than to have wings. To begin with, just let us suppose a spectator to be dying with hunger and to be weary of the choruses of the tragic poets; if he were winged he would fly off, go home to dine and come back with his stomach filled. Some Patroclides, needing to take a crap, would not have to spill it on his cloak, but could fly off, satisfy his requirements, and return. If one of you, it matters not who, had adulterous relations and saw the husband of his mistress in the seats of the senators, he might stretch his wings, fly to her, and, having laid her, resume his place. Is it not the most priceless gift of all, to be winged? Look at Diitrephes! His wings were only wicker-work ones, and yet he got himself chosen Phylarch and then Hipparch; from being nobody, he has risen to be famous; he's now the finest gilded cock of his tribe.

(Pithetaerus *and* Euelpides *return; they now have wings.*)

PITHETAERUS: Halloa! What's this? By Zeus! I never saw anything so funny in all my life.

EUELPIDES: What makes you laugh?

PITHETAERUS: Your little wings. D'you know what you look like? Like a goose painted by some dauber.

EUELPIDES: And you look like a close-shaven blackbird.

PITHETAERUS: We ourselves asked for this transformation, and, as Aeschylus has it, "These are no borrowed feathers, but truly our own."

EPOPS: Come now, what must be done?

PITHETAERUS: First give our city a great and famous name, then sacrifice to the gods.

EUELPIDES: I think so too.

LEADER OF THE CHORUS: Let's see. What shall our city be called?

PITHETAERUS: Will you have a high-sounding Laconian name? Shall we call it Sparta?

EUELPIDES: What! call my town Sparta? Why, I would not use *esparto* for my bed, even though I had nothing but bands of rushes.

PITHETAERUS: Well then, what name can you suggest?

EUELPIDES: Some name borrowed from the clouds, from these lofty regions in which we dwell — in short, some well-known name.

PITHETAERUS: Do you like Nephelococcygia?

LEADER OF THE CHORUS: Oh! capital! truly that's a brilliant thought!

EUELPIDES: Is it in Nephelococcygia that all the wealth of Theogenes and most of Aeschines is?

210

PITHETAERUS: No, it's rather the plain of Phlegra, where the gods withered the pride of the sons of the Earth with their shafts.

LEADER OF THE CHORUS: Oh! capital! truly that's a brilliant thought! But what god shall be its patron? for whom shall we weave the peplus?

EUELPIDES: Why not choose Athené Polias?

PITHETAERUS: Oh! what a well-ordered town it would be to have a female deity armed from head to foot, while Clisthenes was spinning!

LEADER OF THE CHORUS: Who then shall guard the Pelargicon?

PITHETAERUS: A bird.

LEADER OF THE CHORUS: One of us? What kind of bird?

PITHETAERUS: A bird of Persian strain, who is everywhere proclaimed to be the bravest of all, a true chick of Ares.

EUELPIDES: Oh! noble chick!

PITHETAERUS: Because he is a god well suited to, live on the rocks. Come! into the air with you to help the workers who are building the wall; carry up rubble, strip yourself to mix the mortar, take up the hod, tumble down the ladder, if you like, post sentinels, keep the fire smouldering beneath the ashes, go round the walls, bell in hand, and go to sleep up there yourself; then despatch two heralds, one to the gods above, the other to mankind on earth and come back here.

EUELPIDES: As for yourself, remain here, and may the plague take you for a troublesome fellow!

(He departs.)

PITHETAERUS: Go, friend, go where I send you, for without you my orders cannot be obeyed. For myself, I want to sacrifice to the new god, and I am going to summon the priest who must preside at the ceremony. Slaves! slaves! bring forward the basket and the lustral water.

CHORUS *(singing)*: I do as you do, and I wish as you wish, and I implore you to address powerful and solemn prayers to the gods, and in addition to immolate a sheep as a token of our gratitude. Let us sing the Pythian chant in honour of the god, and let Chaeris accompany our voices.

PITHETAERUS *(to the flute-prayer)*: Enough! but, by Heracles! what is this? Great gods! I have seen many prodigious things, but I never saw a muzzled raven. *(The* Priest *arrives.)* Priest! it's high time! Sacrifice to the new gods.

211

PRIEST: I begin, but where is the man with the basket? Pray to the Hestia of the birds, to the kite, who presides over the hearth, and to all the god and goddess-birds who dwell in Olympus.

PITHETAERUS: Oh! Hawk, the sacred guardian of Sunium, oh, god of the storks!

PRIEST: . . . to the swan of Delos, to Leto the mother of the quails, and to Artemis, the goldfinch.

PITHETAERUS: It's no longer Artemis Colaenis, but Artemis the goldfinch.

PRIEST: . . . to Bacchus, the finch and Cybelé, the ostrich and the mother of the gods and mankind.

PITHETAERUS: Oh! sovereign ostrich Cybelé, mother of Cleocritus!

PRIEST: . . . to grant health and safety to the Nephelococcygians as well as to the dwellers in Chios.

PITHETAERUS: The dwellers in Chios! Ah! I am delighted they should be thus mentioned on all occasions.

PRIEST: . . . to the heroes, the birds, to the sons of heroes, to the porphyrion, the pelican, the spoon-bill, the redbreast, the grouse, the peacock, the horned-owl, the teal, the bittern, the stormy petrel, the fig-pecker, the titmouse.

PITHETAERUS: Stop! stop! you drive me crazy with your endless list. Why, wretch, to what sacred feast are you inviting the vultures and the sea-eagles? Don't you see that a single kite could easily carry off the lot at once? Begone, you and your fillets and all; I shall know how to complete the sacrifice by myself.

(The Priest departs.)

CHORUS *(singing)*: It is imperative that I sing another sacred chant for the rite of the lustral water, and that I invoke the immortals, or at least one of them, provided always that you have some suitable food to offer him; from what I see here, in the shape of gifts, there is naught whatever but horn and hair.

PITHETAERUS: Let us address our sacrifices and our prayers to the winged gods.

(A Poet enters.)

POET: Oh, Muse! celebrate happy Nephelococcygia in your hymns.

PITHETAERUS: What have we here? Where did you come from, tell me? Who are you?

POET: I am he whose language is sweeter than honey, the zealous slave of the Muses, as Homer has it.

PITHETAERUS: You a slave! and yet you wear your hair long?

POET: No, but the fact is all we poets are the assiduous slaves of the Muses, according to Homer.

PITHETAERUS: In truth your little cloak is quite holy too through zeal! But, poet, what ill wind drove you here?

POET: I have composed verses in honour of your Nephelococcygia, a host of splendid dithyrambs and parthenia worthy of Simonides himself.

PITHETAERUS: And when did you compose them? How long since?

POET: Oh! 'tis long, aye, very long, that I have sung in honour of this city.

PITHETAERUS: But I am only celebrating its foundation with this sacrifice; I have only just named it, as is done with little babies.

POET: "Just as the chargers fly with the speed of the wind, so does the voice of the Muses take its flight. Oh! thou noble founder of the town of Aetna, thou, whose name recalls the holy sacrifices, make us such gift as thy generous heart shall suggest."

(He puts out his hand.)

PITHETAERUS: He will drive us silly if we do not get rid of him by some present. *(To the* Priest's *acolyte)* Here! you, who have a fur as well as your tunic, take it off and give it to this clever poet. Come, take this fur; you look to me to be shivering with cold.

POET: My Muse will gladly accept this gift; but engrave these verses of Pindar's on your mind.

PITHETAERUS: Oh! what a pest! It's impossible then to get rid of him!

POET: "Straton wanders among the Scythian nomads, but has no linen garment. He is sad at only wearing an animal's pelt and no tunic." Do you get what I mean?

PITHETAERUS: I understand that you want me to offer you a tunic. Hi! you *(to the acolyte)*, take off yours; we must help the poet. Come, you, take it and get out.

POET: I am going, and these are the verses that I address to this city: "Phoebus of the golden throne, celebrate this shivery, freezing city; I have travelled through fruitful and snow-covered plains. Tralalá! Tralalá!"

(He departs.)

PITHETAERUS: What are you chanting us about frosts? Thanks to the tunic, you no longer fear them. Ah! By Zeus! I could not have believed this cursed fellow could so soon have learnt the way to our city. *(To a slave)* Come, take the lustral water and circle the altar. Let all keep silence!

(An Oracle-Monger *enters.)*

ORACLE-MONGER: Let not the goat be sacrificed.

PITHETAERUS: Who are you?

ORACLE-MONGER: Who am I? An oracle-monger.

PITHETAERUS: Get out!

ORACLE-MONGER: Wretched man, insult not sacred things. For there is an oracle of Bacis, which exactly applies to Nephelococcygia.

PITHETAERUS: Why did you not reveal it to me before I founded my city?

ORACLE-MONGER: The divine spirit was against it.

PITHETAERUS: Well, I suppose there's nothing to do but hear the terms of the oracle.

ORACLE-MONGER: "But when the wolves and the white crows shall dwell together between Corinth and Sicyon . . ."

PITHETAERUS: But how do the Corinthians concern me?

ORACLE-MONGER: It is the regions of the air that Bacis indicates in this manner. "They must first sacrifice a white fleeced goat to Pandora, and give the prophet who first reveals my words a good cloak and new sandals."

PITHETAERUS: Does it say sandals there?

ORACLE-MONGER: Look at the book. "And besides this a goblet of wine and a good share of the entrails of the victim."

PITHETAERUS: Of the entrails — does it say that?

ORACLE-MONGER: Look at the book. "If you do as I command, divine youth, you shall be an eagle among the clouds; if not, you shall be neither turtle-dove, nor eagle, nor woodpecker."

PITHETAERUS: Does it say all that?

ORACLE-MONGER: Look at the book.

PITHETAERUS: This oracle in no sort of way resembles the one Apollo dictated to me: "If an impostor comes without invitation to annoy you during the sacrifice and to demand a share of the victim, apply a stout stick to his ribs."

ORACLE-MONGER: You are drivelling.

PITHETAERUS: Look at the book. "And don't spare him, were he an eagle from out of the clouds, were it Lampon himself or the great Diopithes."

ORACLE-MONGER: Does it say that?

PITHETAERUS: Look at the book and go and hang yourself.

ORACLE-MONGER: Oh! unfortunate wretch that I am.

(He departs.)

PITHETAERUS: Away with you, and take your prophecies elsewhere.

(Enter Meton, *with surveying instruments.)*

METON: I have come to you . . .

PITHETAERUS *(interrupting):* Yet another pest! What have you come to do? What's your plan? What's the purpose of your journey? Why these splendid buskins?

METON: I want to survey the plains of the air for you and to parcel them into lots.

PITHETAERUS: In the name of the gods, who are you?

METON: Who am I? Meton, known throughout Greece and at Colonus.

PITHETAERUS: What are these things?

METON: Tools for measuring the air. In truth, the spaces in the air have precisely the form of a furnace. With bent ruler I draw a line from top to bottom; from one of its points I describe a circle with the compass. Do you understand?

PITHETAERUS: Not in the least.

METON: With the straight ruler I set to work to inscribe a square within this circle; in its centre will be the market-place, into which all the straight streets will lead, converging to this centre like a star, which, although only orbicular, sends forth its rays in a straight line from all sides.

PITHETAERUS: A regular Thales! Meton . . .

METON: What d'you want with me?

PITHETAERUS: I want to give you a proof of my friendship. Use your legs.

METON: Why, what have I to fear?

PITHETAERUS: It's the same here as in Sparta. Strangers are driven away, and blows rain down as thick as hail.

METON: Is there sedition in your city?

PITHETAERUS: No, certainly not.

METON: What's wrong then?

PITHETAERUS: We are agreed to sweep all quacks and impostors far from our borders.

METON: Then I'll be going.

PITHETAERUS: I warned you, now, be off, and do your surveying somewhere else.

(He beats him.)

METON: Oh, woe! oh, woe!

(Meton *takes to his heels. He is no sooner gone than an* Inspector *arrives.)*

INSPECTOR: Where are the Proxeni?

215

PITHETAERUS: Who is this Sardanapalus?

INSPECTOR: I have been appointed by lot to come to Nephelococcygia as inspector.

PITHETAERUS: An inspector! and who sends you here, you rascal?

INSPECTOR: A decree of Teleas.

PITHETAERUS: Will you just pocket your salary, do nothing, and get out?

INSPECTOR: Indeed I will; I am urgently needed to be at Athens, to attend the Assembly; for I am charged with the interests of Pharnaces.

PITHETAERUS: Take it then, and get on your way. This is your salary.

(He beats him.)

INSPECTOR: What does this mean?

PITHETAERUS: This is the assembly where you have to defend Pharnaces.

INSPECTOR: You shall testify that they dare to strike me, the inspector.

PITHETAERUS: Are you not going to get out with your urns? It's not to be believed; they send us inspectors before we have so much as paid sacrifice to the gods.

(The Inspector *goes into hiding. A* Dealer in Decrees *arrives.)*

DEALER IN DECREES: "The Nephelococcygians shall adopt the same to the Athenian . . ."

PITHETAERUS: What trouble now? What book is that?

DEALER IN DECREES: I am a dealer in decrees, and I have come here to sell you the new laws.

PITHETAERUS: Which?

DEALER IN DECREES: "The Nephelococcygians shall adopt the same weights, measures and decrees as the Olophyxians."

PITHETAERUS: And you shall soon be imitating the Ototyxians.

(He beats him.)

DEALER IN DECREES: Ow! what are you doing?

PITHETAERUS: Now will you get out of here with your decrees? For I am going to let you see some severe ones.

(The Dealer in Decrees *departs; the* Inspector *comes out of hiding.)*

INSPECTOR *(returning)*: I summon Pithetaerus for outrage for the month of Munychion.

PITHETAERUS: Ha! my friend! are you still there?

(The Dealer in Decrees *also returns.)*

DEALER IN DECREES: "Should anyone drive away the magistrates and not receive them, according to the decree duly posted . . ."

PITHETAERUS: What! rascal! you are back too?

(He rushes at him.)

INSPECTOR: Woe to you! I'll have you condemned to a fine of ten thousand drachmae.

PITHETAERUS: And I'll smash your urns.

INSPECTOR: Do you recall that evening when you crapped on the column where the decrees are posted?

PITHETAERUS: Here! let him be seized. *(The* Inspector *runs off.)* Why, don't you want to stay any longer? But let us get indoors as quick as possible; we will sacrifice the goat inside.

FIRST SEMI-CHORUS *(singing)*: Henceforth it is to me that mortals must address their sacrifices and their prayers. Nothing escapes my sight nor my might. My glance embraces the universe, I preserve the fruit in the flower by destroying the thousand kinds of voracious insects the soil produces, which attack the trees and feed on the germ when it has scarcely formed in the calyx; I destroy those who ravage the balmy terrace gardens like a deadly plague; all these gnawing crawling creatures perish beneath the lash of my wing.

LEADER OF THE FIRST SEMI-CHORUS: I hear it proclaimed everywhere: "A talent for him who shall kill Diagoras of Melos, and a talent for him who destroys one of the dead tyrants." We likewise wish to make our proclamation "A talent to him among you who shall kill Philocrates, the Struthian; four, if he brings him to us alive. For this Philocrates skewers the finches together and sells them at the rate of an obolus for seven. He tortures the thrushes by blowing them out, so that they may look bigger, sticks their own feathers into the nostrils of blackbirds, and collects pigeons, which he shuts up and forces them, fastened in a net, to decoy others." That is what we wish to proclaim. And if anyone is keeping birds shut up in his yard, let him hasten to let them loose; those who disobey shall be seized by the birds and we shall put them in chains, so that in their turn they may decoy other men.

SECOND SEMI-CHORUS *(singing)*: Happy indeed is the race of winged birds who need no cloak in winter! Neither do I fear the relentless rays of the fiery dog-days; when the divine grasshopper,

217

intoxicated with the sunlight, as noon is burning the ground, is breaking out into shrill melody; my home is beneath the foliage in the flowery meadows. I winter in deep caverns, where I frolic with the mountain nymphs, while in spring I despoil the gardens of the Graces and gather the white, virgin berry on the myrtle bushes.

LEADER OF THE SECOND SEMI-CHORUS: I want now to speak to the judges about the prize they are going to award; if they are favourable to us, we will load them with benefits far greater than those Paris received. Firstly, the owls of Laurium, which every judge desires above all things, shall never be wanting to you; you shall see them homing with you, building their nests in your money-bags and laying coins. Besides, you shall be housed like the gods, for we shall erect gables over your dwellings; if you hold some public post and want to do a little pilfering, we will give you the sharp claws of a hawk. Are you dining in town, we will provide you with stomachs as capacious as a bird's crop. But, if your reward is against us, don't fail to have metal covers fashioned for yourselves, like those they place over statues; else, look out! for the day you wear a white tunic all the birds will soil it with their droppings.

PITHETAERUS: Birds! the sacrifice is propitious. But I see no messenger coming from the wall to tell us what is happening. Ah! here comes one running himself out of breath as though he were in the Olympic stadium.

MESSENGER (running back and forth): Where, where, where is he? Where, where, where is he? Where, where, where is he? Where is Pithetaerus, our leader?

PITHETAERUS: Here am I.

MESSENGER: The wall is finished.

PITHETAERUS: That's good news.

MESSENGER: It's a most beautiful, a most magnificent work of art. The wall is so broad that Proxenides, the Braggartian, and Theogenes could pass each other in their chariots, even if they were drawn by steeds as big as the Trojan horse.

PITHETAERUS: That's fine!

MESSENGER: Its length is one hundred stadia; I measured it myself.

PITHETAERUS: A decent length, by Posidon! And who built such a wall?

MESSENGER: Birds — birds only; they had neither Egyptian brickmaker, nor stone-mason, nor carpenter; the birds did it all themselves; I could hardly believe my eyes. Thirty thousand cranes from Libya with a supply of stones, intended for the foundations. The water-rails chiselled them with their beaks. Ten thousand

218

storks where busy making bricks; plovers and other water fowl
carried water into the air.

PITHETAERUS: And who carried the mortar?

MESSENGER: Herons, in hods.

PITHETAERUS: But how could they put the mortar into the hods?

MESSENGER: Oh! it was a truly clever invention; the geese used their
feet like spades; they buried them in the pile of mortar and
then emptied them into the hods.

PITHETAERUS: Ah! to what use cannot feet be put?

MESSENGER: You should have seen how eagerly the ducks carried bricks.
To complete the tale, the swallows came flying to the work,
their beaks full of mortar and their trowels on their backs, just
the way little children are carried.

PITHETAERUS: Who would want paid servants after this? But tell me,
who did the woodwork?

MESSENGER: Birds again, and clever carpenters too, the pelicans, for
they squared up the gates with their beaks in such a fashion
that one would have thought they were using axes; the noise
was just like a dockyard. Now the whole wall is tight everywhere,
securely bolted and well guarded; it is patrolled, bell in hand;
the sentinels stand everywhere and beacons burn on the towers.
But I must run off to clean myself; the rest is your business.

(He departs.)

LEADER OF THE CHORUS *(to* Pithetaerus*)*: Well! what do you say to
it? Are you not astonished at the wall being completed so quickly?

PITHETAERUS: By the gods, yes, and with good reason. It's really not
to be believed. But here comes another messenger from the wall
to bring us some further news! What a fighting look he has!

SECOND MESSENGER *(rushing in)*: Alas! alas! alas! alas! alas! alas!

PITHETAERUS: What's the matter?

SECOND MESSENGER: A horrible outrage has occurred; a god sent by
Zeus has passed through our gates and has penetrated the realms
of the air without the knowledge of the jays, who are on guard
in the daytime.

PITHETAERUS: It's a terrible and criminal deed. What god was it?

SECOND MESSENGER: We don't know that. All we know is, that he has
got wings.

PITHETAERUS: Why were not patrolmen sent against him at once?

SECOND MESSENGER: We have despatched thirty thousand hawks of the
legion of Mounted Archers. All the hook-clawed birds are
moving against him, the kestrel, the buzzard, the vulture, the

219

great-horned owl, they clave the air so that it resounds with the flapping of their wings; they are looking everywhere for the god, who cannot be far away; indeed, if I mistake not, he is coming from yonder side.

PITHETAERUS: To arms, all, with slings and bows! This way, all our soldiers; shoot and strike! Some one give me a sling!

CHORUS (singing): War, a terrible war is breaking out between us and the gods! Come, let each one guard Air, the son of Erebus, in which the clouds float. Take care no immortal enters it without your knowledge.

LEADER OF THE CHORUS: Scan all sides with your glance. Hark! methinks I can hear the rustle of the swift wings of a god from heaven.

(The Machine brings in Iris, in the form of a young girl.)

PITHETAERUS: Hi! you woman! where, where, where are you flying to? Halt, don't stir! keep motionless! not a beat of your wing. (She pauses in her flight.) Who are you and from what country? You must say whence you come.

IRIS: I come from the abode of the Olympian gods.

PITHETAERUS: What's your name, ship or head-dress?

IRIS: I am swift Iris.

PITHETAERUS: Paralus or Salaminia?

IRIS: What do you mean?

PITHETAERUS: Let a buzzard rush at her and seize her.

IRIS: Seize me? But what do all these insults mean?

PITHETAERUS: Woe to you!

IRIS: I do not understand it.

PITHETAERUS: By which gate did you pass through the wall, wretched woman?

IRIS: By which gate? Why, great gods, I don't know.

PITHETAERUS: You hear how she holds us in derision. Did you present yourself to the officers in command of the jays? You don't answer. Have you a permit, bearing the seal of the storks?

IRIS: Am I dreaming?

PITHETAERUS: Did you get one?

IRIS: Are you mad?

PITHETAERUS: No head-bird gave you a safe-conduct?

IRIS: A safe-conduct to me. You poor fool!

PITHETAERUS: Ah! and so you slipped into this city on the sly and into these realms of air-land that don't belong to you.

IRIS: And what other roads can the gods travel?

PITHETAERUS: By Zeus! I know nothing about that, not I. But they won't pass this way. And you still dare to complain? Why, if you were treated according to your deserts, no Iris would ever have more justly suffered death.

IRIS: I am immortal.

PITHETAERUS: You would have died nevertheless. — Oh! that would be truly intolerable! What! should the universe obey us and the gods alone continue their insolence and not understand that they must submit to the law of the strongest in their due turn? But tell me, where are you flying to?

IRIS: I? The messenger of Zeus to mankind, I am going to tell them to sacrifice sheep and oxen on the altars and to fill their streets with the rich smoke of burning fat.

PITHETAERUS: Of which gods are you speaking?

IRIS: Of which? Why, of ourselves, the gods of heaven.

PITHETAERUS: You, gods?

IRIS: Are there others then?

PITHETAERUS: Men now adore the birds as gods, and it's to them, by Zeus, that they must offer sacrifices, and not to Zeus at all!

IRIS *(in tragic style)*: Oh! fool! fool! Rouse not the wrath of the gods, for it is terrible indeed. Armed with the brand of Zeus, Justice would annihilate your race; the lightning would strike you as it did Licymnius and consume both your body and the portions of your palace.

PITHETAERUS: Here! that's enough tall talk. Just listen and keep quiet! Do you take me for a Lydian or a Phrygian and think to frighten me with your big words? Know, that if Zeus worries me again, I shall go at the head of my eagles, who are armed with lightning, and reduce his dwelling and that of Amphion to cinders. I shall send more than six hundred porphyrions clothed in leopards' skins up to heaven against him; and formerly a single Porphyrion gave him enough to do. As for you, his messenger, if you annoy me, I shall begin by getting between your thighs, and even though you are Iris, you will be surprised at the erection the old man can produce; it's three times as good as the ram on a ship's prow!

IRIS: May you perish, you wretch, you and your infamous words!

PITHETAERUS: Won't you get out of here quickly? Come, stretch your wings or look out for squalls!

IRIS: If my father does not punish you for your insults . . .

(The Machine takes Iris away.)

PITHETAERUS: Ha! . . . but just you be off elsewhere to roast younger folk than us with your lightning.

221

CHORUS (singing): We forbid gods, the sons of Zeus, to pass through our city and the mortals to send them the smoke of their sacrifices by this road.

PITHETAERUS: It's odd that the messenger we sent to the mortals has never returned.

(The Herald *enters, wearing a golden garland on his head.)*

HERALD: Oh! blessed Pithetaerus, very wise, very illustrious, very gracious, thrice happy, very . . . Come, prompt me, somebody, do.

PITHETAERUS: Get to your story!

HERALD: All peoples are filled with admiration for your wisdom, and they award you this golden crown.

PITHETAERUS: I accept it. But tell me, why do the people admire me?

HERALD: Oh you, who have founded so illustrious a city in the air, you know not in what esteem men hold you and how many there are who burn with desire to dwell in it. Before your city was built, all men had a mania for Sparta; long hair and fasting were held in honour, men went dirty like Socrates and carried staves. Now all is changed. Firstly, as soon as it's dawn, they all spring out of bed together to go and seek their food, the same as you do; then they fly off towards the notices and finally devour the decrees. The bird-madness is so clear that many actually bear the names of birds. There is a halting victualler, who styles himself the partridge; Menippus calls himself the swallow; Opuntius the one-eyed crow; Philocles the lark; Theogenes the fox-goose; Lycurgus the ibis; Chaerephon the bat; Syracosius the magpie; Midias the quail; indeed he looks like a quail that has been hit hard on the head. Out of love for the birds they repeat all the songs which concern the swallow, the teal, the goose or the pigeon; in each verse you see wings, or at all events a few feathers. This is what is happening down there. Finally, there are more than ten thousand folk who are coming here from earth to ask you for feathers and hooked claws; so, mind you supply yourself with wings for the immigrants.

PITHETAERUS: Ah! by Zeus, there's no time for idling. *(To some slaves)* Go as quick as possible and fill every hamper, every basket you can find with wings. Manes will bring them to me outside the walls, where I will welcome those who present themselves.

CHORUS (singing): This town will soon be inhabited by a crowd of men. Fortune favours us alone and thus they have fallen in love with our city.

222

PITHETAERUS (to the slave Manes, who brings in a basket full of wings): Come, hurry up and bring them along.

CHORUS (singing): Will not man find here everything that can please him — wisdom, love, the divine Graces, the sweet face of gentle peace?

PITHETAERUS (as Manes comes in with another basket): Oh! you lazy servant! won't you hurry yourself?

CHORUS (singing): Let a basket of wings be brought speedily. Come, beat him as I do, and put some life into him; he is as lazy as an ass.

PITHETAERUS: Aye, Manes is a great craven.

CHORUS (singing): Begin by putting this heap of wings in order; divide them in three parts according to the birds from whom they came; the singing, the prophetic and the aquatic birds; then you must take care to distribute them to the men according to their character.

PITHETAERUS (to Manes, who is bringing in another basket): Oh! by the kestrels! I can keep my hands off no longer; you are too slow and lazy altogether.

(He hits Manes, who runs away. A young Parricide enters.)

PARRICIDE (singing): Oh! might I but become an eagle, who soars in the skies! Oh! might I fly above the azure waves of the barren sea!

PITHETAERUS: Ha! it would seem the news was true; I hear someone coming who talks of wings.

PARRICIDE: Nothing is more charming than to fly; I am bird-mad and fly towards you, for I want to live with you and to obey your laws.

PITHETAERUS: Which laws? The birds have many laws.

PARRICIDE: All of them; but the one that pleases me most is that among the birds it is considered a fine thing to peck and strangle one's father.

PITHETAERUS: Yes, by Zeus! according to us, he who dares to strike his father, while still a chick, is a brave fellow.

PARRICIDE: And therefore I want to dwell here, for I want to strangle my father and inherit his wealth.

PITHETAERUS: But we have also an ancient law written in the code of the storks, which runs thus, "When the stork father has reared his young and has taught them to fly, the young must in their turn support the father."

PARRICIDE (petulantly): It's hardly worth while coming all this distance to be compelled to keep my father!

PITHETAERUS: No, no, young friend, since you have come to us with such willingness, I am going to give you these black wings, as though you were an orphan bird; furthermore, some good advice, that I received myself in infancy. Don't strike your father, but take these wings in one hand and these spurs in the other; imagine you have a cock's crest on your head and go and mount and fight; live on your pay and respect your father's life. You're a gallant fellow! Very well, then! Fly to Thrace and fight.

PARRICIDE: By Bacchus! You're right; I will follow your counsel.

PITHETAERUS: It's acting wisely, by Zeus.

(The Parricide *departs, and the dithyrambic poet* Cinesias *arrives.)*

CINESIAS *(singing)*: "On my light pinions I soar off to Olympus; in its capricious flight my Muse flutters along the thousand paths of poetry in turn . . ."

PITHETAERUS: This is a fellow will need a whole shipload of wings.

CINESIAS *(singing)*: ". . . and being fearless and vigorous, it is seeking fresh outlet."

PITHETAERUS: Welcome, Cinesias, you lime-wood man! Why have you come here twisting your game leg in circles?

CINESIAS *(singing)*: "I want to become a bird, a tuneful nightingale."

PITHETAERUS: Enough of that sort of ditty. Tell me what you want.

CINESIAS: Give me wings and I will fly into the topmost airs to gather fresh songs in the clouds, in the midst of the vapours and the fleecy snow.

PITHETAERUS: Gather songs in the clouds?

CINESIAS: 'Tis on them the whole of our latter-day art depends. The most brilliant dithyrambs are those that flap their wings in empty space and are clothed in mist and dense obscurity. To appreciate this, just listen.

PITHETAERUS: Oh! no, no, no!

CINESIAS: By Hermes! but indeed you shall. *(He sings.)* "I shall travel through thine ethereal empire like a winged bird, who cleaveth space with his long neck . . ."

PITHETAERUS: Stop! Way enough!

CINESIAS: ". . . as I soar over the seas, carried by the breath of the winds . . ."

PITHETAERUS: By Zeus! I'll cut your breath short.

(He picks up a pair of wings and begins trying to stop Cinesias' *mouth with them.)*

CINESIAS *(running away)*: ". . . now rushing along the tracks of Notus,

now nearing Boreas across the infinite wastes of the ether."
Ah! old man, that's a pretty and clever idea truly!

PITHETAERUS: What! are you not delighted to be cleaving the air?

CINESIAS: To treat a dithyrambic poet, for whom the tribes dispute with each other, in this style!

PITHETAERUS: Will you stay with us and form a chorus of winged birds as slender as Leotrophides for the Cecropid tribe?

CINESIAS: You are making game of me, that's clear; but know that I shall never leave you in peace if I do not have wings wherewith to traverse the air.

(Cinesias *departs and an* Informer *arrives.*)

INFORMER: What are these birds with downy feathers, who look so pitiable to me? Tell me, oh swallow with the long dappled wings.

PITHETAERUS: Oh! it's a regular invasion that threatens us. Here comes another one, humming along.

INFORMER: Swallow with the long dappled wings, once more I summon you.

PITHETAERUS: It's his cloak I believe he's addressing; it stands in great need of the swallow's return.

INFORMER: Where is he who gives out wings to all comers?

PITHETAERUS: Here I am, but you must tell me for what purpose you want them.

INFORMER: Ask no questions. I want wings, and wings I must have.

PITHETAERUS: Do you want to fly straight to Pellené?

INFORMER: I? Why, I am an accuser of the islands, an informer . . .

PITHETAERUS: A fine trade, truly!

INFORMER: . . . a hatcher of lawsuits. Hence I have great need of wings to prowl round the cities and drag them before justice.

PITHETAERUS: Would you do this better if you had wings?

INFORMER: No, but I should no longer fear the pirates; I should return with the cranes, loaded with a supply of lawsuits by way of ballast.

PITHETAERUS: So it seems, despite all your youthful vigour, you make it your trade to denounce strangers?

INFORMER: Well, and why not? I don't know how to dig.

PITHETAERUS: But, by Zeus! there are honest ways of gaining a living at your age without all this infamous trickery.

INFORMER: My friend, I am asking you for wings, not for words.

PITHETAERUS: It's just my words that give you wings.

INFORMER: And how can you give a man wings with your words?

PITHETAERUS: They all start this way.

INFORMER: How?

PITHETAERUS: Have you not often heard the father say to young men in the barbers' shops, "It's astonishing how Diitrephes' advice has made my son fly to horse-riding." — "Mine," says another, "has flown towards tragic poetry on the wings of his imagination."

INFORMER: So that words give wings?

PITHETAERUS: Undoubtedly; words give wings to the mind and make a man soar to heaven. Thus I hope that my wise words will give you wings to fly to some less degrading trade.

INFORMER: But I do not want to.

PITHETAERUS: What do you reckon on doing then?

INFORMER: I won't belie my breeding; from generation to generation we have lived by informing. Quick, therefore, give me quickly some light, swift hawk or kestrel wings, so that I may summon the islanders, sustain the accusation here, and haste back there again on flying pinions.

PITHETAERUS: I see. In this way the stranger will be condemned even before he appears.

INFORMER: That's just it.

PITHETAERUS: And while he is on his way here by sea, you will be flying to the islands to despoil him of his property.

INFORMER: You've hit it, precisely; I must whirl hither and thither like a perfect humming-top.

PITHETAERUS: I catch the idea. Wait, I've got some fine Corcyraean wings. How do you like them?

INFORMER: Oh! woe is me! Why, it's a whip!

PITHETAERUS: No, no; these are the wings, I tell you, that make the top spin.

INFORMER (as Pithetaerus lashes him): Oh! oh! oh!

PITHETAERUS: Take your flight, clear off, you miserable cur, or you will soon see what comes of quibbling and lying. (The Informer flees. To his slaves) Come, let us gather up our wings and withdraw.

(The baskets are taken away.)

CHORUS (singing): In my ethereal flights I have seen many things new and strange and wondrous beyond belief. There is a tree called Cleonymus belonging to an unknown species; it has no heart, is good for nothing and is as tall as it is cowardly. In springtime it shoots forth calumnies instead of buds and in autumn it strews the ground with bucklers in place of leaves.

Far away in the regions of darkness, where no ray of light ever enters, there is a country, where men sit at the table of the heroes and dwell with them always — except in the evening. Should any mortal meet the hero Orestes at night, he would soon be stripped and covered with blows from head to foot.

(Prometheus *enters, masked to conceal his identity.*)

PROMETHEUS: Ah! by the gods! if only Zeus does not espy me! Where is Pithetaerus?

PITHETAERUS: Ha! what is this? A masked man!

PROMETHEUS: Can you see any god behind me?

PITHETAERUS: No, none. But who are you, pray?

PROMETHEUS: What's the time, please?

PITHETAERUS: The time? Why, it's past noon. Who are you?

PROMETHEUS: Is it the fall of day? Is it no later than that?

PITHETAERUS: This is getting dull!

PROMETHEUS: What is Zeus doing? Is he dispersing the clouds or gathering them?

PITHETAERUS: Watch out of yourself!

PROMETHEUS: Come, I will raise my mask.

PITHETAERUS: Ah! my dear Prometheus!

PROMETHEUS: Sh! Sh! speak lower!

PITHETAERUS: Why, what's the matter, Prometheus?

PROMETHEUS: Sh! Sh! Don't call me by my name; you will be my ruin, if Zeus should see me here. But, if you want me to tell you how things are going in heaven, take this umbrella and shield me, so that the gods don't see me.

PITHETAERUS: I can recognize Prometheus in this cunning trick. Come, quick then, and fear nothing; speak on.

PROMETHEUS: Then listen.

PITHETAERUS: I am listening, proceed!

PROMETHEUS: Zeus is done for.

PITHETAERUS: Ah! and since when, pray?

PROMETHEUS: Since you founded this city in the air. There is not a man who now sacrifices to the gods: the smoke of the victims no longer reaches us. Not the smallest offering comes! We fast as though it were the festival of Demeter. The barbarian gods, who are dying of hunger, are bawling like Illyrians and threaten to make an armed descent upon Zeus, if he does not open markets where joints of the victims are sold.

PITHETAERUS: What! there are other gods besides you, barbarian gods who dwell above Olympus?

PROMETHEUS: If there were no barbarian gods, who would be the patron of Execestides?

PITHETAERUS: And what is the name of these gods?

PROMETHEUS: Their name? Why, the Triballi.

PITHETAERUS: Ah, indeed! 'tis from that no doubt that we derive the word 'tribulation.'

PROMETHEUS: Most likely. But one thing I can tell you for certain, namely, that Zeus and the celestial Triballi are going to send deputies here to sue for peace. Now don't you treat with them, unless Zeus restores the sceptre to the birds and gives you Basileia in marriage.

PITHETAERUS: Who is this Basileia?

PROMETHEUS: A very young damsel, who makes the lightning for Zeus; all things come from her, wisdom, good laws, virtue, the fleet, calumnies, the public paymaster and the triobolus.

PITHETAERUS: Ah! then she is a sort of general manager to the god.

PROMETHEUS: Yes, precisely. If he gives you her for your wife, yours will be the almighty power. That is what I have come to tell you; for you know my constant and habitual goodwill towards men.

PITHETAERUS: Oh, yes! it's thanks to you that we roast our meat.

PROMETHEUS: I hate the gods, as you know.

PITHETAERUS: Aye, by Zeus, you have always detested them.

PROMETHEUS: Towards them I am a veritable Timon; but I must return in all haste, so give me the umbrella; if Zeus should see me from up there, he would think I was escorting one of the Canephori.

PITHETAERUS: Wait, take this stool as well.

(Prometheus *leaves*. Pithetaerus *goes into the thicket*.)

CHORUS *(singing)*: Near by the land of the Sciapodes there is a marsh, from the borders whereof the unwashed Socrates evokes the souls of men. Pisander came one day to see his soul, which he had left there when still alive. He offered a little victim, a camel slit his throat and, following the example of Odysseus, stepped one pace backwards. Then that bat of a Chaerephon came up from hell to drink the camel's blood.

(Posidon *enters, accompanied by* Heracles *and* Triballus.)

POSIDON: This is the city of Nephelococcygia, to which we come as ambassadors. *(To* Triballus*)* Hi! what are you up to? you are throwing your cloak over the left shoulder. Come, fling it quick

228

over the right! And why, pray, does it draggle in this fashion? Have you ulcers to hide like Laespodias? Oh! democracy! whither, oh! whither are you leading us? Is it possible that the gods have chosen such an envoy? You are undisturbed? Ugh! you cursed savage! you are by far the most barbarous of all the gods. — Tell me, Heracles, what are we going to do?

HERACLES: I have already told you that I want to strangle the fellow who dared to wall us out.

POSIDON: But, my friend, we are envoys of peace.

HERACLES: All the more reason why I wish to strangle him.

(Pithetaerus *comes out of the thicket, followed by slaves, who are carrying various kitchen utensils; one of them sets up a table on which he places poultry dressed for roasting.*)

PITHETAERUS: Hand me the cheese-grater; bring me the silphium for sauce; pass me the cheese and watch the coals.

HERACLES: Mortal! we who greet you are three gods.

PITHETAERUS: Wait a bit till I have prepared my silphium pickle.

HERACLES: What are these meats?

PITHETAERUS: These are birds that have been punished with death for attacking the people's friends.

HERACLES: And you are going to season them before answering us?

PITHETAERUS *(looking up from his work for the first time)*: Ah! Heracles! welcome, welcome! What's the matter?

POSIDON: The gods have sent us here as ambassadors to treat for peace.

PITHETAERUS *(ignoring this)*: There's no more oil in the flask.

HERACLES: And yet the birds must be thoroughly basted with it.

POSIDON: We have no interest to serve in fighting you; as for you, be friends and we promise that you shall always have rain-water in your pools and the warmest of warm weather. So far as these points go we are plenipotentiaries.

PITHETAERUS: We have never been the aggressors, and even now we are as well disposed for peace as yourselves, provided you agree to one equitable condition, namely, that Zeus yield his sceptre to the birds. If only this is agreed to, I invite the ambassadors to dinner.

HERACLES: That's good enough for me. I vote for peace.

POSIDON: You wretch! you are nothing but a fool and a glutton. Do you want to dethrone your own father?

PITHETAERUS: What an error. Why, the gods will be much more powerful if the birds govern the earth. At present the mortals are hidden beneath the clouds, escape your observation, and commit

229

perjury in your name; but if you had the birds for your allies, and a man, after having sworn by the crow and Zeus, should fail to keep his oath, the crow would dive down upon him unawares and pluck out his eye.

POSIDON: Well thought of, by Posidon!

HERACLES: My notion too.

PITHETAERUS (to Triballus): And you, what's your opinion?

TRIBALLUS: *Nabaisatreu.*

PITHETAERUS: D'you see? he also approves. But listen, here is another thing in which we can serve you. If a man vows to offer a sacrifice to some god, and then procrastinates, pretending that the gods can wait, and thus does not keep his word, we shall punish his stinginess.

POSIDON: Ah! and how?

PITHETAERUS: While he is counting his money or is in the bath, a kite will relieve him, before he knows it, either in coin or in clothes, of the value of a couple of sheep, and carry it to the god.

HERACLES: I vote for restoring them the sceptre.

POSIDON: Ask Triballus.

HERACLES: Hi! Triballus, do you want a thrashing?

TRIBALLUS: Sure, bashum head withum stick.

HERACLES: He says, "Right willingly."

POSIDON: If that be the opinion of both of you, why, I consent too.

HERACLES: Very well! we accord you sceptre.

PITHETAERUS: Ah! I was nearly forgetting another condition. I will leave Heré to Zeus, but only if the young Basileia is given me in marriage.

POSIDON: Then you don't want peace. Let us withdraw.

PITHETAERUS: It matters mighty little to me. Cook, look to the gravy.

HERACLES: What an odd fellow this Posidon is! Where are you off to? Are we going to war about a woman?

POSIDON: What else is there to do?

HERACLES: What else? Why, conclude peace.

POSIDON: Oh! you blockhead! do you always want to be fooled? Why, you are seeking your own downfall. If Zeus were to die, after having yielded them the sovereignty, you would be ruined, for you are the heir of all the wealth he will leave behind.

PITHETAERUS: Oh! by the gods! how he is cajoling you. Step aside, that I may have a word with you. Your uncle is getting the better of you, my poor friend. The law will not allow you an obolus of the paternal property, for you are a bastard and not a legitimate child.

HERACLES: I a bastard? What's that you tell me?

PITHETAERUS: Why, certainly; are you not born of a stranger woman? Besides, is not Athené recognized as Zeus' sole heiress? And no daughter would be that, if she had a legitimate brother.

HERACLES: But what if my father wished to give me his property on his death-bed, even though I be a bastard?

PITHETAERUS: The law forbids it, and this same Posidon would be the first to lay claim to his wealth, in virtue of being his legitimate brother. Listen; thus runs Solon's law: "A bastard shall not inherit, if there are legitimate children; and if there are no legitimate children, the property shall pass to the nearest kin."

HERACLES: And I get nothing whatever of the paternal property?

PITHETAERUS: Absolutely nothing. But tell me, has your father had you entered on the registers of his phratry?

HERACLES: No, and I have long been surprised at the omission.

PITHETAERUS: Why do you shake your fist at heaven? Do you want to fight? Why, be on my side, I will make you a king and will feed you on bird's milk and honey.

HERACLES: Your further condition seems fair to me. I cede you the young damsel.

POSIDON: But I, I vote against this opinion.

PITHETAERUS: Then it all depends on the Triballus. (To the Triballus) What do you say?

TRIBALLUS: Givum bird pretty gel bigum queen.

HERACLES: He says give her.

POSIDON: Why no, he does not say anything of the sort, or else, like the swallows he does not know how to walk.

PITHETAERUS: Exactly so. Does he not say she must be given to the swallows?

POSIDON (resignedly): All right, you two arrange the matter; make peace, since you wish it so; I'll hold my tongue.

HERACLES: We are of a mind to grant you all that you ask. But come up there with us to receive Basileia and the celestial bounty.

PITHETAERUS: Here are birds already dressed, and very suitable for a nuptial feast.

HERACLES: You go and, if you like, I will stay here to roast them.

PITHETAERUS: You to roast them? you are too much the glutton; come along with us.

HERACLES: Ah! how well I would have treated myself!

PITHETAERUS: Let some one bring me a beautiful and magnificent tunic for the weding.

(The tunic is brought. Pithetaerus and the three gods depart.)

CHORUS (singing): At Phanae, near the Clepsydra, there dwells a people who have neither faith nor law, the Englottogastors, who reap, sow, pluck the vines and the figs with their tongues; they belong to a barbaric race, and among them the Philippi and the Gorgiases are to be found; 'tis these Englottogastorian Phillippi who introduced the custom all over Attica of cutting out the tongue separately at sacrifices.

(A Messenger *enters.)*

MESSENGER *(in tragic style)*: Oh, you, whose unbounded happiness I cannot express in words, thrice happy race of airy birds, receive your king in your fortunate dwellings. More brilliant than the brightest star that illumes the earth, he is approaching his glittering golden palace; the sun itself does not shine with more dazzling glory. He is entering with his bride at his side, whose beauty no human tongue can express; in his hand he brandishes the lightning, the winged shaft of Zeus; perfumes of unspeakable sweetness pervade the ethereal realm. 'Tis a glorious spectacle to see the clouds of incense wafting in light whirlwinds before the breath of the zephyr! But here he is himself. Divine Muse! let thy sacred lips begin with songs of happy omen.

(Pithetaerus *enters, with a crown on his head;*
he is accompanied by Basileia.)

CHORUS *(singing)*: Fall back! to the right! to the left! advance! Fly around this happy mortal, whom Fortune loads with her blessings. Oh! oh! what grace! what beauty! Oh, marriage so auspicious for our city! All honour to this man! 'tis through him that the birds are called to such glorious destinies. Let your nuptial hymns, your nuptial songs, greet him and his Basileia! 'Twas in the midst of such festivities that the Fates formerly united Olympian Heré to the King who governs the gods from the summit of his inaccessible throne. Oh! Hymen! oh! Hymenaeus! Rosy Eros with the golden wings held the reins and guided the chariot; 'twas he, who presided over the union of Zeus and the fortunate Heré. Oh! Hymen! oh! Himenaeus!

PITHETAERUS: I am delighted with your songs, I applaud your verses. Now celebrate the thunder that shakes the earth, the flaming lightning of Zeus and the terrible flashing thunderbolt.

CHORUS *(singing)*: Oh, thou golden flash of the lightning! oh, ye divine shafts of flame, that Zeus has hitherto shot forth! Oh, ye rolling thunders, that bring down the rain! 'Tis by the order of our king that ye shall now stagger the earth! Oh, Hymen! 'tis through thee

232

that he commands the universe and that he makes Basileia, whom he has robbed from Zeus, take her seat at his side. Oh! Hymen! oh! Hymenaeus!

PITHETAERUS *(singing)*: Let all the winged tribes of our fellow-citizens follow the bridal couple to the palace of Zeus and to the nuptial couch! Stretch forth your hands, my dear wife! Take hold of me by my wings and let us dance; I am going to lift you up and carry you through the air.

(Pithetaerus *and* Basileia *leave dancing; the* Chorus *follows them.*)

CHORUS *(singing)*: *Alalaí! Ié Paión! Tenella kállinike!* Loftiest art thou of gods!

Anonymous

HISTORY

Herodotus

Thucydides

Xenophon

HERODOTUS

HERODOTUS (c. 484-425 b. c.) was born in Halicarnassus, in Asia Minor. He lived in Athens for some years, and finally settled as a colonist in Thurii, in Southern Italy.

The achievement of Herodotus is his *History of the Persian Wars*. This is virtually not only an account of a major military and naval conflict between two great nations, the Greeks and the Persians, but a comprehensive survey of contiguous nations as well, an encyclopedic description of their religious rites, social mores, political organization, interspersed with an abundance of illuminating tales and anecdotes of various types.

HISTORY OF THE PERSIAN WARS

Book II — *Account to the Egyptians*

Now the Egyptians, before the reign of their king Psammetichus, believed themselves to be the most ancient of mankind. Since Psammetichus, however, made an attempt to discover who were actually the primitive race, they have been of opinion that while they surpass all other nations, the Phrygians surpass them in antiquity. This king, finding it impossible to make out by dint of inquiry what men were the most ancient, contrived the following method of discovery: He took two children of the common sort, and gave them over to a herdsman to bring up at his folds, strictly charging him to let no one utter a word in their presence, but to keep them in a sequestered cottage, and from time to time introduce goats to their apartment, see that they got their fill of milk, and in all other respects look after them. His object herein was to know, after the indistinct babblings of infancy were over, what word they would first articulate. It happened as he had anticipated. The herdsman obeyed his orders for two years, and at the end of that time, on his one day opening the door of their room and going in, the children both ran up to him with outstretched arms, and distinctly said Becos. When this first happened the herdsman took no notice; but afterwards when he observed, on coming often to see after them, that the word was constantly in their mouths, he informed his lord, and by his command brought the children into his presence. Psammetichus then himself heard them say the word, upon which he proceeded to make inquiry what people there was who called anything bread. In consideration of this circumstance the Egyptians yielded their claims, and admitted the greater antiquity of the Phrygians.

becos, and hereupon he learned that becos was the Phrygian name for

That these were the real facts I learned at Memphis from the priests of Hephaestus. The Greeks, among other foolish tales, relate that Psammetichus had the children brought up by women whose tongues he had previously cut out; but the priests said their bringing up was such as I have stated above. I got much other information also from conversation with these priests while I was at Memphis, and I even went to Heliopolis and to Thebes, expressly to try whether the priests of those places would agree in their accounts with the priests at Memphis. The Heliopolitans have the reputation of being the best skilled in history of all the Egyptians. What they told me concerning their religion it is not my intention to repeat, except the names of their deities, since I believe all men know equally little about the gods. If I relate anything else concerning these matters, it will only be when compelled to do so by the course of my narrative.

Now with regard to mere human matters, the accounts which they gave, and in which all agreed, were the following. The Egyptians, they said, were the first to discover the solar year, and to portion out its course into twelve parts. They obtained this knowledge from the stars. (To my mind they contrive their year much more cleverly than the Greeks, for these last every other year intercalate a whole month, but the Egyptians, dividing the year into twelve months of thirty days each, add every year a space of five days besides, whereby the circuit of the seasons is made to return with uniformity.) The Egyptians, they went on to affirm, first brought into use the names of the twelve gods, which the Greeks adopted from them; and first erected altars, images, and temples to the gods; and also first engraved upon stone the figures of animals. In most of these cases they proved to me that what they said was true. And they told me that the first man who ruled over Egypt was Min, and that in his time all Egypt, except the Thebaic nome, was a marsh, none of the land below lake Moeris, then showing itself above the surface of the water. This is a distance of seven days' sail from the sea up the river.

What they said of their country seemed to me very reasonable. For any one who sees Egypt, without having heard a word about it before, must perceive, if he has only common powers of observation, that the Egypt to which the Greeks go in their ships is an acquired country, the gift of the river. The same is true of the land above the lake, to the distance of three days' voyage, concerning which the Egyptians say nothing, but which is exactly the same kind of country.

236

The following is the general character of the region. In the first place, on approaching it by sea, when you are still a day's sail from the land, if you let down a sounding-line you will bring up mud, and find yourself in eleven fathoms' water, which shows that the soil washed down by the stream extends to that distance.

The length of the country along shore, according to the bounds that we assign to Egypt, namely from the Plinthinetic gulf to lake Serbonis, which extends along the base of Mount Casius, is sixty schoenes. The nations whose territories are scanty measure them by the fathom; those whose bounds are less confined, by the furlong; those who have an ample territory, by the parasang; but if men have a country which is very vast, they measure it by the schoene. Now the length of the parasang is thirty furlongs, but the schoene, which is an Egyptian measure, is sixty furlongs. Thus the coast-line of Egypt would extend a length of 420 miles.

From the coast inland as far as Heliopolis the breadth of Egypt is considerable, the country is flat, without springs, and full of swamps. The length of the route from the sea up to Heliopolis is almost exactly the same as that of the road which runs from the altar of the twelve gods at Athens to the temple of Olympian Zeaus at Pisa. If a person made a calculation he would find but a very little difference between the two routes, not more than about two miles; for the road from Athens to Pisa falls short of 173 miles by exactly two, whereas the distance of Heliopolis from the sea is just the round number.

As one proceeds beyond Heliopolis up the country, Egypt becomes narrow, the Arabian range of hills, which has a direction from north to south, shutting it in upon the one side, and the Libyan range upon the other. The former ridge runs on without a break, and stretches away to the sea called the Red Sea; it contains the quarries whence the stone was cut for the pyramids of Memphis: and this is the point where it ceases its first direction, and bends away in the manner above indicated. In its greatest length from east to west, it is, as I have been informed, a distance of two months' journey; towards the extreme east its skirts produce frankincense. Such are the chief features of this range. On the Libyan side, the other ridge whereon the pyramids stand, is rocky and covered with sand; its direction is the same as that of the Arabian ridge in the first part of its course. Above Heliopolis, then, there is no great breadth of territory for such a country as Egypt, but during four days' sail Egypt is narrow; the valley between the two ranges is a level plain, and seemed to me to be, at the narrowest point, not more than two hundred furlongs across from the Arabian to the Libyan hills. Above this point Egypt again widens.

237

From Heliopolis to Thebes is nine days' sail up the river; the distance is eighty-one schoenes, or 552 miles. If we now put together the several measurements of the country we shall find that the distance along shore is, as I stated above, 420 miles, and the distance from the sea inland to Thebes 700 miles. Further, it is a distance of 206 miles from Thebes to the place called Elephantine.

The greater portion of the country above described seemed to me to be, as the priests declared, a tract gained by the inhabitants. For the whole region above Memphis, lying between the two ranges of hills that have been spoken of, appeared evidently to have formed at one time a gulf of the sea. It resembles (to compare small things with great) the parts about Ilium and Teuthrania, Ephesus, and the plain of the Meander. In all these regions the land has been formed by rivers, whereof the greatest is not to compare for size with any one of the five mouths of the Nile. I could mention other rivers also, far inferior to the Nile in magnitude, that have effected very great changes. Among these not the least is the Achelous, which, after passing through Acarnania, empties itself into the sea opposite the island called Echinades, and has already joined one half of them to the continent.

In Arabia, not far from Egypt, there is a long and narrow gulf running inland from the sea called the Red Sea, of which I will here set down the dimensions. Starting from its innermost recess, and using a row-boat, you take forty days to reach the open main, while you may cross the gulf at its widest part in the space of half a day. In this sea there is an ebb and flow of the tide every day. My opinion is, that Egypt was formerly very much such a gulf as this — one gulf penetrated from the sea washes Egypt on the north, and extended itself towards Ethiopia; another entered from the southern ocean, and stretched towards Syria; the two gulfs ran into the land so as almost to meet each other, and left between them only a very narrow tract of country. Now if the Nile should choose to divert his waters from their present bed into this Arabian gulf, what is there to hinder it from being filled up by the stream within, at the utmost 20,000 years? For my part, I think it would be filled in half the time. How then should not a gulf, even of much greater size, have been filled up in the ages that passed before I was born, by a river that is at once so large and so given to working changes?

Thus I give credit to those from whom I received this account of Egypt, and am myself, moreover, strongly of the same opinion, since I remarked that the country projects into the sea further than the neighbouring shores, and I observed that there were shells upon the hills, and that salt exuded from the soil to such an extent as even to injure the pyramids; and I noticed also that there is but a single hill in all

Egypt where sand is found, namely, the hill above Memphis; and further, I found the country to bear no resemblance either to its borderland Arabia, or to Libya — nay, nor even to Syria, which forms the seaboard of Arabia; but whereas the soil of Libya is, we know, sandy and of a reddish hue, and that of Arabia and Syria inclines to stone and clay, Egypt has a soil that is black and crumbly, as being alluvial and formed of the deposits brought down by the river from Ethiopia.

One fact which I learned of the priests is to me a strong evidence of the origin of the country. They said that when Moeris was king, the Nile overflowed all Egypt below Memphis, as soon as it rose so little as twelve feet. Now Moeris had not been dead 900 years at the time when I heard this of the priests; yet at the present day, unless the river rise twenty-four feet, or, at the very least, twenty-two feet, it does not overflow the lands. It seems to me, therefore, that if the land goes on rising and growing at this rate, the Egyptians who dwell below lake Moeris, in the Delta (as it is called) and elsewhere, will one day, by the stoppage of the inundations, suffer permanently the fate which they told me they expected would some time or other befall the Greeks. On hearing that the whole land of Greece is watered by rain from heaven, and not, like their own, inundated by rivers, they observed, "Some day the Greeks will be disappointed of their grand hope, and then they will be wretchedly hungry"; which was as much as to say, "If God shall some day see fit not to grant the Greeks rain, but shall afflict them with a long drought, the Greeks will be swept away by a famine, since they have nothing to rely on but rain from Zeus, and have no other resource for water."

And in thus speaking of the Greeks the Egyptians say nothing but what is true. But now let me tell the Egyptians how the case stands with themselves. If, as I said before, the country below Memphis, which is the land that is always rising, continues to increase in height at the rate at which it has risen in times gone by, how will it be possible for the inhabitants of that region to avoid hunger, when they will certainly have no rain, and the river will not be able to overflow their corn-lands? At present, it must be confessed, they obtain the fruits of the field with less trouble than any other people in the world, the rest of the Egyptians included, since they have no need to break up the ground with the plough, nor to use the hoe, nor to do any of the work which the rest of mankind find necessary if they are to get a crop; but the husbandman waits till the river has of its own accord spread itself over the fields and withdrawn again to its bed, and then sows his plot of ground, and after sowing turns his swine into it (the swine tread in the corn) after which he has only to await the harvest. The swine serve him also to thrash the grain, which is then carried to the garner.

If then we choose to adopt the views of the Ionians concerning Egypt, we must come to the conclusion that the Egyptians had formerly no country at all. For the Ionians say that nothing is really Egypt but the Delta, which extends along shore from the Watch-tower of Perseus, as it is called, to the Pelusiac Salt-pans, a distance of 300 miles, and stretches inland as far as the city of Cercasorus, where the Nile divides into the two streams which reach the sea at Pelusium and Canobus respectively. The rest of what is accounted Egypt belongs, they say, either to Arabia or Libya. But the Delta, as the Egyptians affirm, and as I myself am persuaded, is formed of the deposits of the river, and has only recently, if I may use the expression, come to light. If then they had formerly no territory at all, how came they to be so extravagant as to fancy themselves the most ancient race in the world? Surely there was no need of their making the experiment with the children to see what language they would first speak. But in truth I do not believe that the Egyptians came into being at the same time with the Delta, as the Ionians call it; I think they have always existed ever since the human race began; as the land went on increasing, part of the population came down into the new country, part remained in their old settlements. In ancient times the Thebais bore the name of Egypt, a district of which the entire circumference is but 700 miles.

If then my judgment on these matters be right, the Ionians are mistaken in what they say of Egypt. If, on the contrary, it is they who are right, then I undertake to show that neither the Ionians nor any of the other Greeks know how to count. For they all say that the earth is divided into three parts, Europe, Asia, and Libya, whereas they ought to add a fourth part, the Delta of Egypt, since they do not include it either in Asia or Libya. For is it not their theory that the Nile separates Asia from Libya? As the Nile therefore splits in two at the apex of the Delta, the Delta itself must be a separate country, not contained in either Asia or Libya.

Book VI — *The Battle of Marathon, 490 B. C. In this conflict the Athenians were victorious over the Persians*

Meantime the Persian pursued his own design, from day to day exhorted by his servant to remember the Athenians, and likewise urged continually by the Pisistratidae, who were ever accusing their countrymen. Moreover it pleased him well to have a pretext for carrying war into Greece, that so he might reduce all those who had refused to give him earth and water. As for Mardonius, since his expedition had succeeded so ill, Darius took the command of the troops from him, and appointed other generals in his stead, who were to lead the host against Eretria and Athens; Datis, who was by descent a Mede, and Artaphernes, the son of Artaphernes, his own nephew. These men received orders to carry Athens and Eretria away captive, and to bring the prisoners into his presence.

So the new commanders took their departure from the court and went down to Cilicia, to the Aleian plain, having with them a numerous and well-appointed land army. Encamping here, they were joined by the sea force which had been required of the several states, and at the same time by the horse-transports which Darius had, the year before, commanded his tributaries to make ready. Aboard these the horses were embarked, and the troops were received by the ships of war; after which the whole fleet, amounting in all to 600 triremes, made sail for Ionia. Thence, instead of proceeding with a straight course along the shore to the Hellespont and to Thrace, they loosed from Samos and voyaged across the Icarian sea through the midst of the islands; mainly, as I believe, because they feared the danger of doubling Mount Athos, where the year before they had suffered so grievously on their passage; but a constraining cause also was their former failure to take Naxos.

When the Persians, therefore, approaching from the Icarian sea, cast anchor at Naxos, which, recollecting what there befell them formerly, they had determined to attack before any other state, the Naxians, instead of encountering them, took to flight, and hurried off to the hills. The Persians however succeeded in laying hands on some, and them they carried away captive, while at the same time they burnt all the temples together with the town. This done, they left Naxos, and sailed away to the other islands.

While the Persians were thus employed, the Delians likewise quitted Delos, and took refuge in Tenos. And now the expedition drew near, when Datis sailed forward in advance of the other ships; which he commanded, instead of anchoring at Delos, to rendezvous at Rhenea, over against Delos, while he himself proceeded to discover whither the Delians had fled, after which he sent a herald to them with this message:

"Why have you fled, O holy men? Why have you judged me so harshly and so wrongfully? I have surely sense enough, even had not the king so ordered, to spare the country which gave birth to the two gods, to spare, I say, both the country and its inhabitants. Come back therefore to your dwellings, and once more inhabit your island." Such was the message which Datis sent by his herald to the Delians. He likewise placed upon the altar 300 talents' worth of frankincense, and offered it.

After this he sailed with his whole host against Eretria, taking with him both Ionians and Aeolians. When he was departed, Delos (at the Delians told me) was shaken by an earthquake, the first and last shock that has been felt to this day. And truly this was a prodigy whereby the god warned men of the evils that were coming upon them. For in the three following generations of Darius the son of Hystaspes, Xerxes the son of Darius, and Artaxerxes the son of Xerxes, more woes befell Greece than in the twenty generations preceding Darius; woes caused in part by the Persians, but in part arising from the contentions among their own chief men respecting the supreme power. Wherefore it is not surprising that Delos, though it had never before been shaken, should at that time have felt the shock of an earthquake. And indeed there was an oracle, which said of Delos:

Delos self will shake, which never yet has been shaken.

Of the above names Darius may be rendered Worker, Xerxes Warrior, and Artaxerxes Great Warrior. And so we might call these kings in our own language with propriety.

The barbarians, setting out from Delos, proceeded to touch at the other islands, and took troops from each, and likewise carried off a number of the children as hostages. Going thus from one to another, they came at last to Carystus; but here the hostages were refused by the Carystians, who said they would neither give any, nor consent to bear arms against the cities of their neighbours, meaning Athens and Eretria. Hereupon the Persians laid siege to Carystus, and wasted the country round, until at last the inhabitants were brought over and agreed to do what was required of them.

Meanwhile the Eretrians, understanding that the Persian armament was coming against them, besought the Athenians for assistance. Nor did the Athenians refuse their aid, but assigned to them as auxiliaries the 4,000 landholders to whom they had allotted the estates of the Chalcidean Hippobatae. At Eretria, however, things were in no healthy state; for though they had called in the aid of the Athenians, yet they were not agreed among themselves how they should act; some of them being minded to leave the city and to take refuge in the heights of Euboea, while others, who looked to receiving a reward from the Persians, were making ready to betray their country. So when these things came to the ears of Aeschines, the son of Nothon, one of the first men in Eretria, he made known the whole state of affairs to the Athenians

242

who were already arrived, and urged them to return home to their own land, and not perish with his countrymen. And the Athenians followed his advice, and crossing over to Oropus, in this way escaped the danger.

The Persian fleet now drew near and anchored at Tamynae, Choereae, and Aegilia, three places in the territory of Eretria. Once masters of these posts, they proceeded forthwith to disembark their horses, and made ready to attack the enemy. But the Eretrians were not minded to sally forth and offer battle; their only care, after it had been resolved not to quit the city, was, if possible, to defend their walls. And now the fortress was assaulted in good earnest, and for six days there fell on both sides vast numbers, but on the seventh day Euphorbus, the son of Alcimachus, and Philagrus, the son of Cyneas, who were both citizens of good repute, betrayed the place to the Persians. These were no sooner entered within the walls than they plundered and burnt all the temples that were in the town, in revenge for the burning of their own temples at Sardis; moreover, they did according to the orders of Darius, and carried away captive all the inhabitants.

The Persians, having thus brought Eretria into subjection, after waiting a few days, sailed for Attica, greatly straitening the Athenians as they approached, and thinking to deal with them as they had dealt with the people of Eretria. And because there was no place in all Attica so convenient for their horse as Marathon, and it lay moreover quite close to Eretria, therefore Hippias, the son of Pisistratus, conducted them thither.

When intelligence of this reached the Athenians, they likewise marched their troops to Marathon, and there stood on the defensive, having at their head ten generals, of whom one was Miltiades.

Now this man's father, Cimon, the son of Stesagoras, was banished from Athens by Pisistratus, the son of Hippocrates. In his banishment it was his fortune to win the four-horse chariot-race at Olympia, whereby he gained the very same honour which had before been carried off by Miltiades, his half-brother on the mother's side. At the next Olympiad he won the prize again with the same mares, upon which he caused Pisistratus to be proclaimed the winner, having made an agreement with him that on yielding him this honour he should be allowed to come back to his country. Afterwards, still with the same mares, he won the prize a third time, whereupon he was put to death by the sons of Pisistratus, whose father was no longer living. They set men to lie in wait for him secretly, and these men slew him near the town-hall in the night-time. He was buried outside the city, beyond what is called the Valley Road, and right opposite his tomb were buried the mares which had won the three prizes. The same success had likewise been achieved once previously, to wit, by the mares of Evagoras the Lacedaemonian, but never except by them. At the time of Cimon's death, Stesagoras, the elder of his two sons, was in the Chersonese, where he lived with Miltiades his uncle; the younger, who was called Miltiades after the founder of the Chersonesite colony, was with his father in Athens.

It was this Miltiades who now commanded the Athenians, after escaping from the Chersonese, and twice nearly losing his life. First he was chased as far as Imbrus by the Phoenicians, who had a great desire to take him and carry him up to the king; and when he had avoided this danger, and, having reached his own country, thought himself to be altogether in safety, he found his enemies waiting for him, and was cited by them before a court and impeached for his tyranny in the Chersonese. But he came off victorious here likewise, and was thereupon made general of the Athenians by the free choice of the people.

And first, before they left the city, the generals sent off to Sparta a herald, one Philippides, who was by birth an Athenian, and by profession and practice a trained runner. This man, according to the account wich he gave to the Athenians on his return, when he was near Mount Parthenium, above Tegea, fell in with the god Pan, who called him by his name, and bade him ask the Athenians, "Why they neglected him so entirely, when he was kindly disposed towards them, and had often helped them in times past, and would do so again in time to come?" The Athenians, entirely believing in the truth of this report, as soon as their affairs were once more in good order, set up a temple to Pan under the Acropolis, and, in return for the message which I have recorded, established in his honour yearly sacrifices and torch-race.

On the occasion of which we speak, when Philippides was sent by the Athenian generals, and, according to his own account, saw Pan on his journey, he reached Sparta on the very next day after quitting the city of Athens. Upon his arrival he went before the rulers, and said: "Men of Lacedaemon, the Athenians beseech you to listen to their aid, and not allow that state, which is the most ancient in all Greece, to be enslaved by the barbarians. Eretria is already carried away captive, and Greece weakened by the loss of no mean city."

Thus did Philippides deliver the message committed to him. And the Spartans wished to help the Athenians, but were unable to give them any present aid, as they did not like to break their established law. It was the ninth day of the month, and they could not march out of Sparta on the ninth, when the moon had not reached the full. So they waited for the full of the moon.

The barbarians were conducted to Marathon by Hippias, the son of Pisistratus, who the night before had seen a strange vision in his sleep. He seemed to have intercourse with his mother, and conjectured the dream to mean that he would be restored to Athens, recover the power which he had lost, and afterwards live to a good old age in his native country. Such was the sense in which he interpreted the vision. He now proceeded to act as guide to the Persians, and in the first place he landed the prisoners taken from Eretria upon the island that is called Aegileia, belonging to the Styreans, after which he brought the fleet to anchor off Marathon, and marshalled the bands of the barbarians as they disembarked. As he was thus employed it chanced that he sneezed and at the same time coughed with more violence than was his wont. Now as he was a man advanced in years, and the greater number of his teeth were loose, it so happened that one of them was driven out with the force of the cough, and fell down into the sand. Hippias took all the pains he could to find it, but the tooth was nowhere to be seen, whereupon he fetched a deep sigh, and said to the bystanders, "After all the land is not ours, and we shall never be able to bring it under. All my share in it is the portion of which my tooth has possession."

So Hippias believed that this fulfilled his dream.

The Athenians were drawn up in order of battle in a precinct belonging to Heracles, when they were joined by the Plataeans, who came in full force to their aid. Some time before, the Plataeans had put themselves under the rule of the Athenians, and these last had already undertaken many labours on their behalf. The occasion of the surrender was the following. The Plataeans suffered grievous things at the hands of the men of Thebes; so, as it chanced that Cleomenes, the son of Anaxandridas, and the Lacedaemonians were in their neighbourhood, they first of all offered to surrender themselves to them. But the Lacedaemonians refused to receive them, and said, "We dwell too far off from you, and ours would be but cold comfort. You might oftentimes be carried into slavery before one of us heard of it. We counsel you rather to give yourselves up to the Athenians, who are your next neighbours, and well able to shelter you."

This they said, not so much out of good will towards the Plataeans as because they wished to involve the Athenians in trouble by engaging them in wars with the Boeotians. The Plataeans, however, when the Lacedaemonians gave them this counsel, complied at once; and when the sacrifice to the Twelve Gods was being offered at Athens, they came and sat as suppliants about the altar, and gave themselves up to the Athenians. The Thebans no sooner learned what the Plataeans had done than instantly they marched out against them, while the Athenians sent troops to their aid. As the two armies were about to join battle, the Corinthians, who chanced to be at hand, would not allow them to engage; both sides consented to take them for arbitrators, whereupon they made up the quarrel, and fixed the boundary-line between the two states upon this condition: that if any of the Boeotians wished no longer to belong to Boeotia, the Thebans should allow them to follow their own inclinations. The Corinthians, when they had thus decreed, departed to their homes; the Athenians likewise set off on their return, but the Boeotians fell upon them during the march, and a battle was fought wherein they were worsted by the Athenians. Hereupon these last would not be bound by the line which the Corinthians had fixed, but advanced beyond those limits, and made the Asopus the boundary-line between the country of the Thebans and that of the Plataeans and Hysians. Under such circumstances did the Plataeans give themselves up to Athens; and now they were come to Marathon to aid the Athenians.

The Athenian generals were divided in their opinions; and some advised not to risk a battle, because they were too few to engage such a host as that of the Medes; while others were for fighting at once, and among these last was Miltiades. He therefore, seeing that opinions were thus divided, and that the less worthy counsel appeared likely to prevail, resolved to go to the Polemarch, and have a conference with him. For the man on whom the lot fell to be Polemarch, at Athens was entitled to give his vote with the ten generals, since anciently the Athenians allowed him an equal right of voting with them. The Polemarch at this juncture was Callimachus of Aphidnae; to him therefore Miltiades went, and said:

"With you it rests, Callimachus, either to bring Athens to slavery, or, by securing her freedom, to leave behind to all future generations a memory beyond even Harmodius and Aristogeiton. For never since the time that the Athenians became a people were they in so great a danger as now. If they bow their necks beneath the yoke of the Medes, the woes which they will have to suffer when given into the power of Hippias are already determined on; if, on the other hand, they fight and overcome, Athens may rise to be the very first city in Greece. How it comes to pass that these things are likely to happen, and how the determining of them in some sort rests with you, I will now proceed to make clear. We generals are ten in number, and our votes are divided; half of us wish to engage, half to avoid a combat. Now, if we do not fight, I look to see a great disturbance at Athens which will shake men's resolutions, and then I fear they will submit themselves; but if we fight the battle before any unsoundness show itself among our citizens, let the gods but give us fair play, and we are well able to overcome

246

the enemy. On you therefore we depend in this matter, which lies wholly in your own power. You have only to add your vote to my side and your country will be free, and not free only, but the first state in Greece. Or, if you prefer to give your vote to them who would decline the combat, then the reverse will follow."

Miltiades by these words gained Callimachus; and the addition of the polemarch's vote caused the decision to be in favor of fighting. Hereupon all those generals who had been desiring of hazarding a battle, when their turn came to command the army, gave up their right to Miltiades. He, however, though he accepted their offers, nevertheless waited, and would not fight, until his own day of command arrived in due course.

Then at length, when his own turn was come, the Athenian battle was set in array, and this was the order of it. Callimachus the polemarch led the right wing, for it was at that time a rule with the Athenians to give the right wing to the polemarch. After this followed the tribes, according as they were numbered, in an unbroken line; while last of all came the Plataeans, forming the left wing. And ever since that day it has been a custom with the Athenians, in the sacrifices and assemblies held each fifth year at Athens, for the Athenian herald to implore the blessing of the gods on the Plataeans conjointly with the Athenians. Now as they marshalled the host upon the field of Marathon, in order that the Athenian front might be of equal length with the Median, the ranks of the centre were diminished, and it became the weakest part of the line, while the wings were both made strong with a depth of many ranks.

So when the battle was set in array, and the victims showed themselves favourable, instantly the Athenians, so soon as they were let go, charged the barbarians at a run. Now the distance between the two armies was little short of a mile. The Persians, therefore, when they saw the Greeks coming on at speed, made ready to receive them, although it seemed to them that the Athenians were bereft of their senses, and bent upon their own destruction; for they saw a mere handful of men coming on at a run without either horsemen or archers. Such was the opinion of the barbarians; but the Athenians in close array fell upon them, and fought in a manner worthy of being recorded. They were the first of the Greeks, so far as I know, who introduced the custom of charging the enemy at a run, and they were likewise the first who dared to look upon the Median garb, and to face men clad in that fashion. Until this time the very name of the Medes had been a terror to the Greeks to hear.

The two armies fought together on the plain of Marathon for a length of time; and in the mid battle, where the Persians themselves and the Sacae had their place, the barbarians were victorious, and broke and pursued the Greeks into the inner country; but on the two wings the Athenians and the Plataeans defeated the enemy. Having so done, they suffered the routed barbarians to fly at their ease, and joining the two wings in one, fell upon those who had broken their own centre, and fought and conquered them. These likewise fled, and now the Athenians hung upon the runaways and cut them down, chasing them all the way to the shore, on reaching which they laid hold of the ships and called aloud for fire.

It was in the struggle here that Callimachus the polemarch, after greatly distinguishing himself, lost his life; Stesilaus too, the son of Thrasilaus, one of the generals, was slain; and Cynaegirus, the son of Euphorion, having seized on a vessel of the enemy's by the ornament at the stern, had his hand cut off by the blow of an axe, and so perished; as likewise did many other Athenians of note and name.

Nevertheless the Athenians secured in this way seven of the vessels, while with the remainder the barbarians pushed off, and taking aboard their Eretrian prisoners from the island where they had left them, doubled Cape Sunium, hoping to reach Athens before the return of the Athenians. The Alcmaeonidae were accused by their countrymen of suggesting this course to them; they had, it was said, an understanding with the Persians, and made a signal to them, by raising a shield, after they were embarked in their ships.

The Persians accordingly sailed round Sunium. But the Athenians with all possible speed marched away to the defense of their city, and succeeded in reaching Athens before the appearance of the barbarians; and as their camp at Marathon had been pitched in a precinct of Heracles, so now they encamped in another precinct of the same god at Cynosarges. The barbarian fleet arrived, and lay to off Phalerum, which was at that time the haven of Athens; but after resting awhile upon their oars, they departed and sailed away to Asia.

There fell in this battle of Marathon, on the side of the barbarians, about 6,400 men; on that of the Athenians, 192. Such was the number of the slain on the one side and the other. A strange prodigy likewise happened at this fight. Epizelus, the son of Cuphagoras, an Athenian, was in the thick of the fray, and behaving himself as a brave man should, when suddenly he was stricken with blindness, without blow of sword or dart, and this blindness continued thenceforth during the whole of his after life. The following is the account which he himself, as I have heard, gave of the matter: he said that a gigantic warrior, with a huge beard, which shaded all his shield, stood over against him, but the ghostly semblance passed him by, and slew the man at his side. Such, as I understand, was the tale which Epizelus told.

Book VII — *Thermopylae. Here the Spartans, under Leonidas, made their memorable stand against the Persians, in 480 B.C.*

King Xerxes pitched his camp in the region of Malis called Trachinia, while on their side the Greeks occupied the straits. These straits the Greeks in general call Thermopylae (the Hot Gates); but the natives and those who dwell in the neighbourhood, called them Pylae (the Gates). Here then the two armies took their stand; the one master of all the region lying north of Trachis, the other of the country extending southward of that place to the verge of the continent.

The Greeks who at this spot awaited the coming of Xerxes were the following: From Sparta, 300 men-at-arms; from Arcadia, 1,000; Tegeans and Mantineans, 500 of each people; 120 Orchomenians, from the Arcadian Orchomenus; and 1,000 from other cities: from Corinth, 400 men: from Phlius, 200; and from Mycenae, eighty. Such was the number from the Peloponnese. There were also present, from Boeotia, 700 Thespians and 400 Thebans.

Besides these troops, the Locrians of Opus and the Phocians had obeyed the call of their countrymen, and sent, the former all the force they had, the latter 1,000 men. For envoys had gone from the Greeks at Thermopylae among the Locrians and Phocians, to call on them for assistance, and to say, "They were themselves but the vanguard of the host, sent to precede the main body, which might every day be expected to follow them. The sea was in good keeping, watched by the Athenians, the Aeginetans, and the rest of the fleet. There was no cause why they should fear; for after all the invader was not a god but a man; and there never had been, and never would be, a man who was not liable to misfortunes from the very day of his birth, and those greater in proportion to his own greatness. The assailant therefore, being only a mortal, must needs fall from his glory." Thus urged, the Locrians and the Phocians had come with their troops to Trachis.

The various nations had each captains of their own under whom they served; but the one to whom all especially looked up, and who had the command of the entire force, was the Lacedaemonian, Leonidas. Now Leonidas was the son of Anaxandridas, who was the son of Leo, who was the son of Eurycratidas, who was the son of Naxander, who was the son of Eurycrates, who was the son of Polydorus, who was the son of Alcamenes, who was the son of Telecles, who was the son of Archelaus, who was the son of Agesilaus, who was the son of Doryssus, who was the son of Labotas, who was the son of Echestratus, who was the son of Agis, who was the son of Eurysthenes, who was the son of Aristodemus, who was the son of Aristomachus, who was the son of Cleodaeus, who was the son of Hyllus, who was the son of Heracles.

Leonidas had come to be king of Sparta quite unexpectedly. Having two elder brothers, Cleomenes and Dorieus, he had no thought of ever mounting the throne. However, when Cleomenes died without male offspring, as Dorieus was likewise deceased, having perished in Sicily, the crown fell to Leonidas, who was older than Cleombrotus, the youngest of the sons of Anaxandridas, and, moreover, was married to the daughter of Cleomenes. He had now come to Thermopylae, accompanied by the 300 men which the law assigned him, whom he had himself chosen from among the citizens, and who were all of them fathers with sons living. On his way he had taken the troops from Thebes, whose number I have already mentioned, and who were under the command of Leontiades the son of Eurymachus. The reason why he made a point of taking troops from Thebes and Thebes only, was that the Thebans were strongly suspected of being well inclined to the Medes. Leonidas therefore called on them to come with him to the war, wishing to see whether they would comply with his demand, or openly refuse, and disclaim the Greek alliance. They, however, though their wishes leant the other way, nevertheless sent the men.

The force with Leonidas was sent forward by the Spartans in advance of their main body, that the sight of them might encourage the allies to fight, and hinder them from going over to the Medes, as it was likely they might have done had they seen Sparta backward. They intended presently, when they had celebrated the Carneian festival, which was what now kept them at home, to leave a garrison in Sparta, and hasten in full force to join the army. The rest of the allies also intended to act similarly; for it happened that the Olympic festival fell exactly at this same period. None of them looked to see the contest at Thermopylae decided so speedily; wherefore they were content to send forward a mere advanced guard. Such accordingly were the intentions of the allies.

The Greek forces at Thermopylae, when the Persian army drew near to the entrance of the pass, were seized with fear, and a council was held to consider about a retreat. It was the wish of the Peloponnesians generally that the army should fall back upon the Peloponnese, and there guard the Isthmus. But Leonidas, who saw with what indignation the Phocians and Locrians heard of this plan, gave his voice for remaining where they were, while they sent envoys to the several cities to ask for help, since they were too few to make a stand against an army like that of the Medes.

While this debate was going on, Xerxes sent a mounted spy to observe the Greeks, and note how many they were, and what they were doing. He had heard, before he came out of Thessaly, that a few men were assembled at this place, and that at their head were certain Lacedaemonians, under Leonidas, a descendant of Heracles. The horseman rode up to the camp, and looked about him, but did not see the whole army; for such as were on the further side of the wall (which had been rebuilt and was now carefully guarded) it was not possible for him to behold; but he observed those on the outside, who were encamped in front of the rampart. It chanced that at this time the Lacedaemonians held the outer guard, and were seen by the spy, some of them engaged in gymnastic exercises, others combing their long hair. At this the spy greatly marvelled, but he counted their number, and when he had taken accurate note of everything, he rode back quietly; for no one pursued after him, or paid any heed to his visit. So he returned, and told Xerxes all that he had seen.

Upon this, Xerxes, who had no means of surmising the truth — namely, that the Spartans were preparing to do or die manfully — but thought it laughable that they should be engaged in such employments, sent and called to his presence Demaratus the son of Ariston, who still remained with the army. When he appeared, Xerxes told him all that he had heard, and questioned him concerning the news, since he was anxious to understand the meaning of such behavior on the part of the Spartans. Then Demaratus said, 'I spoke to you, O King, concerning these men long since, when we had just begun our march upon Greece; you, however, only laughed at my words, when I told you of all this, which I saw would come to pass. Earnestly do I struggle at all times, to speak the truth to you, sire; and now listen to it once more. These men have come to dispute the pass with us, and it is for this that they are now making ready. It is their custom, when they are about to hazard their lives, to adorn their heads with care. Be assured, however, that if you can subdue the men who are here and the Lacedaemonians who remain in Sparta, there is no other nation in all the world which will venture to lift a hand in their defense. You have now to deal with the first kingdom and town in Greece, and with the bravest men."

Then Xerxes, to whom what Demaratus said seemed altogether to surpass belief, asked further, "How was it possible for so small an army to contend with his?"

"Oh King," Demaratus answered, "let me be treated as a liar, if matters fall not out as I say."

But Xerxes was not persuaded any the more. Four whole days he suffered to go by, expecting that the Greeks would run away. When, however, he found on the fifth that they were not gone, thinking that their firm stand was mere impudence and recklessness, he grew wroth, and sent against them the Medes and Cissians, with orders to take them alive and bring them into his presence. Then the Medes rushed forward and charged the Greeks, but fell in vast numbers: others however took the places of the slain, and would not be beaten off, though they suffered terrible losses. In this way it became clear to all, and especially to the king, that though he had plenty of combatants, he had but very few warriors. The struggle, however, continued during the whole day.

Then the Medes, having met so rough a reception, withdrew from the fight; and their place was taken by the band of Persians under Hydarnes, whom the king called his Immortals: they, it was thought, would soon finish the business. But when they joined battle with the Greeks, it was with no better success than the Median detachment — things went much as before — the two armies fighting in a narrow space, and the barbarians using shorter spears than the Greeks, and having no advantage from their numbers. The Lacedaemonians fought in a way worthy of note, and showed themselves far more skilful in fight than their adversaries, often turning their backs, and making as though they were all flying away, on which the barbarians would rush after them with much noise and shouting, when the Spartans at their approach would wheel round and face their pursuers, in this way destroying vast numbers of the enemy. Some Spartans likewise fell in these encounters, but only a very few. At last the Persians, finding that all their efforts to gain the pass availed nothing, and that whether they attacked by divisions or in any other way, it was to no purpose, withdrew to their own quarters.

During these assaults, it is said that Xerxes, who was watching the battle, thrice leaped from the throne on which he sat, in terror for his army.

Next day the combat was renewed, but with no better success on the part of the barbarians. The Greeks were so few that the barbarians hoped to find them disabled, by reason of their wounds, from offering any further resistance; and so they once more attacked them. But the Greeks were drawn up in detachments according to their cities, and bore the brunt of the battle in turns, all except the Phocians, who had been stationed on the mountain to guard the pathway. So when the Persians found no difference between that day and the preceding, they again retired to their quarters.

Now, as the king was at a loss, and knew not how he should deal with the emergency, Ephialtes, the son of Eurydemus, a man of Malis, came to him and was admitted to a conference. Stirred by the hope of receiving a rich reward at the king's hands, he had come to tell him of

252

the pathway which led across the mountain to Thermopylae; by which disclosure he brought destruction on the band of Greeks who had there withstood the barbarians. This Ephialtes afterwards, from fear of the Lacedaemonians, fled into Thessaly; and during his exile, in an assembly of the Amphictyons held at Pylae, a price was set upon his head by the Pylagorae. When some time had gone by, he returned from exile, and went to Anticyra, where he was slain by Athenades, a native of Trachis. Athenades did not slay him for his treachery, but for another reason, which I shall mention in a later part of my history: yet still the Lacedaemonians honoured him none the less. Thus did then Ephialtes perish a long time afterwards.

Besides this there is another story told, which I do not at all believe, that Onetas the son of Phanagoras, a native of Carystus, and Corydallus, a man of Anticyra, were the persons who spoke on this matter to the king, and took the Persians across the mountain. One may guess which story is true, from the fact that the deputies of the Greeks, the Pylagorae, who must have had the best means of ascertaining the truth, did not offer the reward for the heads of Onetas and Corydallus, but for that of Ephialtes of Trachis; and again from the flight of Ephialtes, which we know to have been on this account. Onetas, I allow, although he was not a Malian, might have been acquainted with the path, if he had lived much in that part of the country; but as Ephialtes was the person who actually led the Persians round the mountain by the pathway, I leave his name on record as that of the man who did the deed.

Great was the joy of Xerxes on this occasion; and as he approved highly of the enterprise which Ephialtes undertook to accomplish, he forthwith sent upon the errand Hydarnes, and the Persians under him. The troops left the camp about the time of the lighting of the lamps. The pathway along which they went was first discovered by the Malians of these parts, who soon afterwards led the Thessalians by it to attack the Phocians, at the time when the Phocians fortified the pass with a wall, and so put themselves under covert from danger. And ever since, the path has always been put to an ill use by the Malians.

The course which it takes is the following: Beginning at the Asopus, where the stream flows through the cleft in the hills, it runs along the ridge of the mountain (which is called, like the pathway over it, Anopaea), and ends at the city of Alpenus — the first Locrian town as you come from Malis — by the stone called Black-buttock and the seats of the Cercopians. Here it is as narrow as at any other point.

The Persians took this path, and crossing the Asopus, continued their march through the whole of the night, having the mountains of

Oeta on their right hand, and on their left those of Trachis. At dawn of day they found themselves close to the summit. Now the hill was guarded, as I have already said, by 1,000 Phocian men-at-arms, who were placed there to defend the pathway, and at the same time to secure their own country. They had been given the guard of the mountain path, while the other Greeks defended the pass below, because they had volunteered for the service, and had pledged themselves to Leonidas to maintain the post.

The ascent of the Persians became known to the Phocians in the following manner: During all the time that they were making their way up, the Greeks remained unconscious of it, inasmuch as the whole mountain was covered with groves of oak; but it happened that the air was very still, and the leaves which the Persians stirred with their feet made, as it was likely they would, a loud rustling, whereupon the Phocians jumped up and flew to seize their arms. In a moment the barbarians came in sight, and perceiving men arming themselves, were greatly amazed; for they had fallen in with an enemy when they expected no opposition. Hydarnes, alarmed at the sight, and fearing lest the Phocians might be Lacedaemonians, inquired of Ephialtes to what nation these troops belonged. Ephialtes told him the exact truth, whereupon he arrayed his Persians for battle. The Phocians, galled by the showers of arrows to which they were exposed, and imagining themselves the special object of the Persian attack, fled hastily to the crest of the mountain, and there made ready to meet death; but while their mistake continued, the Persians, with Ephialtes and Hydarnes, not thinking it worth their while to delay on account of the Phocians, passed on and descended the mountain with all possible speed.

The Greeks at Thermopylae received the first warning of the destruction which the dawn would bring on them from the seer Megistias, who read their fate in the victims as he was sacrificing. After this deserters came in, and brought the news that the Persians were marching round by the hills: it was still night when these men arrived. Last of all, scouts came running down from the heights, and brought in the same accounts, when the day was just beginning to break. Then the Greeks held a council to consider what they should do, and here opinions were divided: some were strong against quitting their post, while others contended to the contrary. So when the council had broken up, part of the troops departed and went their ways homeward to their several states; part however, resolved to remain, and stand by Leonidas to the last.

It is said that Leonidas himself sent away the troops who departed, because he tendered their safety, but thought it unseemly that either he or his Spartans should quit the post which they had been especially sent to guard. For my own part, I incline to think that Leonidas gave the order, because he perceived the allies to be out of heart and unwilling to encounter the danger to which his own mind was made up. He therefore commanded them to retreat, but said that he himself could not draw back with honour; knowing that, if he stayed, glory awaited him, and that Sparta in that case would not lose her prosperity. For when the Spartans, at the very beginning of the war, sent to consult the oracle concerning it, the answer which they received from the priestess was that either Sparta must be overthrown by the barbarians, or one of her kings must perish. The prophecy was delivered in hexameter verse, and ran thus:

> Oh! ye men who dwell in the streets of broad Lacedaemon,
> Either your glorious town shall be sacked by the children of
> [Perseus,
> Or, in exchange, must all through the whole Laconian country
> Mourn for the loss of a king, descendant of great Heracles.
> He cannot be withstood by the courage of bulls or of lions,
> Strive as they may; he is mighty as Zeus; there is nought
> [that shall stay him.
> Till he have got for his prey your king, or your glorious city.

The remembrance of this answer, I think, and the wish to secure the whole glory for the Spartans, caused Leonidas to send the allies away. This is more likely than that they quarreled with him, and took their departure in such unruly fashion.

To me it seems no small argument in favour of this view, that the seer also who accompanied the army, Megistias, the Acarnanian, said to have been of the blood of Melampus, and the same who was led by the appearance of the victims to warn the Greeks of the danger which threatened them, received orders to retire (as it is certain he did) from Leonidas, that he might escape the coming destruction. Megistias, however, though bidden to depart, refused, and stayed with the army; but he had an only son present with the expedition, whom he now sent away.

So the allies, when Leonidas ordered them to retire, obeyed him and forthwith departed. Only the Thespians and the Thebans remained with the Spartans; and of these the Thebans were kept back by Leonidas as hostages, very much against their will. The Thespians, on the contrary, stayed entirely of their own accord, refusing to retreat, and declaring that they would not forsake Leonidas and his followers. So they abode with the Spartans, and died with them. Their leader was Demophilus, the son of Diadromes.

At sunrise Xerxes made libations, after which he waited until the time when the market-place is wont to fill, and then began his advance. Ephialtes had instructed him thus, as the descent of the mountain is much quicker, and the distance much shorter, than the way round the hills, and the ascent. So the barbarians under Xerxes began to draw nigh; and the Greeks under Leonidas, as they now went forth determined to die, advanced much further than on previous days, until they reached the more open portion of the pass. Hitherto they had held their station within the wall, and from this had gone forth to fight at the point where the pass was the narrowest. Now they joined battle beyond the defile, and carried slaughter among the barbarians, who fell in heaps. Behind them the captains of the squadrons, armed with whips, urged their men forward with continual blows. Many were thrust into the sea, and there perished; no one heeded the dying. For the Greeks, reckless of their own safety and desperate, since they knew that, as the mountain had been crossed, their destruction was nigh at hand, exerted themselves with the most furious valour against the barbarians.

By this time the spears of the greater number were all shivered, and with their swords they hewed down the ranks of the Persians; and here, as they strove, Leonidas fell fighting bravely, together with many other famous Spartans, whose names I have taken care to learn on account of their great worthiness, as indeed I have those of all the 300. There fell too at the same time very many famous Persians: among them, two sons of Darius, Abrocomes and Hyperanthes, his children by Phratagune, the daughter of Artanes. Artanes was brother of King Darius, being a son of Hystaspes, the son of Arsames; and when he gave his daughter to the king, he made him heir likewise of all his substance; for she was his only child.

Thus two brothers of Xerxes here fought and fell. And now there arose a fierce struggle between the Persians and the Lacedaemonians over the body of Leonidas, in which the Greeks four times drove back the enemy, and at last by their great bravery succeeded in bearing off the body. This combat was scarcely ended when the Persians with Ephialtes approached; and the Greeks, informed that they drew nigh, made a change in the manner of their fighting. Drawing back into the narrowest part of the pass, and retreating even behind the cross wall, they posted themselves upon a hillock, where they stood all drawn up together in one close body, except only the Thebans. The hillock whereof I speak is at the entrance of the straits, where the stone lion stands which was set up in honour of Leonidas. Here they defended themselves to the last, such as still had swords using them, and the others resisting with their hands and teeth; till the barbarians, who in part had pulled down the wall and attacked them in front, in part had gone round and now encircled them upon every side, overwhelmed and buried the remnant left beneath showers of missile weapons.

Thus nobly did the whole body of Lacedaemonians and Thespians behave, but nevertheless one man is said to have distinguished himself above all the rest, to wit, Dieneces the Spartan. A speech which he made before the Greeks engaged the Medes, remains on record. One of the Trachinians told him, "Such was the number of the barbarians, than when they shot forth their arrows the sun would be darkened by their multitude." Dieneces, not at all frightened at these words, but making light of the Median numbers, answered, "Our Trachinian friend brings us excellent tidings. If the Medes darken the sun, we shall have our fight in the shade." Other sayings too of a like nature are said, to have been left on record by this same person.

Next to him two brothers, Lacedaemonians, are reputed to have made themselves conspicuous: they were named Alpheus and Maro, and were the sons of Orsiphantus. There was also a Thespian who gained greater glory than any of his countrymen: he was a man called Dithyrambus, the son of Harmatidas.

The slain were buried where they fell; and in their honour, nor less in honour of those who died before Leonidas sent the allies away, an inscription was set up which said:

> Here did four thousand men from Pelops' land
> Against three hundred myriads bravely stand.

This was in honour of all. Another was for the Spartans alone:

> Go, stranger, and to Lacedaemon tell
> That here, obeying her behests, we fell.

This was for the Lacedaemonians. The seer had the following:

> The great Megistias' tomb you here may view,
>   Whom slew the Medes, fresh from Spercheius' fords.
> Well the wise seer the coming death foreknew,
>   Yet scorned he to forsake his Spartan lords.

These inscriptions, and the pillars likewise, were all set up by the Amphictyons, except that in honour of Megistias, which was inscribed to him (on account of their sworn friendship) by Simonides, the son of Leoprepes.

George Rawlinson

257

THUCYDIDES

THUCYDIDES was a wealthy Athenian. In the Peloponnesian War, a conflict between Sparta and Athens, he commanded an Athenian squadron in 424 B. C., but failed to hold the city of Amphipolis against the Spartan general Brasidas. As a result he went into exile, for twenty years, returning to Athens in 403 B. C.

To acquire material for his *History of the Peloponnesian War,* he traveled in the Peloponnese, consulted participants on both sides, and examined archives and similar sources. His work, in nine books, is virtually the first contemporary history, ending with events in 411 B. C. Thucydides is largely objective, critical, and scrupulous in the verification of factual material.

HISTORY OF THE PELOPONNESIAN WAR

Book II—*The Funeral Oration of Pericles*

The funeral oration of Pericles, delivered before the Athenians in 430 B. C. Essentially, the speech is a glorification of democratic ideals.

In the same winter the Athenians gave a funeral at the public cost to those who had first fallen in this war. It was a custom of their ancestors, and the manner of it is as follows. Three days before the ceremony, the bones of the dead are laid out in a tent which has been erected; and their friends bring to their relatives such offerings as they please. In the funeral procession cypress coffins are borne in cars, one for each tribe; the bonds of the deceased being placed in the coffin of their tribe. Among these is carried one empty bier decked for the missing, that is, for those whose bodies could not be recovered. Any citizen or stranger who pleases, joins in the procession: and the female relatives are there to wail at the burial. The dead are laid in the public sepulchre in the most beautiful suburb of the city, in which those who fall in war are always buried; with the exception of those slain at Marathon, who for their singular and extraordinary valour were interred on the spot where they fell. After the bodies have been laid in the earth, a man chosen by the state, of approved wisdom and eminent reputation, pronounces over them an appropriate panegyric; after which all retire. Such is the manner of the burying; and throughout the whole

258

of the war, whenever the occasion arose, the established custom was observed. Meanwhile these were the first that had fallen, and Pericles, son of Xanthippus, was chosen to pronounce their eulogium. When the proper time arrived, he advanced from the sepulchre to an elevated platform in order to be heard by as many of the crowd as possible, and spoke as follows:

'Most of my predecessors in this place have commended him who made this speech part of the law, telling us that it is well that it should be delivered at the burial of those who fall in battle. For myself, I should have thought that the worth which had displayed itself in deeds, would be sufficiently rewarded by honours also shown by deeds; such as you now see in this funeral prepared at the people's cost. And I could have wished that the reputations of many brave men were not to be imperilled in the mouth of a single individual, to stand or fall according as he spoke well or ill. For it is hard to speak properly upon a subject where it is even difficult to convince your hearers that you are speaking the truth. On the one hand, the friend who is familiar with every fact of the story, may think that some point has not been set forth with that fulness which he wishes and knows it to deserve; on the other, he who is a stranger to the matter may be led by envy to suspect exaggeration if he hears anything above his own nature. For men can endure to hear others praised only so long as they can severally persuade themselves of their own ability to equal the actions recounted: when this point is passed, envy comes in and with it incredulity. However, since our ancestors have stamped this custom with their approval, it becomes my duty to obey the law and to try to satisfy your several wishes and opinion as best I may.

'I shall begin with our ancestors: it is both just and proper that they should have the honour of the first mention on an occasion like the present. They dwelt in the country without break in the succession from generation to generation, and handed it down free to the present time by their valour. And if our more remote ancestors deserve praise, much more do our own fathers, who added to their inheritance the empire which we now possess, and spared no pains to be able to leave their acquisitions to us of the present generation. Lastly, there are few parts of our dominions that have not been augmented by those of us here, who are still more or less in the vigour of life; while the mother country has been furnished by us with everything that can enable her to depend on her own resources whether for war or peace. That part of our history which tells of the military achievement which gave us our several possessions, or of the ready valour with which either we or our fathers stemmed the tide of Hellenic or foreign aggression, is a theme too familiar to my hearers for me to dilate on, and I shall therefore pass it by. But what was the road by which we reached our position, what the form of government under which our greatness grew, what the national habits out of which it sprang; these are questions which I may try to solve before I proceed to my panegyric upon these men; since I think this to be a subject upon which on the present occasion a speaker may properly dwell, and to which the whole assemblage, whether citizens or foreigners, may listen with advantage.

'Our constitution does not copy the laws of neighbouring states; we are rather a pattern to others than imitators ourselves. Its administration favours the many instead of the few; this is why it is called a democracy. If we look to the laws, they afford equal justice to all in their private differences; if to social standing, advancement in public life falls to reputation for capacity, class considerations not being allowed to interfere with merit; nor again does poverty bar the way, if a man is able to serve the state, he is not hindered by the obscurity of his condition. The freedom which we enjoy in our government extends also to our ordinary life. There, far from exercising a jealous surveillance over each other, we do not feel called upon to be angry with our neighbour for doing what he likes, or even to indulge in those injurious looks which cannot fail to be offensive, although they inflict no positive penalty. But all this ease in our private relations does not make us lawless as citizens. Against this fear is our chief safeguard, teaching us to obey the magistrates and the laws, particularly such as regard the protection of the injured, whether they are actually on the statute book, or belong to that code which, although unwritten, yet cannot be broken without acknowledged disgrace.

'Further, we provide plenty of means for the mind to refresh itself from business. We celebrate games and sacrifices all the year round, and the elegance of our private establishments forms a daily source of pleasure and helps to banish the spleen; while the magnitude of our city draws the produce of the world into our harbour, so that to the Athenian the fruits of other countries are as familiar a luxury as those of his own.

'If we turn to our military policy, there also we differ from our antagonists. We throw open our city to the world, and never by alien acts exclude foreigners from any opportunity of learning or observing, although the eyes of an enemy may occasionally profit by our liberality; trusting less in system and policy than to the native spirit of our citizens; while in education, where our rivals from their very cradles by a painful discipline seek for manliness, at Athens we live exactly as we please, and yet are just as ready to encounter every legitimate danger. In proof of this it may be noticed that the Lacedaemonians do not invade our country alone, but bring with them all their confederates; while we Athenians advance unsupported into the territory of a neighbour, and fighting upon a foreign soil usually vanquish with ease men who are defending their homes. Our united force was never yet encountered by any enemy, because we have at once to attend to our marine and to despatch our citizens by land upon a hundred different services; so that, wherever they engage with some such fraction of our strength, a success against a detachment is magnified into a victory over the nation, and a defeat into a reverse suffered at the hands of our entire people. And yet if with habits not of labour but of ease, and courage not of art but of nature, we are still willing to encounter danger, we have the double advantage of escaping the experience of hardships in anticipation and of facing them in the hour of need as fearlessly as those who are never free from them.

'Nor are these the only points in which our city is worthy of admiration. We cultivate refinement without extravagance and knowledge without effeminacy; wealth we employ more for use than for show, and place the real disgrace of poverty not in owning to the fact but in declining the struggle against it. Our public men have, besides politics, their private affairs to attend to, and our ordinary citizens, though occupied with the pursuits of industry, are still fair judges of public matters; for, unlike any other nation, regarding him who takes no part in these duties not as unambitious but as useless, we Athenians are able to judge at all events if we cannot originate, and instead of looking on discussion as a stumbling-block in the way of action, we think it an indispensable preliminary to any wise action at all. Again, in our enterprises we present the singular spectacle of daring and deliberation, each carried to its highest point, and both united in the same persons; although usually decision is the fruit of ignorance, hesitation of reflexion. But the palm of courage will surely be adjudged most justly to those, who best know the difference between hardship and pleasure and yet are never tempted to shrink from danger. In generosity we are equally singular, acquiring our friends by conferring not by receiving favours. Yet, of course, the doer of the favour is the firmer friend of the two, in order by continued kindness to keep the recipient in his debt; while the debtor feels less keenly from the very consciousness that the return he makes will be a payment, not a free gift. And it is only the Athenians who, fearless of consequences, confer their benefits not from calculations of expediency, but in the confidence of liberality.

'In short, I say that as a city we are the school of Hellas; while I doubt if the world can produce a man, who where he has only himself to depend upon, is equal to so many emergencies, and graced by so happy a versatility as the Athenian. And that this is no mere boast thrown out for the occasion, but plain matter of fact, the power of the

261

state acquired by these habits proves. For Athens alone of her contemporaries is found when tested to be greater than her reputation, and alone gives no occasion to her assailants to blush at the antagonist by whom they have been worsted, or to her subjects to question her title by merit to rule. Rather, the admiration of the present and succeeding ages will be ours, since we have not left our power without witness, but have shown it by mighty proofs; and far from needing a Homer for our panegyrist, or other of his craft whose verses might charm for the moment only for the impression which they gave to melt at the touch of fact, we have forced every sea and land to be the highway of our daring, and everywhere, whether for evil or for good, have left imperishable monuments behind us. Such is the Athens for which these men, in the assertion of their resolve not to lose her, nobly fought and died; and well may every one of their survivors be ready to suffer in her cause.

'Indeed if I have dwelt at some length upon the character of our country, it has been to show that our stake in the struggle is not the same as theirs who have no such blessings to lose, and also that the panegyric of the men over whom I am now speaking might be by definite proofs established. That panegyric is now in a great measure complete; for the Athens that I have celebrated is only what the heroism of these and their like have made her, men whose fame, unlike that of most Hellenes, will be found to be only commensurate with their deserts. And if a test of worth be wanted, it is to be found in their closing scene, and this not only in the cases in which it set the final seal upon their merit, but also in those in which it gave the first intimation of their having any. For there is justice in the claim that steadfastness in his country's battles should be as a cloak to cover a man's other imperfections; since the good action has blotted out the bad, and his merit as a citizen more than outweighed his demerits as an individual. But none of these allowed either wealth with its prospect of future enjoyment to unnerve his spirit, or poverty with its hope of a day of freedom and riches to tempt him to shrink from danger. No, holding that vengeance upon their enemies was more to be desired than any personal blessings, and reckoning this to be the most glorious of hazards, they joyfully determined to accept the risk, to make sure of their vengeance and to let their wishes wait; and while committing to hope the uncertainty of final success, in the business before them they thought fit to act boldly and trust in themselves. Thus choosing to die resisting, rather than to live submitting, they fled only from dishonour, but met danger face to face, and after one brief moment, while at the summit of their fortune, escaped, not from their fear, but from their glory.

'So died these men as became Athenians. You, their survivors, must determine to have as unaltering a resolution in the field, though you may pray that it may have a happier issue. And not contented with ideas derived only from words of the advantages which are bound up with the defence of your country, though these would furnish a valuable text to a speaker even before an audience so alive to them as the present, you must yourselves realise the power of Athens, and feed your eyes upon her from day to day, till love of her fills your hearts; and then when all her greatness shall break upon you, you must reflect that it was by courage, sense of duty, and a keen feeling of honour in action that men were enabled to win all this, and that no personal failure in an enterprise could make them consent to deprive their country of their valour, but they laid it at her feet as the most glorious contribution that they could offer. For this offering of their lives made in common by them all they each of them individually received that renown which never grows old, and for a sepulchre, not so much that in which their bones have been deposited, but that noblest of shrines wherein their glory is laid up to be eternally remembered upon every occasion on which deed or story shall fall for its commemoration. For heroes have the whole earth for their tomb; and in lands far from their own, where the column with its epitaph declares it, there is enshrined in every breast a record unwritten with no tablet to preserve it, except that of the heart. These take as your model, and judging happiness to be the fruit of freedom and freedom of valour, never decline the dangers of war. For it is not the miserable that would most justly be unsparing of their lives; these have nothing to hope for; it is rather they to whom continued life may bring reverses as yet unknown, and to whom a fall, if it came, would be most tremendous in its consequences. And surely, to a man of spirit, the degradation of cowardice must be immeasurably more grievous than the unfelt death which strikes him in the midst of his strength and patriotism.

'Comfort, therefore, not condolence is what I have to offer to the parents of the dead who may be here. Numberless are the chances to which, as they know, the life of man is subject; but fortunate indeed are they who draw for their lot a death so glorious as that which has caused your mourning, and to whom life has been so exactly measured as to terminate in the happiness in which it has been passed. Still I know that this is a hard saying, especially when those are in question of whom you will constantly be reminded by seeing in the homes of others blessings of which once you also boasted: for grief is felt not so much for the want of what we have never known, as for the loss of that to which we have been long accustomed. Yet you who are still of an age to beget children must bear up in the hope of having others

263

in their stead; not only will they help you to forget those whom you have lost, but will be to the state at once a reinforcement and a security; for never can a fair or just policy be expected of the citizen who does not, like his fellows, bring to the decision the interests and apprehensions of a father. While those of you who have passed your prime must congratulate yourselves with the thought that the best part of your life was fortunate, and that the brief span that remains will be cheered by the fame of the departed. For it is only the love of honour that never grows old; and honour it is, not gain, as some would have it, that rejoices the heart of age and helplessness.

'Turning to the sons or brothers of the dead, I see an arduous struggle before you. When a man is gone, all are wont to praise him, and should your merit be ever so transcendent, you will still find it difficult not merely to overtake, but even to approach their renown. The living have envy to contend with, while those who are no longer in our path are honoured with a goodwill into which rivalry does not enter. On the other hand, if I must say anything on the subject of female excellence to those of you who will now be in widowhood, it will be all comprised in this brief exhortation. Great will be your natural character; and greatest will be hers who is least talked of among the men whether for good or for bad.

'My task is now finished. I have performed it to the best of my ability, and in words, at least, the requirements of the law are now satisfied. If deeds be in question, those who are here interred have received part of their honours already, and for the rest, their children will be brought up till manhood at the public expense: the state thus offers a valuable prize, as the garland of victory in this race of valour, for the reward both of those who have fallen and their survivors. And where the rewards for merit are greatest, there are found the best citizens.

'And now that you have brought to a close your lamentations for your relatives, you may depart.'

* * *

Book II — *The Plague of Athens*

In the first days of summer the Lacedaemonians and their allies, with two-thirds of their forces as before, invaded Attica, under the command of Archidamus, son of Zeuxidamus, king of Lacedaemon, and sat down and laid waste the country. Not many days after their arrival in Attica the plague first began to show itself among the

264

Athenians. It was said that it had broken out in many places previously in the neighbourhood of Lemnos and elsewhere; but a pestilence of such extent and mortality was nowhere remembered. Neither were the physicians at first of any service, ignorant as they were of the proper way to treat it, but they died themselves the most thickly, as they visited the sick most often; nor did any human art succeed any better. Supplications in the temples, divinations, and so forth were found equally futile, till the overwhelming nature of the disaster at last put a stop to them altogether.

It first began, it is said, in the parts of Ethiopia above Egypt, and thence descended into Egypt and Libya and into most of the king's country. Suddenly falling upon Athens, it first attacked the population in Piraeus, — which was the occasion of their saying that the Peloponnesians had poisoned the reservoirs, there being as yet no wells there — and afterwards appeared in the upper city, when the deaths became much more frequent. All speculation as to its origin and its causes, if causes can be found adequate to produce so great a disturbance, I leave to other writers, whether lay or professional; for myself, I shall simply set down its nature, and explain the symptoms by which perhaps it may be recognised by the student, if it should ever break out again. This I can the better do, as I had the disease myself, and watched its operation in the case of others.

That year then is admitted to have been otherwise unprecedentedly free from sickness; and such few cases as occurred, all determined in this. As a rule, however, there was no ostensible cause; but people in good health were all of a sudden attacked by violent heats in the head, and redness and inflammation in the eyes, the inward parts, such as the throat or tongue, becoming bloody and emitting an unnatural and fetid breath. These symptoms were followed by sneezing and hoarseness, after which the pain soon reached the chest, and produced a hard cough. When it fixed in the stomach, it upset it; and discharges of bile of every kind named by physicians ensued, accompanied by very great distress. In most cases also an ineffectual retching followed, producing violent spasms, which in some cases ceased soon after, in others much later. Externally the body was not very hot to the touch, nor pale in its appearance, but reddish, livid, and breaking out into small pustules and ulcers. But internally it burned so that the patient could not bear to have on him clothing or linen even of the very lightest description; or indeed to be otherwise than stark naked. What they would have liked best would have been to throw themselves into cold water; as indeed was done by some of the neglected sick, who plunged into the rain-tanks in their agonies of unquenchable thirst; though it made no difference whether they drank little or much. Besides this, the miserable feeling of not being able to rest or sleep never ceased to torment them. The body meanwhile did not waste away so long as the distemper was at its height, but held out to a marvel against its ravages; so that when they succumbed, as in most cases, on the seventh or eighth day to the internal inflammation, they had still some strength in them. But if they passed this stage, and the disease descended further into the bowels, inducing a violent ulceration then accompanied by severe diarrhoea, this brought on a weakness which was generally fatal. For the disorder first settled in the head, ran its course from thence through the whole of the body, and even where it did not prove mortal, it still left its mark on the extremities; for it settled in the privy parts, the fingers and the toes, and many escaped with the loss of these, some too with that of their eyes. Others again were seized with an entire loss of memory on their first recovery, and did not know either themselves or their friends.

But while the nature of the distemper was such as to baffle all description, and its attacks almost too grievous for human nature to endure, it was still in the following circumstance that its difference from all ordinary disorders was most clearly shown. All the birds and beasts that prey upon human bodies, either abstained from touching them (though there were many lying unburied), or died after tasting them. In proof of this, it was noticed that birds of this kind actually disappeared; they were not about the bodies, or indeed to be seen at all. But of course the effects which I have mentioned could best be studied in a domestic animal like the dog.

Such then, if we pass over the varieties of particular cases, which were many and peculiar, were the general features of the distemper. Meanwhile the town enjoyed an immunity from all the ordinary disorders; or if any case occurred, it ended in this. Some died in neglect, others in the midst of every attention. No remedy was found that could be used as a specific; for what did good in one case, did harm in another. Strong and weak constitutions proved equally incapable of resistance, all alike being swept away, although dieted with the utmost precaution. By far the most terrible feature in the malady was the dejection which ensued when any one felt himself sickening, for the despair into which they instantly fell took away their power of resistance, and left them a much easier prey to the disorder; besides which, there was the awful spectacle of men dying like sheep, through having caught the infection in nursing each other. This caused the greatest mortality. On the one hand, if they were afraid to visit each other, they perished from neglect; indeed many houses were emptied of their inmates for want of a nurse: on the other, if they ventured to do so, death was the consequence. This was especially the case with such as made any pretensions to goodness: honour made them unsparing in their friends' houses, where even the members of the family were at last worn out by the moans of the dying, and succumbed to the force of the disaster. Yet it was with those who had recovered from the disease that the sick and the dying found most compassion. These knew what it was from experience, and had now no fear for themselves; for the same man was never attacked twice — never at least fatally. And such persons not only received the congratulations of others, but themselves also, in the elation of the moment, half entertained the vain hope that they were for the future safe from any disease whatsoever.

An aggravation of the existing calamity was the influx from the country into the city, and this was especially felt by the new arrivals. As there were no houses to receive them, they had to be lodged at the hot season of the year in stifling cabins, where the mortality raged without restraint. The bodies of dying men lay one upon another, and half-dead creatures reeled about the streets and gathered round all the fountains in their longing for water. The sacred places also in which they had quartered themselves were full of corpses of persons that had died there, just as they were; for as the disaster passed all bounds, men, not knowing what was to become of them, became utterly careless of everything, whether sacred or profane. All the burial rites before in use were entirely upset, and they buried the bodies as best they could. Many from want of the proper appliances, through so many of their friends having died already, had recourse to the most shameless sepultures: sometimes getting the start of those who had raised a pile, they threw their own dead body upon the stranger's pyre and ignited it; sometimes they tossed the corpse which they were carrying on the top of another that was burning, and so went off.

Nor was this the only form of lawless extravagance which owed its origin to the plague. Men now coolly ventured on what they had formerly done in a corner, and not just as they pleased, seeing the rapid transitions produced by persons in prosperity suddenly dying and those who before had nothing succeeding to their property. So they resolved to spend quickly and enjoy themselves, regarding their lives and riches as alike things of a day. Perseverance in what men called honour was popular with none, it was so uncertain whether they would be spared to attain the object; but it was settled that present enjoyment, and all that contributed to it, was both honourable and useful. Fear of gods or law of man there was none to restrain them. As for the first, they judged it to be just the same whether they worshipped them or not, as they saw all alike perishing; and for the last, no one expected to live to be brought to trial for his offences, but each felt that a far severer sentence had been already passed upon them all and hung ever over their heads, and before this fell it was only reasonable to enjoy life a little.

Such was the nature of the calamity, and heavily did it weigh on the Athenians; death raging within the city and devastation without. Among other things which they remembered in their distress was, very naturally, the following verse which the old men said had long ago been uttered:

A Dorian war shall come and with it death.

So a dispute arose as to whether dearth and not death had not been the word in the verse; but at the present juncture, it was of course decided in favour of the latter; for the people made their recollection fit in with their sufferings. I fancy, however, that if another Dorian war should ever afterwards come upon us, and a dearth should happen to accompany it, the verse will probably be read accordingly. The oracle also which had been given to the Lacedaemonians was now remembered by those who knew of it. When the God was asked whether they should go to war, he answered that if they put their might into it, victory would be theirs, and that he would himself be with them. With this oracle events were supposed to tally. For the plague broke out so soon as the Peloponnesians invaded Attica, and never entering Peloponnese (not at least to an extent worth noticing), committed its worst ravages at Athens, and next to Athens, at the most populous of the other towns. Such was the history of the plague.

After ravaging the plain the Peloponnesians advanced into the Paralian region as far as Laurium, where the Athenian silver mines are, and first laid waste the side looking towards Peloponnese, next that which faces Euboea and Andros. But Pericles, who was still general, held the same opinion as in the former invasion, and would not let the Athenians march out against them.

However while they were still in the plain, and had not yet entered the Paralian land, he had prepared an armament of a hundred ships for Peloponnese, and when all was ready put out to sea. On board the ships he took four thousand Athenian heavy infantry, and three hundred cavalry in horse transports, then for the first time made out of old galleys; fifty Chian and Lesbian vessels also joining in the expedition. When this Athenian armament put out to sea, they left the Peloponnesians in Attica in the Paralian region. Arriving at Epidaurus in Peloponnese they ravaged most of the territory, and even had hopes of taking the town by an assault: in this however they were not successful. Putting out from Epidaurus, they laid waste the territory of Troezen, Halieis, and Hermione, all towns on the coast of Peloponnese,

268

and thence sailing to Prasiai, a maritime town in Laconia, ravaged part of its territory, and took and sacked the place itself; after which they returned home, but found the Peloponnesians gone and no longer in Attica.

During the whole time that Peloponnesians were in Attica on the expedition in their ships, men kept dying of the plague both in the armament and in Athens. Indeed it was actually asserted that the departure of the Peloponnesians was hastened by fear of the disorder; as they heard from deserters that it was in the city, and also could see the burials going on. Yet in this invasion they remained longer than in any other, and ravaged the whole country, for they were about forty days in Attica.

* * *

Book VII — *The Sicilian Expedition*

In 415 B. C. a large expedition set out to Sicily, ostensibly to support Segesta, an Athenian ally: but actually to bring Sicily under Athenian domination.

While the Athenians lingered on in this way without moving from where they were, Gylippus and Sicanus now arrived at Syracuse. Sicanus had failed to gain Agrigentum, the party friendly to the Syracusans having been driven out while he was still at Gela; but Gylippus was accompanied not only by a large number of troops raised in Sicily, but by the heavy infantry sent off in spring from Peloponnese, in the merchantmen, who had arrived at Selinus from Libya. They had been carried to Libya by a storm, and having obtained two galleys and pilots from the Cyrenians, on their voyage along shore had taken sides with the Euesperitae and had defeated the Libyans who were besieging them, and from thence coasting on to Neapolis, a Carthaginian mart, and the nearest point to Sicily, from which it is only two days' and a night's voyage, there crossed over and came to Selinus. Immediately upon their arrival the Syracusans prepared to attack the Athenians again by land and sea at once. The Athenian generals seeing a fresh army come to the aid of the enemy, and that their own circumstances, far from improving, were becoming daily worse, and above all distressed by the sickness of the soldiers, now began to repent of not having removed before; and Nicias no longer offering the same opposition, except by urging that there should be no open voting, they gave orders as secretly as possible for all to be prepared to sail out from the camp at a given signal. All was at last ready and they were on the point of sailing away, when an eclipse of the moon, which was then at the full, took place. Most of the Athenians, deeply impressed by this occurrence, now urged the generals to wait; and Nicias, who was somewhat over-addicted to divination and practices of that kind, refused from that moment even to take the question of departure into consideration, until they had waited the thrice nine days prescribed by the soothsayers.

The besiegers were thus condemned to stay in the country; and the Syracusans getting wind of what had happened, became more eager than ever to press the Athenians, who had now themselves acknowledged that they were no longer their superiors either by sea or by land, as otherwise they would never have planned to sail away. Besides which the Syracusans did not wish them to settle in any other part of Sicily, where they would be more difficult to deal with, but desired to force them to fight at sea as quickly as possible, in a position favourable to themselves. Accordingly they manned their ships and practised for as many days as they thought sufficient. When the moment arrived they assaulted on the first day the Athenian lines, and upon a small force of heavy infantry and horse sallying out against them by certain gates, cut off some of the former and routed and pursued them to the lines, where, as the entrance was narrow, the Athenians lost seventy horses and some few of the heavy infantry.

Drawing off their troops for this day, on the next the Syracusans went out with a fleet of seventy-six sail, and at the same time advanced with their land forces against the lines. The Athenians put out to meet them with eighty-six ships, came to close quarters and engaged. The Syracusans and their allies first defeated the Athenian centre, and then caught Eurymedon, the commander of the right wing, who was sailing out from the line more towards the land in order to surround the enemy, in the hollow and recess of the harbour, and killed him and destroyed the ships accompanying him; after which they now chased the whole Athenian fleet before them and drove them ashore.

Gylippus seeing the enemy's fleet defeated and carried ashore beyond their stockades and camp, ran down to the breakwater with some of his troops, in order to cut off the men as they landed and make it easier for the Syracusans to tow off the vessels by the shore being friendly ground. The Tyrrhenians who guarded this point for the Athenians seeing them come on in disorder, advanced out against them and attacked and routed their van, hurling it into the marsh of Lysimeleia. Afterwards the Syracusan and allied troops arrived in greater numbers, and the Athenians fearing for their ships came up

270

also to the rescue and engaged them, and defeated and pursued them to some distance and killed a few of their heavy infantry. They succeeded in rescuing most of their ships and brought them down by their camp; eighteen however were taken by the Syracusans and their allies, and all the men killed. The rest the enemy tried to burn by means of an old merchantman which they filled with faggots and pine-wood, set on fire and let drift down the wind which blew full on the Athenians. The Athenians, however, alarmed for their ships, contrived means for stopping it and putting it out, and checking the flames and the nearer approach of the merchantman, thus escaped the danger.

After this the Syracusans set up a trophy for the sea-fight and for the heavy infantry whom they had cut off up at the lines, where they took the horses; and the Athenians for the rout of the foot driven by the Tyrrhenians into the marsh, and for their own victory with the rest of the army.

The Syracusans had now gained a decisive victory at sea, where until now they had feared the reinforcement brought by Demosthenes, and deep, in consequence, was the despondency of the Athenians, and great their disappointment, and greater still their regret for having come on the expedition. These were the only cities that they had yet encountered, similar to their own in character, under democracies like themselves, which had ships and horses, and were of considerable magnitude. They had been unable to divide and bring them over by holding out the prospect of changes in their governments, or to crush them by their great superiority in force, but had failed in most of their attempts, and being already in perplexity, had now been defeated at sea, where defeat could never have been expected, and were thus plunged deeper in embarrassment than ever.

Meanwhile the Syracusans immediately began to sail freely along the harbour, and determined to close up its mouth, so that the Athenians might not be able to steal out in future, even if they wished. Indeed, the Syracusans no longer thought only of saving themselves, but also how to hinder the escape of the enemy; thinking, and thinking rightly, that they were now much the strongest, and that to conquer the Athenians and their allies by land and sea would win them great glory in Hellas. The rest of the Hellenes would thus immediately be either freed or released from apprehension, as the remaining forces of Athens would be henceforth unable to sustain the war that would be waged against her; while they, the Syracusans, would be regarded as the authors of this deliverance, and would be held in high admiration, not only with all men now living but also with posterity. Nor were these the only considerations that gave dignity to the struggle. They would thus conquer not only the Athenians but also their numerous allies, and conquer not alone, but with their companions-in-arms, commanding side by side with the Corinthians and Lacedaemonians, having offered their city to stand in the van for danger, and having been in a great measure the pioneers of naval success.

Indeed, there were never so many peoples assembled before a single city, if we except the grand total gathered together in this war under Athens and Lacedaemon. The following were the states on either side who came to Syracuse to fight for or against Sicily, to help to conquer or defend the island. Right or community of blood was not the bond of union between them, so much as interest or compulsion as the case might be. The Athenians themselves being Ionians went against the Dorians of Syracuse of their own free will; and the peoples still speaking Attic and using the Athenian laws, the Lemnians, Imbrians, and Aeginetans, that is to say, the then occupants of Aegina, being their colonists, went with them. To these must be also added the Hestiaeans dwelling at Hestiaea in Euboea. Of the rest some joined in the expedition as subjects of the Athenians, others as independent allies, others as mercenaries. To the number of the subjects paying tribute belonged the Eretrians, Chalcidians, Styrians, and Carystians from Euboea; the Ceans, Andrians, and Tenians from the islands; and the Milesians, Samians, and Chians from Ionia. The Chians, however, joined as independent allies, paying no tribute, but furnishing ships. Most of these were Ionians and descended from the Athenians, except the Carystians, who are Dryopes, and although subjects and obliged to serve, were still Ionians fighting against Dorians. Besides these there were men of Aeolic race, the Methymnians, subjects who provided ships, not tribute, and the Tenedians and Aenians who paid tribute. These Aeolians fought against their Aeolian founders, the Boeotians in the Syracusan army, because they were obliged, while the Plataeans, the only native Boeotians opposed to Boeotians, did so upon a just quarrel. Of the Rhodians and Cytherians, both Dorians, the latter, Lacedaemonian colonists, fought in the Athenian ranks against their Lacedaemonian countrymen with Gylippus; while the Rhodians, Argives by race, were compelled to bear arms against the Dorian Syracusans and their own colonists, the Geloans, serving with the Syracusans. Of the islanders round Peloponnese, the Cephallenians and Zacynthians accompanied the Athenians as independent allies, although their insular position really left them little choice in the matter, owing to the maritime supremacy of Athens, while the Corcyraeans, who were not only Dorians but Corinthians, were openly serving against Corinthians and Syracusans, although colonists of the former and of the same race as the latter, under colour of compulsion, but really out of free will through hatred of Corinth. The Messenians, as they are now called in Naupactus and from Pylos, then held by the Athenians, were taken with them to the war. There were also a few Megarian exiles, whose fate it was to be now fighting against the Megarian Selinuntines.

The engagement of the rest was more of a voluntary nature. It was less the league than hatred of the Lacedaemonians and the immediate private advantage of each individual that persuaded the Dorian Argives to join the Ionian Athenians in a war against Dorians; while the Mantineans and other Arcadian mercenaries, accustomed to go against the enemy pointed out to them at the moment, were led by interest to regard the Arcadians serving with the Corinthians as just as much their enemies as any others. The Cretans and Aetolians also served for hire, and the Cretans who had joined the Rhodians in founding Gela, thus came to consent to fight for pay against, instead of for, their colonists. There were also some Acarnanians paid to serve, although they came chiefly for love of Demosthenes and out of goodwill to the Athenians whose allies they were. These all lived on the Hellenic side of the Ionian gulf. Of the Italiots, there were the Thurians and Metapontines, dragged into the quarrel by the stern necessities of a time of revolution; of the Siceliots, the Naxians and the Catanians; and of the barbarians, the Egestaeans, who called in the Athenians, most of the Sicels, and outside Sicily some Tyrrhenian enemies of Syracuse and Iapygian mercenaries.

Such were the peoples serving with the Athenians. Against these the Syracusans had the Camarinaeans their neighbours, the Geolans who live next them, and then passing over the neutral Agrigentines, the Selinuntines settled on the farther side of the island. These inhabit the part of Sicily looking towards Libya; the Himeraeans came from the side towards the Tyrrhenian sea, being the only Hellenic inhabitants in that quarter, and the only people that came from thence to the aid of the Syracusans. Of the Hellenes in Sicily the above peoples joined in the war, all Dorians and independent, and of the barbarians the Sicels only, that is to say, such as did not go over to the Athenians. Of the Hellenes outside Sicily there were the Lacedaemonians, who provided a Spartan to take the command, and a force of Neodamodes or Freedmen, and of Helots; the Corinthians, who alone joined with naval and land forces, with their Leucadian and Ambraciot kinsmen; some mercenaries sent by Corinth from Arcadia; some Sicyonians forced to serve, and from outside Peloponnese the Boeotians. In comparison, however, with these foreign auxiliaries, the great Siceliot cities furnished more in every department — numbers of heavy infantry, ships and horses, and an immense multitude besides having been brought together; while in comparison, again, one may say, with all the rest put together, more was provided by the Syracusans themselves, both from the greatness of the city and from the fact that they were in the greatest danger.

Such were the auxiliaries brought together on either side, all of which had by this time joined, neither party experiencing any subsequent accession. It was no wonder, therefore, if the Syracusans and their allies thought that it would win them great glory if they could follow up their recent victory in the sea-fight by the capture of the whole Athenian armada, without letting it escape either by sea or by land. They began at once to close up the Great Harbour by means of boats, merchant vessels, and galleys moored broadside across its mouth, which is nearly a mile wide, and made all their other arrangements for the event of the Athenians again venturing to fight at sea. There was, in fact, nothing little either in their plans or their ideas.

The Athenians, seeing them closing up the harbour and informed of their further designs, called a council of war. The generals and colonels assembled and discussed the difficulties of the situation; the point which pressed most being that they no longer had provisions for immediate use (having sent on to Catana to tell them not to send any, in the belief that they were going away), and that they would not have any in future unless they could command the sea. They therefore determined to evacuate their upper lines, to enclose with a cross-wall and garrison a small space close to the ships, only just sufficient to hold their stores and sick, and manning all the ships, seaworthy or not, with every man that could be spared from the rest of their land forces, to fight it out at sea, and if victorious, to go to Catana, if not, to burn their vessels, form in close order, and retreat by land for the nearest friendly place they could reach, Hellenic or barbarian. This was no sooner settled than carried into effect: they descended gradually from the upper lines and manned all their vessels, compelling all to go on board who were of age to be in any way of use. They thus succeeded in manning about one hundred and ten ships in all, on board of which they embarked a number of archers and darters taken from the Acarnanians and from the other foreigners, making all other provisions allowed by the nature of their plan and by the necessities which imposed it. All was now nearly ready, and Nicias, seeing the soldiery disheartened by their unprecedented and decided defeat at sea, and by reason of the scarcity of provisions eager to fight it out as soon as possible, called them all together, and first addressed them, speaking as follows: —

'Soldiers of the Athenians and of the allies, we have all an equal interest in the coming struggle, in which life and country are at stake for us quite as much as they can be for the enemy; since if our fleet wins the day, each can see his native city again, wherever that city may be. You must not lose heart, or be like men without any experience, who fail in a first essay, and ever afterwards fearfully forebode a future as disastrous. But let the Athenians among you who have already had experience of many wars, and the allies who have joined us in so many expeditions, remember the surprises of war, and with the hope that fortune will not be always against us, prepare to fight again in a manner worthy of the number which you see yourselves to be.

'Now, whatever we thought would be of service against the crush of vessels in such a narrow harbour, and against the force upon the decks of the enemy, from which we suffered before, has all been considered with the helmsmen, and, as far as our means allowed, provided. A number of archers and darters will go on board, and a multitude that we should not have employed in an action in the open sea, where our science would be crippled by the weight of the vessels; but in the present land-fight that we are forced to make from ship-board all this will be useful. We have also discovered the changes in construction that we must make to meet theirs; and against the thickness of their cheeks, which did us the greatest mischief, we have provided grappling-irons, which will prevent an assailant backing water after charging, if the soldiers on deck here do their duty; since we are absolutely compelled to fight a land battle from the fleet, and it seems to be our interest neither to back water ourselves, nor to let the enemy do so, especially as the shore, except so much of it as may be held by our troops, is hostile ground.

'You must remember this and fight on as long as you can, and must not let yourselves be driven ashore, but once alongside must make up your minds not to part company until you have swept the heavy infantry from the enemy's deck. I say this more for the heavy infantry than for the seamen, as it is more the business of the men on deck; and our land forces are even now on the whole the strongest. The sailors I advise, and at the same time implore, not to be too much daunted by their misfortunes, now that we have our decks better armed and a greater number of vessels. Bear in mind how well worth preserving is the pleasure felt by those of you who through your knowledge of our language and imitation of our manners were always considered Athenians, even though not so in reality, and as such were honoured throughout Hellas, and had your full share of the advantages of our empire, and more than your share in the respect of our subjects and in protection from ill treatment. You, therefore, with whom alone we freely share our empire, we now justly require not to betray that empire in its extremity, and in scorn of Corinthians, whom you have often conquered, and of Siceliots, none of whom so much as presumed to stand against us when our navy was in its prime, we ask you to repel them, and to show that even in sickness and disaster your skill is more than a match for the fortune and vigour of any other.

'For the Athenians among you I add once more this reflexion: — you left behind you no more such ships in your docks as these, no more heavy infantry in their flower; if you do aught but conquer, our enemies here will immediately sail thither, and those that are left of us at Athens will become unable to repel their home assailants, reinforced by these new allies. Here you will fall at once into the hands of the Syracusans — I need not remind you of the intentions with which you attacked them — and your countrymen at home will fall into those of the Lacedaemonians. Since the fate of both thus hangs upon this single battle — now, if ever, stand firm, and remember, each and all, that you who are now going on board are the army and navy of the Athenians, and all that is left of the state and the great name of Athens, in whose defence if any man has any advantage in skill or courage, now is the time for him to show it, and thus serve himself and save all.'

After this address Nicias at once gave orders to man the ships. Meanwhile Gylippus and the Syracusans could perceive by the preparations which they saw going on that the Athenians meant to fight at sea. They had also notice of the grappling-irons, against which they specially provided by stretching hides over the prows and much of the upper part of their vessels, in order that the irons when thrown might slip off without taking hold. All being now ready, the generals and Gylippus addressed them in the following terms: —

'Syracusans and allies, the glorious character of our past achievements and the no less glorious results at issue in the coming battle are, we think, understood by most of you, or you would never have thrown yourselves with such ardour into the struggle; and if there be any one not as fully aware of the facts as he ought to be, we will declare them to him. The Athenians came to this country first to effect the conquest of Sicily, and after that, if successful, of Peloponnese and the rest of Hellas, possessing already the greatest empire yet known, of present or former times, among the Hellenes. Here for the first time they found in you men who faced their navy which made them masters everywhere; you have already defeated them in the previous sea-fight, and will in all likelihood defeat them again now. When men are once checked in what they consider their special excellence, their whole opinion of themselves suffers more than if they had not at first believed in their superiority, the unexpected shock to their pride causing them to give way more than their real strength warrants; and this is probably now the case with the Athenians.

'With us it is different. The original estimate of ourselves which gave us courage in the days of our unskilfulness has been strengthened, while the convictions super-added to it that we must be the best seamen of the time, if we have conquered the best, has given a double measure of hope to every man among us; and, for the most part, where there is the greatest hope, there is also the greatest ardour for action. The means to combat us which they have tried to find in copying our armament are familiar to our warfare, and will be met by proper provisions; while they will never be able to have a number of heavy infantry on their decks, contrary to their custom, and a number of darters (born landsmen, one may say, Acarnanians and others, embarked afloat, who will not know how to discharge their weapons when they have to keep still), without hampering their vessels and falling all into confusion among themselves through fighting not according to their own tactics. For they will gain nothing by the number of their ships — I say this to those of you who may be alarmed by having to fight against odds — as a quantity of ships in a confined space will only be slower in executing the movements required, and most exposed to injury from our means of offence. Indeed, if you would know the plain truth, as we are credibly informed, the excess of their sufferings and the necessities of their present distress have made them desperate; they have no confidence in their force, but wish to try their fortune in the only way they can, and either to force their passage and sail out, or after this to retreat by land, it being impossible for them to be worse off than they are.

'The fortune of our greatest enemies having thus betrayed itself, and their disorder being what I have described, let us engage in anger, convinced that, as between adversaries, nothing is more legitimate than to claim to sate the whole wrath of one's soul in punishing the aggressor, and nothing more sweet, as the proverb has it, than the vengeance upon an enemy, which it will now be ours to take. That enemies they are and mortal enemies you all know, since they came here to enslave our country, and if successful had in reserve for our men all that is most dreadful, and for our children and wives all that is most dishonourable, and for the whole city the name which conveys the greatest reproach. None should therefore relent to think it gain if they go away without further danger to us. This they will do just the same, even if they get the victory; while if we succeed, as we may expect, in chastising them, and in handing down to all Sicily her ancient freedom strengthened and confirmed, we shall have achieved no mean triumph. And the rarest dangers are those in which failure brings little loss and success the greatest advantage.'

After the above address to the soldiers on their side, the Syracusan generals and Gylippus now perceived that the Athenians were manning their ships, and immediately proceeded to man their own also. Meanwhile Nicias, appalled by the position of affairs, realising the greatness and the nearness of the danger now that they were on the point of putting out from shore, and thinking, as men are apt to think in great crises, that when all has been done they have still something left to do, and when all has been said that they have not yet said enough, again called on the captains one by one, addressing each by his father's name and by his own, and by that of his tribe, and adjured them not to belie their own personal renown, or to obscure the hereditary virtues for which their ancestors were illustrious; he reminded them of their country, the freest of the free, and of the unfettered discretion allowed in it to all to live as they pleased; and added other arguments such as men would use at such a crisis, and which, with little alteration, are made to serve on all occasions alike — appeals to wives, children, and national gods, — without caring whether they are thought commonplace, but loudly invoking them in the belief that they will be of use in the consternation of the moment. Having thus admonished them, not, he felt, as he would, but as he could, Nicias withdrew and led the troops to the sea, and ranged them in as long a line as he was able, in order to aid as far as possible in sustaining the courage of the men afloat; while Demosthenes, Menander, and Euthydemus, who took the command on board, put out from their own camp and sailed straight to the barrier across the mouth of the harbour and to the passage left open, to try to force their way out.

The Syracusans and their allies had already put out with about the same number of ships as before, a part of which kept guard at the outlet, and the remainder all around the rest of the harbour, in order to attack the Athenians on all sides at once; while the land forces held themselves in readiness at the points at which the vessels might put into the shore. The Syracusan fleet was commanded by Sicanus and Agatharchus, who had each a wing of the whole force, with Python and the Corinthians in the centre. When the rest of the Athenians came up to the barrier, with the first shock of their charge they overpowered the ships stationed there, and tried to undo the fastenings; after this, as the Syracusans and allies bore down upon them from all quarters, the action spread from the barrier over the whole harbour, and was more obstinately disputed than any of the preceding ones. On either side the rowers showed great zeal in bringing up their vessels at the boatswains' orders, and the helmsmen great skill in manoeuvering, and great emulation one with another; while the ships once alongside, the soldiers on board did their best not to let the service on deck be outdone by the others; in short, every man strove to prove himself the first in his particular department. And as many ships were engaged in a small compass (for these were the largest fleets fighting in the narrowest space ever known, being together little short of two hundred), the regular attacks with the beak were few, there being no opportunity of backing water or of breaking the line; while the collisions caused by one ship chancing to run foul of another, either in flying from or attacking a third, were more frequent. So long as a vessel was coming up to the charge the men on the decks rained darts and arrows and stones upon her; but once alongside, the heavy infantry tried to board each other's vessel, fighting hand to hand. In many quarters also it happened, by reason of the narrow room, that a vessel was charging an enemy on one side and being charged herself on another, and that two, or sometimes more ships had perforce got entangled round one, obliging the helmsmen to attend to defence here, offence there, not to one thing at once, but to many on all sides; while the huge din caused by the number of ships crashing together not only spread terror, but made the orders of the boatswains inaudible. The boatswains on either side in the discharge of their duty and in the heat of the conflict shouted incessantly orders and appeals to their men; the Athenians they urged to force the passage out, and now if ever to show their mettle and lay hold of a safe return to their country; to the Syracusans and their allies they cried that it would be glorious to prevent the escape of the enemy, and conquering, to exalt the countries that were theirs. The generals, moreover, on either side, if they saw any in any part of the battle backing ashore without being forced to do so, called out to the captain by name and asked him — the Athenians, whether they were retreating because they thought the thrice hostile shore more their own than that sea which had cost them so much labour to win; the Syracusans, whether they were flying from the flying Athenians, whom they well knew to be eager to escape in whatever way they could.

Meanwhile the two armies on shore, while victory hung in the balance, were a prey to the most agonising and conflicting emotions; the natives thirsting for more glory than they had already won, while the invaders feared to find themselves in even worse plight than before. Then all of the Athenians being set upon their fleet, their fear for the event was like nothing they had ever felt; while their view of the struggle was necessarily as chequered as the battle itself. Close to the scene of action and not all looking at the same point at once, some saw their friends victorious and took courage, and fell to calling upon heaven not to deprive them of salvation, while other who had their eyes turned upon the losers, wailed and cried aloud, and, although spectators, were more overcome than the actual combatants. Others, again, were gazing at some spot where the battle was evenly disputed; as the strife was protracted without decision, their swaying bodies reflected the agitation of their minds, and they suffered the worst agony of all, ever just within reach of safety or just on the point of destruction. In short, in that one Athenian army as long as the sea-fight remained doubtful there was every sound to be heard at once, shrieks, cheers, 'We win,' 'We lose,' and all the other manifold exclamations that a great host would necessarily utter in great peril; and with the men in the fleet it was nearly the same; until at last the Syracusans and their allies, after the battle had lasted a long while, put the Athenians to flight, and with much shouting and cheering chased them in open rout to the shore. The naval force, one one way, one another, as many as were not taken afloat, now ran ashore and rushed from on board their ships to their camp; while the army, no more divided, but carried away by one impulse, all with shrieks and groans deplored the event, and ran down, some to help the ships, others to guard what was left of their wall, while the remaining and most numerous part already began to consider how they should save themselves. Indeed, the panic of the present moment had never been surpassed. They now suffered very nearly what they had inflicted at Pylos; as then the Lacedaemonians with the loss of their fleet lost also the men who had crossed over to the island, so now the Athenians had no hope of escaping by land, without the help of some extraordinary accident.

The sea-fight having been a severe one, and many ships and lives having been lost on both sides, the victorious Syracusans and their allies now picked up their wrecks and dead, and sailed off to the city and set up a trophy. The Athenians, overwhelmed by their misfortune, never even thought of asking leave to take up their dead or wrecks, but wished to retreat that very night. Demosthenes, however, went to Nicias and gave it as his opinion that they should man the ships they had left and make another effort to force their passage out next morning; saying that they had still left more ships fit for service than the enemy, the Athenians having about sixty remaining as against less than fifty of their opponents. Nicias was quit of his mind; but when they wished to man the vessels, the sailors refused to go on board, being so utterly overcome by their defeat as no longer to believe in the possibility of success.

Accordingly they all now made up their minds to retreat by land. Meanwhile the Syracusan Hermocrates suspecting their intention, and impressed by the danger of allowing a force of that magnitude to retire by land, establish itself in some other part of Sicily, and from thence renew the war, went and stated his views to the authorities, and pointed out to them that they ought not to let the enemy get away by night, but that all the Syracusans and their allies should at once march out and block up the roads and seize and guard the passes. The authorities were entirely of his opinion, and thought that it ought to be done, but on the other hand felt sure that the people, who had given themselves over to rejoicing and were taking their ease after a great battle at sea, would not be easily brought to obey; besides, they were celebrating a festival, having on that day a sacrifice to Heracles, and most of them in their rapture at the victory had fallen to drinking at the festival, and would probably consent to anything sooner than to take up their arms and march out at that moment. For these reasons, the thing appeared impracticable to the magistrates; and Hermocrates, finding himself unable to do anything further with them, had now recourse to the following stratagem of his own. What he feared was that the Athenians might quietly get the start of them by passing the most difficult places during the night; and he therefore sent, as soon as it was dusk, some friends of his own to the camp with some horsemen who rode up within earshot and called out to some of them, as though they were well-wishers of the Athenians, and told them to tell Nicias (who had in fact some correspondence who informed him of what went on inside the town), not to lead off the army by night as the Syracusans were guarding the roads, but to make his preparations at his leisure and to retreat by day. After saying this they departed; and their hearers informed the Athenian generals, who put off going for that night on the strength of this message, not doubting its sincerity.

Since after all they had not set out at once, they now determined to stay also the following day to give time to the soldiers to pack up as well as they could the most useful articles, and, leaving everything else behind, to start only with what was strictly necessary for their personal subsistence. Meanwhile the Syracusans and Gylippus marched out and blocked up the roads through the country by which the Athenians were likely to pass, and kept guards at the fords of the stream and rivers, posting themselves so as to receive them and stop the army where they thought best; while their fleet sailed up to the beach and towed off the ships of the Athenians. Some few were burned by the Athenians themselves as they had intended; the rest the Syracusans lashed on to their own at their leisure as they had been thrown up on shore, without any one trying to stop them, and conveyed to the town.

After this, Nicias and Demosthenes now thinking that enough had been done in the way of preparation, the removal of the army took place upon the second day after the sea-fight. It was a lamentable scene, not merely from the single circumstance that they were retreating

281

after having lost all their ships, their great hopes gone, and themselves and the state in peril; but also in leaving the camp there were things most grievous for every eye and heart to contemplate. The dead lay unburied, and each man as he recognised a friend among them shuddered with grief and horror; while the living whom they were leaving behind, wounded or sick, were to the living far more shocking than the dead, and more to be pitied than those who had perished. These fell to entreating and bewailing until their friends knew not what to do, begging them to take them and loudly calling to each individual comrade or relative whom they could see, hanging upon the necks of their tent-fellows in the act of departure, and following as far as they could, and when their bodily strength failed them, calling again and again upon heaven and shrieking aloud as they were left behind. So that the whole army being filled with tears and distracted after this fashion, found it not easy to go, even from an enemy's land, where they had already suffered evils too great for tears and in the unknown future before them feared to suffer more. Dejection and self-condemnation were also rife among them. Indeed they could only be compared to a starved-out town, and that no small one, escaping; the whole multitude upon the march being not less than forty thousand men. All carried everything they could which might be of use, and the heavy infantry and troopers, contrary to their wont, while under arms carried their own victuals, in some cases for want of servants, in others through not trusting them; as they had long been deserting and now did so in greater numbers than ever. Yet even thus they did not carry enough, as there was no longer food in the camp. Moreover their disgrace generally, and the universality of their sufferings, however to a certain extent alleviated by being borne in company, were still felt at the moment a heavy burden, especially when they contrasted the splendour and glory of their setting out with the humiliation in which it had ended. For this was by far the greatest reverse that ever befell an Hellenic army. They had come to enslave others, and were departing in fear of being enslaved themselves: they had sailed out with prayer and paeans, and now started to go back with omens directly contrary; traveling by land instead of by sea, and trusting not in their fleet but in their heavy infantry. Nevertheless the greatness of the danger still impending made all this appear tolerable.

Nicias seeing the army dejected and greatly altered, passed along the ranks and encouraged and comforted them as far as was possible under the circumstances, raising his voice still higher and higher as he went from one company to another in his earnestness, and in his anxiety that the benefit of his words might reach as many as possible: —

'Athenians and allies, even in our present position we must still hope on, since men have here now been saved from worse straits than this; and you must not condemn yourselves too severely either because of your disasters or because of your present unmerited sufferings. I myself who am not superior to any of you in strength — indeed you see how I am in my sickness — and who in the gifts of fortune am, I think, whether in private life or otherwise, the equal of any, am now exposed to the same danger as the meanest among you; and yet my life has been one of much devotion towards the gods, and of much justice and without offence towards men. I have, therefore, still a strong hope for the future, and our misfortunes do not terrify me as much as they might. Indeed we may hope that they will be lightened: our enemies have had good fortune enough; and if any of the gods was offended at our expedition, we have been already amply punished. Others before us have attacked their neighbours and have done what men will do without suffering more than they could bear; and we may now justly expect to find the gods more kind, for we have become fitter objects of their pity than their jealousy. And then look at yourselves, mark the numbers and efficiency of the heavy infantry marching in your ranks, and not give way too much to despondency, but reflect that you are yourselves at once a city wherever you sit down, and that there is no other in Sicily that could easily resist your attack, or expel you when once established. The safety and order of the march is for yourselves to look to; the one thought of each man being that the spot on which he may be forced to fight must be conquered and held as his country and stronghold. Meanwhile we shall hasten on our way night and day alike, as our provisions are scanty; and if we can reach some friendly place of the Sicels, whom fear of the Syracusans still keeps true to us, you may forthwith consider yourselves safe. A message has been sent on to them, with directions to meet us with supplies of food. To sum up, be convinced, soldiers, that you must be brave, as there is no place near for your cowardice to take refuge in, and that if you now escape from the enemy, you may all see again what your hearts desire, while those of you who are Athenians will raise up again the great power of the state, fallen though it be. Men make the city and not walls or ships without men in them.'

As he made this address, Nicias went along the ranks, and brought back to their place any of the troops that he saw straggling out of the line; while Demosthenes did as much for his part of the army, addressing them in words very similar. The army marched in a hollow square, the division under Nicias leading, and that of Demosthenes following, the heavy infantry being outside and the baggage-carriers and the bulk of the army in the middle. When they arrived at the ford of the river Anapus they there found drawn up a body of the Syracusans and allies, and routing these, made good their passage and pushed on, harassed by the charges of the Syracusan horse and by the missiles of their light troops. On that day they advanced about four miles and a half, halting for the night upon a certain hill. On the next day they started early and got on about two miles further, and descended into a place in the plain and there encamped, in order to procure some eatables from the houses, as the place was inhabited, and to carry on with them water from thence, as for many furlongs in front, in the direction in which they were going, it was not plentiful. The Syracusans meanwhile went on and fortified the pass in front, where there was a steep hill with a rocky ravine on each side of it, called the Acraean cliff. The next day the Athenians advancing found themselves impeded by the missiles and charges of the horse and darters, both very numerous, of the Syracusans and allies; and after fighting for a long while, at length retired to the same camp, where they had no longer provisions as before, it being impossible to leave their position by reason of the cavalry.

Early next morning they started afresh and forced their way to the hill, which had been fortified, where they found before them the enemy's infantry drawn up many shields deep to defend the fortification, the pass being narrow. The Athenians assaulted the work, but were greeted by a storm of missiles from the hill, which told with the greater effect through its being a steep one, and unable to force the passage, retreated again and rested. Meanwhile occurred some claps of thunder and rain, as often happens towards autumn, which still further disheartened the Athenians, who thought all these things to be omens of their approaching ruin. While they were resting Gylippus and the Syracusans sent a part of their army to throw up works in their rear on the way by which they had advanced; however, the Athenians immediately sent some of their men and prevented them; after which they retreated more towards the plain and halted for the night. When they advanced the next day the Syracusans surrounded and attacked them on every side, and disabled many of them, falling back if the Athenians advanced and coming on if they retired, and in particular assaulting their rear, in the hope of routing them in detail, and thus striking a panic into the whole army. For a long while the Athenians persevered in this fashion, but after advancing for four or five furlongs halted to rest in the plain, the Syracusans also withdrawing to their own camp.

During the night Nicias and Demosthenes, seeing the wretched condition of their troops, now in want of every kind of necessary, and numbers of them disabled in the numerous attacks of the enemy, determined to light as many fires as possible, and to lead off the army, no longer by the same route as they had intended, but towards the sea in the opposite direction to that guarded by the Syracusans. The whole of this route was leading the army not to Catana but to the other side of Sicily, towards Camarina, Gela, and the other Hellenic and barbarian towns in that quarter. They accordingly lit a number of fires and set out by night. Now all armies, and the greatest most of all, are liable to fears and alarms, especially when they are marching by night through an enemy's country and with the enemy near; and the Athenians falling into one of these panics, the leading division, that of Nicias, kept together and got on a good way in front, while that of Demosthenes, comprising rather more than half the army, got separated and marched on in some disorder. By morning, however, they reached the sea, and getting into the Helorine Road, pushed on in order to reach the river Cacyparis, and to follow the stream up through the interior, where they hoped to be met by the Sicels whom they had sent for. Arrived at the river, they found there also a Syracusan party engaged in barring the passage of the ford with a wall and a palisade, and forcing this guard, crossed the river and went on to another called the Erineus, according to the advice of their guides.

Meanwhile, when day came and the Syracusans and allies found that the Athenians were gone, most of them accused Gylippus of having let them escape on purpose, and hastily pursuing by the road which they had no difficulty in finding that they had taken, overtook them about dinner-time. They first came up with the troops under Demosthenes, who were behind and marching somewhat slowly and in disorder, owing to the night-panic above referred to, and at once attacked and engaged them, the Syracusan horse surrounding them with more ease now that they were separated from the rest, and hemming them in on one spot. The division of Nicias was five or six miles on in front, as he led them more rapidly, thinking that under the circumstances their safety lay not in staying and fighting, unless obliged, but in retreating as fast as possible, and only fighting when forced to do so. On the other hand, Demosthenes was, generally speaking, harassed more incessantly, as his post in the rear left him the first exposed to the attacks of the enemy; and now, finding that the Syracusans were in pursuit, he omitted to push on, in order to form his men for battle, and so lingered until he was surrounded by his pursuers and himself and the Athenians with him placed in the most distressing position, being huddled into an enclosure with a wall all around it, a road on this side and on that, and olive-trees in great number, where missiles were showered in upon them from every quarter. This mode of attack the Syracusans had with good reason adopted in preference to fighting at close quarters, as to risk a struggle with desperate men was now more for the advantage of the

Athenians than for their own; besides, their success had now become so certain that they began to spare themselves a little in order not to be cut off in the moment of victory, thinking too that, as it was, they would be able in this way to subdue and capture the enemy.

In fact, after plying the Athenians and allies all day long from every side with missiles, they at length saw that they were worn out with their wounds and other sufferings; and Gylippus and the Syracusans and their allies made a proclamation, offering their liberty to any of the islanders who chose to come over to them; and some few cities went over. Afterwards a capitulation was agreed upon for all the rest with Demosthenes, to lay down their arms on condition that no one was to be put to death either by violence or imprisonment or want of the necessaries of life. Upon this they surrendered to the number of six thousand in all, laying down all the money in their possession, which filled the hollows of four shields, and were immediately conveyed by the Syracusans to the town.

Meanwhile Nicias with his division arrived that day at the river Erineus, crossed over and posted his army upon some high ground upon the other side. The next day the Syracusans overtook him and told him that the troops under Demosthenes had surrendered, and invited him to follow their example. Incredulous of the fact, Nicias asked for a truce to send a horseman to see and upon the return of the messenger with the tidings that they had surrendered, sent a herald to Gylippus and the Syracusans, saying that he was ready to agree with them on behalf of the Athenians to repay whatever money the Syracusans had spent upon the war if they would let his army go; and offered until the money was paid to give Athenians as hostages, one for every talent. The Syracusans and Gylippus rejected this proposition, and attacked this division as they had the other, standing all round and plying them with missiles until the evening. Food and necessaries were as miserably wanting to the troops of Nicias as they had been to their comrades; nevertheless they watched for the quiet of the night to resume their march. But as they were taking up their arms the Syracusans perceived it and raised their paean, upon which the Athenians, finding that they were discovered, laid them down again, except about three hundred men who forced their way through the guards and went on during the night as they were able.

As soon as it was day Nicias put his army in motion, pressed, as before, by the Syracusans and their allies, pelted from every side by their missiles, and struck down by their javelins. The Athenians pushed on for the Assinarus, impelled by the attacks made upon them from every side by a numerous cavalry and the swarm of other arms, fancying that they should breathe more freely if once across the river, and driven on also by their exhaustion and craving for water. Once there they rushed in, and all order was at an end, each man wanting to cross first, and the attacks of the enemy making it difficult to cross at all; forced to huddle together, they fell against and trod down one another, some dying immediately upon the javelins, others getting entangled together and stumbling over the articles of baggage, without being able to rise again. Meanwhile the opposite bank, which was steep, was lined by the Syracusans, who showered missiles down upon the Athenians, most of them drinking greedily and heaped together in disorder in the hollow bed of the river. The Peloponnesians also came down and butchered them, especially those in the water, which was thus immediately spoiled, but which they went on drinking just the same, mud and all, bloody as it was, most even fighting to have it.

At last, when many dead now lay piled one upon another in the stream, and part of the army had been destroyed at the river, and the few that escaped thence cut off by the cavalry, Nicias surrendered himself to Gylippus, whom he trusted more than he did the Syracusans, and told him and the Lacedaemonians to do what they liked with him, but to stop the slaughter of the soldiers. Gylippus, after this, immediately gave others to make prisoners; upon which the rest were brought together alive, except a large number secreted by the soldiery, and a party was sent in pursuit of the three hundred who had got through the guard during the night, and who were now taken with the rest. The number of the enemy collected as public property was not considerable; but that secreted was very large, and all Sicily was filled with them, no convention having been made in their case as for those taken with Demosthenes. Besides this, a large portion were killed outright, the carnage being very great, and not exceeded by any in this Sicilian war. In the numerous other encounters upon the march, not a few also had fallen. Nevertheless many escaped, some at the moment, others served as slaves, and then ran away subsequently. These found refuge at Catana.

The Syracusans and their allies now mustered and took up the spoils and as many prisoners as they could, and went back to the city. The rest of their Athenian and allied captives were deposited in the quarries, this seeming the safest way of keeping them; but Nicias and Demosthenes were butchered, against the will of Gylippus, who thought that it would be the crown of his triumph if he could take the enemy's generals to Lacedaemon. One of them, as it happened, Demosthenes, was one of her greatest enemies, on account of the affair of the island and of Pylos; while the other, Nicias, was for the same reasons one of her greatest friends, owing to his exertions to procure the release of the prisoners by persuading the Athenians to make peace. For these reasons the Lacedaemonians felt kindly towards him; and it was in this that Nicias himself mainly confided when he surrendered to Gylippus. But some of the Syracusans who had been in correspondence with him were afraid, it was said, of his being put to the torture and troubling their success by his revelations; others, especially the Corinthians, of his escaping, as he was wealthy, by means of bribes, and living to do them further mischief; and these persuaded the allies and put him to death. This or the like was the cause of the death of a man who, of all the Hellenes in my time, least deserved such a fate, seeing that the whole course of his life had been regulated with strict attention to virtue.

The prisoners in the quarries were at first hardly treated by the Syracusans. Crowded in a narrow hole, without any roof to cover them, the heat of the sun and the stifling closeness of the air tormented them during the day, and then the nights, which came on autumnal and chilly, made them ill by the violence of the change; besides, as they had to do everything in the same place for want of room, and the bodies of those who died of their wounds or from the variation in the temperature, or from similar causes, were left heaped together one upon another, intolerable stenches arose; while hunger and thirst never ceased to afflict them, each man during eight months having only half a pint of water and a pint of corn given him daily. In short, no single suffering to be apprehended by men thrust into such a place was spared them. For some seventy days they thus lived all together, after which all, except the Athenians and any Siceliots or Italiots who had joined in the expedition, were sold. The total number of prisoners taken it would be difficult to state exactly, but it could not have been less than seven thousand.

This was the greatest Hellenic achievement of any in this war, or, in my opinion, in Hellenic history; at once most glorious to the victors, and most calamitous to the conquered. They were beaten at all points and altogether; all that they suffered was great; they were destroyed, as the saying is, with a total destruction, their fleet, their army — everything was destroyed, and few out of many returned home.

R. Crawley

XENOPHON

XENOPHON (C. 430 - C. 354 B. C.) was a wealthy Athenian who became a follower of Socrates. He served in the Persian Army under Cyrus the younger, was presented with an estate by Sparta, and died at Corinth.

Among his works are the *Anabasis,* describing the adventures of Greek mercenary troops under Cyrus the younger: *Cyropaedia,* a biography of Cyrus the elder: *Hellenica,* a sequel to Thucydides' history: and *Memorabilia,* memoirs of Socrates, in four books.

Book III — *Anabasis — A Council of Greek Generals*

What the Greeks did in their march up the country with Cyrus, until the time of the battle, and what occurred after Cyrus was dead, when the Greeks set out to return with Tissaphernes in reliance on a truce, has been related in the preceding part of the work.

After the generals were made prisoners, and such of the captains and soldiers as had accompanied them were put to death, the Greeks were in great perplexity, reflecting that they were not far from the king's residence; that there were around them, on all sides, many hostile nations and cities; that no one would any longer secure them opportunities of purchasing provisions; that they were distant from Greece not less than ten thousand stadia; that there was no one to guide them on the way; that impassable rivers would intercept them in the midst of their course; that the Barbarians who had gone up with Cyrus had deserted them; and that they were left utterly alone, having no cavalry to support them, so that it was certain, even if they defeated their enemies, that they would not kill a man of them, and that, if they were defeated, none of themselves would be left alive; reflecting, I say, on these circumstances, and being disheartened at them, few of them tasted food for that evening, few kindled fires, and many did not come to the place of arms during the night, but lay down to rest where they severally happened to be, unable to sleep for sorrow and longing for their country, their parents, their wives and children, whom they never expected to see again. In this state of mind they all went to their resting-places.

There was in the army a certain Xenophon, an Athenian, who accompanied it neither in the character of general, nor captain, nor common soldier, but it had happened that Proxenus, an old guest-friend of his, had sent for him from home, giving him a promise that, if he came, he would recommend him to the friendship of Cyrus, whom he considered, he said, as a greater object of regard than his own country. Xenophon, on reading the letter, consulted Socrates the Athenian, as to the propriety of making the journey; and Socrates, fearing that if he attached himself to Cyrus it might prove a ground of accusation against him with his country, because Cyrus was thought to have zealously assisted the Lacedaemonians in their war with Athens, advised Xenophon to go to Delphi, and consult the god respecting the expedition. Xenophon, having gone thither accordingly, inquired of Apollo to which of the gods he should sacrifice and pray, in order most honorably and successfully to perform the journey which he contemplated, and, after prosperously accomplishing it, to return in safety. Apollo answered him that "he should sacrifice to the gods to whom it was proper for him to sacrifice." When he returned, he repeated the oracle to Socrates, who, on hearing it, blamed him for not asking Apollo in the first place, whether it were better for him to go or stay at home; whereas, having settled with himself that he would go, he only asked how he might best go; "but since you have," said he, "put the question thus, you must do what the god has directed." Xenophon, therefore, having sacrificed to the gods, that Apollo commanded, set sail, and found Proxenus and Cyrus at Sardis, just setting out on their march up the country, and was presented to Cyrus. Proxenus desiring that he should remain with them, Cyrus joined in the same desire, and said that as soon as the expedition was ended, he would send him home again. The expedition was said to be intended against the Pisidians. Xenophon accordingly joined in the enterprise, being thus deceived, but not by Proxenus; for he did not know that the movement was against the king, nor did any other of the Greeks, except Clearchus. When they arrived in Cilicia, however, it appeared manifest to every one that it was against the king that their force was directed; but, though they were afraid of the length of the journey, and unwilling to proceed, yet the greater part of them, out of respect both for one another and for Cyrus, continued to follow him; of which number was Xenophon.

When this perplexity occurred, Xenophon was distressed as well as the other Greeks, and unable to rest, but having at length got a little sleep, he had a dream in which, in the midst of a thunder-storm, a bolt seemed to him to fall upon his father's house, and the house in consequence became all in a blaze. Being greatly frightened, he immediately awoke, and considered his dream as in one respect favorable (inasmuch as, being in troubles and dangers, he seemed to behold a great light from Jupiter), but in another respect he was alarmed (because the dream appeared to him to be from Jupiter who was a king, and the fire to blaze all around him), lest he should be unable to escape from the king's territories, but should be hemmed in on all sides by inextricable difficulties.

What it betokens, however, to see such a dream, we may conjecture from the occurrences that happened after the dream. What immediately followed was this. As soon as he awoke, the thought that first occurred to him was, "Why do I lie here? The night is passing away. With daylight it is probable that the enemy will come upon us; and if we once fall into the hands of the king, what is there to prevent us from being put to death with ignominy, after witnessing the most grievous sufferings among our comrades, and enduring every severity of torture ourselves? Yet no one concerts measures, or takes thought, for our defense, but we lie still, as if we were at liberty to enjoy repose. From what city, then, do I expect a leader to undertake our defense? What age am I waiting for to come to myself? Assuredly I shall never be older, if I give myself up to the enemy to-day." After these reflections he arose, and called together, in the first place, the captains that were under Proxenus.

When they were assembled, he said, "For my part, captains, I can not sleep, nor, I should think, can you, nor can I lie still any longer, when I consider in what circumstances we are placed; for it is plain that the enemy did not openly manifest hostility toward us, until they thought that they had judiciously arranged their plans; but on our side no one takes any thought how we may best maintain a contest with them. Yet if we prove remiss, and fall into the power of the king, what may we not expect to suffer from a man who cut off the head and hand of his own brother by the same mother and father, even after he was dead, and fixed them upon a stake? What may not we, I say, expect to suffer, who have no relative to take our part, and who have marched against him to make him a subject instead of a monarch, and to put him to death if it should lie in our power? Will he not proceed to every extremity, that by reducing us to the last degree of ignominious suffering, he may inspire all men with a dread of ever taking the field against him? We must, however, try every expedient not to fall into his hands. For myself, I never ceased, while the truce lasted, to consider ourselves as objects of pity, and to regard the king and his people as objects of envy, as I contemplated how extensive and valuable a country they possessed, how great an abundance of provisions, how many slaves and cattle, and how vast a quantity of gold and raiment; while, on the other hand, when I reflected on the condition of our own soldiers, that we had no share in any of all these blessings, unless we bought it, and knew that few of us had any longer money to buy, and that our oaths restrained us from getting provisions otherwise than by buying, I sometimes, on taking all these circumstances into consideration, feared the continuance of peace more than I now fear war. But since they have put an end to peace, their own haughtiness, and our mistrust, seem likewise to be brought to an end; for the advantages which I have mentioned lie now as prizes between us, for whichsoever of us shall prove the better men; and the gods are the judges of the contest, who, as is just, will be on our side; since the enemy have offended them by perjury, while we, though seeing many good things to tempt us, have resolutely abstained from all of them through regard to our oaths; so that, as it seems to me, we may advance to the combat with much greater confidence than they can feel. We have bodies, moreover, better able than theirs to endure cold, and heat, and toil; and we have, with the help of the gods, more resolute minds; while the enemy, if the gods, as before, grant us success, will be found more obnoxious to wounds and death than we are. But possibly others of you entertain the same thoughts; let us not, then, in the name of heaven, wait for others to come and exhort us to noble deeds, but let us be ourselves the first to excite others to exert their valor. Prove yourselves the bravest of the captains, and more worthy to lead than those who are now leaders. As for me, if you wish to take the start in the course, I am willing to follow you, or, if you appoint me to be a leader, I shall not make my youth an excuse, but shall think myself sufficiently mature to defend myself against harm."

Thus spoke Xenophon; and the captains, on hearing his observations, all desired him to be their leader, except a certain Apollonides, who resembled a Boeotian in his manner of speaking; this man said that "whoever asserted they could gain safety by any other means than by obtaining, if he could, the king's consent to it, talked absurdly"; and at the same time began to enumerate the difficulties surrounding them. But Xenophon, interrupting him, said, "O most wonderful of men! you neither understand what you see, nor remember what you hear. Yet you were on the same spot with those here present, when the king, after Cyrus was dead, being in high spirits at the circumstance, sent to demand that we should deliver up our arms; and, when we, refusing to deliver them up, and appearing in full armor, went and encamped over against him. what means did he not try, sending deputies, asking for a truce, and supplying us with provisions until he obtained a truce? But when, on the other hand, our generals and captains went to confer with the Barbarians, as you now advise us to do, without their arms, and relying on the truce, were they not beaten, goaded, insulted, and are they not unable, wretched men, to die, though, I should think, greatly longing for death? And do you, knowing all these occurrences, say to those who exhort us to defend ourselves, talk absurdly, and advise us to go again to try persuasion? To me, O captains, it seems that we should no longer admit this man into the same service with ourselves, but take from him his captaincy, and laying baggage on his back, make use of him in that capacity; for he disgraces both his own country and all Greece, inasmuch as, being a Greek, he is of such a character." Here Agasias of Stymphalus, proceeding to speak, said, "But this man, assuredly, has nothing to do either with Boeotia or with Greece at all, for I have observed that he has both his ears bored, like a Lydian." Such indeed was the case; and they accordingly expelled him.

The rest, proceeding to the different divisions of the troops, called up the general wherever there was a general surviving, and the lieutenant-general where the general was dead, and the captain wherever there was a captain surviving. When they were all come together, they sat down before the place where the arms were piled; and the generals and captains assembled were about a hundred in all. The time when the meeting took place was about midnight.

Hieronymus, a native of Elis, the oldest of all the captains that had served under Proxenus, was the first to speak, as follows: "It has seemed proper to us, O generals and captains, on contemplating the present state of our affairs, to meet together ourselves, and to call upon you to join us, that we may determine, if we can, on some plan for our benefit. But do you, Xenophon, first represent to the assembly what you have already observed to us." Xenophon accordingly said, "We are all aware that the king and Tissaphernes have made prisoners of as many of us as they could; and it is evident that they are forming designs against the rest of us, that they may put us to death if they can. But on our parts I think that every means should be adopted in order that we may not fall into the Barbarians' hands, but rather that they, if we can accomplish it, may fall into ours. Be well assured then, that you, who have now met together in such numbers, have upon you a most important responsibility; for all the soldiers look to you, and, if they see you dispirited, they will themselves lose courage, but if both you yourselves appear well prepared to meet the enemy, and exhort others to be equally prepared, be certain that they will follow you, and strive to imitate you. Perhaps, too, it is right that you should show some superiority over them; for you are their generals, their officers, and their captains, and, when there was peace, you enjoyed

293

advantages over them in fortune and honor; and now, in consequence, when war arises, you ought to prove yourselves pre-eminent over the multitude, and to take the lead in forming plans for them, and should it ever be necessary, in toiling for them. And, in the first place, I think that you will greatly benefit the army, if you take care that generals and captains be chosen, as soon as possible, in the room of those whom we have lost; for without commanders nothing honorable or advantageous can be achieved, I may say in one word, anywhere, but least of all in the field of battle. Good order conduces to safety, but want of order has already proved fatal to many. Again, when you have appointed as many commanders as are requisite, I consider that if you were to assemble and encourage the rest of the soldiers, you would act very suitably to the occasion; for you perhaps observe, as well as myself, how dejectedly they have now come to the place of arms, and how dejectedly they go upon guard, so that, while they are in such a condition, I know not for what service any one could employ them, whether required by night or by day. But if any one could change the direction of their thoughts, so that they may not merely contemplate what they are likely to suffer, but what they may be able to do, they will become much more eager for action; for you are certain that it is neither numbers nor strength which gives the victory in war, but that whichsoever side advances on the enemy with the more resolute courage, their opponents, in general, cannot withstand their onset. I have also remarked, fellow-soldiers, that such as are eager in the field to preserve their lives at any rate, for the most part perish wretchedly and ignominiously, while I see that such as reflect that death is to all men common and inevitable, and seek in battle only to fall with honor, more frequently, from whatever cause, arrive at old age, and live, while they live, with greater happiness. Being aware, then, of these facts, it behooves us, such are the circumstances in which we are placed, both to prove ourselves to be brave soldiers, and to exhort others to be so likewise." Having spoken thus, he stopped.

After him Cheirisophus said, "Till the present moment, O Xenophon, I knew nothing of you, except having heard that you were an Athenian, but now I have to praise you both for what you say and what you do, and could wish that there were very many like you; for it would be a general good. And now," he added, "let us not delay, my fellow-soldiers, but proceed at once, you who want them, to choose commanders, and when you have elected them, come to the center of the camp, and bring those that are chosen; and we will then call the rest of the soldiers together there. And let Tolmides the herald," said he, "come with us." As he said this, he rose up, that the necessary measures might not be delayed, but carried at once into execution.

There were accordingly chosen commanders, Timasion, a Dardanian in the room of Clearchus, Xanthicles an Achaean in that of Socrates, Cleanor an Arcadian in that of Agias, Philesius an Achaean in that of Menon, and Xenophon of Athens in that of Proxenus.

Book IV — *The March of the Greeks*

When they had crossed, and had ranged themselves in order about noon, they proceeded through the country of Armenia, consisting wholly of plains and gently sloping hills, a distance of not less than five parasangs; for there were no villages near the river, in consequence of the hostilities with the Carduchi. The village, however at which they at length arrived, was of considerable size, and contained a palace for the satrap; upon most of the houses there were towers, and provisions were in great plenty.

Hence they proceeded, two days' journey, a distance of ten parasangs, until they passed round the sources of the river Tigris. From hence they advanced, three days' journey, fifteen parasangs, to the river Teleboas, a stream not large, indeed, but of much beauty; and there were many villages on its banks. This part of the country was called Western Armenia. The deputy-governor of it was Tiribazus, who was an intimate friend of the king; and no one else, when he was present, assisted the king to mount his horse. He now rode up with a body of cavalry, and sending forward an interpreter, said that he wished to speak with the commanders. The generals thought proper to hear what he had to say, and advancing within hearing, asked what he wanted. He replied, that he wished to make a treaty with them, on the conditions that he himself should not hurt the Greeks, and that the Greeks should not burn the houses, but should be at liberty to take such provisions as they required. This proposal was agreeable to the generals, and they concluded a treaty upon these terms.

Hence they proceeded, three days' march, a distance of fifteen parasangs, through a plain; and Tiribazus followed them with his troops, keeping at a distance of about ten stadia. They then came to a palace, with several villages around it stored with abundance of provisions. While they were encamped, there fell a great quantity of snow in the night; and in the morning it was thought advisable that the companies and officers should take up their quarters in the neighboring villages; for they perceived no enemy, and it appeared to be safe on account of the quantity of the snow. Here they found all kinds of excellent provisions, cattle, corn, old wines of great fragrance, dried grapes, and vegetables of all kinds.

Some of the soldiers, however, who had strolled away from the camp, brought word that they had caught sight of an enemy, and that many fires had been visible during the night. The generals thought it unsafe, therefore, for the troops to quarter apart, and resolved to bring the whole army together again. They accordingly assembled, for it seemed to be clearing up. But as they were passing the night here, there fell a vast quantity of snow, so that it covered both the arms and the men as they lay on the ground. The snow cramped the baggage-cattle, and they were very reluctant to rise; for, as they lay, the snow that had fallen upon them served to keep them warm, when it had not dropped off. But when Xenophon was hardy enough to rise, without his outer garment, and to cleave wood, some one else then rose, and, taking the wood from him, cleft it himself. Soon after, the rest got up, and lighted fires and anointed themselves; for abundance of ointment was found there, made of hog's-lard, seasamum, bitter almonds, and turpentine, which they used instead of oil. Of the same materials an odoriferous unguent was found.

After this it was resolved to quarter again throughout the villages, under shelter; and the soldiers went off with great shouting and delight to the cottages and provisions. Those who had set fire to the houses, when they quitted them before, paid the penalty of having to encamp uncomfortably in the open air. Hence they dispatched in the night Democrates of Temenos, giving him a detachment of men, to the hills where the stragglers said that they had seen the fires; they selected him because he was thought on several former occasions to have brought exact information concerning such matters, reporting what was, just as it appeared, and what was not, as not existing. Having gone, he said that he saw no fires, but he brought with him a captive that he had taken, having a Persian bow and quiver, and a short battle-ax, such as the Amazons have. Being asked of what country he was, he said that he was a Persian, and that he was going from the army of Tiribazus to get provisions. They then asked him how large the army was, and for what purpose it was assembled. He said that Tiribazus had his own troops, and some mercenaries from the Chalybes and Taochians; and that he was prepared to attack the Greeks in their passage over the mountains, at a narrow defile through which lay their only road.

The generals, on hearing this, resolved to collect the army, and, leaving a guard, with Sophaenetus the Stymphalian as commander over those who stayed behind, proceeded to march without delay, taking the man who had been captured for their guide. After they had passed the mountains, the peltasts, who went before the rest, and were the first to discover the enemy's camp, did not wait for the heavy-armed men, but ran forward with a shout to attack it. The Barbarians, hearing the noise, did not stand their ground, but fled; some of them however were killed, and about twenty horses taken, as was also the tent of Tiribazus, and in it some couches with silver feet, and drinking-cups, and some prisoners, who said that they were bakers and cup-bearers. When the officers of the heavy-armed troops heard what had taken place, they resolved upon marching back as fast as possible to their own camp, lest any attempt should be made on those who had been left there. Calling in the men immediately, therefore, by sound of trumpet, they returned to the camp the same day.

The next day it was thought necessary to march away as fast as possible, before the enemy's force should be re-assembled, and get possession of the pass. Collecting their baggage at once, therefore, they set forward through a deep snow, taking with them several guides; and, having the same day passed the height on which Tiribazus had intended to attack them, they encamped. Hence they proceeded three days' journey through a desert tract of country, a distance of fifteen parasangs, to the river Euphrates, and passed it without being wet higher than the middle. The sources of the river were said not to be far off. From hence they advanced three days' march, through much snow and a level plain, a distance of fifteen parasangs; the third day's march was extremely troublesome, as the north wind blew full in their faces, completely parching up everything and benumbing the men. One of the augurs, in consequence, advised that they should sacrifice to the wind; and a sacrifice was accordingly offered; when the vehemence of the wind appeared to every one manifestly to abate. The depth of the snow was a fathom; so that many of the baggage cattle and slaves perished with about thirty of the soldiers. They continued to burn fires through the whole night, for there was plenty of wood at the place of encampment. But those who came up late could get no wood; those therefore who had arrived before, and had kindled fires, would not admit the late comers to the fire unless they gave them a share of the corn or other provisions that they had brought. Thus they shared with each other what they respectively had. In the places where the fires were made, as the snow melted, there were formed large pits that reached down to the ground; and here there was accordingly opportunity to measure the depth of the snow.

From hence they marched through snow the whole of the following day, and many of the men contracted the bulimia. Xenophon, who commanded in the rear, finding in his way such of the men as had fallen down with it, knew not what disease it was. But as one of those acquainted with it, told him that they were evidently affected with bulimia, and that they would get up if they had something to eat, he went round among the baggage, and, wherever he saw anything eatable, he gave it out, and sent such as were able to run to distribute it among those diseased, who, as soon as they had eaten, rose up and continued their march. As they proceeded, Cheirisophus came, just as it grew dark, to a village, and found, at a spring, in front of the rampart, some women and girls belonging to the place fetching water. The women asked them who they were; and the interpreter answered, in the Persian language, that they were people going from the king to the satrap. They replied that he was not there, but about a parasang off. However, as it was late, they went with the water-carriers within the rampart, to the head man of the village; and here Cheirisophus and as many of the troops as could come up, encamped; but of the rest, such as were unable to get to the end of the journey, spent the night on the way without food or fire; and some of the soldiers lost their lives on that occasion. Some of the enemy too, who had collected themselves into a body, pursued our rear, and seized any of the baggage-cattle that were unable to proceed, fighting with one another for the possession of them. Such of the soldiers, also, as had lost their sight from the effects of the snow, or had their toes mortified by the cold, were left behind. It was found to be a relief to the eyes against the snow, if the soldiers kept something black before them on the march, and to the feet, if they kept constantly in motion, and allowed themselves no rest, and if they took off their shoes in the night; but as to such as slept with their shoes on, the straps worked into their feet, and the soles were frozen about them; for when their old shoes had failed them, shoes of raw hides had been made by the men themselves from the newly-skinned oxen. From such unavoidable sufferings, some of the soldiers were left behind, who, seeing a piece of ground of a black appearance, from the having disappeared there, conjectured that it must have melted; and it had in fact melted in the spot from the effect of a fountain, which was sending up vapor in a woody hollow close at hand. Turning aside thither, they sat down and refused to proceed further. Xenophon, who was with the rear-guard, as soon as he heard this, tried to prevail on them by every art and means not to be left behind, telling them, at the same time, that the enemy were collected, and pursuing them in great numbers. At last he grew angry; and they told him to kill them, as they were quite unable to go forward. He then thought it the best course to strike a terror, if possible, into the enemy that were behind, lest they should fall upon the exhausted soldiers. It was now dark, and the enemy were advancing with a great noise, quarreling about the booty that they had taken; when such of the rear-guard as were not disabled, started up, and rushed toward them, while the tired men, shouting as loud as they could, clashed their spears against their shields. The enemy, struck with alarm, threw themselves among the snow into the hollow, and no one of them afterward made themselves heard from any quarter.

Xenophon, and those with him, telling the sick men that a party should come to their relief next day, proceeded on their march, but before they had gone four stadia, they found other soldiers resting by the way in the snow, and covered up with it, no guard being stationed over them. They roused them up, but they said that the head of the army was not moving forward. Xenophon, going past them, and sending on some of the ablest of the peltasts, ordered them to ascertain what it was that hindered their progress. They brought word that the whole army was in that manner taking rest. Xenophon and his men, therefore, stationing such a guard as they could, took up their quarters there without fire or supper. When it was near day, he sent the youngest of his men to the sick, telling them to rouse them and oblige them to proceed. At this juncture Cheirisophus sent some of his people from the village to see how the rear were faring. The young men were rejoiced to see them, and gave them the sick to conduct to the camp, while they themselves went forward, and, before they had gone twenty stadia, found themselves at the village in which Cheirisophus was quartered. When they came together, it was thought safe enough to lodge the troops up and down in the villages. Cheirisophus accordingly remained where he was, and the other officers, appropriating by lot the several villages that they had in sight, went to their respective quarters with their men.

Here Polycrates, an Athenian captain, requested leave of absence, and, taking with him the most active of his men, and hastening to the village which Xenophon had been allotted, surprised all the villagers, and their head man, in their houses, together with seventeen colts that were bred as a tribute for the king, and the head man's daughter, who had been but nine days married; her husband was gone out to hunt mares, and was not found in any of the villages. Their houses were under ground, the entrance like the mouth of a well, but spacious below; there were passages dug into them for the cattle, but the people descended by ladders. In the houses were goats, sheep, cows, and fowls, with their young; all the cattle were kept on fodder within the walls. There was also wheat, barley, leguminous vegetables, and barley-wine, in large bowls; the grains of barley floated in it even with the brims of the vessels, and reeds also lay in it, some larger and some smaller, without joints; and these, when any one was thirsty, he was able to take in his mouth, and suck. The liquor was very strong, unless one mixed water with it, and a very pleasant drink to those accustomed to it.

Xenophon made th echief man of his village sup with him, and told him to be of good courage, assuring him that he should not be deprived of his children, and that they would not go away without filling his house with provisions in return for what they took, if he would but prove himself the author of some service to the army till they should reach another tribe. This he promised, and, to show his goodwill, pointed out where some wine was buried. This night, therefore, the soldiers rested in their several quarters in the midst of great abundance, setting a guard over the chief, and keeping his children at the same time under their eye. The following day Xenophon took the head man and went with him to Cheirisophus, and wherever he passed by a village, he turned aside to visit those who were quartered in it, and found them in all parts feasting and enjoying themselves; nor would they anywhere let them go till they had set refreshments before them; and they placed everywhere upon the same table, lamb, kid, pork, veal, and fowl, with plenty of bread both of wheat and barley. Whenever any person, to pay a compliment, wished to drink to another, he took him to the large bowl, where he had to stoop down and drink, sucking like an ox. The chief they allowed to take whatever he pleased, but he accepted nothing from them; where he found any of his relatives, however, he took them with him.

When they came to Cheirisophus, they found his men also feasting in their quarters, crowned with wreaths made of hay, and Armenian boys, in the Barbarian dress, waiting upon them, to whom they made signs what they were to do as if they had been deaf and dumb. When Cheirisophus and Xenophon had saluted one another, they both asked the chief man, through the interpreter who spoke the Persian language, what country it was. He replied that it was Armenia. They then asked him for whom the horses were bred; and he said that they were a tribute for the king, and added that the neighboring country was that of Chalybes, and told them in what direction the road lay. Xenophon then went away, conducting the chief back to his family, giving him the horse that he had taken, which was rather old, to fatten and offer in sacrifice (for he had heard that it had been consecrated to the sun), being afraid, indeed, that it might die, as it had been injured by the journey. He then took some of the young horses, and gave one of them to each of the other generals and captains. The horses in this country were smaller than those of Persia, but far more spirited. The chief instructed the men to tie little bags round the feet of the horses, and other cattle, when they drove them through the snow, for without such bags they sunk up to their bellies.

When the eighth day was come, Xenophon committed the guide to Cheirisophus. He left the chiefs all the members of his family, except his son, a youth just coming to mature age; him he gave in charge to

Episthenes of Amphipolis, in order that if the father should conduct them properly, he might return home with him. At the same time they carried to his house as many provisions as they could, and then broke up their camp, and resumed their march. The chief conducted them through the snow, walking at liberty. When he came to the end of the third day's march, Cheirisophus was angry at him for not guiding them to some villages. He said that there were none in that part of the country. Cheirisophus then struck him, but did not confine him; and in consequence he ran off in the night, leaving his son behind him. This affair, the ill-treatment and neglect of the guide, was the only cause of dissension between Cheirisophus and Xenophon during the march. Episthenes conceived an affection for the youth, and, taking him home, found him extremely attached to him.

After this occurrence, they proceeded seven days' journey, five parasangs each day, till they came to the river Phasis, the breadth of which is a plethrum. Hence they advanced two days' journey, ten parasangs; when, on the pass that led over the mountains into the plain, the Chalybes, Taochi, and Phasians were drawn up to oppose their progress. Cheirisophus, seeing these enemies in possession of the height, came to a halt, at the distance of about thirty stadia, that he might not approach them while leading the army in a column. He accordingly ordered the other officers to bring up their companies, that the whole force might be formed in line.

When the rear-guard was come up, he called together the generals and captains, and spoke to them as follows: "The enemy, as you see, are in possession of the pass over the mountains; and it is proper for us to consider how we may encounter them to the best advantage. It is my opinion, therefore, that we should direct the troops to get their dinner and that we ourselves should hold a council, in the mean time, whether it is advisable to cross the mountain to-day, or to-morrow." "It seems best to me," exclaimed Cleanor, "to march at once, as soon as we have dined and resumed our arms, against the enemy; for if we waste the present day in inaction, the enemy who are now looking down upon us will grow bolder, and it is likely that, as their confidence is increased, others will join them in greater numbers."

After him Xenophon said, "I am of opinion that if it is necessary to fight, we ought to make our arrangements so as to fight with the greatest advantage; but that if we propose to pass the mountains as easily as possible, we ought to consider how we may incur the fewest wounds and lose the fewest men. The range of hills, as far as we see, extends more than sixty stadia in length; but the people nowhere seem to be watching us except along the line of road; and it is therefore better, I think, to endeavor to try to seize unobserved some part of the unguarded range, and to get possession of it, if we can, beforehand, than to attack a strong post and men prepared to resist us. For it is far less difficult to march up a steep ascent without fighting than along a level road with enemies on each side; and, in the night, if men are not obliged to fight, they can see better what is before them than by day if engaged with enemies; while a rough road is easier to the feet to those who are marching without molestation, than a smooth one to those who are pelted on the head with missiles. Nor do I think it at all impracticable for us to steal a way for ourselves, as we can march by night, so as not to be seen, and can keep at such a distance from the enemy as to allow no possibility of being heard. We seem likely, too, in my opinion, if we make a pretended attack on this point, to find the rest of the range still less guarded; for the enemy will so much the more probably stay where they are. But why should I speak doubtfully about stealing? For I hear that you Lacedaemonians, O Cheirisophus, such of you at least as are of the better class, practice stealing from your boyhood, and it is not a disgrace, but an honor, to steal whatever the law does not forbid; while, in order that you may steal with the utmost dexterity, and strive to escape discovery, it is appointed by law that, if you are caught stealing, you are scourged. It is now high time for you, therefore, to give proof of your education, and to take care that we may not receive many stripes." "But I hear that you Athenians also," rejoined Cheirisophus, "are very clever at stealing the public money, though great danger threatens him that steals it; and that your best men steal it most, if indeed your best men are thought worthy to be your magistrates; so that it is time for you likewise to give proof of your education."

"I am then ready," exclaimed Xenophon, "to march with the rearguard, as soon as we have supped, to take possession of the hills. I have guides too; for our light-armed men captured some of the marauders following us by lying in ambush; and from them I learn that the mountains are not impassable, but are grazed over by goats and oxen, so that if we once gain possession of any part of the range, there will be tracks also for our baggage-cattle. I expect also that the enemy will no longer keep their ground, when they see us upon a level with them on the heights, for they will not now come down to be upon a level with us." Cheirisophus then said, "But why should you go, and leave the charge of the rear? Rather send others, unless some volunteers present themselves." Upon this Aristonymus of Methydria came forward with his heavy-armed men, and Aristeas of Chios and Nichomachus of Oeta with their light-armed; and they made an arrangement, that as soon as they should reach the top, they should light a number of fires. Having settled these points, they went to dinner; and after dinner Cheirisophus led forward the whole army ten stadia toward the enemy, that he might appear to be fully resolved to march against them on that quarter.

When they had taken their supper, and night came on, those appointed for the service went forward and got possession of the hills; the other troops rested where they were. The enemy, when they saw the heights occupied, kept watch and burned a number of fires all night. As soon as it was day, Cheirisophus, after having offered sacrifice, marched forward along the road; while those who had gained the heights advanced by the ridge. Most of the enemy, meanwhile, stayed at the pass, but a part went to meet the troops coming along the heights. But before the main bodies came together, those on the ridge closed with one another, and the Greeks had the advantage, and put the enemy to flight. At the same time the Grecian peltasts ran up from the plain to attack the enemy drawn up to receive them, and Cheirisophus followed at a quick pace with the heavy-armed men. The enemy at the pass, however, when they saw those above defeated, took to flight. Not many of them were killed, but a great number of shields were taken, which the Greeks, by hacking them with their swords, rendered useless. As soon as they had gained the ascent, and had sacrificed and erected a trophy, they went down into the plain before them, and arrived at a number of villages stored with abundance of excellent provisions.

J. S. Watson

PHILOSOPHY

Plato

Aristotle

Epictetus

P L A T O

PLATO (c. 429-347 B. C.) was one of the greatest philosophical minds of all time. An Athenian of distinguished family, he spent much time in association with the philosopher Socrates. After the death of Socrates in 399 B. C., Plato left Athens and traveled widely. On his return to Athens he founded the Academy, virtually the first university in the western world. Here he taught for some forty years.

He is the author of some twenty-five philosophical dialogues, the *Apology*, and a number of letters: all of which are extant. Plato's influence was pervasive in succeeding centuries, and affected even Arab thought. Particularly associated with Platonic philosophy are the Theory of Ideas, the conceptual outline of an ideal state in the *Republic,* and questions on epistemology.

APOLOGY

In the *Apology* Socrates defends his way of life and his philosophical views.

How you, O Athenians, have been affected by my accusers, I cannot tell; but I know that they almost made me forget who I was — so persuasively did they speak; and yet they have hardly uttered a word of truth. But of the many falsehoods told by them, there was one which quite amazed me; — I mean when they said that you should be upon your guard and not allow yourselves to be deceived by the force of my eloquence. To say this, when they are certain to be detected as soon as I opened my lips and proved myself to be anything but a great speaker, did indeed appear to me most shameless — unless by the force of eloquence they mean the force of truth; for if such is their meaning, I admit that I am eloquent. But in how different a way from theirs! Well, as I was saying, they have scarcely spoken the truth at all; but from me you shall hear the whole truth: not, however, delivered after their manner in a set oration duly ornamented with words and phrases. No, by heaven! but I shall use the words and arguments which occur to me at the moment; for I am confident in the justice of my cause: at my time of life I ought not to be appearing before you, O men of Athens, in the character of a juvenile orator — let no one expect it of me. And I must beg of you to grant me a favour: —If I defend myself in my accustomed manner, and you hear me using the words which I have been in the habit of using in the agora, at the tables of the money-changers, or anywhere else, I would ask you not to be surprised, and not to interrupt me on this account. For I am more than seventy years of age, and appearing now for the first time in a court of law, I am quite a stranger to the language of the place; and therefore I would have you regard me as if I were really a stranger, whom you would excuse if he spoke in his native tongue, and after the fashion of his country: — Am I making an unfair request of you? Never mind the manner, which may or may not be good; but think only of the truth of my words, and give heed to that: let the speaker speak truly and the judge decide justly.

And first, I have to reply to the older charges and to my first accusers, and then I will go on to the later ones. For of old I have had many accusers, who have accused me falsely to you during many years; and I am more afraid of them than of Anytus and his associates, who are dangerous, too, in their own way. But far more dangerous are the others, who began when you were children, and took possession of your minds with their falsehoods, telling of one Socrates, a wise man, who speculated about the heaven above, and searched into the earth beneath, and made the worse appear the better cause. The disseminators of this tale are the accusers whom I dread; for their hearers are apt to fancy that such enquirers do not believe in the existence of the gods. And they are many, and their charges against me are of ancient date, and they were made by them in the days when you were more impressible than you are now — in childhood, or it may have been in youth —and the cause when heard went by default, for there was none to answer. And hardest of all, I do not know and cannot tell the names of my accusers; unless in the chance case of a comic poet. All who from envy and malice have persuaded you — some of them having first convinced themselves — all this class of men are most difficult to deal with; for I cannot have them up here, and cross-examine them, and therefore I must simply fight with shadows in my own defence, and argue when there is no one who answers. I will ask you then to assume with me, as I was saying, that my opponents are of two kinds; one recent, the other ancient: and I hope that you will see the propriety of my answering the latter first, for these accusations you heard long before the others, and much oftener.

Well, then, I must make my defence, and endeavour to clear away in a short time, a slander which has lasted a long time. May I succeed, if to succeed be for my good and yours, or likely to avail me in my cause! The task is not an easy one; I quite understand the nature of it. And so leaving the event with God, in obedience to the law I will now make my defence.

I will begin at the beginning, and ask what is the accusation which has given rise to the slander of me, and in fact has encouraged Meletus to prefer this charge against me. Well, what do the slanderers say? They shall be my prosecutors, and I will sum up their words in an affidavit: 'Socrates is an evil-doer, and a curious person, who searches into things under the earth and in heaven, and he makes the worse appear the better cause; and he teaches the aforesaid doctrines to others.' Such is the nature of the accusation: it is just what you have yourselves seen in the comedy of Aristophanes, who has introduced a man whom he calls Socrates, going about and saying that he walks on air, and talking a deal of nonsense concerning matters of which I do not pretend to know either much or little — not that I mean to speak disparagingly of any one who is a student of natural philosophy. I should be very sorry if Meletus could bring so grave a charge against me. But the simple truth is, O Athenians, that I have nothing to do with physical speculations. Very many of those here present are witnesses to the truth of this, and to them I appeal. Speak then, you who have heard me, and tell your neighbours whether any of you have ever known me hold forth in few words or in many upon such matters. . . . You hear their answer. And from what they say of this part of the charge you will be able to judge of the truth of the rest.

As little foundation is there for the report that I am a teacher, and take money; this accusation has no more truth in it than the other. Although, if a man were really able to instruct mankind, to receive money for giving instruction would, in my opinion, be an honour to him. There is Gorgias of Leontium, and Prodicus of Ceos, and Hippias of Elis, who go the round of the cities, and are able to persuade the young men to leave their own citizens by whom they might be taught for nothing, and come to them whom they not only pay, but are thankful if they may be allowed to pay them. There is at this time a Parian philosopher residing in Athens, of whom I have heard and I came to hear of him in this way: — I came across a man who has spent a world of money on the Sophists, Callias, the son of Hipponicus, and knowing that he had sons, I asked him: 'Callias,' I said, 'if your two sons were foals or calves, there would be no difficulty in finding some one to put over them; we should hire a trainer of horses, or a farmer probably, who would improve and perfect them in their own proper virtue and excellence; but as they are human beings, whom are you thinking of placing over them? Is there any one who understands human and political virtue? You must have thought about the matter, for you have sons; is there any one?' 'There is,' he said. 'Who is he?'

said I; 'and of what country? and what does he charge?' 'Evenus the Parian,' he replied; 'he is the man, and his charge is five minae.' Happy is Evenus, I said to myself, if he really has this wisdom, and teaches at such a moderate charge. Had I the same, I should have been very proud and conceited; but the truth is that I have no knowledge of the kind.

I dare say, Athenians, that some one among you will reply, 'Yes, Socrates, but what is the origin of these accusations which are brought against you; there must have been something strange which you have been doing? All these rumours and this talk about you would never have arisen if you had been like other men; tell us, then, what is the cause of them, for we should be sorry to judge hastily of you.' Now I regard this as a fair challenge, and I will endeavour to explain to you the reason why I am called wise and have such an evil fame. Please to attend them. And although some of you may think that I am joking, I declare that I will tell you the entire truth. Men of Athens, this reputation of mine has come of a certain sort of wisdom which I possess. If you ask me what kind of wisdom, I reply, wisdom such as may perhaps be attained by man, for to that extent I am inclined to believe that I am wise; whereas the persons of whom I was speaking have a superhuman wisdom, which I may fail to describe, because I have it not myself; and he who says that I have, speaks falsely, and is taking away my character. And here, O men of Athens, I must beg you not to interrupt me, even if I seem to say something extravagant. For the word which I will speak is not mine. I will refer you to a witness who is worthy of credit; that witness shall be the God of Delphi — he will tell you about my wisdom, if I have any, and of what sort it is. You must have known Chaerephon; he was early a friend of mine, and also a friend of yours, for he shared in the recent exile of the people, and returned with you. Well, Chaerephon, as you know, was very impetuous in all his doings, and he went to Delphi and boldly asked the oracle to tell him whether — as I was saying, I must beg you not to interrupt — he asked the oracle to tell him whether any one was wiser than I was, and the Pythian prophetess answered, that there was no man wiser. Chaerephon is dead himself; but his brother, who is in court, will confirm the truth of what I am saying.

Why do I mention this? Because I am going to explain to you why I have such an evil name. When I heard the answer, I said to myself, What can the god mean? and what is the interpretation of his riddle? for I know that I have no wisdom, small or great. What then can he mean when he says that I am the wisest of men? And yet he is a god, and cannot lie; that would be against his nature. After long consideration, I thought of a method of trying the question. I reflected that if I could only find a man wiser than myself, then I might go to the god with a refutation in my hand. I should say to him, 'Here is a man who is wiser than I am; but you said that I was the wisest.' Accordingly I went to one who had the reputation of wisdom, and observed him — his name I need not mention; he was a politician whom I selected for examination — and the result was as follows: When I began to talk with him, I could not help thinking that he was not really wise, although he was thought wise by many, and still wiser by himself; and thereupon I tried to explain to him that he thought himself wise, but was not really wise; and the consequence was that he hated me, and his enmity was shared by several who were present and heard me. So I left him, saying to myself, as I went away: Well, although I do not suppose that either of us knows anything really beautiful and good, I am better off than he is, — for he knows nothing, and thinks that he knows; I neither know nor think that I know. In this latter particular, then, I seem to have slightly the advantage of him. Then I went to another who had still higher pretensions to wisdom, and my conclusion was exactly the same. Whereupon I made another enemy of him, and of many others besides him.

Then I went to one man after another, being not unconscious of the enmity which I provoked, and I lamented and feared this: But necessity was laid upon me, — the word of God, I thought, ought to be considered first. And I said to myself, Go I must to all who appear to know, and find out the meaning of the oracle. And I swear to you, Athenians, by the dog I swear! — for I must tell you the truth — the result of my mission was just this: I found that the men most in repute were all but the most foolish; and that others less esteemed were really wiser and better. I will tell you the tale of my wanderings and of the 'Herculean' labours, as I may call them, which I endured only to find at last the oracle irrefutable. After the politicans, I went to the poets; tragic, dithyrambic, and all sorts. And there, I said to myself, you will be instantly detected; now you will find out that you are more ignorant than they are. Accordingly, I took them some of the most elaborate passages in their own writings, and asked what was the meaning of them — thinking that they would teach me something. Will you believe me? I am almost ashamed to confess the truth, but I must say that there is hardly a person present who would not have talked better about their poetry than they did themselves. Then I knew that not by wisdom do poets write poetry, but by a sort of genius and inspiration; they are like diviners or soothsayers who also say many fine things, but do not understand the meaning of them. The poet appeared to me to be much in the same case; and I further observed that upon the strength of their poetry they believed themselves to be the wisest of men in other things in which they were not wise. So I departed, conceiving myself to be superior to them for the same reason that I was superior to the politicians.

At last I went to the artisans, for I was conscious that I knew nothing at all, as I may say, and I was sure that they knew many fine things; and here I was not mistaken, for they did know many things of which I was ignorant, and in this they certainly were wiser than I was. But I observed that even the good artisans fell into the same error as the poets; — because they were good workmen they thought that they also knew all sorts of high matters, and this defect in them overshadowed their wisdom; and therefore I asked myself on behalf of the oracle, whether I would like to be as I was, neither having their knowledge nor their ignorance, or like them in both; and I made answer to myself and to the oracle that I was better off as I was.

This inquisition has led to my having many enemies of the worst and most dangerous kind, and has given occasion also to many calumnies. And I am called wise, for my hearers always imagine that I myself possess the wisdom which I find wanting in others: but the truth is, O men of Athens, that God only is wise; and by his answer he intends to show that the wisdom of men is worth little or nothing; he is not speaking of Socrates, he is only using my name by way of illustration, as if he said, He, O men, is the wisest, who, like Socrates, knows that his wisdom is in truth worth nothing. And so I go about the world, obedient to the god, and search and make enquiry into the wisdom of any one, whether citizen or stranger, who appears to be wise; and if he is not wise, then in vindication of the oracle I show him that he is not wise; and my occupation quite absorbs me, and I have no time to give either to any public matter of interest or to any concern of my own, but I am in utter poverty by reason of my devotion to the god.

There is another thing: — young men of the richer classes, who have not much to do, come about me of their own accord; they like to hear the pretenders examined, and they often imitate me, and proceed to examine others; there are plenty of persons, as they quickly discover, who think that they know something, but really know little or nothing; and then those who are examined by them instead of being angry with themselves are angry with me: This confounded Socrates, they say; this villainous misleader of youth! — and then if somebody asks them, Why, what evil does he practice or teach? they do not know, and cannot tell; but in order that they may not appear to be at a loss, they repeat the ready-made charges which are used against all philosophers about teaching things up in the clouds and under the earth, and having no gods, and making the worse appear the better cause; for they do not like to confess that their pretence of knowledge has been detected — which is the truth; and as they are numerous and ambitious and energetic, and are drawn up in battle array and have persuasive tongues, they have filled your ears with their loud and inveterate calumnies. And this is the reason why my three accusers, Meletus and Anytus and Lycon, have set upon me; Meletus, who has a quarrel with me on behalf of the poets; Anytus, on behalf of the craftsmen and politicians; Lycon, on behalf of the rhetoricians: and as I said at the beginning, I cannot expect to get rid of such a mass of calumny all in a moment. And this, O men of Athens, is the truth and the whole truth; I have concealed nothing, I have dissembled nothing. And yet, I know that my plainness of speech makes them hate me, and what is their hatred but a proof that I am speaking the truth? — Hence has arisen the prejudice against me; and this is the reason of it, as you will find out either in this or in any future enquiry.

I have said enough in my defence against the first class of my accusers; I turn to the second class. They are headed by Meletus, that good man and true lover of his country, as he calls himself. Against these, too, I must try to make a defence: — Let their affidavit be read: it contains something of this kind: It says that Socrates is a doer of evil, who corrupts the youth; and who does not believe in the gods of the state, but has other new divinities of his own. Such is the charge; and now let us examine the particular counts. He says that I am a doer of evil, and corrupt the youth; but I say, O men of Athens, that Meletus is a doer of evil, in that he pretends to be in earnest when he is only in jest, and is so eager to bring men to trial from a pretended zeal and interest about matters in which he really never had the smallest interest. And the truth of this I will endeavour to prove to you.

Come hither, Meletus, and let me ask a question of you. You think a great deal about the improvement of youth?

Yes, I do.

Tell the judges, then, who is their improver; for you must know, as you have taken the pains to discover their corrupter, and are citing and accusing me before them. Speak, then, and tell the judges who their improver is. — Observe, Meletus, that you are silent, and have nothing to say. But is not this rather disgraceful, and a very considerable proof of what I was saying, that you have no interest in the matter. Speak up, friend, and tell us who their improver is.

The laws.

But that, good sir, is not my meaning. I want to know who the person is, who, in the first place, knows the laws.

The judges, Socrates, who are present in court.

What, do you mean to say, Meletus, that they are able to instruct and improve youth?

Certainly they are.

What, all of them, or some only and not others?

All of them.

By the goddess Herè, that is good news! There are plenty of improvers, then. And what do you say of the audience, — do they improve them?

Yes, they do.

And the senators?

Yes, the senators improve them.

But perhaps the members of the assembly corrupt them? — or do they improve them?

They improve them.

Then every Athenian improves and elevates them; all with the exception of myself; and I alone am their corrupter? Is that what you affirm?

That is what I stoutly affirm.

I am very unfortunate if you are right. But suppose I ask a question: How about horses? Does one man do them harm and all the world good? Is not the exact opposite the truth? One man is able to do them good, or at least not many;—the trainer of horses, that is to say, does them good, and others who have to do with them rather injure them? Is not that true, Meletus, of horses, or of any other animals? Most assuredly it is; whether you and Anytus say yes or no. Happy indeed would be the condition of youth if they had one corrupter only, and all the rest of the world were their improvers. But you, Meletus, have sufficiently shown that you never had a thought about the young: your carelessness is seen in your not caring about the very things which you bring against me.

And now, Meletus, I will ask you another question — by Zeus I will: Which is better, to live among bad citizens, or among good ones? Answer, friend, I say; the question is one which may be easily answered. Do not the good do their neighbours good, and the bad do them evil?

Certainly.

And is there any one who would rather be injured than benefited by those who live with him? Answer, my good friend, the law requires you to answer — does any one like to be injured?

Certainly not.

And when you accuse me of corrupting and deteriorating the youth, do you allege that I corrupt them intentionally or unintentionally?

Intentionally, I say.

But you have just admitted that the good do their neighbours good, and evil do them evil. Now, is that a truth which your superior wisdom has recognized thus early in life, and am I, at my age, in such darkness and ignorance as not to know that if a man with whom I have to live is corrupted by me, I am very likely to be harmed by him; and yet I corrupt him, and intentionally, too, — so you say, although neither I nor any other human being is ever likely to be convinced by you. But either I do not corrupt them, or I corrupt them unintentionally; and on either view of the case you lie. If my offence is unintentional, the law has no cognizance of unintentional offences: you ought to have taken me privately, and warned and admonished me; for if I had been better advised, I should have left off doing what I only did unintentionally — no doubt I should; but you would have nothing to say to me and refused to teach me. And now you bring me up in this court, which is a place not of instruction, but of punishment.

It will be very clear to you, Athenians, as I was saying, that Meletus has no care at all, great or small, about the matter. But still I should like to know, Meletus, in what I am affirmed to corrupt the young. I suppose you mean, as I infer from your indictment, that I teach them not to acknowledge the gods which the state acknowledges, but some other new divinities or spiritual agencies in their stead. These are the lessons by which I corrupt the youth, as you say.

Yes, that I say emphatically.

Then, by the gods, Meletus, of whom we are speaking, tell me and the court, in somewhat plainer terms, what you mean! for I do not as yet understand whether you affirm that I teach other men to acknowledge some gods, and therefore that I do believe in gods, and am not an entire atheist — this you do not lay to my charge, — but only you say that they are not the same gods which the city recognizes — the charge is that they are different gods. Or, do you mean that I am an atheist simply, and a teacher of atheism?

I mean the latter — that you are a complete atheist.

What an extraordinary statement! Why do you think so, Meletus? Do you mean that I do not believe in the godhead of the sun or moon, like other men?

I assure you, judges, that he does not: for he says that the sun is stone, and the moon earth.

Friend Meletus, you think that you are accusing Anaxagoras: and you have but a bad opinion of the judges, if you fancy them illiterate to such a degree as not to know that these doctrines are found in the books of Anaxagoras the Clazomenian, which are full of them. And so, forsooth, the youth are said to be taught them by

313

Socrates, when there are not unfrequently exhibitions of them at the theatre (price of admission one drachma at the most); and they might pay their money, and laugh at Socrates if he pretends to father these extraordinary views. And so, Meletus, you really think that I do not believe in any god?

I swear by Zeus that you believe absolutely in none at all.

Nobody will believe you, Meletus, and I am pretty sure that you do not believe yourself. I cannot help thinking, men of Athens, that Meletus is reckless and impudent, and that he has written this indictment in a spirit of mere wantonness and youthful bravado. Has he not compounded a riddle, thinking to try me? He said to himself: — I shall see whether the wise Socrates will discover my facetious contradiction, or whether I shall be able to deceive him and the rest of them. For he certainly does appear to me to contradict himself in the indictment as much as if he said that Socrates is guilty of not believing in the gods, and yet of believing in them — but this is not like a person who is in earnest.

I should like you, O men of Athens, to join me in examining what I conceive to be his inconsistency; and do you, Meletus, answer. And I must remind the audience of my request that they would not make a disturbance if I speak in my accustomed manner:

Did ever man, Meletus, believe in the existence of human beings, and not of human beings? . . . I wish, men of Athens, that he would answer, and not be always trying to get up an interruption. Did ever any man believe in horsemanship, and not in horses? or in flute-playing, and not in flute-players? No, my friend; I will answer to you and to the court, as you refuse to answer for yourself. There is no man who ever did. But now please to answer the next question: Can a man believe in spiritual and divine agencies, and not in spirits or demigods?

He cannot.

How lucky I am to have extracted that answer, by the assistance of the court! But then you swear in the indictment that I teach and believe in divine or spiritual agencies (new or old, no matter for that); at any rate, I believe in spiritual agencies, — so you say and swear in the affidavit; and yet if I believe in divine things, how can I help believing in spirits or demigods; — must I not? To be sure I must; and therefore I may assume that your silence gives consent. Now what are spirits or demigods? are they not either gods or the sons of gods?

Certainly they are.

But this is what I call the facetious riddle invented by you: the demigods or spirits are gods, and you say first that I do not believe in gods, and then again that I do believe in gods; that is, if I believe in demigods. For if the demigods are the illegitimate sons of gods, whether by the nymphs or by any other mothers, of whom they are said to be the sons — what human being will ever believe that there are no gods if they are the sons of gods? You might as well affirm the existence of mules, and deny that of horses and asses. Such nonsense, Meletus, could only have been intended by you to make trial of me. You have put this into the indictment because you had nothing real of which to accuse me. But no one who has a particle of understanding will ever be convinced by you that the same man can believe in divine and superhuman things, and yet not believe that there are gods and demigods and heroes.

I have said enough in answer to the charge of Meletus: any elaborate defence is unnecessary; but I know only too well how many are the enmities which I have incurred, and this is what will be my destruction if I am destroyed; — not Meletus, nor yet Anytus, but the envy and detraction of the world, which has been the death of many good men, and will probably be the death of many more; there is no danger of my being the last of them.

Some one will say: And are you not ashamed, Socrates, of a course of life which is likely to bring you to an untimely end? To him I may fairly answer: There you are mistaken: a man who is good for anything ought not to calculate the chance of living or dying; he ought to consider in doing anything he is doing right or wrong — acting the part of a good man or of a bad. Whereas, upon your view, the heroes who fell at Troy were not good for much and the son of Thetis above all, who altogether despised danger in comparison with disgrace; and when he was so eager to slay Hector, his goddess mother said to him, that if he avenged his companion Patroclus, and slew Hector, he would die himself — 'Fate,' she said, in these or the like words, 'waits for you next after Hector;' he, receiving this warning, utterly despised danger and death, and instead of fearing them, feared rather to live in dishonour, and not to avenge his friend. 'Let me die forthwith,' he replies, 'and be avenged of my enemy, rather than abide here by the beaked ships, a laughing-stock and a burden on the earth.' Had Achilles any thought of death and danger? For wherever a man's place is, whether the place which he has chosen or that in which he has been placed by a commander, there he ought to remain in the hour of danger; he should not think of death or of anything but of disgrace. And this, O men of Athens, is a true saying.

Strange, indeed, would be my conduct, O men of Athens, if I who, when I was ordered by the generals whom you chose to command me at Potidaea and Amphipolis and Delium, remained where they placed me, like any other man, facing death — if now, when, as I conceive and imagine, God orders me to fulfil the philosopher's mission of searching into myself and other men, I were to desert my post through fear of death, or any other fear; that would indeed be strange, and I might justly be arraigned in court for denying the existence of the gods, if I disobeyed the oracle because I was afraid of death, fancying that I was wise when I was not wise. For the fear of death is indeed the pretence of wisdom, and not real wisdom, being a pretence of knowing the unknown; and no one knows whether death, which men in their fear apprehend to be the greatest evil, may not be the greatest good. Is not this ignorance of a disgraceful sort, the ignorance which is the conceit that a man knows what he does not know? And in this respect only I believe myself to differ from men in general, and may perhaps claim to be wiser than they are: — that whereas I know but little of the world below, I do not suppose that I know; but I do know that injustice and disobedience to a better, whether God or man, is evil and dishonourable, and I will never fear or avoid a possible good rather than a certain evil. And therefore if you let me go now, and are not convinced by Anytus, who said that since I had been prosecuted I must be put to death: (or if not that I ought never to have been prosecuted at all); and that if I escape now, your sons will all be utterly ruined by listening to my words — if you say to me, Socrates, this time we will not mind Anytus, and you shall be let off, but upon one condition, that you are not to enquire and speculate in this way any more, and that if you are caught doing so again you shall die; — if this was the condition on which you let me go, I should reply: Men of Athens, I honour and love you; but I shall obey God rather than you, and while I have life and strength I shall never cease from the practice and teaching of philosophy, exhorting any one whom I meet and saying to him after my manner: You, my friend, — a citizen of the great and mighty and wise city of Athens, — are you not ashamed of heaping up the greatest amount of money and honour and reputation, and caring so little about wisdom and truth and the greatest improvement of the soul, which you never regard or heed at all? and if the person with whom I am arguing, says: Yes, but I do care; then I do not leave him or let him go at once; but I proceed to interrogate and examine and cross-examine him, and if I think that he has no virtue in him, but only says that he has, I reproach him with undervaluing the greater, and overvaluing the less. And I shall repeat the same words to every one whom I meet, young and old, citizen and alien, but especially to the citizens inasmuch as they are my brethren. For know that this is the command of God; and believe that no greater good has ever happened in the state than my service to the

God. For I do nothing but go about persuading you all, old and young alike, not to take thought for your persons or your properties, but first and chiefly to care about the greatest improvement of the soul. I tell you that virtue is not given by money, but that from virtue comes money and every other good of man, public as well as private. This is my teaching, and if this is the doctrine which corrupts the youth, I am a mischievous person. But if any one says that this is not my teaching, he is speaking an untruth. Wherefore, O men of Athens, I say to you, do as Anytus bids or not as Anytus bids, and either acquit me or not; but whichever you do, understand that I shall never alter my ways, not even if I have to die many times.

Men of Athens, do not interrupt, but hear me; there was an understanding between us that you should hear me to the end: I have something more to say, at which you may be inclined to cry out; but I believe that to hear me will be good for you, and therefore I beg that you will not cry out. I would have you know, that if you kill such an one as I am, you will injure yourselves more than you will injure me. Nothing will injure me, not Meletus nor yet Anytus — they cannot, for a bad man is not permitted to injure a better than himself. I do not deny that Anytus may, perhaps, kill him, or drive him into exile, or deprive him of civil rights; and he may imagine, and others may imagine, that he is inflicting a great injury upon him: but there I do not agree. For the evil of doing as he is doing — the evil of unjustly taking away the life of another — is greater far.

And now, Athenians, I am not going to argue for my own sake, as you may think, but for yours, that you may not sin against the God by condemning me, who am his gift to you. For if you kill me you will not easily find a successor to me, who, if I may use such a ludicrous figure of speech, am a sort of gadfly, given to the state by God; and the state is a great and noble steed who is tardy in his motions owing to his very size, and requires to be stirred into life. I am that gadfly which God has attached to the state, and all day long and in all places am always fastening upon you, arousing and persuading and reproaching you. You will not easily find another like me, and therefore I would advise you to spare me. I dare say that you may feel out of temper (like a person who is suddenly awakened from sleep), and you think that you might easily strike me dead as Anytus advises, and then you would sleep on for the remainder of your lives, unless God in his care of you sent you another gadfly. When I say that I am given to you by God, the proof of my mission is this: — if I had been like other men, I should not have neglected all my own concerns or patiently seen the neglect of them during all these years, and have been doing yours, coming to you individually like a father or elder brother, exhorting you to regard virtue; such conduct, I say, would be unlike human nature. If I had gained anything, or if my exhortations had been paid, there would have been some sense in my doing so; but now, as you will perceive, not even the imprudence of my accusers dares to say that I have ever exacted or sought pay of any one; of that they have no witness. And I have a sufficient witness to the truth of what I say — my poverty.

Some one may wonder why I go about in private giving advice and busying myself with the concerns of others, but do not venture to come forward in public and advise the state. I will tell you why. You have heard me speak at sundry times and in divers places of an oracle or sign which comes to me, and is the divinity which Meletus ridicules in the indictment. This sign, which is a kind of voice, first began to come to me when I was a child; it always forbids but never commands me to do anything which I am going to do. This is what deters me from being a politician. And rightly, as I think. For I am certain, O men of Athens, that if I had engaged in politics, I should have perished long ago, and done no good either to you or to myself. And do not be offended at my telling you the truth; for the truth is, that no man who goes to war with you or any other multitude, honestly striving against the many lawless and unrighteous deeds which are done in a state, will save his life; he who will fight for the right, if he would live even for a brief space, must have a private station and not a public one.

I can give you convincing evidence of what I say, not words only, but what you value far more — actions. Let me relate to you a passage of my own life which will prove to you that I should never have yielded to injustice from any fear of death, and that 'as I should have refused to yield' I must have died at once. I will tell you a tale of the courts, not very interesting perhaps, but nevertheless true. The only office of state which I ever held, O men of Athens, was that of senator: the tribe Antiochis, which is my tribe, had the presidency at the trial of the generals who had not taken up the bodies of the slain after the battle of Arginusae; and you proposed to try them in a body, contrary to law, as you all thought afterwards; but at the time I was the only one of the Prytanes who was opposed to the illegality, and I gave my vote against you; and when the orators threatened to impeach and arrest me, and you called and shouted, I made up my mind that I would run the risk, having law and justice with me, rather than take part in your injustice because I feared imprisonment and death. This happened in the days of the democracy. But when the oligarchy of the Thirty was in power, they sent for me and four others into the rotunda, and bade us bring Leon the Salaminian from Salamis, as they wanted to put him to death. This was a specimen of the sort of commands which they were always giving with the view of implicating as many as possible in their crimes; and then I showed, not in word only but in deed, that, if I may be allowed to use such an expression, I cared not a straw for death, and that my great and only care was lest I should do an unrighteous or unholy thing. For the strong arm of that oppressive power did not frighten me into doing wrong; and when we came out of the rotunda the other four went to Salamis and fetched Leon, but I went quietly home. For which I might have lost my life, had not the power of the Thirty shortly afterwards come to an end. And many will witness to my words.

Now do you really imagine that I could have survived all these years, if I had led a public life, supposing that like a good man I had always maintained the right and had made justice, as I ought, the first thing? No indeed, men of Athens, neither I nor any other man. But I have been always the same in all my actions, public as well as private, and never have I yielded any base compliance to those who are slanderously termed my disciples, or to any other. Not that I have any regular disciples. But if any one likes to come and hear me while I am pursuing my mission, whether he be young or old, he is not excluded. Nor do I converse only with those who pay; but any one, whether he be rich or poor, may ask and answer me and listen to my words; and whether he turns out to be a bad man or a good one, neither result can be justly imputed to me; for I never taught or professed to teach him anything. And if any one says that he has ever learned or heard anything from me in private which all the world has not heard, let me tell you that he is lying.

But I shall be asked, Why do people delight in continually conversing with you? I have told you already, Athenians, the whole truth about this matter: they like to hear the cross-examination of the pretenders to wisdom; there is amusement in it. Now this duty of cross-examining other men has been imposed upon me by God; and has been signified to me by oracles, visions, and in every way in which the will of divine power was ever intimated to any one. This is true, O Athenians; or, if not true, would be soon refuted. If I am or have been corrupting the youth, those of them who are now grown up and become sensible that I gave them bad advice in the days of their youth should come forward as accusers, and take their revenge; or if they do not like to come themselves, some of their relatives, fathers, brothers, or other kinsmen, should say what evil their families have suffered at my hands. Now is their time. Many of them I see in the court. There is Crito, who is of the same age and of the same deme with myself, and there is Critobulus his son, whom

I also see. Then again there is Lysanias of Sphettus, who is the father of Aeschines — he is present; and also there is Antiphon of Cephisus, who is the father of Epigenes; and there are the brothers of several who have associated with me. There is Nicostratus the son of Theosdotides, and the brother of Theodotus (now Theodotus himself is dead, and therefore he, at any rate, will not seek to stop him); and there is Paralus the son of Demodocus, who had a brother Theages; and Adeimantus the son of Ariston, whose brother Plato is present; and Aeantodorus, who is the brother of Apollodorus, whom I also see. I might mention a great many others, some of whom Meletus should have produced as witnesses in the course of his speech; and let him still produce them, if he has forgotten — I will make way for him. And let him say, if he has any testimony of the sort which he can produce. Nay, Athenians, the very opposite is the truth. For all these are ready to witness on behalf of the corrupter, of the injurer of their kindred, as Meletus and Anytus call me; not the corrupted youth only — there might have been a motive for that — but their uncorrupted elder relatives. Why should they too support me with their testimony? Why, indeed, except for the sake of truth and justice, and because they know that I am speaking the truth, and that Meletus is a liar.

Well, Athenians, this and the like of this are all the defence which I have to offer. Yet a word more. Perhaps there may be some one who is offended at me, when he calls to mind how he himself on a similar, or even a less serious occasion, prayed and entreated the judges with many tears, and how he produced his children in court, which was a moving spectacle, together with a host of relations and friends; whereas I, who am probably in danger of my life, will do none of these things. The contrast may occur to his mind, and he may be set against me, and vote in anger because he is displeased at me on this account. Now if there be such a person among you, — mind, I do not say that there is, — to him I may fairly reply: My friend, I am a man, and like other men, a creature of flesh and blood, and not 'of wood or stone,' as Homer says; and I have a family, yes, and sons, O Athenians, three in number, one almost a man, and two others who are still young; and yet I will not bring any of them hither in order to petition you for an acquittal. And why not? Not from any self-assertion or want of respect for you. Whether I am or am not afraid of death is another question, of which I will not now speak. But, having regard to public opinion, I feel that such conduct would be discreditable to myself, and to you, and to the whole state. One who has reached my years, and who has a name for wisdom, ought not to demean himself. Whether this question of me be deserved or not, at any rate the world has decided that Socrates is in some way superior to other men. And if those among you who are said to be superior in wisdom and courage, and any other virtue, demean themselves in this way, how shameful is their conduct! I have seen men of reputation, when they have been condemned, behaving in the strangest manner: they seemed to fancy that they were going to suffer something dreadful if they died, and that they could be immortal if you only allowed them to live; and I think that such are a dishonour to the state, and that any stranger coming would have said of them that the most eminent men of Athens, to whom the Athenians themselves give honour and command, are no better than women. And I say that these things ought not to be done by those of us who have a reputation; and if they are done, you ought not to permit them; you ought rather to show that you are far more disposed to condemn the man who gets up a doleful scene and makes the city ridiculous, than him who holds his peace.

But, setting aside the question of public opinion, there seems to be something wrong in asking a favour of a judge, and thus procuring an acquittal, instead of informing and convincing him. For his duty is, not to make a present of justice, but to give judgment; and he has sworn that he will judge according to the laws, and not according to his own good pleasure; and we ought not to encourage you, nor should you allow yourself to be encouraged, in this habit of perjury — there can be no piety in that. Do not then require me to do what I consider dishonourable and impious and wrong, especially now, when I am being tried for impiety on the indictment of Meletus. For if, O men of Athens, by force of persuasion and entreaty I could overpower your oaths, then I should be teaching you to believe that there are no gods, and in defending should simply convict myself of the charge of not believing in them. But that is not so — far otherwise. For I do believe that there are gods, and in a sense higher than that in which any of my accusers believe in them. And to you and to God I commit my cause, to be determined by you as is best for you and me.

* * *

There are many reasons why I am not grieved, O men of Athens, at the vote of condemnation. I expected it, and am only surprised that the votes are so nearly equal; for I had thought that the majority against me would have been far larger; but now, had thirty votes gone over the other side, I should have been acquitted. And I may say, I think, that I have escaped Meletus. I may say more; for without the assistance of Anytus and Lycon, any one may see that he would not have had a fifth part of the votes, as the law requires, in which case he would have incurred a fine of a thousand drachmae.

And so he proposes death as the penalty. And what shall I propose on my part, O men of Athens? Clearly that which is my due. And what is my due? What return shall be made to the man who has never had the wit to be idle during his whole life; but has been careless of what the many care for — wealth, and family interests, and military offices, and speaking in the assembly, and magistracies, and plots, and parties. Reflecting that I was really too honest a man to be a politician and live, I did not go where I could do no good to you or to myself; but where I could do the greatest good privately to every one of you, thither I went, and sought to persuade every man among you that he must look to himself, and seek virtue and wisdom before he looks to his private interests, and look to the state before he looks to the interests of the state; and that this should be the order which he observes in all his actions. What shall be done to such an one? Doubtless some good thing. O men of Athens, if he has his reward; and the good should be of a kind suitable to him. What would be a reward suitable to a poor man who is your benefactor, and who desires leisure that he may instruct you? There can be no reward so fitting as maintenance in the Prytaneum, O men of Athens, a reward which he deserves far more than the citizen who has won the prize at Olympia in the horse or chariot race, whether the chariots were drawn by two horses or by many. For I am in want, and he has enough; and he only gives you the appearance of happiness, and I give you the reality. And if I am to estimate the penalty fairly, I should say that maintenance in the Prytaneum is the just return.

Perhaps you think that I am braving you in what I am saying now, as in what I said before about the tears and prayers. But this is not so. I speak rather because I am convinced that I never intentionally wronged any one, although I cannot convince you — the time has been too short; if there were a law at Athens, as there is in other cities, that a capital cause should not be decided in one day, then I believe that I should have convinced you. But I cannot in a moment refute great slanders; and, as I am convinced that I never wronged another, I will assuredly not wrong myself. I will not say of myself that I deserve any evil, or propose any penalty. Why should I? Because I am afraid of the penalty of death which Meletus proposes? When I do not know whether death is a good or an evil, why should I propose a penalty which would certainly be an evil? Shall I say imprisonment? And why should I live in prison, and be the slave of the magistrates of the year — of the Eleven? Or shall the penalty

322

be a fine, and imprisonment until the fine is paid? There is the same objection. I should have to lie in prison, for money I have none, and cannot pay. And if I say exile (and this may possibly be the penalty which you will affix) I must be blinded by the love of life, if I am so irrational as to expect that when you, who are my own citizens, cannot endure my discourses and words, and have found them so grievous and odious that you will have no more of them, others are likely to endure me. No indeed, men of Athens, that is not very likely. And what a life should I lead, at my age, wandering from city to city, ever changing my place of exile, and always being driven out! For I am quite sure that wherever I go, there, as here, the young men will flock to me; and if I drive them away, their elders will drive me out at their request; and if I let them come, fathers and friends will drive me out for their sakes.

Some one will say: Yes, Socrates, but cannot you hold your tongue, and then you may go into a foreign city, and no one will interfere with you? Now I have great difficulty in making you understand my answer to this. For if I tell you that to do as you say would be a disobedience to the God, and therefore that I cannot hold my tongue, you will not believe that I am serious; and if I say again that daily to discourse about virtue, and of those other things about which you hear me examining myself and others, is the greatest good of man, and that the unexamined life is not worth living, you are still less likely to believe me. Yet I say what is true, although a thing of which it is hard for me to persuade you. Also, I have never been accustomed to think that I deserve to suffer any harm. Had I money I might have estimated the offence at what I was able to pay, and not have been much the worse. But I have none, and therefore I must ask you to proportion the fine to my means. Well, perhaps I could afford a mina, and therefore I propose that penalty: Plato, Crito, Critobulus, and Apollodorus, my friends here, bid me say thirty minae, and they will be the sureties. Let thirty minae be the penalty; for which sum they will be ample security to you.

* * *

Not much time will be gained, O Athenians, in return for the evil name which you will get from the detractors of the city, who will say that you killed Socrates, a wise man; for they will call me wise, even although I am not wise, when they want to reproach you. If you had waited a little while, your desire would have been fulfilled in the course of nature. For I am far advanced in years, as you may perceive, and not far from death. I am speaking now not to all of you, but only to those who have condemned me to death. And I have another thing to say to them: You think that I was convicted because I have no words of the sort which would have procured my acquittal — I mean, if I had thought fit to leave nothing undone or unsaid. Not so; the deficiency which led to my conviction was not of words — certainly not. But I had not the boldness or impudence or inclination to address you as you would have liked me to do, weeping and wailing and lamenting, and saying and doing many things which you have been accustomed to hear from others, and which, as I maintain, are unworthy of me. I thought at the time that I ought not to do anything common or mean when in danger: nor do I now repent of the style of my defence; I would rather die having spoken after my manner, than speak in your manner and live. For neither in war nor yet at law ought I or any man to use every way of escaping death. Often in battle there can be no doubt that if a man will throw away his arms, and fall on his knees before his pursuers, he may escape death; and in other dangers there are other ways of escaping death, if a man is willing to say and do anything. The difficulty, my friends, is not to avoid death, but to avoid unrighteousness; for that runs faster than death. I am old and move slowly, and the slower runner has overtaken me, and my accusers are keen and quick, and the faster runner, who is unrighteousness, has overtaken them. And now I depart hence condemned by you to suffer the penalty of death, — they too go their ways condemned by the truth to suffer the penalty of villainy and wrong; and I must abide by my award— let them abide by theirs. I suppose that these things may be regarded as fated, — and I think that they are well.

And now, O men who have condemned me, I would fain prophesy to you; for I am about to die, and in the hour of death men are gifted with prophetic power. And I prophesy to you who are my murderers, that immediately after my departure punishment far heavier than you have inflicted on me will surely await you. Me you have killed because you wanted to escape the accuser, and not to give an account of your lives. But that will not be as you suppose: far otherwise. For I say that there will be more accusers of you than there are now; accusers whom hitherto I have restrained: and as they are younger they will be more inconsiderate with you, and you will be more offended at them. If you think that by killing men you can prevent some one from censuring your evil lives, you are mistaken; that is not a way of escape which is either possible or honourable: the easiest and the noblest way is not to be disabling others, but to be improving yourselves. This is the prophecy which I utter before my departure to the judges who have condemned me.

Friends, who would have acquitted me, I would like also to talk with you about the thing which has come to pass, while the magistrates are busy, and before I go to the place at which I must die. Stay then a little, for we may as well talk with one another, while there is time. You are my friends, and I should like to show you the meaning of this event which has happened to me. O my judges — for you I may truly call judges—I should like to tell you of a wonderful circumstance. Hitherto the divine faculty of which the internal oracle is the source has constantly been in the habit of opposing me even about trifles, if I was going to make a slip or error in any matter; and now as you see there has come upon me that which may be thought, and is generally believed to be, the last and worst evil. But the oracle made no sign of opposition, either when I was leaving my house in the morning, or when I was on my way to the court, or while I was speaking, at anything which I was going to say; and yet I have often been stopped in the middle of a speech, but now in nothing I either said or did touching the matter in hand has the oracle opposed me. What do I take to be the explanation of this silence? I will tell you. It is an intimation that what has happened to me is a good, and that those of us who think that death is an evil are in error. For the customary sign would surely have opposed me had I been going to evil and not to good.

Let us reflect in another way, and we shall see that there is great reason to hope that death is a good; for one of two things — either death is a state of nothingness and utter unconsciousness, or, as men say, there is a change and migration of the soul from this world to another. Now if you suppose that there is no consciousness, but a sleep like the sleep of him who is undisturbed even by dreams, death will be an unspeakable gain. For if a person were to select the night in which his sleep was undisturbed even by dreams, and were to compare with this the other days and nights of his life, and then were to tell us how many days and nights he had passed in the course of his life better and more pleasantly than this one, I think that any man, I will not say a private man, but even the great king will not find many such days or nights, when compared with the others. Now if death be of such a nature, I say that to die is gain; for eternity is then only a single night. But if death is the journey to another place, and there, as men say, all the dead abide, what good, O my friends and judges, can be greater than this? If indeed when the pilgrim arrives in the world below, he is delivered from the professors of justice in this world, and finds the true judges who are said to give judgment there, Minos and Rhadamanthus and Aeacus and Triptolemus, and other sons of God who were righteous in their own life, that pilgrimage will be worth making. What would not a man give if he might converse with Orpheus and Musaeus and Hesiod and Homer? Nay, if this be true, let me die again and again. I myself, too, shall have a wonderful interest in there meeting and conversing with Palamedes, and Ajax the son of Telamon, and any other ancient hero who has suffered death through an unjust judgment; and there will be no small pleasure, as I think, in comparing my own sufferings with theirs. Above all, I shall then be able to continue my search into true and false knowledge; as in this world, so also in the next; and I shall find out who is wise, and who pretends to be wise, and is not. What would not a man give, O judges, to be able to examine the leader of the great Trojan expedition; or Odysseus or Sisyphus, or numberless others, men and women too! What infinite delight would there be in conversing with them and asking them questions! In another world they do not put a man to death for asking questions: assuredly not. For besides being happier than we are, they will be immortal, if what is said is true.

Wherefore, O judges, be of good cheer about death, and know of a certainty, that no evil can happen to a good man, either in life or after death. He and his are not neglected by the gods; nor has my own approaching end happened by mere chance. But I see clearly that the time had arrived when it was better for me to die and be released from trouble; wherefore the oracle gave no sign. For which reason, also, I am not angry with my condemners, or with my accusers; they have done me no harm, although they did not mean to do me any good; and for this I may gently blame them.

Still I have a favour to ask of them. When my sons are grown up, I would ask you, O my friends, to punish them; and I would have you trouble them, as I have troubled you, if they seem to care about riches, or anything, more than about virtue; or if they pretend to be something when they are really nothing, — then reprove them, as I have reproved you, for not caring about that for which they ought to care, and thinking that they are something when they are really nothing. And if you do this, both I and my sons will have received justice at your hands.

The hour of departure has arrived, and we go our ways — I to die, and you to live. Which is better God only knows.

Benjamin Jowett

ARISTOTLE

ARISTOTLE (384-322 B. C.), the *Master of those that know,* as Dante called him, was the supreme polymath. He ranged over every known field of knowledge and classified the resultant findings into the major categories. He established the principles of reasoning and pioneered in the biological sciences.

Born at Stagira in Thrace, the son of Nicomachus, a physician, Aristotle, at the age of seventeen, became a pupil of Plato, at the Academy, remaining there many years. Here he started on those zoological researches that laid the basis of his reputation as an independent investigator. For some time he was a tutor to Alexander the Great, who probably gave him financial aid.

In 335 Aristotle founded his own school, the Lyceum, where he supervised research in various directions, collected a vast library, and also gave lectures. The school had a covered court — a peripatos — and hence Aristotle's followers were later known as Peripatetics.

Accused of impiety, Aristotle left Athens, so that the Athenians would not 'sin twice against philosophy.' In 322 he died in Chalcis.

Aristotle investigated the basis of dramatic structure, examined political theory and organization, astronomy and memory, life and death, the soul, dreams, cosmic teleology, and the evolutionary processes. In his writings he left a body of postulates and factual data that made him for long centuries afterward the primary philosopher, whose *ipsissima verba* held definitive and authoritative finality. His major contributions centre on the foundations of dialectics as he developed this study in his *Prior Analytics* and *Posterior Analytics*. Basically, Aristotle was the great classifier, the ultimate master of synthesis.

THE NICOMACHEAN ETHICS

Book I — *The God. Different Ends. Happiness.*

Every art and every scientific system, and in like manner every course of action and deliberate preference, seems to aim at some good; and consequently *the good* has been well defined as *that which all things aim at.*

But there appears to be a kind of difference in ends; for some are energies; others again beyond these, certain works; but wherever there are certain ends besides the actions, there the works are naturally better than the energies.

327

Now since there are many actions, arts, and sciences, it follows that there are many ends; for of medicine the end is health; of ship-building, a ship; of generalship, victory; of economy, wealth. But whatever of such arts are contained under any one faculty, (as, for instance, under horsemanship is contained the art of making bridles, and all other horse furniture; and this and the whole art of war is contained under generalship; and in the same manner other arts are contained under different faculties;) in all these the ends of the chief arts are more eligible than the ends of the subordinate ones; because for the sake of the former, the latter are pursued. It makes, however, no difference whether the energies themselves, or something else besides these, are the ends of actions, just as it would make no difference in the sciences above mentioned.

If, therefore, there is some end of all that we do, which we wish for on its own account, and if we wish for all other things on account of this, and do not choose everything for the sake of something else (for thus we should go on to infinity, so that desire would be empty and vain), it is evident that this must be *the good*, and the greatest good. Has not, then, the knowledge of this end a great influence on the conduct of life? and, like archers, shall we not be more likely to attain that which is right, if we have a mark? If so, we ought to endeavour to give an outline at least of its nature, and to determine to which of the sciences or faculties it belongs.

Now it would appear to be the end of that which is especially the chief and master science, and this seems to be the political science; for it directs what sciences states ought to cultivate, what individuals should learn, and how far they should pursue them. We see, too, that the most valued faculties are comprehended under it, as, for example, generalship, economy, rhetoric. Since, then, this science makes use of the practical sciences, and legislates respecting what ought to be done, and what abstained from, its end must be *the good* of man. For although the good of an individual and a state be the same, still that of a state appears more important and more perfect both to obtain and to preserve. To discover the good of an individual is satisfactory, but to discover that of a state or a nation is more noble and divine. This, then, is the object of my treatise, which is of a political kind.

The subject would be sufficiently discussed, if it were explained so far as the subject-matter allows; for exactness is not to be sought in all treatises alike, any more than in all productions of mechanic art. But things honourable and things just, the consideration of which falls within the province of political science, admit of such vast difference and uncertainty, that they seem to exist by law only, and not in the nature of things. Things good have also a similar uncertainty, because from them calamities have befallen many. For some, we know, have perished through wealth, and others through courage. We must be content, then, when treating of, and drawing conclusions from such subjects, to exhibit the truth roughly, and in outline; and when dealing with contingent matter, to draw conclusions of the same kind.

According to the same rule ought we to admit each assertion; for it is the part of an educated man to require exactness in each class of subjects, only so far as the nature of the subject admits; for it appears nearly the same thing to allow a mathematician to speak persuasively, as to demand demonstrations from an orator.

Now each individual judges well of what he knows, and of these he is a good judge. In each particular science, therefore, he is a good judge who has been instructed in them; and universally, he who has been instructed in all subjects. Therefore a young man is not a proper person to study political science, for he is inexperienced in the actions of life: but these are the subjects and grounds of this treatise. Moreover, being inclined to follow the dictates of passion, he will listen in vain, and without benefit, since the end is not knowledge, but practice. But it makes no difference, whether he be a youth in age, or a novice in character; for the defect arises not from age, but from his life and pursuits being according to the dictates of passion; for to such persons knowledge becomes useless, as it does to the incontinent; but to those who regulate their appetites and actions according to reason, the knowledge of these subjects must be very beneficial. Concerning the student, and in what manner he is to admit our arguments, and what we propose to treat of, let this much be prefaced.

But let us resume the subject from the commencement. Since all knowledge and every act of deliberate preference aims at some good, let us show what that is, which we say that the political science aims at, and what is the highest good of all things which are done. As to its name, indeed, almost all men are agreed; for both the vulgar and the educated call it *happiness;* but they suppose that to live well and do well are synonymous with being happy. But concerning the nature of happiness they are at variance, and the vulgar do not give the same definition of it as the educated; for some imagine it to be an obvious and well-known object — such as pleasure, or wealth, or honour; but different men think differently of it: and frequently even the same person entertains different opinions respecting it at different times; for, when diseased, he believes it to be health; when poor, wealth; but, conscious of their own ignorance, they admire those who say that it is something great, and beyond them. Some, again, have supposed that, besides these numerous goods, there is another self-existent good, which is to all these the cause of their being goods. Now, to examine all the opinions would perhaps be rather unprofitable; but it will be sufficient to examine those which lie most upon the surface, or seem to be most reasonable.

Let it not, however, escape our notice, that arguments from principles differ from arguments to principles; for well did Plato also propose doubts on this point, and inquire whether the right way is from principles or to principles; just as in the course from the starting-point to the goal, or the contrary. For we must begin from those things that are known; and things are known in two ways; for some are known to ourselves, others are generally known; perhaps, therefore, we should begin from the things known to ourselves.

Whoever, therefore, is to study with advantage the things which are honourable and just, and in a word the subjects of political science, must have been well and morally educated; for the point from whence we must begin is *the fact*, and if this is satisfactorily proved, it will be unnecessary to add *the reason*. Such a student either possesses, or would easily acquire, the principles. But let him who possesses neither of these qualifications, hear the sentiments of Hesiod: —

> Far does the man all other men excel,
> Who, from his wisdom, thinks in all things well.
> Wisely considering, to himself a friend,
> All for the present best, and for the end.
> Nor is the man without his share of praise,
> Who well the dictates of the wise obeys:
> But he that is not wise himself, nor can
> Hearken to wisdom, is a useless man.

Hesiod: *Works and Days*

But let us return to the point where we commenced this digression; for men seem not unreasonably to form their notion of *the good*, and of happiness, from observing the different lives which men lead. The many and most sordid class suppose it to be pleasure, and therefore they are content with a life of enjoyment.

For there are three kinds of lives which are most prominent — first, that just mentioned; secondly, the political; and, thirdly, the contemplative.

Now, the vulgar appear entirely slavish, deliberately preferring the life of brutes; but they find a reason for what they do, because many persons in positions of authority are led by the same passions as Sardanapalus.

But those who are educated, and fond of active pursuits, suppose it to be honour, for this may be almost said to be the end of political life; but it appears to be too superficial for the object of our inquiry; for it seems to reside rather in those who confer, than in those who receive, honour; but we have a natural conception, that the good is something peculiarly one's own, and difficult to be taken away. Moreover, men seem to pursue honour in order that they may believe themselves to be good; at any rate they seek to be honoured by wise men, and by their acquaintances, and on account of virtue: it is plain therefore, that, at least in their opinion, virtue is superior. But perhaps it may rather be supposed that virtue is the end of the political life; but this appears too incomplete, for it seems possible for a man, while in possession of virtue, either to sleep or be inactive through life; and besides this, to suffer the greatest misfortunes and calamities. But no one would pronounce a man happy who lives such a life as this, unless he were defending a favourite hypothesis. Enough, therefore, of these things; for we have treated of them sufficiently in our encyclic works.

The third life is the contemplative; which we shall make the subject of future consideration.

But the money-getting life does violence to our natural inclinations; and it is obvious that riches are not the good which we are in search of! for they are merely useful, and for the sake of some other end. One would therefore rather suppose, that *the good* is one of the ends before mentioned, for they are loved on their own account; but even they do not appear to be so, although many arguments have been expended upon them. Let these things be dismissed from our consideration.

But perhaps it would be better to examine the theory of a universal good, and to inquire what is meant by it, although such an inquiry involves difficulties, because men who are our friends have introduced the doctrine of *ideas*. But perhaps it would seem to be better, and even necessary, at least for the preservation of truth, that we should even do away with private feelings, especially as we are philosophers; for both being dear to us, it is a sacred duty to prefer truth.

But those who introduced this doctrine, did not suppose ideas of those things in which they predicated priority and posteriority, and therefore they did not establish an idea of number. But the good is predicated in substance, in quality, and in relation. But the self-existent and the essence are naturally prior to that which is related; for this is like an offshoot, and an accident of the essence; so that there cannot be any common idea in these.

331

Again, since the good is predicated in as many ways as being (for it is predicated in essence, as God and intellect; and in quality, as the virtues; and in quantity, as the mean; and in relation, as utility; and in time, as opportunity; and in place, as a habitation, and so on), it is evident, that it cannot be anything common, universal, and one: for then it would not have been predicated in all the categories, but in one only.

Again, since of things which are comprehended under one idea there is also one science, there would then be some one science of all goods; but now there are many sciences, even of goods which fall under the same category; as, for instance, under the category of opportunity; for in war there is the science of generalship, but in disease, that of medicine; and again, in the category of the mean, in diet, there is the science of medicine; in labours, that of gymnastics.

But one might doubt as to what they mean by the term *self*-anything, since in self-man and man there is one and the same definition of man; for as far as they are man, they will not differ. But if so, neither will the good and the self-good differ, so far as they are good; nor yet will the self-good be more a good from being eternal; if the white which is of long duration is not whiter than that which lasts but for a day.

But the Pythagoreans seem to speak more plausibly on the subject when they place unity in the co-ordinate series of goods; whom Speusippus also seems to have followed.

The subject, however, may be discussed in another point of view; and what has been said admits of dispute, because our arguments are not applicable to every good; but those things which are pursued and loved on their own account, are predicated under one species, whilst the things which produce these, or in any way preserve them, or prevent the contrary, are said to be goods on account of these, and after another manner. It is evident, then, that goods may be so-called in two ways; some on their own account, the others on account of the former. Having, therefore, separated those which are good on their own account, from those which are useful, let us consider whether they are predicated under one *idea*.

Now, what kind of goods may we assume to be goods on their own account? May we assume all those which are pursued even when alone, such as wisdom, sight, and some pleasures and honours? for these, even if we pursue them on account of something else, one would nevertheless class among things good on their own account: or is there nothing else good *per se* besides the idea? so that, in this view of the subject, the doctrine of the idea is without foundation. But if these also belong to the class of goods on their own account, the definition of good must necessarily show itself to be the same in all these; just as the definition of whiteness in snow, and white lead; but of honour, and prudence, and pleasure, the definitions are distinct and different in the very point which constitutes them goods. The good, therefore, is not anything common under one idea.

In what sense, then, is the term good predicated of these different things? For they are not like things which are homonymous accidentally; is it because they all proceed from one, or tend towards one good? or is it not rather predicated analogically? For as in the body sight is a good, so is intellect in the soul; and, in like manner, different things are goods under different circumstances.

But perhaps these questions should be dismissed for the present, for it would more properly belong to another branch of philosophy to discuss them minutely. The same observation may be applied to the doctrine of the idea; for if there is some one good predicated in common, or something separate, independent by itself, it is obvious it would neither be practical nor capable of being acquired by man; but something of this kind is the object of our present inquiry.

Perhaps, however, some might think that it were well to know it, with a view to those goods which are to be possessed and acted upon; for having this as pattern, we shall better know the goods which are so relatively to ourselves: and if we know them, we shall obtain them. Certainly this position has some plausibility, but it appears to be at variance with the sciences; for all of them, although aspiring after some good, and seeking to supply that which is deficient, omit the knowledge of this; and yet, that all artists should be ignorant of an aid of such consequence, and never inquire for it, is not at all reasonable. It is likewise difficult to say how a weaver or carpenter would be benefited with reference to his own art, by knowing the self-good; and how will he who has contemplated the idea itself be a more skilful physician, or a more able general? for the physician does not appear to regard health in this manner, but the health of man, or rather, perhaps, that of a particular individual; for he cures individual cases. Let it be sufficient, then, to have said so much on these subjects.

Now let us again return to the good we are in search of, and inquire what it is; for it seems to be different in different courses of action and arts; for it is different in the art of medicine, in generalship, and in like manner in the rest. What then is the good in each? Is it not that, for the sake of which the other things are done? Now in the art of medicine this is health; in the art of generalship, victory; in architecture, a house; in different arts, different ends. But in every action and deliberate preference, it is the end; since for the sake of this all men do everything else. So that if there is any end of all human actions, this must be the practical good; but if more ends than one, these must be it. By a different path, therefore, our argument has arrived at the same point; and this we must attempt to explain still farther.

Since ends appear to be more than one, and of these we choose some for the sake of others, as, for instance, riches, musical instruments, and universally all instruments whatever, it is plain that they are not all perfect. But the chief good appears to be something perfect; so that if there is some one end which is alone perfect, that must be the very thing which we are in search of; but if there are many, it must be the most perfect of them. Now we say, that the object pursued for its own sake is more perfect than that pursued for the sake of another; and that the object which is never chosen on account of another thing, is more perfect than those which are eligible both by themselves, and for the sake of that other; in fine, we call that completely perfect, which is always eligible for its own sake, and never on account of anything else.

Of such a kind does happiness seem in a peculiar manner to be; for this we always choose on its own account, and never on account of anything else. But honour, and pleasure, and intellect, and every virtue we choose partly on their own account (for were no further advantage to result from them, we should choose each of them), but we choose them also for the sake of happiness, because we suppose that we shall attain happiness by their means; but no one chooses happiness for the sake of these, nor in short for the sake of anything else.

But the same result seems also to arise from self-sufficiency, for the perfect good appears to be self-sufficient; but we attribute self-sufficiency not to him who leads, for himself alone, a solitary life, but to him who lives also for his parents and children, and wife, and, in short, for his friends and fellow-citizens; since man is naturally a social being. Some limit, however, must be assigned; for, if we go so far as to include parents and descendants, and the friends of friends, we may go on to infinity. But this must be made the subject of future investigation. We define *the self-sufficient* as that which, when separated from everything else, makes life eligible, and in want of nothing; and such we suppose the nature of happiness to be; and moreover, we suppose it the most eligible of all things, even when not reckoned together with any other good; but more eligible, doubtless, even when reckoned together with the smallest good; for the part added becomes an excess of good; but of two goods the greater is always more eligible. Happiness, then, appears something perfect and self-sufficient, being the end of all human actions.

But, perhaps, to say that happiness is the greatest good, appears like stating something which is already granted; and it is desirable that we should explain still more clearly what it is. Perhaps, then, this may be done, if we take the peculiar work of man; for as to the musician, and statuary, and to every artist, and in short to all who have any work or course of action, the good and excellence of each appears to consist in their peculiar work; so would it appear to be with man, if there is any peculiar work belonging to him. Are there, then certain peculiar works and courses of action belonging to the carpenter and shoemaker; and is there no peculiar work of man, but is he by nature without a work? or, as there appears to be a certain work peculiarly belonging to the eye, the hand, and the foot, and, in fine, to each of the members, in like manner would not one assume a certain work besides all these peculiarly belonging to man?

What, then, must this peculiar work be? For life man appears to share in common with plants; but his *peculiar* work is the object of our inquiry: we must, therefore, separate the life of nutrition and growth. Then a kind of sensitive life would next follow; but this also he appears to enjoy in common with the horse, the ox, and every animal. There remains, therefore, a certain practical life of a being which possesses reason; and of this one part is, as it were, obedient to reason, the other as possessing it, and exercising intellect. But this life also being spoken of in two ways, we must take that according to energy; for that appears to be more properly so-called. Now if the work of man is an energy of the soul according to reason, or not without reason; and if we say that the work of man, and of a good man, is the same generically, as in the case of a harper, and a good harper (and so, in short, in all cases, superiority in each particular excellence being added to each particular work); for it is the work of a harper to play, of a good harper to play well: and if we assume the peculiar work of man to be a kind of life, and this life an energy of the soul and actions performed with reason; and the peculiar work of a good man to be the same things done well, and honourably; and everything to be complete according to its proper excellence: if, I repeat, these things are true, it follows, that man's chief good is *an energy of the soul according to virtue*; but if the virtues are more than one, according to the best and most perfect virtue; and besides this, we must add, in a perfect life: for as neither one swallow, nor one day, makes a spring; so neither does one day, nor a short time, make a man blessed and happy.

Let this then be *the good* in its general outlines; for it is necessary, perhaps, first to sketch, then afterwards to complete the drawing. But it would seem to be incumbent upon every one to improve and distinctly delineate the figures which are correctly sketched, and time would seem to be the discoverer of such features as these, or at least a good assistant; whence also proceed the improvements in the arts; for it is the duty of every one to supply deficiencies. But it is necessary to bear in mind what has been mentioned already, and not to demand exactness equally in all subjects, but in each according to its subject-matter, and just so far as is appropriate to the system to which it belongs: for the carpenter and geometrician examine a right angle with different views; the one, so far as it is useful for his work, whilst the other investigates its nature and properties; for his object is the contemplation of the truth, for he is a contemplator of the truth. In the same manner, then, must we act in all other instances, that the mere accessories may not become more numerous than the works themselves. Nor, indeed, is the cause to be required in all cases alike; but it suffices in some, as for instance, in first principles, that their existence be clearly shown; but the existence is the first and the principle.

Now of principles some are perceived by induction, others by sensation, others by a certain habit, and different principles in different ways; but we must endeavour to trace each of them in the manner in which they are formed by nature; and we must use our utmost endeavours that they be well defined, for that has great weight in the discussions which follow. For the principle seems to be more than the half of the whole, and many of the subjects of our inquiry seem to become clear by means of this.

But we must consider the subject of happiness not only as regards the conclusion which we have drawn, and the premises from which our arguments are derived, but also as regards the statements of others concerning it; for all the properties of a thing accord with the truth; but the truth is at once discordant with falsehood.

Now, goods being divided into three classes, and some being called external, others said to belong to the soul, and others to the body, we call those belonging to the soul, the superior, and good, in a higher sense than the others; but we assume, that the actions and energies of the soul belong to the soul. So that our assertion would be correct, according to this opinion at least, which is ancient, and allowed by philosophers, that certain actions and energies are the end; for thus it becomes one of the goods of the soul, and not one of the external ones.

Also, that the happy man lives well, and does well, harmonizes with our definition; for we have almost defined happiness as a kind of well living, and well doing.

Again, all the qualities required in happiness appear to exist in our definition; for to some it seems to be virtue, to others prudence, and to others a kind of wisdom: to some, again, these, or some one of these, with pleasure, or at least, not without pleasure; others, again, include external prosperity: but of these opinions, many ancient writers support some; a few celebrated philosophers the others; but it is reasonable to suppose that none of these have totally erred, but that in some one particular, at least, they are for the most part right.

Now with those, who say that it is every virtue, or some virtue, our definition accords; for to this virtue belongs the energy. But perhaps it makes no slight difference whether we conceive the chief good to consist in possession, or in use; in habit, or in energy. For it is possible, that the habit, though really existing, should cause the performance of no good thing; as in the case of a man who is asleep, or in any other way is incapable of acting: but that the energy should do so is impossible; for of necessity it will act, and will act well. But as in the Olympic games, it is not the most beautiful and the strongest who are crowned, but those who engage in the conflict (for some of these are the conquerors); thus it is those only who act aright, who obtain what is honourable and good in life. Moreover, their life is of itself pleasant; for to be pleased, is one of the goods of the soul; but that is to every man pleasant, with reference to which he is said to be fond of such a thing; as, for example, a horse to the man who is fond of horses, and a spectacle to the man who is fond of spectacles; in like manner also, things just to the lover of justice; and, in a word, virtuous things to the lover of virtue.

Now the things that are pleasant to the generality of mankind, are at variance with each other, because they are not naturally pleasant; but things naturally pleasant, are pleasant to those who are fond of that which is honourable; and such are always the actions according to virtue; so that to these men they are pleasant, even of themselves. Their life therefore stands in no need of the addition of pleasure, as a kind of appendage or amulet, but possesses pleasure in itself; for, besides what has been said, the man who does not take pleasure in honourable actions, has no title to be called good; for neither would any person call that man just, who takes no pleasure in acting justly; nor that man liberal, who takes no pleasure in liberal actions; and in the other cases in like manner. But if this is the case, the actions of virtue must be pleasant of themselves; and yet they are also good and honourable, and each of these in the highest degree, if, indeed, the good man judges rightly concerning them; but he judges as we said. Happiness, therefore, is the best, the most honourable, and the most pleasant of all things; and these qualities are not divided, as in the Delian inscription:

> That which is most just is most honourable,
> and health is the most desirable, and the obtaining
> what we love the most pleasant:

for all these qualities exist in the best energies; and these, or the best one of them, we say that happiness is. But, nevertheless, it appears to stand in need of the addition of external goods, as we said; for it is impossible, or not easy, for one who is not furnished with external means, to do honourable actions; for many things are done, as it were, by means of instruments, by friends, by money, or political influence. And if deprived of some things, men sully their happiness, as for instance, of noble birth, good children, or beauty: for the man of deformed appearance, and of ignoble birth, and the solitary and childless man, is not at all likely to be happy: and still less perhaps is he likely to be so whose children or friends are utterly wicked, or have been good, and are dead. As, therefore, we said there seems to be need of the addition of this sort of external prosperity; whence some people set down good fortune as synonymous with happiness, and others virtue.

Hence also a question is raised, whether happiness is acquired by learning, by habit, or by exercise of any other kind; or whether it is produced in a man by some heavenly dispensation, or even by chance. Now, if there is any other thing which is the gift of God to men, it is reasonable to suppose that happiness is a divine gift, and more than anything else, inasmuch as it is the best of human things. But this, perhaps, would more fitly belong to another kind of investigation: but, even if it be not sent from heaven, but is acquired by means of virtue, and of some kind of teaching or exercise, it appears to be one of the most divine of things; for the prize and end of virtue seems to be something which is best, godlike, and blessed. It must also be common to many; for it is possible, that by means of some teaching and care, it should exist in every person who is not incapacitated for virtue. But if it is better that people should be happy by these means, than by chance, it is reasonable to suppose it is so, since natural productions are produced in the best way in which it is possible for them to be produced; and likewise the productions of art, and of every efficient cause, and especially of the best cause. But to commit the greatest and the noblest of things to chance would be very inconsistent. Now the thing we are at present in search of receives additional clearness from the definition; for happiness has been said to be a kind of energy of the soul according to virtue; but of the remaining goods it is necessary that some exist in it, and that others should be naturally assistant and useful, instrumentally. But this will agree with what we stated in the

338

beginning; for we set down the end of the political science as the good; and this devotes its principal attention to form the characters of the citizens, to make them good, and dispose them to honourable actions.

It is with reason, then, that we do not call an ox, a horse, or any other beast, happy; for none of them are able to participate in this kind of energy. For this cause, also, a child cannot be called happy; for from his time of life he is not yet able to perform such actions; but those who are so-called, are called happy from hope; for, as we said, there is need of perfect virtue, and of perfect life. For the changes of life are numerous, and the accidents of fortune various; and it is possible for the man in the enjoyment of the greatest prosperity to become involved in great calamities in the time of his old age, as is related in the story of Priam, in the Iliad; and no man will call him happy, who has experienced such misfortunes and died miserably.

Are we, then to call no other man happy as long as he lives, but is it necessary, as Solon says, to look to the end? But if we must lay down this rule, is he then happy when he is dead? Or is this altogether absurd, especially in us who assert happiness to be a kind of energy? But if we do not call the dead man happy, and even Solon does not mean this, but that a person might then securely call a man happy, as beyond the reach of evils and misfortunes, even this assertion admits of some dispute. For if there is some good and evil to the man who is alive, and who is not aware of it, there may be supposed to be some to the dead man also, as honours and dishonours, and the good and evil fortunes of children and descendants generally. But this too occasions some difficulty; for when a man has lived happily till his old age, and has died in the same manner, it is possible that various changes may happen to his descendants, and that some of them should be good, and enjoy a life according to their deserts, while others obtain the contrary one; but it is clearly possible for them, taking into consideration the distance of time, to stand in every imaginable relation towards their parents. Now it would be absurd, if the dead man were to participate in their changes, and be at one time happy, and then again miserable; and it would also be absurd, that the fortunes of children should not, in any instance, or at any time, reach to and affect the parents.

But we must return to the doubt originally started; for perhaps from its solution the present question might receive elucidation. Now, if it is necessary to look to the end, and then to call every man happy, not because he is, but because he has been, happy, how can it be otherwise than absurd, if, when he is happy, the thing which really exists in him shall be unable to be truly said of him, because we do not choose to call living men happy on account of the changes of life, and because we have in our mind conceived happiness to be something permanent, and by no means easily admitting of change, and because good and evil fortune come frequently round to the same persons? for it is clear, that if we constantly attend to the chances of fortune, we shall frequently call the same man at one time happy, and at another miserable, exhibiting the happy man as a kind of chameleon, and as placed upon an insecure foundation.

Or is this following of the accidents of fortune in no way right? for goodness and badness do not depend upon these, but human life, as we said, stands in need of external goods as additions; but virtuous energies are the essential constituents of happiness, and the contrary energies of the contrary to happiness. But the question we have just started bears testimony to the definition; for stability does not exist in any human thing so much as in virtuous energies; for these seem to be more permanent even than the sciences, and the most honourable of these are likewise the most stable, because happy men most frequently and most constantly pass their lives in them; for this seems to be the reason why there is no forgetfulness of them. Therefore, the thing which we are in search of will exist in the happy man, and throughout his life he will be of this character; for he always, or most of all men, will live in the practice and contemplation of virtuous actions, and he will bear the accidents of fortune most nobly, and in every case, and altogether suitably, as a man in reality good, and a faultless cube. But since the accidents of fortune are numerous, and differ in greatness and smallness, small instances of good fortune, and likewise of the opposite, clearly will not influence the balance of life; but great and numerous accidents, if on the side of good fortune, will make life more happy, for they naturally unite in giving additional embellishment, and the use of them become honourable and good; but if they happen on the other side, they crush and spoil the happiness; for they bring on sorrows, and are impediments to many energies. But nevertheless, even in these, the honourable is conspicuous, whenever a man bears with equanimity many and great misfortunes, not from insensibility, but because he is high-spirited and magnanimous.

But if the energies are the essential constituents of the happiness or the misery of life, as we said, no happy man can ever become miserable; for he will never do hateful and worthless actions; for we conceive that the man who is in reality good and wise, bears every accident of fortune in a becoming manner, and always acts in the most honourable manner that the circumstances admit of, just as the good general makes the most skilful use of the army he has, and the good shoemaker of the skins that are given him makes the most elegant shoe, and all other artificers in the same manner. But if this is the case, the happy man can never become miserable; yet he would not

340

be perfectly blessed, if he were to be involved in calamities like Priam's. Not that for this reason he is variable, or easily liable to change; for he will neither be moved from his happiness easily, nor by common misfortunes, but only by great and numerous ones; and after these, he cannot become happy again in a short time: but if he does at all, it will be after the lapse of some long and perfect period of time, having in the course of it successfully attained to great and honourable things. What then hinders us from calling that man happy, who energizes according to perfect virtue, and is sufficiently furnished with external goods, and that not for a short time, but for the full period of his life? or must we add, that he is to go on living in the same manner, and die accordingly? since the future is to us invisible. But happiness we set down as in every way and altogether the end, and perfect. But if this be true, we shall call those men blessed amongst the living, in whom the things we have mentioned exist, and will continue to exist, but only blessed as men. And let these subjects have been thus far defined.

But it appears a very unfriendly idea, and one contrary to universal opinion, to suppose that the fortunes of descendants and friends do not in the smallest degree affect the dead man. But since the accidents of fortune that occur are numerous, and differ in various ways, and some of them come more home, and others less, it seems to be a tedious and endless task to discuss them individually; but perhaps it would be sufficient if what we say were said generally and in outline.

If, then, as in the case of misfortunes occurring to one's self, some have weight and influence in life, while others appear lighter; the same exactly is the case with those which happen to all our friends. But it makes a great difference whether each misfortune happens to living or to dead persons; much greater difference than it makes in a tragedy, whether atrocious and horrible crimes are supposed to have been committed previously, or form part of the action of the play. We may then, in this way, come to a conclusion respecting the extent of this difference; or rather, perhaps, respecting the answer to the question about the dead, and their participation in good and its opposites; for it appears from these observations, that, even if anything reaches them, whether good or evil, it must be weak and small, either absolutely, or relatively to them; or, if not this, it must be of such extent and description as not to make those happy who are not already happy, nor to deprive those who are happy of their happiness. Therefore the good fortune of their friends seems in some degree to affect the dead, and in like manner their ill fortunes; but only in such a manner and to such an extent as neither to make the happy unhappy, nor to do anything else of this kind.

These points being determined, let us next consider happiness, whether it be one of things praised or rather of things honourable;

for it is clear that it is not one of the faculties. Now, everything that is praised seems to be praised because it is of a certain character, and has a certain relation to something; for we praise the just man, and the brave man, and the good man generally, and virtue, on account of their works and actions; and the strong man, and the good runner, and everyone else whom we praise, because he naturally is of a certain character, and has a certain relation to something that is good and excellent.

But this is clear from the praises that are given to the gods; for they appear ridiculous when referred to us; but this happens because praises are bestowed relatively to some standard, as we said. But if praise belongs to things of this kind, it is clear that it does not belong to the best things, but something greater and better is bestowed upon them, as also seems to be the case: for we predicate blessedness and happiness of the gods, and of the most godlike of men; and likewise of the most godlike of goods; for no man praises happiness as he would justice, but calls it blessed, as being something more divine and excellent.

But Eudoxus also appears to have pleaded well for the claim of pleasure to the highest place; for he thought that its not being praised, when it was one of the goods, proved it to be superior to all things praised; but God and the highest good are of this kind, for everything else is referred to these; for praise is of virtue, for from this men are able to perform honourable actions; but encomiums are of works, as well bodily as mental. But to discuss these matters with exactness belongs perhaps more properly to those who study encomiums; but for our purpose it is clear, from what has been said, that happiness is one of the things honourable and perfect. And this seems to be the case, from its being a principle; for, for the sake of this all of us do everything else; but we assume the principle and the cause of goods to be something honourable and divine.

But since happiness is a certain energy of the soul according to perfect virtue, we must next consider the subject of virtue; for thus, perhaps, we should see more clearly respecting happiness. But he who in reality is skilled in political philosophy, appears to devote the principal part of his study to this; for he wishes to make the citizens good and obedient to the laws; but we have an example of this in the legislators of the Cretans and Lacedaemonians, and any others who may have become like them. But if this is the peculiar study of political philosophy, it is clear that the investigation would be consistent with our original plan.

We must therefore next examine virtue, that is to say, of course, human virtue; for the good which we were in search of is human good, and the happiness, human happiness; but by human happiness we mean, not that of the body, but that of the soul; and happiness, too, we define to be an energy of the soul. But if these things are true, it is evidently necessary for the political philosopher to have some knowledge of what relates to the soul; just as it is necessary for the man who intends to cure the eyes, to study the whole body; and still more, in proportion as political philosophy is more honourable and excellent than the science of medicine; and the best educated physicians take a great deal of pains in acquiring a knowledge of the human body.

The student of political philosophy must therefore study the soul, but he must study it for the sake of these things, and only so far as is sufficient for the objects which he has in view; for greater exactness requires more labour perhaps than the subject in hand demands. But some things are said about it sufficiently in my exoteric discourses; and these we must make use of: as, for instance, that one part of it is irrational, and the other possessing reason. But whether these things are really separate, like the members of the body, and everything that is capable of division; or whether, being by nature indivisible, they are only in word two, as in a circumference the convex and concave side, matters not for our present purpose.

But of the irrational part, one division is like that which is common, and belonging to plants; that, I mean, which is the cause of nourishment and growth: for a person might assert that such a faculty of life as this exists in all beings that are nourished, even in embryos, and the very same in perfect beings; for it is more reasonable to call it the same than any other. The excellence of this part, therefore, appears common to other beings, and not peculiar to man; for this part of the soul, and its faculties, seem to energize principally in sleep; but the good and the bad man are in sleep least distinguishable; whence men say, that for half their lives there is no difference between the happy and the miserable. But it is reasonable that this should be the case; for sleep is the inaction of the soul, so far forth as it is called good or bad; except if some emotions in a small degree reach it, and in this manner the visions of good men become better than those of the generality. But enough of these things; we must therefore put aside the part which consists in nourishment, since it has naturally no connection with human virtue.

Now another natural power of the soul appears to be irrational, but to participate in reason in some sort; for we praise the reason of the continent and incontinent man, and that part of the soul which is endued with reason; for it exhorts us aright, and to the best actions. But there seems to be in man something else by nature contrary to reason, which contends with and resists reason. For, in reality, just as the paralyzed limbs of the body, when we intend to move them to the right hand, are turned aside the opposite way to the left, so it is with the soul; for the impulses of the incontinent are directed towards the contraries. But in the case of the body we see the part that is turned aside, in the soul we do not see it; but perhaps we must no less believe that there is in the soul something contrary to reason, which opposes and resists it; but how if differs it matters not. But this part also seems, as we said, to partake of reason; at least in the continent man it obeys reason; but in the temperate or brave man it is perhaps still more ready to listen to reason; for in them it entirely agrees with reason.

The irrational part therefore appears to be two-fold; for the part which is common to plants does not at all partake of reason; but the part which contains the desires and the appetites generally in some sense partakes of reason, in that it is submissive and obedient to it. Thus, in fact, we say that a man has regard for his father and friends, but not in the same sense in which we use the expression *logon echein* in mathematics. But the giving of advice, and all reproaching and exhorting, prove that the irrational part is in some sense persuaded by reason. But if it is necessary to say that this has reason likewise, the part which has reason will be twofold also; one part properly and in itself, the other as though listening to the suggestions of a parent.

But virtue also is divided according to this difference; for we call some of the virtues intellectual, others moral — wisdom, and intelligence, and prudence, we call intellectual, but liberality and temperance, moral; for when speaking of the moral character of a man, we do not say that he is wise or intelligent, but that he is meek or temperate; but we praise the wise man also according to his habits; but praiseworthy habits we call virtues.

R. W. Browne

344

EPICTETUS

EPICTETUS (c. 55 - c. 135 A. D.) was a Stoic philosopher. Formerly a slave, he was granted freedom and taught philosophy at Rome. Banished by the Emperor Domitian, Epictetus settled in Nicopolis, in Greece, and taught there until his death. One of his followers, Arrian, collected the lectures of Epictetus, of which four books are extant. The *Manual* or *Encheiridion* is a summary, also by Arrian, of Epictetus' philosophy.

DISCOURSES

Of the things which are in our power, and not in our power.

Of all the faculties (except that which I shall soon mention), you will find not one which is capable of contemplating itself, and, consequently, not capable either of approving or disapproving. How far does the grammatic art possess the contemplating power? As far as forming a judgment about what is written and spoken. And how far music? As far as judgment about melody. Does either of them then contemplate itself? By no means. But when you must write something to your friend, grammar will tell you what words you should write; but whether you should write or not, grammar will not tell you. And so it is with music as to musical sounds; but whether you should sing at the present time and play on the lute, or do neither, music will not tell you. What faculty then will tell you? That which contemplates both itself and all other things. And what is this faculty? The rational faculty; for this is the only faculty that we have received which examines itself, what it is, and what power it has, and what is the value of this gift, and examines all other faculties: for what else is there which tells us that golden things are beautiful, for they do not say so themselves? Evidently it is the faculty which is capable of judging of appearances. What else judges of music, grammar, and the other faculties, proves their uses, and points out the occasions for using them? Nothing else.

What then should a man have in readiness in such circumstances? What else than this? What is mine, and what is not mine; and what is permitted to me, and what is not permitted to me. I must die. Must

I then die lamenting? I must be put in chains. Must I then also lament? I must go into exile. Does any man then hinder me from going with smiles and cheerfulness and contentment? Tell me the secret which you possess. I will not, for this is in my power. But I will put you in chains. Man, what are you talking about? Me in chains? You may fetter my leg, but my will not even Zeus himself can overpower. I will throw you into prison. My poor body, you mean. I will cut your head off. When then have I told you that my head alone cannot be cut off? These are the things which philosophers should meditate on, which they should write daily, in which they should exercise themselves.

What then did Agrippinus say? He said, "I am not a hindrance to myself." When it was reported to him that his trial was going on in the Senate, he said: "I hope it may turn out well; but it is the fifth hour of the day" — this was the time when he was used to exercise himself and then take the cold bath, — "let us go and take our exercise." After he had taken his exercise, one comes and tells him, "You have been condemned." "To banishment," he replies, "or to death?" "To banishment". "What about my property?" "It is not taken from you." "Let us go to Aricia then," he said, "and dine."

How a man on every occasion can maintain his proper character

To the rational animal only is the irrational intolerable; but that which is rational is tolerable. Blows are not naturally intolerable. How is that? See how the Lacedaemonians endure whipping when they have learned that whipping is consistent with reason. To hang yourself is not intolerable. When then you have the opinion that it is rational, you go and hang yourself. In short, if we observe, we shall find that the animal man is pained by nothing so much as by that which is irrational; and, on the contrary, attracted to nothing so much as to that which is rational.

Only consider at what price you sell your own will: if for no other reason, at least for this, that you sell it not for a small sum. But that which is great and superior perhaps belongs to Socrates and such as are like him. Why then, if we are naturally such, are not a very great number of us like him? Is it true then that all horses become swift, that all dogs are skilled in tracking footprints? What then, since I am naturally dull, shall I, for this reason, take no pains? I hope not. Epictetus is not superior to Socrates; but if he is not inferior, this is enough for me; for I shall never be a Milo, and yet I do not neglect my body; nor shall I be a Croesus, and yet I do not neglect my property; nor, in a word, do we neglect looking after anything because we despair of reaching the highest degree.

How a man should proceed from the principle of God being the father of all men to the rest.

If a man should be able to assent to this doctrine as he ought, that we are all sprung from God in an especial manner, and that God is the father both of men and of gods, I suppose that he would never have any ignoble or mean thoughts about himself. But if Caesar should adopt you, no one could endure your arrogance; and if you know that you are the son of Zeus, will you not be elated? Yet we do not so; but since these two things are mingled in the generation of man, body in common with the animals, and reason and intelligence in common with the gods, many incline to this kinship, which is miserable and mortal; and some few to that which is divine and happy. Since then it is of necessity that every man uses everything according to the opinion which he has about it, those, the few, who think that they are formed for fidelity and modesty and a sure use of appearances have no mean or ignoble thoughts about themselves; but with the many it is quite the contrary. For they say, What am I? A poor, miserable man, with my wretched bit of flesh. Wretched, indeed; but you possess something better than your bit of flesh. Why then do you neglect that which is better, and why do you attach yourself to this?

Through this kinship with the flesh, some of us inclining to it become like wolves, faithless and treacherous and mischievous; some become like lions, savage and bestial and untamed; but the greater part of us become foxes, and other worse animals. For what else is a slanderer and malignant man than a fox, or some other more wretched and meaner animal? See then and take care that you do not become some one of these miserable things.

THE ENCHEIRIDION

I

Of things some are in our power, and others are not. In our power are opinion, movement towards a thing, desire, aversion, turning from a thing; and in a word, whatever are our acts. Not in our power are the body, property, reputation, offices, and in a word, whatever are not our own acts. And the things in our power are by nature free, not subject to restraint or hindrance; but the things not in our power are weak, slavish, subject to restraint, in the power of others. Remember then, that if you think the things which are by nature slavish to be free, and the things which are in the power of others to be your own, you will be hindered, you will lament, you will be disturbed, you will blame both gods and men; but if you think that only which is your own to be your own, and if you think that what is another's, as it really is, belongs to another, no man will ever compel you, no man will hinder you, you will never blame any man, you will accuse no man, you will do nothing involuntarily, no man will harm you, you will have no enemy for you will not suffer any harm.

If then you desire such great things remember that you must not lay hold of them with a small effort; but you must leave alone some things entirely, and postpone others for the present. But if you wish for these things also, and power and wealth, perhaps you will not gain even these very things because you aim also at those former things; certainly you will fail in those things through which alone happiness and freedom are secured. Straightway then practice saying to every harsh appearance: You are an appearance, and in no manner what you appear to be. Then examine it by the rules which you possess, and by this first and chiefly, whether it relates to the things which are in our power or to things which are not in our power; and if it relates to anything which is not in our power, be ready to say that it does not concern you.

II

Remember that desire contains in it the profession of obtaining that which you desire; and the profession in aversion is that you will not fall into that which you attempt to avoid; and he who fails in his desire is unfortunate; and he who falls into that which he would avoid is unhappy. If then you attempt to avoid only the things contrary to nature which are within your power you will not be involved in any of the things which you would avoid. But if you attempt to avoid disease, or death, or poverty, you will be unhappy. Take away then aversion from all things which are not in our power, and transfer it to the things contrary to nature which are in our power. But destroy desire completely for the present. For if you desire anything which is not in our power, you must be unfortunate; but of the things in our power, and which it would be good to desire, nothing yet is before you. But employ only the power of moving towards an object and retiring from it; and these powers indeed only slightly and with exceptions and with remission.

III

In everything which pleases the soul, or supplies a want, or is loved, remember to add this to the notion: What is the nature of each thing, beginning from the smallest? If you love an earthen vessel, say it is an earthen vessel which you love; for when it has been broken you will not be disturbed. If you are kissing your child or wife, say that it is a human being whom you are kissing, for when the wife or child dies you will not be disturbed.

IV

When you are going to take in hand any act remind yourself what kind of an act it is. If you are going to bathe, place before yourself what happens in the bath; some splashing the water, others pushing against one other, others abusing one another, and some stealing; and thus with more safety you will undertake the matter, if you say to yourself, I now intend to bathe, and to maintain my will in a manner conformable to nature. And so you will do in every act; for thus if any hindrance to bathing shall happen let this thought be ready. It was not this only that I intended, but I intended also to maintain my will in a way conformable to nature; but I shall not maintain it so if I am vexed at what happens.

V

Men are disturbed not by the things which happen, but by the opinions about the things; for example, death is nothing terrible, for if it were it would have seemed so to Socrates; for the opinion about death that it is terrible, is the terrible thing. When then we are impeded, or disturbed, or grieved, let us never blame others, but ourselves—that is, our opinions. It is the act of an ill-instructed man to blame others for his own bad condition; it is the act of one who has begun to be instructed, to lay the blame on himself; and of one whose instruction is completed, neither to blame another, nor himself.

VI

Be not elated at any advantage which belongs to another. If a horse when he is elated should say, I am beautiful, one might endure it. But when you are elated, and say, I have a beautiful horse, you must know that you are elated at having a good horse. What then is your own? The use of appearances. Consequently when in the use of appearances you are conformable to nature, than be elated, for then you will be elated at something good which is your own.

VII

As on a voyage when the vessel has reached a port, if you go out to get water it is an amusement by the way to pick up a shellfish or some bulb, but your thoughts ought to be directed to the ship, and you ought to be constantly watching if the captain should call, and then you must throw away all those things, that you may not be bound and pitched into the ship like sheep. So in life also, if there be given to you instead of a little bulb and a shell a wife and child, there will be nothing to prevent you from taking them. But if the captain should call, run to the ship and leave all those things without regard to them. But if you are old, do not even go far from the ship, lest when you are called you make default.

VIII

Seek not that the things which happen should happen as you wish; but wish the things which happen to be as they are, and you will have a tranquil flow of life.

George Long

ORATORY

Demosthenes

Aeschines

DEMOSTHENES

DEMOSTHENES (384-322 B. C.) was the most famous of all Greek orators. His study of rhetoric and law brought him numerous private law cases: but his chief reputation rests on his public political speeches.

Demosthenes' most notable speech is *On The Crown*, a contrast between Demosthenes' private life and that of the prosecutor, the orator Aeschines.

The Oration of Demosthenes on the Crown

In this speech Demosthenes analyzes the political situation, relates his public services, and contrasts his own policies in opposition to those of Aeschines. In the course of the speech, relevant decrees, letters and various lists are read into the public record.

In the first place, ye men of Athens, I make my prayer to all the powers of heaven, that such affection as I have ever invariably discovered to this state, and all its citizens, you, now, may entertain for me, upon this present trial. And (what concerns you nearly, what essentially concerns your religion and your honour) — that the Gods may so dispose your minds, as to permit me to proceed in my defence, not as directed by my adversary, (that would be severe indeed!) but by the laws, and by our oath, in which, to all the other equitable clauses, we find this expressly added — each party shall have equal audience. This imports not merely that you shall not pre-judge, not merely that the same impartiality shall be shewn to both; but still further, that the contending parties shall each be left at full liberty to arrange, and to conduct his pleading, as his choice or judgment may determine.

In many instances hath Aeschines the intire advantage in this cause. Two there are of more especial moment. First, as to our interests in the contests, we are on terms utterly unequal: for they are by no means points of equal import, for me to be deprived of your affections, and for him to be defeated in his prosecution. As to me — but, when I am entering on my defence, let me suppress every thing ominous, sensible as I must be of this the advantage of my adversary. — In the next place, such is the natural disposition of mankind, that invective and accusation are heard with pleasure: while they who speak their own praises are received with impatience. His, then, is the part which commands a favourable acceptance; that which must prove offensive to every single hearer is reserved for me. If, to guard against this disadvantage, I should decline all mention of my own actions, I know not by what means I could refute the charge, or establish my pretensions to this honour. If, on the other hand, I enter into a detail of my whole conduct, private and political, I must be obliged to speak perpetually of myself. Here then I shall endeavour to preserve all possible moderation; and what the circumstances of the case necessarily extort from me must, in justice, be imputed to him who first moved a prosecution so extraordinary.

I presume, ye Judges, ye will acknowledge, that in this Ctesiphon and I are equally concerned; that it calls for my attention no less than his. For, in every case, it is grievous and severe to be deprived of our advantages; and especially when they are wrested from us by an enemy. But to be deprived of your favour, and affections, is a misfortune the most severe, as these are advantages the most important. And if such be the object of the present contest, I hope, and it is my general request to this tribunal, that, while I endeavour to defend myself fairly and equitably, against this charge, ye will hear me as the laws direct, those laws, which their first author, Solon, the man so tender of our interests, so true a friend to liberty, secured, not by enacting only, but by the additional provision of that oath imposed on you, ye Judges, not, as I conceive, from any suspicion of your integrity, but from a clear conviction, that, as the prosecutor, who is first to speak, hath the advantage of loading his adversary with invectives and calumnies, the defendant could not possibly prevail against them, unless each of you, who are to pronounce sentence, should, with a reverend attention to that duty which you owe to Heaven, favourably admit the just defence of him who is to answer, vouchsafe an impartial and equal audience to both parties, and thus form your decision, on all that hath been urged by both.

As I am, on this day, to enter into an exact detail of all my conduct, both in private life, and in my public administration, here permit me to repeat those supplications to the Gods with which I first began, and, in your presence, to offer up my prayers, first, that I may be received by you, on this occasion, with the same affection, which I have ever felt for this state and all its citizens; and, in the next place, that Heaven may direct your minds to that determination, which shall prove most conducive to the general honour of all, and most exactly consonant to the religious engagements of each individual.

Had Aeschines confined his accusation to those points only on which he founded his impeachment, I too should have readily proceeded to support the *legality* of the decree. But, as he hath been less copious upon other subjects, as he hath pressed me with various allegations, most of them grossest falsehoods, I deem it necessary, and it is but just that I first speak a few words of these, that none of you may be influenced by matters foreign to the cause, and no propositions conceived against me, when I come to the chief point of my defence.

As to all that scandalous abuse which he hath vented against my private character, mark, on what a plain and equitable issue I rest the whole. — If you know me to be such a man as he alledges, (for I am no stranger; my life hath been spent among you;) suffer me not to speak, no, though my public administration may have had the most transcendent merit: rise up at once, and pronounce my condemnation. But if you have ever esteemed, if you have known, me to be much superior to him, of a family more reputable; inferior to no citizen of common rank, either in character or birth, (to say more might seem arrogant and offensive;) then let him be denied all confidence in other matters: for here is a plain proof that he hath equally been false in all: and let me be now favoured with the same regard which I have experienced on many former trials. — Yes, Aeschines! — depraved as is your heart, your understanding here appears equally depraved! To imagine that I could be diverted from the account of all my political transactions by turning aside to these your personal scurrilities! I shall not proceed thus: I am not so infatuated: no, I shall first examine all that falsehood and virulence with which you have loaded my administration; — and then proceed to those calumnies with which he hath so licentiously abused my private character, if this audience can endure the odious detail.

To proceed then to the articles on which I am accused. These are many and grievous: some of that kind, against which the laws denounce severe, nay the utmost, punishments. But the whole scheme of this prosecution discovers all the rancour of enmity, all the extravagance, and virulence, and insolence of malice: which, I call the Gods to witness, is neither right, nor constitutional, nor just. True it is, that no man should be denied the privilege of appearing and speaking before the people: but this privilege never should be perverted to the purposes of animosity and envy. *Yet thus hath he abused it.* For, had he really been witness of my crimes against the state, and of crimes so heinous, as he hath now set forth with such theatrical solemnity, he might have resorted to the legal punishments, while the facts were recent: had he seen me acting so as to merit an impeachment, he might have impeached: had I proposed illegal decrees, he might in due form have accused me of illegal decrees; or whatever other crimes his malice hath now falsely urged against me; or whatever other instances of guilt he had discovered in my conduct; there are laws against them all, there are punishments, there are legal forms of procedure, which might have condemned me to severest penalties. Here was his resource. And did it appear that he had proceeded thus, that he had thus embraced the legal advantages against me, then, had he been consistent in the present prosecution. But now, as he hath deviated from the regular and equitable method, as he hath declined all attempts to convict me, while the facts were recent; and, after so long an interval, hath collected such an heap of calumny, of ribaldry and scandal; it is evident he but acts a part: while I am the person really accused, he affects the form of proceeding only against this man: while on the very face of the prosecution there appears a malicious design against me, he dares not point his malice at the real object, but labours to destroy the reputation of another. So that to all the other arguments obvious to be urged, with all the force of truth, in defence of Ctesiphon, I might fairly add one more: That, whatever be our particular quarrels, justice requires that they should be discussed between ourselves: that we ourselves, I say, should support the contest, and not seek for some innocent victim to sacrifice to our animosities. This is the severest injustice. No! he cannot pursue Ctesiphon on my account; and that he hath not directed his impeachment against me, can proceed but from a consciousness that such impeachment could not be supported.

Here then I might rest my cause, as it is natural to conclude, from what hath now been offered, that all the several articles of his accusation must be equally unjust, and equally devoid of truth. But it is my purpose to examine them distinctly, one by one; and especially his injurious falsehoods relative to the Peace and Embassy, where he would transfer the guilt of those actions upon me, which he himself committed, in conjunction with Philocrates. And here, my fellow-citizens, it is necessary nor is it foreign to the purpose, to recall to your remembrance the state of our affairs in those times, that, together with each conjuncture, ye may have a clear view of each particular transaction.

At that period then, when the Phocian war broke out, (not by my means, for I had no share in public business at that time) such were, in the first place, the dispositions of this state, that we wished the safety of the Phocians, although we saw the injustice of their conduct; and what calamity soever the Thebans might have suffered would have given us pleasure, as we are incensed, and not without reason and justice, against this people: indeed, they had not used their success at Leuctra with moderation. Then, Peloponnesus was all divided: those who hated the Lacedaemonians were not strong enough to destroy them; nor could the governors, appointed by Lacedaemon, maintain their authority in the several cities: but they, and all, were every-where involved in desperate contention and disorder. Philip, perceiving this, (for it was no secret) and lavishing his gold on the traitors in the several states, aided the confusion, and inflamed them still more violently against each other. Thus did he contrive to make the faults and errors of other men subservient to his own interests, so as to rise to that height of power which threatened all Greece. — And now, when men began to sink under the calamity of a long-protracted war; when the then insolent, but now unhappy Thebans, were on the point of being compelled, in the face of Greece, to fly to you for protection; Philip, to prevent this, to keep the states from uniting, promised a peace, to you; to them, a reinforcement. What was it then, which so far conspired with his designs, that you fell into snare by an error almost voluntary? The cowardice shall I call it? Or the ignorance of the other Greeks? Or rather a combination of both? Who, while you were maintaining a tedious and incessant war, and this in the common cause, (as was evident in fact) never once provided for your support, neither by money, nor by troops, nor by any assistance whatever. This conduct you received with a just and a becoming resentment, and readily listened to the overtures of Philip. Hence were you prevailed on to grant the peace, not by any promises of mine, as he hath falsely asserted. And it must appear, upon a fair examination, that the iniquity and corruption of these men, in the course of that treaty, have been the real cause of all our present difficulties. But I shall now proceed to a faithful and exact detail of this whole transaction; conscious, that, if any instances of guilt ever so heinous should appear in it, not one can be fairly charged on me.

The first who ever moved or mentioned a peace was Aristodemus the player. The man who seconded his instances, and proposed the decree, and who, with him, had hired out his services on this occasion, was Philocrates, your accomplice, Aeschines, not mine: no! though you rear out your falsehoods 'till you burst. — They who united with them in support of this measure, (from what motives I shall not now inquire) were Eubulus and Cephisophon. I had no part in it at all. And, though this be really the fact, though it be proved by the evidence of truth itself, yet so abandoned is he to all sense of shame, as to dare not only to assert that I was the author of this peace, but that I prevented the state from concluding it in conjunction with the general assembly of the Greeks. —— O thou — by what name can I properly call thee? When thou wert present, when thou sawest me depriving the state of an interest so important, a conjunction of such moment, as thou now describest with so much pomp, didst thou express thy indignation? Didst thou rise up, to explain, to inforce, that guilt of which thou now accusest me? And, had Philip purchased this my important service of preventing the union of the Greeks, surely it was not thy part to be silent, but to cry aloud, to testify, to inform these thy fellow-citizens. But this was never done: thy voice was never once heard on this occasion. — And, in fact, no embassy was at that time sent to any of the Grecian states: they had all discovered their sentiments long before; such is the absurdity of his assertions. And, what is still worse, these his falsehoods are principally directed against the honour of our state. For, if you called on the other Greeks to take up arms, and at the same time sent out your ministers to Philip to treat for peace, this was the act of an Eurybatus, not the part of this city, not the procedure of honest men. But this is not the fact: no! For what purpose could ye have sent to them at that period? For a peace? They were all at peace. For a war? We were then actually deliberating about the treaty. Upon the whole, therefore, it doth not appear that I was at all the agent, or at all the author of this first peace: nor can he produce the least reasonable evidence to support those other falsehoods he hath urged against me.

Again, from the time when this state had agreed to peace, examine fairly what course of conduct each of us adopted. Thus shall you clearly see who was Philip's agent upon every occasion; who acted for you, and sought the real interest of his country.

I, on my part, proposed a decree in the senate, that our ambassador should embark, with all expedition, for such place as they were informed was the present residence of Philip, and receive his oaths of ratification. But they, even after my decree had passed, declined to pay the due obedience. — And here, Athenians! I must explain the import and moment of this my decree. It was the interest of Philip that the interval between our acceding, and his swearing to the treaty, should be as long; your's, that it should be as short as possible. And why? You had abandoned all warlike preparations, not only from the day when you had sworn to the peace, but from the moment you had first conceived an expectation of it: he, on the contrary, redoubled his attention to all military affairs, through the whole intervening period; concluding, (and it proved a just conclusion) that whatever places he could wrest from us, previous to his oaths of ratification, he might retain them all securely, and that no one could think of rescinding the treaty upon that account. This I foresaw, I weighed it maturely, and hence proposed this decree, that they should repair to Philip, and receive his oaths, with all expedition: that so he should be obliged to ratify the treaty, while the Thracians, your allies, yet kept possession of those places; the object of this man's ridicule, Serrium, Myrtium, and Ergyskè: not that Philip, by seizing such of them as were most convenient to his purposes, should become master of all Thrace; not that he should acquire vast treasures; not that he should gain large reinforcements, and thus execute all his future schemes, with ease. —— Here is a decree which Aeschines hath never mentioned, never quoted. But, because I moved in the senate that the ambassadors of Macedon should be introduced, he inveighs against me as highly criminal. What should I have done? Was I to move that they should not be introduced? The men who came purposedly to treat with us? Was I to forbid that any feats should be appointed for them in the theatre? Why, they might have purchased feats at the common trifling price! Was I to shew my concern for Athens by such minute savings, while, like him and his accomplices, I sold our capital interests to Philip? No! —— Take my decree, which he, though well acquainted with it, hath passed over in silence. — Read!

THE DECREE

"In the Archonship of Mnesiphilus, on the nineteenth day of the month Ecatombaeon, the Pandionian tribe presiding. — Demosthenes, son of Demosthenes, of the Paeanian tribe, proposed the following decree:

"Whereas Philip, by his Ambassadors sent to Athens to confer about a peace, hath agreed and concluded on the terms: it is resolved by the senate and people of Athens, in order to the final execution of this treaty, agreeably to the resolutions and conventions of a formed assembly, that five ambassadors be chosen from the community of Athens: which ambassadors thus chosen shall depart, and without delay repair to such place as, they shall be informed, is the place of Philip's residence, and with all possible expedition mutually receive and take the oaths necessary for ratification of the treaty concluded, as aforesaid, with the people of Athens, including the allies on each side. — The persons chosen into this commission are Eubulus, Aeschines, Cephisophon, Democrates, and Cleon."

When, by this decree, I had approved my attachment to the state, not to the interests of Philip, our excellent ambassadors sat down in perfect indifference, three whole months, in Macedon, although within the space of ten, or rather of three or four days, they might have arrived at the Hellespont, tendered the oaths, and thus saved the towns before he had reduced them. For he would not have attempted the least hostility in our presence; or, if he had, we might have refused his ratification, and disappointed his hopes of peace: for he could not have enjoyed both; a peace and his conquests also.

Such was the first instance of Philip's artifice in this negotiation, and of the corruption of these wicked men: for which I then denounced, and now, and ever must, denounce perpetual war and opposition against these enemies of Heaven. — I proceed to point out another, and a still more flagrant instance of iniquity. When Philip had in due form acceded to the treaty, having first possessed himself of Thrace by means of those ministers who refused obedience to my decree, he bribed them once again not to depart from Macedon, until he had completed his armament against the Phocians; lest a fair report of his designs and preparation should prompt you to issue forth, steer your course to Thermopylae, as on a former occasion; and block up the streights of Euboeca with your navy. He resolved that the news of his preparations, and his passage through the streights, should arrive together. And such were his apprehensions, such the violence of his terror, lest, when he had gained the streights, before he had completed the destruction of Phocis, ye should be informed of his motions, resolve to assist this state, and thus defeat his grand design; that he again bribed this wretch, not in conjunction with the other deputies, but now, apart and by himself, to make such representations, and to give you such assurances, as effectually ruined all our interests.

And here, my fellow-citizens, I desire, I beseech you to bear in mind, through the whole course of this dispute, that, if Aeschines had urged nothing against me foreign to his cause, I too should have confined myself to the great point in contest. But as he hath recurred to every charge, every invective which malice could suggest; it becomes necessary for me to make some short reply to all the several crimes alledged against me.

What then were the declarations which he made at this juncture, and which proved so fatal to our interests? That you ought not to be violently alarmed at Philip's passage through the streights; that the event would answer to your most sanguine wishes, if you but continued quiet; that in two or three days you should hear, that he had entered into strict friendship with those who seemed the object of his hostilities, and that he had become their enemy, with whom he now united. "For it is not words," said he, in all the solemnity of language, "that form the estrict band of friendship, but a similarity of interests. And it is equally the interest of all, of Philip, of the Phocians, and of Athens, to be relieved from the insolence and stupidity of the Thebans." —

And what were the immediate consequences? The unhappy Phocians were speedily destroyed, and their cities razed to their foundations: you who had relied on his assurances, and continued quiet, were shortly obliged to leave your lands desolate, and collect your property within these walls: while he received his gold. And, still further, the inveterate hatred of the Thebans and Thessalians fell, with all its weight, on Athens, while Philip's conduct was attended with applause and popularity. To prove these things, read the decree of Callisthenes, and the letter received from Philip. They both confirm the truth of my assertions. — Read!

THE DECREE

"In the Archonship of Mnesiphilus, on the twenty-first day of the month of Maemacterion, in an assembly extraordinary convened by authority of the generals, prytanes, and senate, at the motion of Callisthenes, it is

RESOLVED

"That no citizen of Athens be permitted, on any pretence whatever, to pass the night in the country: but that every man shall confine himself within the city, or the precincts of the Piraeus, excepting only such persons as may be appointed to the defence of some post. That every such person shall be obliged to maintain his station, without presuming to absent himself, either by night or day. That whoever refuses to pay due obedience to this resolution and decree, shall incur the penalties ordained for traitors, unless he can alledge some necessary cause to be approved of by the general immediately in command, the treasurer, and the secretary of the senate, who shall have the sole power of judging of such allegations. That all effects now in the country shall be instantly removed; those within the distance of one hundred and twenty stadia, into the city or Piraeus: those at any greater distance, to Eleusis, Phylè, Aphidna, Rhamnusium, and Sunium."

Were these the hopes which induced you to conclude the peace? Were these the promises, with which this hireling amused you? — Now read the letter soon afterwards received from Philip.

THE LETTER

"Philip, king of Macedon, to the senate and people of Athens, health.

360

"Know ye that we have passed the streights of Thermopylae, and reduced Phocis. We have stationed our garrisons in such towns as have submitted and acknowledged our authority. Those which have presumed to resist our force we have taken by assault, reduced the inhabitants to slavery, and razed their habitations to the ground. But, being informed that you are making dispositions for the support of these people, we, by these presents, recommend to you to spare yourselves the pains of such an ineffectual attempt. Your conduct must certainly appear extremely inequitable and extravagant, in arming against us, with whom you have so lately concluded a treaty. If you have determined to shew no regard to your engagements, we shall only wait for the commencement of hostilities, to exert a resolution on our part, no less vigorous and formidable."

You hear how he announces his intention in this letter: how explicitly he declares to his allies, "I have taken these measures in despight of the Athenians, and to their eternal mortification. If ye are wise then, ye Thebans and Thessalians, ye will regard them as enemies, and submit to me with an entire confidence." These are not his words indeed; but thus he would gladly be understood. And by these means did he acquire such an absolute dominion over their affections, that, blind and insensible to all consequences, they suffered him to execute the utmost schemes of his ambition. Hence, all the calamities which the wretched Thebans experience at this day. While he, who was the great agent and co-adjutor in procuring this implicit confidence; he who in this place uttered his falsehoods and deceived you by his flattering assurances; he it is who affects a deep concern at the misfortunes of Thebes, who displays them in such pathetic terms; although he himself be the real author both of these and the calamities of Phocis, and of all others, which the Greeks have suffered. Yes, Aeschines, you must be affected deeply with these events, you must indeed feel compassion for the Thebans: you who have acquired possessions in Boeotia, you who enjoy the fruits of their lands: and I must surely rejoice at their misery; I who was instantly demanded by the man who had inflicted it.

But I have been led insensibly to some particulars, which I may shortly introduce with more propriety. I now return to the proof of my assertion, that the corruption and iniquity of these men have been the real cause of our present difficulties. —— When Philip had contrived to deceive you so effectually, by means of those who, during their embassy, had sold themselves to this prince, and never reported one word of truth to your assemblies; when the wretched Phocians also had been betrayed, and their cities levelled with the ground; — what followed? —

The miscreant Thessalians and the stupid Thebans regarded Philip as their friend, their benefactor, their saviour: he was every thing with them: nor could they bear a word which tended to oppose these sentiments. On your part, although ye looked with a just suspicion on the progress of affairs, although ye felt the utmost indignation, yet still ye adhered to the treaty: for it was not possible to act, single as ye were. The other Greeks too, equally abused with you, and equally disappointed in their hopes, were yet determined to the same pacific conduct, though Philip, in effect, had long since made war upon them. For when, in the circuit of his expedition, he had destroyed the Illyrians, and the Triballians, and even some Grecian states; when a certain set of men had seized the opportunity of a peace, issued forth from the several cities, and, repairing to Macedon, had there received his bribes, (of which number Aeschines was one) then were the real objects of his hostilities discovered, and then was the attack made on the several states. Whether they yet perceived this attack, or no, is another question, a question which concerns not me: I was ever violent in forewarning, in denouncing the danger here, and in every place to which I was deputed. But, in fact, the states were all unsound. Those who had the conduct and administration of affairs, had been gained by gold: while their private citizens and popular assemblies were either blind to all consequences, or caught by the fatal bait of temporary ease and quiet. And such was the general infatuation that each community conceived, that they alone were to be exempted from the common calamity, nay, that they could derive their own security from the public danger. To this I must impute it, that the many found their inordinate and ill-timed indolence exchanged for slavery: while their statesmen, who imagined that they were selling every thing but themselves, found at length, that they had first sold themselves. Instead of friends and guests (so were they stiled, while they were receiving their bribes) now, are they called flatterers, enemies to Heaven, and every other odious name so justly merited. For it is not the interest of the traitor that is at all regarded by the man who bribes him; nor, when the purchased service hath been once obtained, is the traitor ever admitted into his future confidence. If he were, no man could be happier than the traitor. But this is not the case, my fellow-citizens! How should it? No! impossible! When the votary of ambition hath once obtained his object, he also becomes master of his vile agents: and, as he knows their baseness, then, then, he detests them, he keeps them at a wary distance, he spurns them from him. Reflect on former events: their time indeed is passed: but men of sense may always find a time to derive instruction from them. Lasthenes was called the friend of Philip, until he had betrayed Olynthus; Timoläus, until he had destroyed the Thebans;

Eudicus and Simo, until they had given him the dominion of Thessaly; then were they driven away with scorn, then were they loaded with every kind of wretchedness; and traitors in disgrace were dispersed through the whole nation. How was Aristratus received at Sicyon? How Periläus at Megara? Are they not in abject infamy? And, hence, it evidently appears, that he who is most vigilant in defence of his country, and most zealous in his opposition to such men, is really a friend to you, Aeschines, and your venal, traitorous faction, (as his conduct makes it necessary to bribe you;) and that your safety and your gains depend intirely on the number of such patriots, and their obstinate aversion to your counsels. If left to yourselves, ye must have long since perished.

And now, as to the transactions of those times, I might say more; but I have already said what I deem more than sufficient. To him must it be imputed, who hath disgorged all the foulness of his own iniquity upon me, which it was necessary to wipe away, for the sake of those who were born since the events I speak of. To you, ye Judges, the detail must be tedious and disgusting. Before I had uttered one word, you were well informed of his prostitution. He calls it friendship and intimate connexion. Thus hath he just now expressed it. — "He who reproaches me with the intimacy of Alexander!" — I reproach thee with the intimacy of Alexander! — How couldn't thou obtain it? How couldn't thou aspire to it? I could never call thee the friend of Philip; no, nor the intimate of Alexander. I am not so mad. — Unless we are to call those menial servants, who labour for their wages, the friends and intimates of those who hire them. — But how can this be? Impossible! No! I formerly called you the hireling of Philip; I now call you the hireling of Alexander: and so do all these our fellow-citizens. If you doubt it, ask them: or I shall ask them for you. — Ye citizens of Athens, do you account Aeschines the hireling, or the intimate of Alexander! — You hear their answer.

I now proceed to my defence against the several articles of his impeachment, and to the particulars of my ministerial conduct, that Aeschines (although he knows them well) may hear the reasons on which I justly claim the honour of this decree, and might claim still greater honours. —— Take the impeachment. — Read it.

THE IMPEACHMENT

"In the Archonship of Chaerondas, on the sixth day of the month Elaphaebolion. Aeschines, son of Atrometus, of the Cothocidian tribe, impeached Ctesiphon, son of Leosthenes, of the Anaphlystian tribe, before the Archon, of a violation of the laws.

363

"Forasmuch as he hath been author of an illegal Decree, importing, that a golden Crown should be conferred on Demosthenes, son of Demosthenes, of the Paeanian tribe; and that proclamation should be made in the theatre, during the grand festival of Bacchus, and the exhibition of the new tragedies, that the people of Athens had conferred this golden crown upon the said Demosthenes, on acount of his virtue, and affectionate attachment to Greece in general, and to Athens in particular; as also, on account of that magnanimity and steady zeal in speaking and acting for the interests of this state, which he hath ever discovered, and still discovers, upon every occasion, to the utmost of his power. —— All which clauses are false, and re-pugnant to our laws. As it is enacted,

"First, that no man shall enter false allegation into our public acts.

"Secondly, that no man, yet accountable for any office of trust, shall receive a crown; whereas Demosthenes was director of the fortifications, and manager of the theatrical funds.

"Lastly, that no crown shall be proclaimed in the theatre during the festival, or dramatic entertainments, but in the senate-house, if the crown be granted by the senate; if by the commons, in the Pnyx, and in full assembly."

Thomas Leland

364

AESCHINES

AESCHINES (C. 390-380 B. C.) was an Athenian orator. Exiled, he later returned to Athens, where he conducted a school. He was a political enemy of the orator Demosthenes, who accused him of bribery. Among his speeches are *On the Embassy,* that involved Demosthenes' charge of treason on Aeschines' part: and *Against Ctesiphon.*

The Oration of Aeschines Against Ctesiphon

An attack on the illegality of Ctesiphon's action in conferring
a crown on Demosthenes

You see, Athenians! what forces are prepared, what numbers formed and arrayed, what soliciting through the assembly, by a certain party;—and all this, to oppose the fair and ordinary course of justice in the state. As to me, I stand here in firm reliance, first on the immortal gods, next on the laws, and you; convinced that sanction never can have greater weight with you, than law and justice.

It were to be wished, indeed, that the presidents of our senate, and of our popular assembly, would attend with due care to the order of their debates; that the laws ordained by Solon to secure the decency of public speaking might still preserve their force; that so, our elder citizens might first arise in due and decent form, (as these laws direct) without tumult or confusion; and each declare, in order, the salutary counsels of his sage experience: that, after these, our other citizens who chose to speak, might severally, and in order, according to their ages, propose their sentiments on every subject. Thus, in my opinion, would the course of government be more exactly regulated; and thus would our assemblies be less frequently engaged in trials. But now, when these institutions, so confessedly excellent, have lost their force; when men propose illegal resolutions, without reserve or scruple; when others are found to put them to the vote, not regularly chosen to preside in our assemblies, but men who have raised themselves to this dignity by intrigue; when if any of the other senators on whom the lot of presidency hath fairly fallen, should discharge his office faithfully, and report your voices truly, there are men who threaten to impeach him, men who invade our rights, and regard the administration as their private property; who have secured their vassals, and raised themselves to sovereignty; who have suppressed such judicial procedures as are founded on established laws, and in the decision of those appointed by temporary decrees consult their passions; now, I say, that most sage and virtuous proclamation is no longer heard: "Who is disposed to speak, of those above fifty years old?" and then, "Who of the other citizens in their turns?" Nor is the indecent licence of our speakers any longer restrained by our laws by our magistrates; no, nor by the presiding tribe, which contains a full tenth part of the community.

If such be our situation, such the present circumstances of the state, and of this you seem convinced; one part alone of our polity remains; (as far as I may presume to judge:) prosecutions of those who violate the laws. Should you suppress these; should you permit them to be suppressed; I freely pronounce your fate; that your government must be gradually and imperceptibly given up to the power of a few. You are not to be informed, Athenians, that there are three different modes of government established in the world; the monarchical, the government of the few, and the free republic. In the two former, the administration is directed by the pleasure of the ruling powers; in free states, it is regulated by established laws. It is then a truth, of which none should be ignorant, which every man should impress deeply on his mind; that when he enters the tribunal, to decide a case of violation of the laws, he that day gives sentence of his own liberties. Wisely therefore hath our legislator prescribed this, as the first clause in the oath of every judge: "I will give my voice agreeably to the laws;" well knowing, that when the laws are preserved sacred in every state, the freedom of their constitution is most effectually secured. Let these things be ever kept in memory, that your indignation may be kindled against all those whose decrees have been illegal. Let not any of their offences be deemed of little moment, but all of the greatest importance: nor suffer your rights to be wrested from you, by any power; neither by the combinations of your generals, who, by conspiring with our public speakers, have frequently involved the state in danger; nor by the solicitations of foreigners, who have been brought up to screen some men from justice, whose administration hath been notoriously illegal. But as each man among you, would be ashamed to desert from his post in battle; to think it shameful to abandon the post this day assigned to you by the laws, that of guardians of the constitution.

Let it also be remembered, that the whole body of our citizens hath now committed their state, their liberties, into your hands. Some of them are present, awaiting the event of this trial: others are called away to attend on their private affairs. Shew the due reverence to these; remember your oaths and your laws: and if we convict Ctesiphon of having proposed decrees illegal, false, and detrimental to the state, reverse these illegal decrees, assert the freedom of your constitution, and punish those who have administered your affairs in opposition to your laws, in contempt of your constitution, and in total disregard of your interest. If, with these sentiments impressed upon your minds, you attend to what is now to be proposed, you must, I am convinced, proceed to a decision just and religious; a decision of the utmost advantage to yourselves, and to the state.

As to the general nature of this prosecution, thus far have I premised, and, I trust, without offence. Let me now request your attention to a few words about the laws relative to persons accountable to the public, which have been violated by the decree proposed by Ctesiphon.

In former times there were found magistrates of the most distinguished rank, and entrusted with the management of our revenues, who in their several stations were guilty of the basest corruption, but who, by forming an interest with the speakers in the senate, and in the popular assembly, anticipated their accounts by public honours and declarations of applause. Thus when their conduct came to a formal examination, their accusers were involved in great perplexity; their judges in still greater. For many of the persons thus subject to examination, though convicted, on the clearest evidence, of having defrauded the public, were yet suffered to escape from justice; and no wonder. The judges were ashamed that the same man, in the same city, possibly in the same year, should be publicly honoured in our festivals, that proclamation should be made, "that the people had conferred a golden crown upon him, on account of his integrity and virtue;" that the same man, I say, in a short time after, when his conduct had been brought to an examination, should depart from the tribunal, condemned of fraud. In their sentence, therefore, the judges were necessarily obliged to attend, not to the nature of these offences, but to the reputation of the state.

Some of our magistrates observing this, framed a law, (and its excellence is undeniable) expressly forbidding any man to be honoured with a crown, whose conduct had not yet been submitted to the legal examination. But, notwithstanding all the precaution of the framers of this law, pretences were still found of force sufficient to defeat its intention. Of these you are to be informed, lest you should be unwarily betrayed into error. Some of those who in defiance of the laws have moved, that men who yet stood accountable for their conduct, should be crowned, are still influenced by some degree of decency (if this can

riety be said of men who propose resolutions directly sub-
the laws:) they still seek to cast a kind of veil upon their
nce are they sometimes careful to express their resolutions in
er, 'that the man whose conduct is not yet submitted to
examination, shall be honoured with a crown,' "when his accounts
"have first been examined, and approved." But this is no less injurious
to the state; for by these crowns and public honours is his conduct
prejudged, and his examination anticipated: while the author of such
resolutions demonstrates to his hearers, that his proposal is a violation
of the laws, and that he is ashamed of his offence. But Ctesiphon (my
countrymen) hath at once broken through the laws relative to the
examination of our magistrates; he hath scorned to recur to that subterfuge now explained: he hath moved you to confer a crown upon
Demosthenes, previous to any account, to any examination of his conduct: at the very time while he was yet employed in the discharge of
his magistracy.

But there is another evasion of a different kind, to which they are
to recur. These offices, say they, to which a citizen is elected by an
occasional decree, are by no means to be accounted *magistracies*, but
commissions or *agencies*. Those alone are magistrates whom the proper
officers appoint by lot in the temple of Theseus, or the people elect by
suffrage in their ordinary assemblies; such as generals of the army,
commanders of the cavalry, and such-like: all other are but commis-
sioners, who are but to execute a particular decree. To this their plea
I shall oppose your own law, a law enacted from a firm conviction,
that it must at once put an end to all such evasions. In this it is expressly
declared, that all offices whatever, appointed by the voices of the
people, shall be accounted magistracies. In one general term the author
of this law hath included all. All hath he declared magistrates, whom
the votes of the assembly have appointed: and particularly the inspector of public works. — Now Demosthenes inspected the repair of our
walls, the most important of public works. — Those who have been
entrusted with any public money for more than thirty days. Those
who are intitled to preside in a tribunal. But the inspectors of works
are intitled to this privilege. — What then doth the law direct? That
all such should assume, not their commission, but their magistracy,
having first been judicially approved: (for even the magistrates appointed by lot are not exempted from this previous inquiry, but must
be first approved, before they assume their office.) These are also
directed by the law to submit the accounts of their administration to
the legal officers, as well as every other magistrate. And for the truth
of what I now advance, to the laws themselves do I appeal. — Read.

368

Here then you find that what these men call commissions or agencies, are declared to be magistracies. It is your part to bear this in memory; to oppose the law to their presumption; to convince them that you are not to be influenced by the wretched, sophistical artifice, that would defeat the force of laws by words; and that the greater their address in defending their illegal proceedings, the more severely must they feel your resentment. For the public speaker should ever use the same language with the law. Should he at any time speak in one language, and the law pronounce another, to the just authority of law, should you grant your voices, not to the shameless presumption of the speaker.

To that argument on which Demosthenes relies, as utterly unanswerable, I would now briefly speak. — This man will say, "I am director of the fortifications. I confess it. But I have expended of my own money, for the public service, and additional sum of one hundred minae, and enlarged the work beyond my instructions; for what then, am I to account? Unless a man is to be made accountable for his own beneficence." — To this evasion you shall hear a just and good reply. —— In this city of so antient an establishment, and a circuit so extensive, there is not a man exempted from account, who has the smallest part in the affairs of state. This I shall shew, first in instances scarcely creditable. Thus, the priests and priestesses are by the laws obliged to account for the discharge of their office: all in general, and each in particular; although they have received no more than an honorary pension, and have had no other duty but of offering up their prayers for us to the Gods. And this is not the case of single persons only, but of whole tribes, as the *Eumolpidae,* the *Ceryces,* and all the others. Again, the Trierarchs are by the law made accountable for their conduct: although no public money hath been committed to their charge; although they have not embezzled large portions of your revenue, and accounted but for a small part; although they have not affected to confer bounties on you, while they really but restored your own property; no; they confessedly expended their paternal fortunes to approve their zealous affection for your service; and not our Trierarchs alone, but the greatest assemblies in the state, are bound to submit to the sentence of our tribunals. First, the law directs, that the council of the Areopagus shall stand accountable to the proper officers, and submit their august transactions to a legal examination: thus our greatest judicial body stands in perpetual dependence upon your decisions. Shall the members of this council then be precluded from the honour of a crown? — Such has been the ordinance from times the most remote. — And have they no regard to public honour? — So scrupulous is their regard, that it is not deemed sufficient, that their conduct should not be notoriously criminal, their least irregularity is severely punished; a discipline too rigorous for our delicate orators. Again, our lawgiver directs, that the senate of five hundred shall be bound to account for their conduct; and so great dissidence doth he express of those who have not yet rendered such account, that in the very beginning of the law it is ordained, "that no magistrate, who hath not yet passed through the ordinary examination, shall be permitted to go abroad." — But here a man may exclaim, "What! In the name of Heaven, am I, because I have been in office, to be confined to the city?" — *Yes, and with good reason;* lest, when you have secreted the public money, and betrayed your trust, you might enjoy your perfidy by flight. Again, the laws forbid the man who hath not yet accounted to the state, to dedicate any part of his effects to religious purposes, to deposit any offering in a temple, to accept of an adoption into any family, to make any alienation of his property: and to many other instances is the prohibition extended. In one word, our lawgiver hath provided that the fortunes of such persons shall be secured as a pledge to the community, until their accounts are fairly examined and approved. Nay, further, suppose there be a man who hath neither received nor expended any part of the public money, but hath only been concerned in some affairs relative to the state. Even such a one is bound to submit his accounts to the proper officers. — "But how can the man, who hath neither received nor expended, pass such accounts?" — The law hath obviated this difficulty, and expressly prescribed the form of his accounts. It directs that it shall consist of this declaration: "I have not received, neither have I disposed of any public money." To confirm the truth of this, hear the laws themselves.

THE LAWS

When Demosthenes therefore shall exult in his evasion, and insist that he is not to be accountable for the additional fund which he bestowed freely on the state, press him with this reply: "It was then your duty, Demosthenes, to have permitted the usual and legal proclamation to be made: Who is disposed to prosecute?" and to have given an opportunity to every citizen that pleased to have urged on his part, that you bestowed no such additional fund: but that, on the contrary, having been trusted with ten talents for the repair of our fortifications, you really expended but a small part of this great fund. Do not assume an honour to which you have no pretensions: do not wrest their suffrages from your judges: do not act in presumptuous contempt of the laws, but with due submission yield to their guidance. Such is the conduct that must secure the freedom of our constitution."

As to the evasions on which these men rely, I trust that I have spoken sufficiently. That Demosthenes really stood accountable to the state, at the time when this man proposed his decree; that he was really a magistrate, as manager of the theatrical funds; a magistrate, as inspector of the fortifications; that his conduct in either of these offices had not been examined, had not obtained the legal approbation, I shall now endeavour to demonstrate from the public records. Read, in whose Archonship, in what month, on what day, in what assembly, Demosthenes was chosen into the office of manager of the theatrical funds. So shall it appear that, during the execution of this office, the decree was made, which conferred this crown upon him. —Read.

THE COMPUTATION OF THE TIMES

If then I should here rest my cause, without proceeding further, Ctesiphon must stand convicted; convicted, not by the arguments of his accuser, but by the public records. In former times, Athenians, it was the custom that the state should elect a comptroller, who, in every presidency of each tribe, was to return to the people an exact state of the finances. But by the implicit confidence which you reposed in Eubulus, the men who were chosen to the management of the theatrical money, executed this office of comptroller, (I mean before the law of Hegemon was enacted) together with the offices of receiver, and of inspector of our naval affairs: they were charged with the building of our arsenals, with the repair of our roads; in a word, they were entrusted with the conduct of almost all our public business. I say not this to impeach their conduct, or to arraign their integrity I mean but to convince you, that our laws have expressly directed, that no man yet accountable for his conduct in any one office, even of the smallest consequence, shall be intitled to the honour of a crown, until his accounts have been regularly examined and approved: and that Ctesiphon hath yet presumed to confer this honour on Demosthenes, when engaged in every kind of public magistracy. At the time of this decree, he was a magistrate as inspector of the fortifications, a magistrate as entrusted with public money, and, like other officers of the state, imposed fines, and presided in tribunals. These things I shall prove by the testimony of Demosthenes and Ctesiphon themselves. For in the Archonship of Chaerondas, on the 22d of the month Thargelion, was a popular assembly held, in which Demosthenes obtained a decree, appointing a convention of the tribes on the 2d of the succeeding month;

and on the third his decree directed still further, that supervisors should be chosen, and treasurers, from each tribe, for conducting the repairs of our fortifications. And justly did he thus direct; that the public might have the security of good and responsible citizens, who might return a fair account of all disbursements.——Read these decrees.

THE DECREES

Yes. But you will hear it urged in answer, that to this office of inspector of the works he was not appointed in the general assembly, either by lot or suffrage. This is an argument on which Demosthenes and Ctesiphon will dwell with the utmost confidence. My answer shall be easy, plain, and brief; but first I would premise a few things on this subject. Observe, Athenians! Of magistracy there are three kinds. First, those appointed by lot or by election. Secondly, the men who have managed public money for more than thirty days, or have inspected public works. To these the law adds another species, and expressly declares, that all such persons as, in consequence of a regular appointment, have enjoyed the right of jurisdiction, shall, when approved, be accounted magistrates. So that, should we take away the magistrates appointed by lot or suffrage, there yet remains the last kind, of those appointed by the tribes, or the thirds of tribes, or by particular districts, to manage public money, all which are declared to be magistrates from the time of their appointment. And this happens in cases like that before us, where it is a direction to the tribes to make canals, or to build ships of war. For the truth of this, I appeal to the laws themselves.——Read.——

THE LAW

Let it be remembered, that, as I have already observed, the sentence of the law is this, that all those appointed to any office by their tribes shall act as magistrates, when first judicially approved. But the Pandionian tribe hath made Demosthenes a magistrate, by appointing him an inspector of the works; and for this purpose he hath been entrusted with public money to the amount of near ten talents. Again, another law expressly forbids any magistrate, who yet stands accountable for his conduct, to be honoured with a crown. You have sworn to give sentence according to the laws. Here is a speaker who hath brought in a decree for granting a crown to a man yet accountable for his conduct. Nor hath he added that saving clause, "when his accounts have first been passed." I have proved the point of illegality from the testimony of your laws, from the testimony of your decrees, and from

372

that of the opposite parties. How then can any man support a prosecution of this nature with greater force and clearness?

But further, I shall now demonstrate that this decree is also a violation of the law, by the manner in which it directs that this crown shall be proclaimed. The laws declare in terms, the most explicit, that, if any man receives a crown from the senate, the proclamation shall be made in the senate house; if by the people, in the assembly: never in any other place. Read this law.

THE LAW

And this institution is just and excellent. The author of this law seems to have been persuaded, that a public speaker should not ostentatiously display his merits before foreigners; that he should be contented with the approbation of this city, of these his fellow-citizens; without practising vile arts to procure a public honour. So thought our lawgiver. What are the sentiments of Ctesiphon? Read his decree.

THE DECREE

You have heard, Athenians, that the law directs, in every case where a crown is granted by the people, that the proclamation shall be made in presence of the people, in the Pnyx, in full assembly: never in any other place. Yet Ctesiphon hath appointed proclamation to be made in the theatre: not contented that the act itself should violate our laws, he hath presumed to change the scene of it. He confers this honour, not while the people are assembled, but while the new tragedies are exhibiting; not in the presence of the people, but of the Greeks; that they too may know, on what kind of man our honours are conferred.

And now when the illegal nature of this decree is so incontestably established, the author, assisted by his confederate Demosthenes, hath yet recourse to subtleties, in order to evade the force of justice. These I must explain; I must so guard you against them, that you may not be surprised by their pernicious influence.——These men can by no means deny, that our laws expressly direct, that a crown conferred on any citizen by the people shall be proclaimed in the assembly, and in no other place. But, to defend their conduct, they produce a law relative to our festivals: of this they but quote a part, that they may more effectually deceive you: and thus recur to an ordinance by no means applicable to the case before us. Accordingly they will tell you, there are in this state two laws enacted relative to proclamations. One is, that which I have now produced expressly forbidding the proclamation

373

of a crown granted by the people to be issued in any other place, but the assembly. The other, say they, is contrary to this: it allows the liberty of proclaiming a crown so conferred, in the theatre, when the tragedies are exhibited, provided always, that the people shall so determine by their voices. On this law it is (thus will they plead) that Ctesiphon has founded his decree. To this artifice I shall oppose your own laws, my assistants, my constant reliance, through the whole course of this prosecution. If this be so; if such a custom hath been admitted into our government; that laws repealed are still allowed to hold their place amidst those in full force; that two, directly contradictory to each other, are enacted on the same subjects; what shall we pronounce on that polity, where the laws command and forbid the very same things? But this is by no means the case: and never may your public acts be exposed to such disorder! The great lawgiver, to whom we owe our constitution, was not inattentive to guard against such dangers. It is his express direction, that, in every year, our body of laws shall be adjusted by the legal inspectors, in the popular assembly; and if, after due examination and inspection, it shall appear, that a law hath been enacted contradictory to a former law; or that any one, when repealed, shall still hold its place among those actually in force; or that any more than one have been enacted on the same subject; that, in all such cases, the laws shall be transcribed and fixed up in public on the statues of our heroes; that the presidents shall convene the assembly, shall specify the authors of these several laws, and that the proper officer shall propose the question to the people, that they may by their voices repeal some, and establish others.

Thomas Leland

SATIRE

Lucian

375

LUCIAN

LUCIAN (c. 120-c. 180 A.D.) is the author of some eighty sketches, largely in dialogue form. In these pieces he satirizes many types of pretensions: philosophical, religious, and social, as well as human foibles and vanities.

Dialogues of the Gods — I

Prometheus obtains his release from Zeus by a Prophecy

PROMETHEUS: Set me free, O Zeus, for I have already endured dreadful sufferings.

ZEUS: Set you free, say you? you who ought to have heavier fetters, and all Caucasus heaped on your head; and not only your liver gnawed by sixteen vultures, but also your eyes scooped out, in return for your fashioning such animals as men, and for stealing my fire, and fabricating women. As for the tricks you put upon me in your distribution of the flesh meats, in offering me bones wrapped up in fat, and reserving the better portion of the pieces for yourself, why need I speak?

PROMETHEUS: Have I then not paid enough penalty, nailed for such a long period of time to Caucasus, supporting that most cursed of winged creatures, the vulture, with my liver?

ZEUS: Not an infinitesimal part that of what you ought to suffer.

PROMETHEUS: Yet you shall not release me without recompense. But I will impart something to you, Zeus, exceedingly important.

ZEUS: You are for outwitting me, Prometheus.

PROMETHEUS: And what advantage should I gain? For you will not be ignorant hereafter of the whereabouts of Caucasus; neither will you be in want of chains, should I be caught playing you any trick.

ZEUS: Say, first, what sort of equivalent you will pay, of so much importance to us.

PROMETHEUS: If I tell you for what purpose you are now on your travels, shall I have credit with you, when I prophesy about the rest?

ZEUS: Of course.

PROMETHEUS: You are off to Thetis, to an intrigue with her.

ZEUS: That indeed you have correct knowledge of. But what then, after that? For you seem to have some inkling of the truth.

PROMETHEUS: Don't have anything to do with the Nereid, Zeus: for, if she should be pregnant by you, her progeny will treat you exactly as you, too, treated —

ZEUS: This do you assert — that I shall be expelled from my kingdom?

PROMETHEUS: Heaven forbid, Zeus! Intercourse with her, however, threatens something of the kind.

ZEUS: Good-bye to Thetis, then. And as for you, for these timely warnings Hephaestus shall set you free.

2: Zeus threatens to put Eros in Fetters

EROS: Well, if I have really done wrong at all, Zeus, pardon me; for I am but an infant, and still without sense.

ZEUS: You an infant — you the Eros, who are far older than Iapetus? Because you have not grown a beard, and don't show gray hairs, do you really claim on that account to be considered an infant, when, in fact, you are an old scamp?

EROS: But what great injury have I — the old scamp, as you call me — done you, that you intend putting me in irons?

ZEUS: Consider, accursed rascal, whether they are trifling injuries you have done me, you, who make such sport of me, that there is nothing which you have not turned me into — satyr, bull, gold, swan, eagle — but not any one of them have you made to be in love with me at all; nor have I perceived that, for anything that depends upon you, I have been agreeable to any woman; but I am obliged to have recourse to juggling tricks against them, and to conceal my proper self, while they are really in love with the bull or swan, and, if they have but a glimpse of me, they die of fear.

EROS: Naturally enough, Zeus, for, being mortal women, they can't endure the sight of your person.

ZEUS: How is it, then, that Branchus and Hyacinthus love Apollo?

EROS: But even from him the beauty, Daphne, fled away, for all his flowing locks and beardless chin. If you wish to be loved, don't shake your aegis, and don't take your thunderbolt with you; but make yourself as agreeable as you can, letting down you locks on both sides of \your face, and tying them up again under your coronet; wear a fine purple dress, put on golden sandals, step along keeping time to the sounds of the pipe and cymbals, and you will see that more women will follow you than all the Maenads of Bacchus.

ZEUS: Get away with you. I would not take the offer of being loved, on condition of becoming such a figure.

EROS: Then, Zeus, don't wish to love, either: that, at all events, is an easy matter.

ZEUS: Not so; but I do wish to love, and to enjoy their society in a less vexatious fashion. Upon this, and this condition alone, I let you go.

Dialogues of the Sea-Gods — II

Polyphemus complains to Poseidon, his father, of his treatment at the hands of Odysseus

CYCLOPS *(blubbering)*: O father, what have I endured at the hands of the accursed stranger, who made me drunk and put out my eye, assaulting me when I was lulled to sleep.

POSEIDON: Who dared to do this, my poor Polyphemus?

CYCLOPS: In the first instance, he called himself Outis; but, when he had got clear away, and was out of reach of my arrow, he said that his name was Odysseus.

POSEIDON: I know whom you speak of — him of Ithaka, and he was on his return-voyage from Ilium. But how did he do it, for he is, by no means, a man of too much courage?

CYCLOPS: Returning from my accustomed tending of my flocks, I caught a number of fellows in my cave, evidently having designs on my herds: for, when I placed the stone block against the door — the rock is of huge size — and had lighted the fire by igniting the tree which I brought from the mountain, evidently they appeared to be trying to conceal themselves. Well, when I had got hold of some of them, I devoured them for a pack of thieves, as was reasonable. Hereupon that most villainous rascal, whether he was Outis or Odysseus, pours out a sort of drug and gives me to drink — sweet, indeed, and of delicious smell, but most insidious, and which caused great disorder in my head: for immediately upon my drinking everything seemed to me to be in a whirl, and the cave itself was turned upside down, and I was no longer at all in my senses; and, at last, I was dragged down into sleep. Then sharpening the bar, and igniting it besides, he blinded me as I slept, and from that time, I am a blind man, at your service, Poseidon.

POSEIDON: How soundly you slept, my son, that you did not jump up while you were being blinded! But as for this Odysseus, then, how did he escape? For he could not — I am well assured that he could not — move away the rock from the door.

CYCLOPS: Yes, but it was I who removed it, that I might the better catch him as he was going out; and, sitting down close to the door, I groped for him with extended hands, letting only my sheep pass out to pasture, after having given instructions to the ram what he was to do in my place.

POSEIDON: I understand, they slipped away under them unnoticed. But you ought to have shouted, and called the rest of the Cyclopes to your aid against him.

CYCLOPS: I did summon them, father, and they came. But when they asked the sneaking rascal's name, and I said it was Outis, thinking I was in a mad fit, they took themselves off at once. Thus the cursed fellow tricked me with his name; and what especially vexes me is, that actually throwing my misfortune in my teeth, "Not even," says he, "will your father Poseidon cure you."

POSEIDON: Never mind, my child, for I will revenge myself upon him, that he may learn that, even if it is not possible for me to heal the mutilation of people's eyes, at all events the fate of voyagers is in my hands. And he is still at sea.

Dialogues of the Dead — I

Diogenes commissions Polydeukes, about to return to the upper world, to inform Menippus of the condition of things in the land of shades, and to deliver admonitory messages to various sorts of men.

DIOGENES: Polydeukes, I entrust to you the task, as soon as ever you reach the upper world — for it is your turn, I believe, to return to life again to-morrow — if you anywhere catch sight of Menippus, the Dog (and you would probably find him at Korinth, near the Kraneium, or in the Lyceium, deriding the philosophers as they quarrel one with another), to say to him: "Diogenes bids you, Menippus, if things above ground have been sufficiently ridiculed by you, to come hither, to laugh at many more matters. For there your laughter was yet questionable, and frequent was the objection, but who knows altogether what is to come after life? But here you will not cease laughing on firm grounds, as I do now, and most of all when you see the rich, and viceroys, and princes to be so humble and obscure, and distinguishable by their lamentations alone, and that they are soft-hearted and mean-spirited, recollecting their life above." This tell him, and, further, to come with his scrip filled with a quantity of lupines;

and, if he anywhere find on the cross-roads a supper for Hekate set out, or a purificatory egg, or anything of the sort, let him bring it.

POLYDEUKES: Well, I will give this message, Diogenes. But describe him, that I may know quite certainly what manner of man he is as to looks.

DIOGENES: An old fellow, bald, with a little old cloak, with many a hole in it, exposed to every wind of heaven, and variegated with rags and tatters; and he is for ever laughing, and, for the most part, jeers at those loud-talking philosophers.

POLYDEUKES: It will be easy to find him by those tokens, at all events.

DIOGENES: Are you willing that I give you some commission with respect to those philosophers themselves?

POLYDEUKES: Speak: for that will not be any trouble either.

DIOGENES: In a word, then, exhort them to cease their trifling nonsense, and quarreling about the nature of the universe, and generating "horns" for each other, and making "crocodiles" and teaching the young to engage in such futile rubbish.

POLYDEUKES: But they will say that I am an ignorant and uneducated fellow to denounce their philosophy.

DIOGENES: Do you, however, bid them from me to go and howl with a plague to them.

POLYDEUKES: This message, too, I will give them, Diogenes.

DIOGENES: And to the rich, my dearest pet of a Polydeukes, convey this message from me: 'Why, O fools, do you guard your gold so religiously; and why do you punish yourselves, calculating the interest of your money, and heaping talents upon talents, who must shortly come hither with only a single obulus?"

POLYDEUKES: This, too, shall be told to them.

DIOGENES: Yes, and say to the handsome and the strong, to Megillus of Corinth and Damoxenus the Wrestler, that with us there is neither auburn hair, nor bright nor black eyes, nor a blush upon the cheek any longer, nor well-strung nerves, nor strong shoulders: but all is for us, as they say, "one and the same dust" — skulls bare of all beauty.

POLYDEUKES: It will be no trouble either to say this to the handsome and strong.

DIOGENES: And to the poor, Mr. Laconian — and they are numerous enough, grieving at their lot, and bewailing their destitution — say that they are not to weep or lament; explain to them the perfect equality here; and that they will see those who are rich are in no way better off than themselves. And your Lacedaemonians reprove from me for this, if you like — telling them that they have become remiss and degenerate.

POLYDEUKES: Not a word, Diogenes, about the Lacedaemonians, for I certainly will not tolerate it. But as to what you were saying in regard to the rest, I will deliver your messages.

DIOGENES: Let us leave them alone, since such is your pleasure: do you, however, convey from me my words to those whom I before mentioned.

16: Cheiron imparts to Menippus his reason for preferring Hades to Heaven and Immortality

MENIPPUS: I heard, Cheiron, that though divine, you had a great desire to die.

CHEIRON: You heard quite right, Menippus; and I have died, as you see, when I might have been immortal.

MENIPPUS: Pray, what love of death possessed you, a thing undesired by most people?

CHEIRON: I will tell you, as you are not altogether without sense. I had no longer any pleasure to get from immortality.

MENIPPUS: It was no pleasure to you to live and see the light of day?

CHEIRON: No, Menippus, for I, for my part, hold pleasure to be something which is variable, and not simple. But I was always living and in the enjoyment of the same things — sin, light, food; and there were the same seasons, and everything happened, each in its own order, following, as it were, one after the other — I became, therefore, satiated with them: for my pleasure was dependent not on its permanence, but on the not being constantly participant in it.

MENIPPUS: You are right, Cheiron; but how do you endure the state of things in Hades, ever since you came here by preference?

CHEIRON: Not disagreeably, Menippus, for your equality is very democratic, and the circumstance of being in daylight or in darkness brings no difference with it: besides, one has not to be thirsty nor hungry, as up above, for we are without all those wants.

MENIPPUS: Take care, Cheiron, that you are not caught in your own words, and your argument does not came round to the same thing.

CHEIRON: How do you mean?

MENIPPUS: That if everlasting sameness and similarity of human life was the cause of your ennui, here, too, the sameness of things must be equally matter for satiety for you; and you will be obliged to seek some means of migrating from here, also, to another life, a thing which, I imagine, is impossible.

CHEIRON: What should one do, then, Menippus?

MENIPPUS: According to what is commonly said, I suppose that a sensible man is pleased and content with his present circumstances, and thinks none of them intolerable.

20: Aeakus introduces Menippus to the ghosts of celebrated figures of antiquity

MENIPPUS: In the name of Pluto, Aeakus, be my chaperon, and conduct me round all the sights of Hades.

AEAKUS: No easy thing, Menippus, to do everything. As regards, however, the principal sights, learn as follows: — that this creature here is Kerberus you are aware; and this ferryman, who conveyed you across, and the lake, and Pyriphlegethon, you have seen but now at your entering —

MENIPPUS: I know all that, and you, that you are the gate-keeper, and I saw the king, and the Erinyes: but point out to me the men of old times, and especially those of them who are famous.

AEAKUS: This is Agamemnon, and this is Achilleus, and this Idomeneus close by, and this Odysseus; next are Aias and Diomedes, and the most valiant of the Hellenes.

MENIPPUS: Bah! Homer, what creatures are the principal ornaments of your rhapsodies, that are tossed about on the ground, shapeless, mere dust all of them, and empty trumpery, in very truth "fleeting forms!" And this fellow, Aeakus, who is he?

AEAKUS: It is Cyrus, and this Kroesus, and the one above him Sardanapalus, and the one above them Midas; and he here is Xerxes.

MENIPPUS *(to Xerxes)*: Then, vile refuse, it was at your bridging the Hellespont that Hellas shuddered, and at your ambition to sail through the mountains? And what a figure, too, is the famous Kroesus! And as for Sardanapalus, Aeakus, just permit me to give him a cuff on the ear.

AEAKUS: By no means, for you would shiver his skull in pieces, it is so like a woman's.

MENIPPUS: Well, then, I will, at least, certainly spit upon him for a woman-man.

AEAKUS: Would you like me to show the philosophers, too?

MENIPPUS: In heaven's name, yes.

AEAKUS: First of all, this is your celebrated Pythagoras.

MENIPPUS: Good-day to you, Euphorbus, or Apollo, or whatever you like to be.

PYTHAGORAS: The same to you, with all my heart, Menippus.

MENIPPUS: Have you no longer a golden thigh?

PYTHAGORAS: Why, no; but come, let me see if your wallet contains anything eatable.

382

MENIPPUS: Beans, my dear sir — so that's not in your way of eating.

PYTHAGORAS: Only give them to me. Other opinions hold among the dead; for I have learned that beans and one's parents' heads are not all on an equality here.

AEAKUS: This is Solon, the son of Exekestides, and that Thales, and by their side Pittakos and the rest; and there are seven in all, as you observe.

MENIPPUS: These, Aeakus, are the only ones of all of them without grief and cheerful. But the one covered with cinders, for all the world like a loaf baked in the ashes, who blossoms all over with blisters, who is he?

AEAKUS: Empedokles, Menippus, come from Aetna, half-boiled.

MENIPPUS: Fine Sir of the brazen foot, what possessed you that you threw yourself into the craters of Aetna?

EMPEDOKLES: A sort of melancholy madness, Menippus.

MENIPPUS: Not so, by heaven! but vain-glory and puffed-up pride, and much drivelling — these things burned you to ashes, slippers and all, not unworthy of your fate. But the clever trick did you no good; for you clearly were proved to have died. — Sokrates, however, wherever in the world is he, pray?

AEAKUS: He is generally talking nonsense, with Nestor and Palamedes.

MENIPPUS: None the less I would wish to have a look at him, if he is anywhere here.

AEAKUS: Do you see the bald-headed man?

MENIPPUS: All of them are bald-headed together. So that would be the distinguishing mark of all.

AEAKUS: I mean the snub-nosed one.

MENIPPUS: That, too, is all one; for they are the whole lot of them all snub-nosed.

SOKRATES: Is it me you are inquiring for, Menippus?

MENIPPUS: Yes, indeed, Sokrates.

SOKRATES: How go things in Athens?

MENIPPUS: Many of the young men say they are engaged in philosophy. And if one were to regard their ways of dressing and walking alone, they are tip-top philosophers.

SOKRATES: I have seen very many of them.

MENIPPUS: But you have observed, I suppose, in what style Aristippus came to you, and Plato himself; the one reeking of perfume, and the other after having thoroughly learned the art of courting Sicilian despots.

SOKRATES: But about me what opinions do they entertain?

MENIPPUS: You are a lucky fellow, Sokrates, as to that sort of thing, at all events. All, in fact, consider you to have been an admirable

man, and to have known everything; and that, too — for one
must, I suppose, tell the truth — when you knew nothing.

SOKRATES: And I myself kept telling them that, but they would imagine
the thing was pretended ignorance on my part.

MENIPPUS: And who are these about you?

SOKRATES: Charmides, and Phaedrus, and the son of Kleinias.

MENIPPUS: Well done, Sokrates; for even here you pursue your peculiar
profession, and don't altogether despise the handsome fellows.

SOKRATES: Why, what else could I engage in more pleasantly? However,
do you, please, recline close by us.

MENIPPUS: No, faith, for I shall go off to join Kroesus and Sardanapalus,
to take up my abode in their neighbourhood. I think, in fact, that
I shall laugh not a little in listening to their doleful lamentations.

AEAKUS: I, too, will now be off, for fear that some one or other of the
dead may get clear away without my perceiving him. As for the
remaining sights you shall see them at another time, Menippus.

MENIPPUS: Take yourself off at once; indeed, these sights here are quite
sufficient, Aeakus.

H. Williams

SELECTIVE BIBLIOGRAPHY

Bury, J. B. A History of Greece to the Death of Alexander the Great. New York: Modern Library, Random House, 1937.

Cooper, Lane. The Greek Genius and Its Influence. New Haven: Yale University Press, 1917.

Cornford, F. M. Before and After Socrates. Cambridge: University Press, 1932.

Farrington, Benjamin. Greek Science. 2 volumes. Pelican, 1949.

Fowler, W. W. The City-State of the Greeks and the Romans. 2nd. Edition. New York: The Macmillan Co., 1907.

Jaeger, Werner. Paideia. 3 volumes. Oxford: Blackwell, 1939-44. Translated by Gilbert Highet.

Kitto, H. D. F. Greek Tragedy. London: Methuen and Co., 1935.

Kitto, H. D. F. The Greeks. Pelican, 1951.

Nilsson, Martin P. A History of Greek Religion. Oxford: Clarendon Press, 1925.

Rose, H. J. A. A Handbook of Greek Literature from Homer to the Age of Lucian. London: Methuen and Co., 1934.

Symonds, J. A. Studies of the Greek Poets. 3rd. ed. London: A and C Black, 1893.

Tarn, W. W. Hellenistic Civilization. 2nd. ed. London: Edwin Arnold, 1927.